SHOT IN COLD BLOOD

The first shot struck Buzz Clinton's right ear. The next two bullets hit him in the shoulder blade and the armpit. The fourth bullet hit him in the back of the neck and exited out of his tongue. When the bullet pierced his spinal column and cord, it dropped him to the ground almost instantly. As he fell, his body turned, exposing his right side, allowing the next bullet—the fatal bullet—to enter his chest, ricochet off his rib cage, pierce his lungs, aorta and heart. With the amount of internal bleeding that occurred at this point, and Buzz's lungs, aorta and heart all punctured, he had likely drowned in his own blood. Even though this all took place in a matter of seconds, he likely felt a great deal of pain as he died and, most certainly, knew what was happening to him.

It was possible he lived between five and six minutes.

BOOK YOUR PLACE ON OUR WEBSITE AND MAKE THE READING CONNECTION!

We've created a customized website just for our very special readers, where you can get the inside scoop on everything that's going on with Zebra, Pinnacle and Kensington books.

When you come online, you'll have the exciting opportunity to:

- View covers of upcoming books
- Read sample chapters
- Learn about our future publishing schedule (listed by publication month *and author*)
- Find out when your favorite authors will be visiting a city near you
- Search for and order backlist books from our online catalog
- Check out author bios and background information
- Send e-mail to your favorite authors
- Meet the Kensington staff online
- Join us in weekly chats with authors, readers and other guests
- Get writing guidelines
- AND MUCH MORE!

**Visit our website at
http://www.kensingtonbooks.com**

LETHAL GUARDIAN

M. WILLIAM PHELPS

PINNACLE BOOKS
Kensington Publishing Corp.
http://www.kensingtonbooks.com

Some names have been changed to protect the privacy of individuals connected to this story.

PINNACLE BOOKS are published by

Kensington Publishing Corp.
850 Third Avenue
New York, NY 10022

All Kensington titles, imprints and distributed lines are available at special quantity discounts for bulk purchases for sales promotion, premiums, fund-raising, educational or institutional use. Special book excerpts or customized printings can also be created to fit specific needs. For details, write or phone the office of the Kensington Special Sales Manager: Kensington Publishing Corp., 850 Third Avenue, New York, NY 10022. Attn. Special Sales Department. Phone: 1-800-221-2647.

Zebra and the Z logo Reg. U.S. Pat. & TM Off.

First Printing: June 2004
10 9 8 7 6 5 4 3 2 1

Printed in the United States of America

For Tommy Louis

The world is what it is; men who are nothing,
who allow themselves to become nothing,
have no place in it.
—V. S. Naipaul, A Bend in the River

Day by day with love.
— Anson "Buzz" Clinton

TABLE OF CONTENTS

Author's Note

All of the people, places and events in this book are real. Over the course of about sixteen months of research and writing, which included dozens of interviews with many of the key players involved in the case, I established a comprehensive understanding of the facts and events herein and wrote about them. Some sources have chosen to remain anonymous, and I have honored that request by either changing their names (the first time any name in the book appears in italics means that I have either chosen myself to change the name or that person has requested it) or keeping it out of the narrative altogether. Over the course of my research, I uncovered many new and exclusive pieces of the story that have never been reported. It is through that underlying presence of the truth that this entire case can, for the first time, be exposed to the public. Courageous individuals chose to come forward and help me find the truth, and I am forever indebted to them.

The information and the dialogue in this book are based on trial testimony, court records, interviews with key sources, hundreds of pages of police reports, interviews conducted by the police, search warrants, arrest warrants, international documents, hundreds of pages of reports by the Department of Child and Youth Services in the state of Connecticut, diaries, letters, cards, affidavits and other items I uncovered while doing research. I carefully reconstructed the events in this book through the study of all these documents and interviews. All dialogue is actual speech to the best of the recollection of those involved. To keep the narrative flowing, in some instances dialogue was reconstructed using interviews, court records, trial transcripts and a cautious and tedious study of the rather extensive list of documents made available to me.

Furthermore, every person involved in the story I tell in this book had a chance—some had multiple chances—to talk to me. Some did, some didn't. When someone chose not to talk to me, I simply backed up whatever part of his story I was writing about with other key sources: police reports, court transcripts, other documents and interviews.

I encourage anyone with the guts and the courage to learn and accept the truth to take an objective look at this case—and as you read this book, I urge you to purge your mind of what you've heard, read or think you know about this case. For the first time, it is all here. Remember, I made up nothing in this book. All of it—from the thoughts of people to the dialogue to the trial testimony to the scores of interviews I conducted over the course of about a year and a half—is based on factual evidence uncovered during the investigation process of my research.

History cannot be rewritten.

Please visit my Web site at www.mwilliamphelps.com for more information.

Hit and Run

Chapter 1

Early in the evening on March 10, 1994, *Christine Roy** indicated to her husband, *Steven,* that she was in the mood to go shopping. Christine's sister was getting married in a few months, and it was time, she insisted, they found her a gift.

"We've been putting it off long enough, Steven."

For seven years, the Roys had lived an unpretentious life in Uncasville, Connecticut, a postage-stamp-size rural community just north of New London. Today, Uncasville is the site of the Mohegan Sun, one of Connecticut's two casinos.

Already eight years into a successful career as an architect, Christine was comfortable with her life in suburbia: good job, nice home, loving husband, healthy child.

What more did she need?

At about 7:00 P.M., Christine and Steven loaded their three-year-old son, *Brendan,* into their car, and took off for the Bridal Mall, located in a small shopping center on the East Lyme–Niantic border, about a half hour's drive from Uncasville.

It was supposed to be just another casual trip to the mall.

* * *

* Italics on first use represents pseudonym.

Connecticut would suffer record snowfall amounts by the time the 1993 to 1994 winter was over—a total of eighty-three inches, the largest since record keeping had begun in the state back in 1905. Still, it wasn't snowfall amounts that had Connecticut residents on edge in 1994. The Victorian-like countryside and postcard ambiance of one of New England's crown jewels had been riddled with crime throughout the past twelve months. By year's end, there would be more than 214 murders, the most Connecticut had seen in the last thirty-five years. Seven out of every one hundred thousand residents would be murdered in some violent manner: shot, stabbed, run over, strangled, beaten, clubbed. People were talking about it all over the state: at the post office, general store, boat launches, PTA meetings, town council. Everywhere.

Murder and death.

It wasn't just happening in the more populated cities, like Hartford, New Haven or Bridgeport. The smaller towns—Old Lyme, Old Saybrook, Waterford, Uncasville, Essex, Deep River, Ledyard—had all been touched in one way or another by murder.

These were quiet coastal towns. People left their doors unlocked overnight and wide open during hot and humid summer evenings. Neighbors borrowed sugar and eggs from one another. Murder rates this high were expected to the south, in New York and New Jersey.

But Connecticut? The Nutmeg State?

When Christine and Steven Roy left their Uncasville home, it had been cloudy, around fifty degrees. A slight drizzle had been falling. With any luck, they could get down to the Bridal Mall and back home inside of an hour and a half and put Brendan to bed on time.

Traveling south on Interstate 95, the main highway that

runs from Florida to Boston, Massachusetts, snaking along the Connecticut coastline as it cuts through the southern part of the state, Steven pulled off the interstate and onto Exit 72, a half-mile stretch of road that connects I-95 to Route 156. The Bridal Mall was off to the left. At the bottom of the connector was Rocky Neck State Park Beach, one of the many sprawling public beaches along Connecticut's pristine coastline. Drive down Route 156 a bit and York Correctional Facility for Women is set back a short distance from the road, nearly in the backyard of the Lyme Tavern, a favorite local gin mill.

As the Roys approached the end of the exit, Christine noticed two cars off to the right side of the road. Through the foggy windshield, it looked to Christine as if both cars had just stopped for no apparent reason.

It was odd. There wasn't much of anything going on in East Lyme at *any* time of the day or night, let alone a rainy Thursday evening in March at 7:20 P.M.

"What's that?" Steven asked, driving slowly, pulling up about one hundred yards in back of where the cars were parked.

There was a small compact car—light in color, Christine remembered later—on the side of the road. In front of it, there was a beat-up 1981 Pontiac Firebird with the driver's-side door wide open, headlights on, just up ahead of the blue car.

"Looks like an accident," Christine said. "Pull up a bit closer, Steven. Hurry up."

Lying not too far away from the Pontiac Firebird, Christine noticed, was a male, perhaps in his early twenties. Skinny, but in good shape, he had short black hair, a lumberjack-type dress shirt, jeans, sneakers, no jacket—and lay on the road curled up in a fetal position as if he were asleep.

"It's odd," Christine said to Steven, "he's not moving. . . ."

As they approached, Christine saw the taillights on the second car light up. She could see clearly that a "tall, lanky man" was driving the car.

As Steven began to pull over and stop, the man driving the blue car sped off. Christine later recalled it with the cliché: "Like a bat out of hell."

"Follow that car," Christine shouted. "He just hit that guy." She was frantic, pointing at the car. "Go, Steven. Go! What are you waiting for? . . ."

"No way. I'm not following anybody."

"He just hit that guy, Steven—we need to get his license plate number!"

Steven later recalled that he "wasn't about to go chasing some maniac when I had my son in the backseat."

When they got closer to the Firebird, they could see that it had Maine license plates, with a cardboard temporary Connecticut license plate tucked in the back windshield, as if it were a For Sale sign. A car battery sat on the floorboard in back of the driver's seat. A baby seat sat empty in the passenger-side backseat.

Oddly, the car was still running.

As Steven called 911 from his cell phone, Christine approached the man lying in the road and immediately noticed a large pool of blood, about the size of a garbage can cover, underneath the man's head and shoulders.

Moving in for a closer look, she saw that the man's face was covered with blood.

Someone had to stay with Brendan. So when Steven stopped the car to let Christine out, she ran toward the man, thinking he was still alive and in need of immediate help.

At 7:23 P.M., Steven got through to 911. Unbeknownst to him, someone else had already phoned it in a few minutes earlier.

A second car had since pulled off to the shoulder, and the driver, a woman in her midthirties, got out of her car and began walking toward Christine, who was now standing over the man staring down at him.

After a moment, Christine leaned down and, with her right hand, pushed the locks of her long brown hair over and around her ears so she could go in for a closer look without saturating her hair with the man's blood.

"My husband's calling 911," Christine said to the woman.

They couldn't see the man's face. Or tell if he was breathing. Nonetheless, he was lying still as a brick, on his side, eyes closed, with a large pool of blood around his head, which, they assumed, had leaked out of his ear.

Christine wanted to touch him, feel for a pulse, but she couldn't bring herself to do it. "I had never seen a body like that before," she recalled. "I was horrified and confused."

"What happened?" the woman asked Christine.

"I don't know."

Again leaning over the man, staring at him, wanting to poke and prod him as if he were a cat or a dog that had been struck by a car, Christine said as loud as she could, "Hello? Can you hear me?"

The women then looked at each other and shrugged.

A moment later, Christine stood up. Looking at the idling Pontiac Firebird, its driver's-side door wide open, its headlights still on, she began to speculate about what had happened: *The guy had had some type of aneurysm while driving, became disoriented, pulled over, got out of his car and, while walking into the road to flag someone down for help, keeled over. No. He wasn't dead. He was just in shock! But what about the car that had sped away as we pulled up? A hit-and-run?*

It was almost 7:45 P.M. now, and the connector was beginning to jam up with cars that had pulled over to see what was going on. Within moments, a man got out of his car and ran up to where Christine and the other woman were standing. Looking at both women, he asked, "Did one of you hit him?"

"No," they both said.

"I'm an EMT," the man then said.

"Good! Can you do CPR or *something* on the guy?" Christine suggested.

The EMT looked down at the man. All that blood. He wasn't moving. All that blood. "No way. There's no way I'm doing *that*."

You bastard. You are not *going to do CPR?* Christine thought, but didn't say anything.

Steven then ran up, leaned down, and began touching the man. "At that point, he was still warm," Steven said later.

The mild weather throughout the day had given way to more seasonal temperatures as the evening progressed. With the man's body still warm, they agreed that whatever had happened must have just occurred.

"It looked like he had pulled over, stumbled a step or two and just fell down where he was."

Steven wasn't going to waste precious time. He and the EMT bent down and rolled the man over. Christine, by this point, had gone back to the car to stay with Brendan.

Almost instantly, after turning him faceup, Steven and the EMT could see the source of all the blood: it had run out of his nose, ears and mouth. Upon further examination, they could tell he wasn't breathing. There also appeared to be an imprint of tire tracks on his pant legs, Steven later recalled.

"He looks to be in his twenties," one of them said, checking to see if he had a pulse. "He's dead."

By this time, Joe Dunn, a local cop from the East Lyme Police Department, who had gotten called by dispatch at around 7:30 P.M., and had been only about a mile and a half away, barreled up to the scene and parked his cruiser in front of the body, blocking it so no one would mistakenly drive over it. It was dark. With the thick and dense woods on each side of the road, the connector ran through what amounted to a tunnel of trees. Some frustrated driver, late for a date or just having a fit of road rage, might try to whisk past the scene and end up either hitting someone who was standing around or running over the body.

Detective Mike Foley, of the Eastern District Major Crime Squad (ED-MCS), in Norwich, Connecticut, had always been a "detailed" and careful cop. Balding, with a thin, pencillike mustache, Foley was often teased by other detectives because he looked so quintessentially Irish. Richard "Reggie" Wardell, a colleague of Foley's, had been with the Connecticut State Police since 1975. Besides being quite a bit taller, Wardell could have doubled for actor Joe Pesci—right down to his brushed-back haircut, mannerisms and the way he talked with his hands. Wardell had been raised in New Jersey and, after being denied a position with the Pennsylvania State Police because of affirmative action, got a job with the Connecticut State Police.

Foley, Wardell and Detective Peter Cleary, who worked for the Crime Scene Unit of the state police, had gone out for pizza at a local East Lyme restaurant only about a mile from the Rocky Neck connector. It was about 7:30 P.M. when they arrived. They all had the following day off. A fellow colleague, Donny Richardson, who had stopped by to say hi on his way home, but had since left, returned only minutes later.

He had a surprised look on his face . . . *You guys actually think you're going to have the night off?*

"There's a body up on the highway," Richardson said. He had just taken the call in his cruiser.

"You *have* to be kidding me?" Wardell balked.

"You're foolin' with us, Donny, right?" Foley said.

No sooner had Richardson spoken, when all of their pagers went off.

Mike Foley then made the call into dispatch. "Get to that scene," the dispatcher ordered.

"The crime scene van is in Colchester, though," Foley said. Colchester was about an hour away. They were only minutes away from the connector.

"Get to that scene! We'll have someone pick up the van and bring it over."

The first thing Officer Joe Dunn did when he got to the scene was check for "responsiveness by attempting to establish an airway." But the man's mouth, Dunn noticed, was full of blood. Getting air into his lungs would be impossible.

Dunn then realized that the man's shirt was also covered with blood, so he ripped it open to see if he could find out what had happened.

Just then, Dunn realized that it had not been a hit and run—at least not in a conventional sense—as so many combing the scene had been suggesting. There were two small holes, clearly visible to Dunn, in the man's chest: one above his left nipple, the other near his armpit on the same side. There was no blood in or around the holes; they looked like tiny moon craters, as if someone had poked the man with an ice pick or something sharp and round.

Dunn knew from experience that they weren't stab wounds. By the looks of it, someone had shot the man. And they weren't close-range wounds, either; he had apparently been hit from afar. Close-range wounds leave starlike marks—like a balloon knot—on the skin around the wound. Gases from the weapon char and tear the skin apart.

Looking more closely at the man's face, Dunn noticed something else—he recognized the man. It was Anson

"Buzz" Clinton, a local "hustler" in town Dunn had had some contact with on several occasions.

"I had dealt with him . . . in the past regarding domestic disturbances. And had also seen him several times in local drinking establishments," Dunn later said.

On January 7, 1994, only two months before Buzz Clinton was found dead, he and his family celebrated his twenty-eighth birthday. They were all looking forward to where Buzz's life was heading. A rather popular guy in the Old Lyme–East Lyme area, Buzz had the build of a featherweight boxer: lean, cut, muscular. Whether from genetics or the hours of hard manual labor he had done throughout his short life, Buzz could eat all day long and retain his bodybuilder shape without worry. One of the stars of his high-school wrestling and gymnastics teams, quite striking in his pretty-boy manner, Buzz had an uncanny likeness to pop sensation Ricky Martin, back when Martin was fronting the boy band Menudo as a teenager.

With his feathered-back dark brown hair and blue eyes, Buzz had no trouble getting the ladies. But he also had a reputation in some crowds for being a troublemaker. Buzz was always looking to cut a deal to make some money on the side, former friends recalled. Married for a second time when he was murdered, his first marriage lasted only about a month, and, some claimed, was rife with dysfunction, drug and alcohol abuse and violence.

Chapter 2

Officer Joe Dunn, now standing over Buzz's body staring at his blood-drenched face, had spoken with Buzz back in January, only weeks ago. Buzz had been drinking. He'd been fighting with his wife, the former Kim Carpenter, and her family over custody of Rebecca, Kim's daughter from a previous relationship. Kim's sister, Beth Ann Carpenter, was an elegant and beautiful lawyer. In her own right, she seemed to be a beacon of sanity during a situation that had gotten completely out of hand. Beth Ann had helped her mother, Cynthia, wage a savage battle for custody of Rebecca back in 1991. When Buzz met Kim in 1992, he had become entangled in the custody fight. There had been countless court battles. Custody had been granted to the elder Carpenters and then returned back to Kim Clinton. By the beginning of 1994, with Buzz threatening to take Rebecca and Kim and move cross-country, Rebecca's grandfather Richard "Dick" Carpenter and Buzz had been arguing and fighting fiercely just about every time they ran into each other.

One night, Buzz called the East Lyme Police Department in a fury. Joe Dunn had taken the call.

"I'm living in town in an apartment . . . ," Buzz said, his voice wrought with rage and alcohol. "I haven't gotten along well with my father-in-law."

"Go on. What's the problem?"

"My father-in-law, Dick Carpenter, and I have cross complaints against each other filed at the Old Lyme Police Department. He came over here tonight. I told him to leave."

"Did he?"

"Yes, but . . . I want him arrested and a restraining order placed against him."

Dunn then explained to Buzz that no crime had been committed.

"He hasn't trespassed—"

But Buzz interrupted and became angrier, Dunn recalled later. Then Buzz began to shout.

"If the feud continues," he said clearly, "one of us will end up dead. And if I end up dead, you'll know who did it!"

"You should file a restraining order against him, Mr. Clinton. But you have to do that through the courts, not us."

"Maybe I'll kill him first and end the problem," Buzz said before hanging up.

On two separate occasions, Joe Dunn had either arrested Buzz or participated in the arrest. Both instances involved domestic disputes, either between Buzz and his wife, Kim, or Buzz and his in-laws.

The day after Buzz had made that rather threatening phone call to Joe Dunn, he called back. Sober now, he wanted to explain himself, saying how he felt bad about the previous night's call. He had been drinking, he explained. He was fed up. Things were getting out of hand with his in-laws.

"It's because of my wife," Buzz said, "that [the Carpenters and I] don't get along."

"If the problem continues," Dunn advised, "I suggest you get that restraining order."

Officer Joe Dunn was standing on the Rocky Neck connector now, shaking his head, staring down at Buzz

Clinton's lifeless body as it lay in a pool of blood. Buzz's skin was turning yellow. It had warmed up a few degrees as a slight drizzle began to fall again, and rigor mortis was beginning to set in.

Dunn radioed for backup. He needed to get the Connecticut State Police homicide division out there as soon as possible. Any rookie cop—which Dunn wasn't, by any means—knew the first twenty-four to forty-eight hours after a murder were crucial. The more time the killer had immediately following his crime, the less the chances were he'd ever be caught.

As Steven and Christine Roy wandered around the scene, which was overflowing with onlookers and rubberneckers, they were finally informed that the man they had found lying on the road, most likely, had been shot. It wasn't an aneurysm or a hit and run.

It was murder.

After learning this, Christine concluded that the man in the car she had seen speed off was probably the murderer.

Oh, my goodness, she told herself, holding her child tighter.

About fifteen minutes later, when the state police showed up and began questioning Steven about what had happened and what he had seen, one of the detectives, Steven recalled later, indicated to him that they already had a suspect—and it wasn't the guy in the car who had sped off.

With about 3.5 million residents, 90 percent of which are white, Connecticut is a tad over five thousand square miles. Bridgeport, about twenty-five miles from the New York border, is Connecticut's largest city with about 140,000 people. The entire southern portion of the state—among the towns are Greenwich, Stamford, Old Lyme, East Lyme, New London, Waterford, Old Saybrook,

New Haven—borders the Atlantic Ocean and contains some of the most sought-after real estate in New England.

The Constitution State, as it was dubbed in 1959, holds bragging rights to being the first among America's fifty states to develop the typewriter, newspaper, nuclear submarine, artificial heart, color television, hamburger, vacuum cleaner, pay telephone, dictionary and revolver.

With Hartford, the state capital, situated in the middle of the state, many outsiders view the financially suffering city as nothing more than a pit stop between New York City and Boston.

Connecticut has twelve state police barracks spread throughout the state's eight counties, 169 towns. Meriden (Central), Litchfield (Western) and Norwich (Eastern) house the Connecticut State Police's Major Crime Squad District Headquarters.

The ED-MCS, in Norwich, is about an hour from the East Lyme ramp where Buzz Clinton had been found dead. The crime squads take their work seriously. Territory is everything. If Buzz had been shot just fifteen feet south of where he was found, it would have been Central District's case.

The Major Crime Squads are responsible "for all major case investigations—homicides, sexual assaults, armed robberies, arsons—for the forty-two towns situated in the eastern portion of the state." In addition to its primary responsibilities of investigating violent crime, the ED-MCS serves the offices of the state's attorneys in Tolland, Windham, Middlesex and New London Counties, and also "assists and supports" twelve police departments within the Eastern District, helping out with "crime processing and major crime investigations."

At about 8:30 P.M., Joe Dunn turned the crime scene over to several state troopers and the ED-MCS. Yellow crime-scene tape was unspooled, and an area about the size of a football field, with Buzz's body in the middle, was cordoned off.

It was time for the big boys with the gold badges to step in and begin reconstructing exactly what had happened. Containing the crime scene and getting a handle on it were critical. One mistake, and the integrity of an entire investigation could be compromised.

As plainclothes detectives began to scour the area, looking for any possible pieces of trace evidence—a single strand of hair, a cigarette butt, shell casings, tire tracks, linen, gum, *anything*—troopers began gathering witnesses who had been hanging around, waiting, wondering. It was getting colder. With drizzle falling, the road had developed a slight glaze that sparkled like diamond dust. Locating evidence—if, in fact, the killer or killers had left any—was getting tougher by the minute.

By 8:40 P.M., local emergency personnel had tried reviving Buzz, but their efforts were fruitless. He had been dead at least an hour already, maybe longer.

Murders may take years to solve, but it's those clues picked up in the first two days that always become the key pieces of evidence. The East Lyme crime scene, however, as it appeared to ED-MCS detectives from a first look, offered little, if any, evidence. Buzz's Firebird would be towed away, taken to the lab and scoured for clues. But that would take days.

Temperatures plummeted as the drizzle finally subsided. Within minutes, detectives began gathering any information they could from several of the witnesses who had arrived on the scene after Christine and Steven Roy, who were still standing over by their car, talking to troopers. Buzz's body, now spread out on the pavement in somewhat of a Christ-on-the-cross fashion, was still out in the open and uncovered. In all the chaos, no one had thought to place a sheet over him.

Dressed in a cherry red, button-up shirt (which had been opened from top to bottom by Joe Dunn), Buzz lay in a pool of his own blood, urine and feces. The large pool of blood around his head had seeped into the ground and mixed with whatever rainwater had accumulated around him. It was easy to tell that he had been moved at some point after his death. There was a large blood spot to his left that appeared smudged—like pencil markings on paper—as if he'd been dragged. There were also blotches of blood toward his feet—more smudges, detectives guessed, from when one of the witnesses or Joe Dunn had rolled him over.

Detectives Reggie Wardell and Mike Foley, of the ED-MCS, after viewing the body and discussing how they were going to go about processing the scene, walked over to where Christine and Steven Roy had been waiting. It had been a long night for the couple. What started out as a simple trip to the Bridal Mall ended as a scene out of a TV movie of the week. Steven was tired, Christine shaken. Brendan, who had held up fairly well throughout the night, was beginning to whine now.

"We're going to have to separate the two of you and ask you guys some questions," one of the detectives said.

"Fine," Steven answered. "Let's just get this over with so we can go home." *If only we had left our house five minutes sooner or later . . .*

Christine had been appalled that one of the first things Joe Dunn had done when he'd arrived on the scene earlier, after looking at Buzz lying on the ground near their car, was to walk over to the Roys' Pontiac Grand Am and begin circling it with his flashlight out, checking to see if maybe the Roys has struck and killed him. She was wondering now if the detectives were going to be hostile and accusatory, pressing questions on them for which they didn't have any answers.

As one of the detectives and Christine walked past

Buzz's body en route to a police cruiser, Christine could see that Buzz's body was beginning to show signs of death. She put her hands over her mouth. "I had never really seen something so graphic before," she recalled. While everything had been going on, she never had time to stop and think about what had actually happened. But now the anxiety of the entire night settled on her: She and Steven had come upon the scene of a murder as it was just winding down, and they had possibly even seen the murderer drive away.

"At that point," she later said, "I was beginning to comprehend what had happened. I was really, really scared. I didn't even want to look at [Buzz]. Everything was becoming so real."

"Can't anyone cover that body?" Christine asked as she and one of the detectives proceeded by Buzz's body.

"Sure, ma'am."

It was pitch black out now. The only hint of light was coming from the blue and red flashes protruding off the tops of the many police cruisers surrounding the scene. Out on Interstate 95, traffic was backed up for miles. Drivers were being stopped by state troopers and asked questions.

Buzz Clinton had not always gotten along well with his parents, DaLoyd "Dee" and Anson "Buck" Clinton. But the Clintons, of course, loved Buzz, along with their other children, Suzanne and Billy. Shortly before Buzz was killed, he and his new wife, Kim, had lived out in the back of the Clintons' ranch-style home, situated on the top of a hill off Old Stagecoach Road, in Old Lyme, on about fifty acres. It was a little apartment Buzz had converted from an old toolshed. Just four months ago, though, Buzz and Kim had moved out of "the shed" and into their own apartment in East Lyme, just down the road from where Buzz now lay dead in the road.

When he was single and living at home, Buzz was always getting kicked out of the house. Dee had a typical mother-son relationship with him, and she always bent over backward to help out and give him whatever she could. But when he failed to live by her rules, they butted heads like rams, and Dee would have no other choice but to ask him to leave. Months later, Buzz would promise to be a good little boy and Dee would allow him back.

"Buzz was a complex person and, at the same time, very simple," Dee said later. "[He was] not perfect, and most of my gray hair I got from him. He always tried to do at least two things at the same time. He could make me smile and make me want to wring his neck . . . often at the same time . . . I used to tell Buzz, 'There is no expiration date on your birth certificate, so make every day count.' Buzz packed a lot of living in such a short time."

Dee had left her Old Lyme home for a shopping trip at about 7:10 P.M. on the night of Buzz's murder. Here she was now, however, at about 8:30 P.M., still sitting in a traffic jam—and she had no idea it had been created by the death of her son. From where she was on Exit 72, about one hundred yards from the crime scene, Dee could even see the police's yellow tape and the sheet troopers had, only recently, placed over Buzz's body.

"I hear somebody got hit by a car," a passerby said to Dee as she sat and worked on a crossword puzzle, waiting for traffic to move again.

"No kidding," Dee responded.

The connector was a parking lot by this point. Cops were still roaming around, asking questions, not letting motorists pass.

In no hurry, Dee was content in waiting for whatever

the holdup was. Traffic would move soon enough, and she would be on her way. Kim, her daughter-in-law, who was at home waiting on Dee to pick her and Buzz's kids up to go shopping, would have to understand.

Detectives soon realized that finding actual forensic evidence on the road or in the field that ran parallel to the crime scene was probably going to be like finding a pine needle in a pile of grass. It was wet, dark, cold. And there really wasn't much of anything around besides two spent shell casings on the road near Buzz's body, which detectives guessed had come from the murder weapon. Beyond that, there really wasn't much more the scene offered other than speculation and theory.

As Christine Roy made her way through the small crowd of state troopers, witnesses and onlookers, toward the detective's vehicle where she was going to be interviewed, Steven Roy was being grilled by another detective about one hundred yards away.

"Why were you on the road tonight?"

"We were going to buy a gift for my . . ."

"Where?"

"Just up the road at the Bridal Shop—"

"What time did you come upon the body?"

"I don't know exactly . . . maybe seven-thirty. . . ."

"Did you touch the body?"

"Yes, but I—"

"Where?"

"I rolled him over with the other guy, the EMT. I think that officer was there, too."

"Right to left, or left to right?"

Specifics: *What? Where? When? Why?* Any cop would have asked the same repetitive questions. Details were still fresh in Steven's mind, even if he didn't realize it himself. He and his wife were the first people on the crime scene. Moving the body was a mistake. But Steven wasn't an investigator. He was looking to save Buzz's life, as most people would have done.

Still, the fact of the matter remained—the first person at a crime scene can change the entire scope of the investigation.

Meanwhile, the detective interviewing Christine was a bit more relaxed. Christine did most of the talking, explaining exactly what she saw, along with when and where she saw it. At first, the detective had very few questions, letting Christine rattle on about nothing. He could tell she was nervous, scared. There was no sense in putting pressure on her. It would only confuse her more.

But then she mentioned the car she had seen driving away from the scene as they pulled up—and the detective's eyeballs nearly popped out of his skull.

"What did the guy driving the car look like?"

"Tall. Very, very tall. Lanky. He was thin."

"That's good. What make, model and year of car are we talking about?"

"I have no idea. . . . Blue, maybe? I don't know."

Dickey Morris, the East Lyme fire marshal on the scene, had dated Christine Roy's neighbor some years ago. When Christine saw Dickey out of the corner of her eye, she felt a little bit more comfortable. However, she couldn't remember what appeared to be the most significant piece of information available to detectives at this point: the make, model and license plate number of, possibly, the murderer's vehicle.

By 10:00 P.M., Detective John Turner, ED-MCS's case manager, arrived. Turner was an eleven-year veteran of the Connecticut State Police, spending the past several with the ED-MCS. He was just under six feet tall and completely bald, save for a ring of gray hair just above his ears and around his head

Quiet, rarely showing emotion, Turner liked to listen and think about things, then maybe come up with an angle and ask specific questions geared toward that theory. When he felt he could get the information he was looking for out of someone, he went for it. Growing up in Everett, Massachusetts, Turner had an unmistakable Boston inflection to his voice. Cops on the force liked Turner. They respected him.

"John was the best processor of evidence and organizer we ever had," colleague Reggie Wardell later said. "No one did more for [Buzz's murder] case than John. You can't do anything perfectly, but John did, as humanly possible, the perfect job."

Turner knew exactly where to look for what he wanted when he approached a crime scene. The first thing he noticed was the positioning of Buzz's car. He had been told by other detectives that the headlights were still on when the first troopers arrived. The car had even been running, they said.

Turner approached the car.

There was a car battery sitting on the floorboard behind the driver's seat, and a baby's seat in the back.

He made a note.

Then he took out a camera and began snapping photographs of the car, inside and out.

When he walked over to the body, he first noticed how Buzz's shirt had been pulled open. To the right of Buzz's chest, Turner saw gunshot wounds. He could tell by looking at the body that it had been rolled over, but the area surrounding it, he noted, was clean. Just beyond the body, about twenty feet, he located a spent projectile.

Detective Mike Foley was roaming around the scene making sketches of things. There wasn't much: a body, a bullet, a car and a long stretch of road that on any other night would have been as dark and desolate as a cemetery. But Foley needed to note where everything had been found. The distances: yards, inches and feet. It all might seem like a waste of time to a layperson, but when

Turner, Foley and the rest of the ED-MCS had a chance to calculate everything, the distance between Buzz's body and his car just might be the turning point in the entire case. Who could know at this point?

Meanwhile, Steven Roy was still being questioned.

"Did you, Mr. Roy, drive down to the Lyme Tavern and make your 911 call?" one of the detectives asked.

"No. I called from my car," Steven said. "We have a cell phone."

"Well, someone made a 911 call from the Lyme Tavern—you're saying that *wasn't* you?"

"No! That was definitely not me."

Then, after asking several specific questions, one of the cops, Steven later recalled, made an odd statement.

"The cop that was questioning me . . . started going through how many murders had taken place in East Lyme over the past ten years—and he started naming them. And then he started saying that whoever did this . . . they were going to get them because they had a one hundred percent track record."

"We've gotten every single person!" the cop said.

Steven was overwhelmed. *Why are you telling me this? Why are you gloating? What kind of cop brags about this stuff?*

"Is that right?" Steven replied when the detective took a minute to catch his breath. He had no idea what else to say.

"Then," Steven remembered later, "they said there was bad blood between Dick Carpenter and Buzz Clinton. I didn't even know who these people were. The names meant nothing to me. But the cop said, 'We've had numerous calls about the two of them. Buzz has a restraining order against Mr. Carpenter. That's the first person we're going to talk to about this.' It was almost as if he was telling me, 'We're so good, we already have a suspect.'"

Under the most perfect conditions, it takes between eight and twelve hours for a body to begin show signs of death. In the cold weather, it can take even longer. Here it was, not yet three hours after the murder of twenty-eight-year-old Buzz Clinton, his body still warm to the touch, and the Connecticut State Police had a suspect?

The last thing in the world any good investigator wanted to do was jump to erroneous conclusions and begin pointing his finger at someone with whom he had no evidence to target. At best, it was shoddy police work and unprofessional; at worst, it would lead to sure legal trouble down the road—and a guilty man might end up free on a technicality.

Chapter 3

Former Willimantic, Connecticut, police officer Marty Graham joined the Connecticut State Police in 1982. By 1987, he was working as a plainclothes detective for Troop C, in Stafford, Connecticut, and joined the ED-MCS a few years later. At six-feet four inches, Graham skyed over most of his colleagues and was considered the jokester of the bunch. With his military-cropped hair and seemingly continuous smile, Graham brought to the job a much-needed reprise from the day-in and day-out business of death, violence and abuse of all kinds.

Detective Foley, who had been at the East Lyme crime scene for most of the night, received orders for him and Graham to take a ride over to Buzz and Kim's apartment just a few minutes away. The two veteran detectives would have the grave job of notifying Kim Clinton that her husband had been murdered.

It was 12:40 A.M., Friday morning, March 11, 1994, when they arrived.

A small, one-bedroom apartment, with a breathtaking view of the Atlantic Ocean out back that might make Robin Leach quiver with envy, the apartment was free-dom for Buzz and Kim. Finally out on their own, starting a life together with their two kids, they no longer had to depend on Buzz's parents for shelter.

Buzz was studying to become a nurse. He had just

recently gotten his nurse's aid certificate—a CNA, a certified nurse's aide degree. Things were getting better by the moment. In fact, he had been mentioning lately that he and Kim were maybe going to move out to Arizona with the kids and begin anew, meet different people. A change of pace.

Most important, though, was to get away from Kim's family. Arizona would be a way for Buzz and Kim to rid themselves of the dysfunction the Carpenters—sister Beth Ann, younger brother Richard, father Dick and mother Cynthia—had brought into their lives.

Kim was blond, slightly overweight and, without airs, a plain Jane. Soft-spoken and somewhat introverted, she had been at war with her family for the past two years, fighting with them in and out of court for custody of her daughter Rebecca.

It had turned into an all-out battle, often pitting Buzz against Dick and Cynthia. They couldn't see eye to eye on anything. The Carpenters felt Kim and Buzz were incompetent parents. They wanted full custody of Rebecca.

Buzz complemented Kim's passiveness. Whereas Kim couldn't speak up for herself during intimidating situations with her family, Buzz, never one to be afraid to speak his mind, would step in and take control.

As Graham and Foley made their way around Kim's apartment, allowing the weight of what they had told her to sink in, Graham later said Kim never shed a tear, as if she had been expecting a visit like this since the day she met Buzz.

"He's not coming home, ma'am," Marty said. "Do you understand that?"

"Yes," Kim said.

It was one of the toughest parts of the job, notifying someone that a loved one was dead. Cops dreaded having to make the midnight phone calls and surprising knocks on the door—especially when the victim had kids. Nevertheless, it was the only way for a cop to get to the truth. The clock on that twenty-four-hour to forty-eight-hour time period was ticking. Foley and Graham were looking to learn who Buzz was and, possibly, who might have wanted him dead.

Kim showed them photos of Buzz for identification.

"That's him," both detectives confirmed.

Graham took out his notepad and began asking questions. Initially, all interviews with immediate family members begin with a sketch of the family.

"Buzz and I," Kim said, still not showing any sign of emotion, "have one daughter, Briana. I'm . . . I'm pregnant with our second child."

The detectives looked at each other. They had noticed when they walked in that Kim had looked a little big around the midsection.

Jesus Christ.

There was a photo of another child on the table next to where they were sitting. Graham picked it up.

"Who's this?"

"Rebecca. She'll be four in August."

A cute little towhead with penetrating blue eyes, Rebecca had her hands in her mouth when the photograph had been taken. Mother and daughter, the cops easily calculated, could have been twins.

"So, that's not Buzz's daughter, then?"

"No. John Gaul is Rebecca's dad. He lives in Groton. He pays me ten dollars a week in child support."

Kim then began describing her Ledyard, Connecticut, roots. "My father and brother do landscaping," she said. "It's my father's business. My sister, Beth Ann, is an attorney."

"What about Buzz's family?"

"He has an ex-wife, Lisa. She lives in Meriden and

recently got married. He has a four-year-old son with Lisa, Michael."

"Child support?"

"He was behind on his payments—about three hundred. He's supposed to pay twenty, twenty-five dollars a week, but we don't have much money, and . . . well . . . he has . . . he *had* a court date scheduled for March twenty-third."

She continued, telling them about Buzz's eleven-year-old sister, Suzanne, and his little brother, Billy, who was nine.

"Where was Buzz working, Mrs. Clinton?" Graham asked.

With that, Kim got up and walked toward the kitchen.

"What is it?" Foley asked.

"He was working at Pettipaug Manor, a convalescent home in Essex, as a nursing assistant for the past year," Kim said softly.

There was something wrong. Seemingly, just the mention of Pettipaug had dredged up a sour feeling.

"He hadn't been working for the past two weeks, though," Kim continued. "He was going to be working at the Groton Regency Nursing Home. A girl, *Natalie Farmer,* used to give him rides to work at Pettipaug. Paula Hunt, who also worked with Natalie and Buzz at Pettipaug, had called Natalie's husband one day and told him that Buzz and Nat were fooling around. There's another girl, Tammy. She may have also worked at Pettipaug . . . I don't know. Buzz might have been fooling around with her, too."

If what Kim was saying were true, Buzz's social life, Graham and Foley figured, was a tangled web of adultery and extramarital affairs. Whenever that was the case, experience told them, the motive for murder existed.

A jealous husband? A jilted lover?

At this point, it was important to get Kim to describe,

as best she could remember, Buzz's final hours. Where was he going when he was murdered? To meet someone? Out for a drink? Rendezvousing with a lover?

Kim explained that Buzz had gotten up at 8:00 A.M. and had stayed home while she went to the bank and then shopping. By 11:00 A.M., Kim said, she returned home with groceries and she and Buzz talked a bit and then just hung around the apartment. Around 1:00 P.M., Cynthia Carpenter came by and picked up Rebecca for a scheduled, court-ordered visit with the child. Buzz and Cynthia, as they often did, exchanged a few hostile remarks, Kim said, but nothing out of the ordinary.

With Rebecca gone, Buzz phoned Stop & Shop in Groton and asked about Kim's paycheck. She had been working at Stop & Shop for several years. Buzz liked to go pick up her paycheck, cash it and pay what bills he could. It wasn't much money, but it helped. They had been late on their rent, and Buzz wanted it paid.

A Stop & Shop manager had told Buzz the check was ready. "But make sure you have a note from Kim allowing you to pick it up!"

Kim said she wrote Buzz a note right after he got off the phone. He then left in his Pontiac Firebird.

As promised, Buzz drove to Undersea Warfare Center in New London and signed over Kim's check for the rent. Before leaving, Buzz had his landlord sign an application he had with him so they could apply for rent subsidy. If approved, Catholic Charities would pay any excess rent he and Kim couldn't afford each month.

By 4:10 P.M., as it started to rain a bit harder than it had throughout the day, Buzz was at home telling Kim what he'd been doing all day.

That's when things got a little sketchy. Buzz, Kim said, received a phone call at about 6:15 P.M. From what she could tell by hearing only Buzz's end of the call, someone was interested in buying his tow truck, which he'd had for sale for about a month. Buzz had placed an ad in the local *Bargain News* just two weeks ago. The truck had been good to Buzz. He had made money with it, but he just couldn't keep up with the maintenance: transmission, brakes, oil changes. Something was always wrong with the thing. Buzz had just recently repainted it and wanted to sell it to use the money to move to Arizona.

"Who was that?" Kim asked Buzz when he hung up the phone.

"I think I have the truck sold," Buzz said. "I'm meeting this guy at seven. But I have to go to my mother's first to pick up a battery."

Within minutes, Buzz left. It was about 6:30 P.M., Kim told Graham and Foley.

It was the last time she had ever seen or heard from her husband again.

During the course of the interview, Foley and Graham learned several things that could take them in any number of directions. But the most vital piece of information thus far was something Kim had said about a guy named Charlie Snyder. She said that Charlie, the owner and operator of Blonders Used Auto Parts, in nearby Waterford, and Buzz had not been getting along well lately. Buzz had owed Charlie about $1,500 for some auto parts Charlie had fronted him for his tow truck. Charlie would give Buzz auto parts under the agreement that Buzz would either pay him off when he got the money, or work it off, towing junk cars into Blonders. They had a love-hate relationship. As long as Buzz lived up to his responsibilities, Charlie later said, "I would give him the shirt off my back."

For the past few weeks, however, Buzz had been ducking Charlie's phone calls and avoiding Blonders. Charlie had even called the apartment a few days before and left Buzz a threatening message on his answering machine:

"If you don't pay me my money, I'm going to break your fucking legs."

Charlie Snyder grew up in Bloomfield, Connecticut, near the north end of Hartford. It was considered one of the toughest sections of the city, often leading in rape, murder and drug trade statistics. Red-haired, freckle-faced and scrawny, Charlie didn't fit into the black neighborhoods he frequented, and he learned quickly that survival on the street meant he had to be rough, regardless how big or strong he was.

After graduating from Bloomfield High School in 1972, Charlie bounced around for a while and spent some time in Europe. In 1982, not really sure of what he wanted to do, he saw an ad for a computer technician job at a local junkyard. He didn't know the first thing about computers or how to fix them. But he walked into the job as if he were the only one who could do it.

"It was one of those things," Snyder, who had turned forty a few days before Buzz was murdered, said, "where you look in the paper for a job and decide you can do it. I had no idea what I was doing."

Once he began working at it, Charlie figured the job out easily, then put his name into a pool of employment agencies. Gary Blonders, a local bigwig in the used-auto junk business, soon hired Charlie to put a computer system in Blonders Used Auto. When they sat and talked one day, Gary realized he could use Charlie in other areas and hired him as a salesman. By 1983, Charlie owned the Waterford Blonders.

As time passed, Charlie built a reputation in the Waterford area, a town sandwiched between New London and Old Lyme, for being the go-to guy if one needed cash. His name was known well on the streets.

"How come my shit never got ripped off?" Charlie

recalled later. "Because people knew there'd be a price. There was one time when one of my places got broken into. The cops caught the guys in the act. One of the guys went to jail, got out on bail and now walks with a limp. The message is out there. *I* didn't spread it. Buzz knew that if he didn't pay me what he owed me, he'd have to pay a price."

As Graham and Foley worked up a list of people to interview, at about midnight on March 11, John Turner and Pete Cleary went to interview someone whose name they'd gotten from Buzz's address book: a local kid named Rob Ferguson, who, they were told, might either know who would want Buzz dead, or commit the murder himself.

Ferguson and Buzz had run into each other on occasion throughout the past nine years, but they had recently met at a local bar. Buzz mentioned something about having a tow truck business and needing a space to rent, and Ferguson explained how he'd just opened a car-detailing place in town, Finishing Touch, and could rent out part of his garage.

"I saw him nearly every day," Ferguson told Turner and Cleary. "I began to learn about his personal life."

As Ferguson told it, Buzz had been having problems with drugs. Ferguson had never seen Buzz take drugs, he said, but being an ex-addict himself, he knew when someone was on drugs. He also mentioned that Buzz continually talked about the child custody case going on between Kim, Buzz and Kim's parents.

"Buzz told me that Kim's father had even grabbed him around the neck one time. But instead of fighting, Buzz just left to avoid being arrested."

Then the name Natalie Farmer came up again. Ferguson confirmed that Buzz had been having an affair with her for the past few weeks.

Turner asked Ferguson about Charlie Snyder.

"Yeah," Ferguson said, "Buzz had just mentioned yesterday that Blonders was going down . . . because some agency was going to begin checking the cars on the lot to make sure they had the proper titles. Charlie, before I kicked Buzz out of the garage on February twenty-third for not paying *me* rent, was calling here every day looking for him."

Turner and Cleary ended up with a five-page statement from Ferguson, which detailed his whereabouts for the night. Ferguson said the last time he saw Buzz was on March 9, at about 11:00 A.M. Buzz had cashed a check at the Lyme Tavern. Interesting to Turner and Cleary was the fact that Ferguson placed himself (at the time of the murder) at the Lyme Tavern. He even said a friend of his had come into the bar and mentioned something about an "incident" on the Rocky Neck connector that involved a "dead man" who was driving a Firebird with Maine plates. When Ferguson heard that, he said, he rushed over to Buzz and Kim's apartment to find out if she knew anything.

"It was about nine," Ferguson recalled.

"Do you or anyone you know own a gun?" Turner asked.

"The only person . . . I know [who] owns a gun is Buzz. He showed it to me twice. I think it's a twenty-two."

Turner and Cleary promised they'd be back in a day or two.

Chapter 4

On Friday, March 11, Dr. H. Wayne Carver, the chief medical examiner from Farmington, Connecticut, determined that Buzz had been killed by "multiple gunshot wounds to the body." Five shots in all. The doctor ruled his death, to no one's surprise, a homicide—one of over two hundred that would pass through the medical examiner's office by year's end.

It wasn't difficult for Dr. Carver to figure out which gunshot killed Buzz: one of the bullets had punctured both of his lungs, heart and aorta. In theory, Buzz had drowned in his own blood. What became an issue later, however, was a debate over how much Buzz had likely suffered. By studying his wounds, one might easily conclude that Buzz didn't die a quick and painless death.

There was no definitive way to determine the actual order in which the bullets had entered Buzz's body, which would have, quite convincingly, given the doctor a clearer picture of how much he had suffered, along with where the murderer was standing at the time he fired. So when Dr. Carver sat down to write his report, the best he could do was describe exactly what he found.

The first bullet extracted from Buzz's body had entered through the soft part of his right ear, which Dr. Carver opined was fired on him "from the front toward the back." The second wound he examined had originated in "the

back of his neck, just to the right of midline," slightly
below the earlobe. It had traveled "from the back of him
toward the front, slightly left." During its trek, the bullet
"passed through the bones that stick out of the back of
[the] spinal column and support the spinal cord, and frac-
tured them." Oddly, as it proceeded through his neck,
through his tonsils and into the back of his tongue, it went
straight through the tongue on a flat line, finally exiting
out of the tip of it, loosening two of his bottom teeth and
grazing the inside of his lip. The third bullet went "in on
the upper right portion of his back . . . [near] the middle
of his shoulder blade and went upward toward his [left]
side and toward the front, then went through the shoulder apparatus and ended near the front of the shoulder
apparatus," or his middle, upper back. The fourth entered
through "a little graze on the arm, right side . . . [and]
went from the back of his body toward the front, from the
right side toward the left. It went through the thick muscular part of the shoulder attachment and came out . . . in
the front of the muscular part of the right side of the chest
[but] did not enter the chest cavity." Number five was,
without a doubt, the wound that killed Buzz. It had entered "on the right chest, two inches above the nipple,
went from the front of his body toward the back, on the
right side toward the left and somewhat downwards, went
through both lungs, the heart and the aorta . . . then
ended [its trajectory] toward the back left, lower chest." It
was only one of two bullets the doctor had extracted.

   In all likelihood, considering the injuries Buzz sustained, the position of his body when Steven and Christine
Roy arrived on the scene, and the fact that the medical examiner extracted only two bullets from his body, the
sequence of his injuries could have perhaps happened
only one way:

   The first shot was likely the one that had struck Buzz's
right ear. When this happened, his natural reflex told him

to grab hold of it with his right arm, which exposed the entire back, right side of his body to his killer, allowing the next two bullets to hit him in the shoulder blade area and the armpit area. From there, the next wound was likely in the neck area—the bullet that hit him in the back of the neck and exited out of his tongue. When the bullet pierced his spinal column and cord, it dropped him to the ground almost instantly, perhaps like a puppet whose strings had been cut. The impact of these four wounds and the shock his body suffered from the injuries probably forced it to spin around. As he fell, his body turned a bit, exposing his right side, allowing the next bullet—the fatal bullet—to enter his chest, ricochet off his rib cage, pierce his lungs, aorta and heart. This was obvious from the shape of the bullet: it was frayed and ripped open like a chunk of lead that had been blown apart from the inside out. With the amount of internal bleeding that occurred at this point, and Buzz's lungs, aorta and heart all punctured, he had likely drowned in his own blood. The only comforting notion about this theory is that Buzz probably didn't feel anything because he had been paralyzed by the last shot. Nevertheless, even though this all took place in a matter of seconds, he likely felt a great deal of pain as he died and, most certainly, knew what was happening to him. Some say it was possible he could have lived for between five and six minutes after the fatal shot.

What was clearly evident from the beginning was that Buzz's killer was one of the best shots many of the ED-MCS detectives had ever seen. It had been dark, Buzz was moving toward his killer when he was shot. Still, his killer had managed to strike him five times with a .38-caliber revolver. As Reggie Wardell and John Turner later put it, most cops aren't capable of such accuracy.

Factoring this efficiency didn't mean Buzz had been killed by a professional. It hadn't been a clean job, like a mob hit, for example. Buzz's killer most probably was a person full of rage or resentment. Perhaps he was someone who had never killed before, but had just snapped. Buzz had gotten out of his car, walked a few feet and was mowed down in a fury of gunfire. From all the evidence collected, there had been every reason to believe that very little thought had been put into the murder—especially considering where it took place.

Dr. Carver also found several abrasions on Buzz's lower torso: "He had one on the upper body and several on his leg."

There was no way to prove it, and Dr. Carver disagreed, but it was possible the killer had run Buzz over as he lay helpless, bleeding, suffocating on his own blood. Reggie Wardell was present during the autopsy. Cops often take part in autopsies because they can ask questions as they come up during the procedure. The ED-MCS had always emphasized the importance of its cops being at autopsies.

Wardell had taken Buzz's clothes and laid them out on a gurney near his body to take photographs. "I remember seeing clothing on Buzz's body that indicated debris or markings," Wardell recalled. "I personally had the impression then that he was run over."

Buzz's blood had been screened for everything: cocaine, heroin, alcohol. The only drug Dr. Carol Fletterick, a toxicologist, found was caffeine.

In Buzz's front pocket, investigators found one Bic lighter, his "yellow metal" wedding band and $5.62.

Christine and Steven Roy had spent better nights in their marriage. When all was said and done, they had been at the crime scene for nearly four hours. By midnight, March 11, they had arrived back home flustered and confused at the thought of having witnessed a murder.

Christine still wasn't sure of the make and model of the

vehicle she'd spied leaving the scene. She wanted to help the cops, of course, but for the life of her, she just couldn't remember what model car it was.

As she made her way to work the following day, Christine kept her eyes open for a car similar to the one she had seen. She knew she would recognize it if she ever saw it again. For some reason, the taillights stuck out. They were different, she thought. Larger. More pronounced. *Nissan,* she told herself while driving. *It was definitely a Nissan.*

Later that morning, at about 11:30, John Turner and Reggie Wardell showed up at Christine's work unannounced to ask her a few follow-up questions. They had a book of photos: every type of vehicle imaginable.

Maybe she could pick out the vehicle in a lineup?

Taking her time, Christine looked at each vehicle carefully, as if she were scouring a book of mug shots looking for a perp. One of the ideas investigators had during that first twenty-four-hour period was: *find the car, find the killer.*

"I know the taillights went all the way across the back of the car," Christine said as she browsed through the book. But she still wasn't sure.

For about an hour, Christine scanned every car in the book, but she still couldn't pin down a positive identification.

"I just don't see the car, sorry."

"Here's my card," Turner said. "Call me if you think of anything else."

Later that afternoon, as Christine made her way through traffic on Interstate 84 on her way home from work, she spotted a car on the highway that immediately looked familiar. It was, as she had first thought, a Nissan Pulsar. The taillights, like on the car she had seen, went across the back of the entire car. It was definitely the same type of vehicle.

When she got home, she phoned Turner. He was gone, so she left him a voice mail message: "I figured it out," Christine said with some excitement in her voice. "It was a Nissan Pulsar. . . . Call me back, please."

To her surprise, nobody from the Connecticut State Police ever returned her call. In fact, she wouldn't hear back from them again for *seven* years.

As it turned out, as Turner and Wardell began to examine Buzz's life further, they had no reason to think that Christine Roy could be much help—for they were concentrating now on a number of suspects, one of whom they were certain killed Buzz.

During the early-morning hours of March 11, someone by the name of *Victor Page,* a local kid who'd had his share of troubles with the law in the past, had phoned the state police. Without identifying himself, Page told a trooper how on the night of the murder, at about 7:30, he'd watched two cars exit I-95 near Exit 72 and pull over to the side of the road. One, Page said, was a Firebird with Maine license plates. The other was a '78 or '82 Impala or Caprice, two tone in color, maybe maroon or silver.

It had no license plate.

During the day, Turner and Wardell tried tracking Page down, but they couldn't find him.

What they didn't know, however, was that Victor Page owned a blue Nissan.

Detectives spread out. From the interview Marty Graham and Mike Foley had conducted with Kim Clinton, several names emerged that could lead to the profile of a possible killer. There were several people Buzz knew who had, at one time or another, said some pretty nasty things about him. There were several more to whom Buzz had owed money. There were others who had even threatened him on occasion.

Every last threat and altercation Buzz had gotten into had to be taken seriously—no matter who had made it. There was even a state trooper who had had words with

Buzz sometime before his murder. Dee Clinton told detectives she thought for sure the trooper had tracked Buzz down and murdered him. She also said that Buzz had had problems with crack and alcohol in the past but had gone into detox and licked both problems. Perhaps he was back on dope and had burned a dealer?

Both matters had to be considered.

Rob Ferguson was another person who had to be looked at more closely. Buzz and Rob had been friends, true. But also enemies. They had worked together. Drank together. Hung out together.

On the night of March 10, Rob had stopped by Buzz and Kim's apartment in East Lyme. He'd already confessed to that. When he arrived, he said, he was looking for Buzz. Kim was at home preparing the kids for bed. It wasn't, Kim later remembered, a typical conversation: "Where's Buzz? When is he going to be home?" Instead, Rob seemed worried, nervous, Kim stated. He had a beer in his hand, and there was someone in the car waiting for him.

"Someone with a Pontiac Firebird with Maine plates," Rob told Kim, "was shot twice on the Rocky Neck connector."

"Where'd you hear that?"

"Kippy told me. I was at the Lyme Tavern."

"What?"

Rob took a pull from his beer. Then, "You should call the East Lyme Police Department and find out what's going on."

"I will."

"Call me when you find out anything."

The conversation had taken about five minutes. But ten minutes later, Rob phoned Kim and asked if she had heard anything.

Kim said she hadn't.

When detectives interviewed Rob a second and third

time, he admitted to having been involved in an insurance scam with Buzz. Buzz had smashed into Rob's car, and they had agreed to split the insurance money. Then he told another detective that Charlie Snyder had called the shop and threatened Buzz. When Reggie Wardell interviewed Rob, he asked him straight out, "Did you kill Buzz?"

"No!" Rob shot back.

"Were you involved in any way?"

"No, damn it! I wasn't."

"Do you know who might have been?"

"No."

Detective Paul Poissant, another detective from the ED-MCS, tracked down twenty-seven-year-old Kevin Myers, an unemployed mechanic who had known Buzz fairly well. The purpose of the interview was to find out what the relationship between Myers and Buzz had been like. Rob Ferguson had given Myers's name to detectives. Myers was part of the crowd. He, Rob and Buzz had been pretty tight at one time.

Myers said he had known Buzz for about four years and had worked for him on occasion, up until about three weeks ago.

"Buzz had always paid me on time, if not early," Myers said.

Poissant asked him about Buzz's friends.

"There's some people around town who owe Buzz money for car work."

"When was the last time you spoke to him?"

"About two days ago, over the phone. The last time I saw him was about three weeks ago, the day I stopped working for him."

Myers knew that Buzz had been murdered before Poissant told him. Although the story had been plastered all over the area newspapers and local television, Poissant was still curious as to how Myers had found out.

"I saw his father this morning. He told me."

Myers further explained that he knew of no drug use history of Buzz's. But more than that, Myers had just recently been fired from Blonders for stealing and using cocaine. Charlie Snyder, himself a reformed addict, had little tolerance for drug users.

"What else can you tell me, Kevin?"

"I know that he was having problems with his father-in-law."

There it was again—another indication that Buzz and Dick Carpenter had an ongoing spat that Buzz had been telling people about.

Poissant made a note. While writing, he asked, "Okay . . . what about Rob Ferguson?"

"Rob and Buzz got along fine. There were a few problems here and there, but nothing bad."

"What about women? Did Buzz screw around?"

Myers said he knew for a fact that Buzz had been cheating on Kim with someone. ". . . I'm not sure of her name."

Poissant finally wanted to know more about one of their main suspects, Charlie Snyder.

"Do you know him?"

"Yeah, I know Charlie," Myers said, looking away.

"Tell me about him."

"Well, Charlie was always accusing people of owing him money. He liked to threaten people, too."

After a few more questions, Poissant said thanks and told Myers that someone would be in touch with him soon.

From the look of things, it was time to put some pressure on Charlie Snyder.

Chapter 5

Before ED-MCS detectives could focus on Charlie Snyder, they had some groundwork to cover first. It had only been twenty-four hours since the discovery of Buzz's body, and there was no sense in hurrying the investigative process along. Information was coming in at a pretty good clip. There was no need to push it. Follow the evidence. Follow the leads. Let them dictate what to do next.

Detectives John Szamocki and Marty Graham were assigned to interview Buzz's present father-in-law, Richard "Dick" Carpenter, on March 11, at about 10:30 A.M.—the one man who, according to some, had good reason to kill Buzz.

Ledyard, Connecticut, where the Carpenters lived, was quite a ride from East Lyme, but only a few miles away the ED-MCS headquarters, in Norwich.

Dick and Cynthia Carpenter grew up in Ledyard, which is a mere pinpoint on the map of New England. About sixty miles northeast of Hartford, Ledyard is sandwiched between two major industrial cities: Norwich and Groton. Settled in 1863, Ledyard encompasses some forty square miles, and before the state of Connecticut allowed it to become the home of the Mashantucket Pequot Indian Casino—or Foxwoods, a full-fledged casino with thousands of gaming tables and slot machines—it housed about fifteen thousand residents. It was suburban heaven.

Quiet. Laid-back. Countrified. Corn stands were common in the summer and pumpkin stands in the fall. Clapboarded ranch-style homes and refurbished colonials date back to the seventeenth century. Farmland, winding roads and hidden trails to break horses and ride motorbikes were scattered all about.

Dick Carpenter, a twenty-two-year U.S. Navy man, retired in the early 1980s and started a landscaping business, which had done well throughout the years. People in Ledyard knew Dick. They liked him. Trusted his work. Cynthia Carpenter, ever so prudish, a smart woman by many standards, became an Advanced Practice Board–certified practical nurse, consulting in nursing homes and psychiatric nursing. She was even certified to write prescriptions. Her educational credentials ran the gamut: a nursing degree, a bachelor's, two masters.

Dick Carpenter had a full shock of concrete-gray-and-black hair, a bulging Santa Claus stomach—the same as any beer-guzzling construction worker—large, beefy hands and stubby arms and legs. He wore shirts too small and pants too tight. He wasn't all that tall, at about five feet nine inches, but at approximately 250 pounds, he wasn't someone who had any trouble taking care of himself, either.

Stone-faced and shell-shocked when he answered the door on March 11, Dick resembled an old-time farmer from out West, right down to his blue jeans, glaring belt buckle and plaid shirt.

By the looks of the Carpenters' yard on Indiantown Road, located in Ledyard's south end, it wasn't too difficult to tell that Dick was a blue-collar man all the way. There were skeletons of rusty cars and trucks, old machines, tractors, rusty truck plows, rusty tools and, oddly enough, several different types of lawn ornaments spread throughout the yard, sort of just dumped there as if the place were a cemetery for old and unwanted machinery and crafts. Ironically, waist-high grass grew wild in certain sections of the landscaper's yard and leaves were piled everywhere. The paint on the house, a dull puke green, flaked to the touch and, in some areas, had fallen like confetti around the base of the home. Doors, windows and shutters needed to be replaced. Set back a bit from the road, the modest home couldn't compare to anything out of *House & Garden*, but it had a kitchen, one-and-a-half baths and enough bedrooms to raise a family.

Just down the road, the Mashantucket Pequot Indian tribe—owners and operators of the world's largest casino, a massive structure with a hotel that rose out of the trees like a skyscraper just across the street from the Carpenters' home—had its main reservation office, where the rather tall tepeelike structure that welcomed arrivals to the reservation stood erect.

So far, detectives had several people suggesting that Dick was the point man in the death of his son-in-law. As bold as it was, there was even one cop who had told the Roys on the night of the murder that Dick had had something to do with it. But it was all talk. Detectives had no proof. If they had, they wouldn't be showing up in Ledyard without an arrest warrant.

What was well documented, however, was that Dick and Buzz had hated each other with a fevered passion that had sometimes manifested into pushing and shoving. They argued just about every time they were in the same room together, and they were heard on many occasions threatening each other. A burly man, nearly twice the size of Buzz, Dick could have possibly broken Buzz in two with one arm if he'd wanted to.

But murder?

A seven-year veteran of the Connecticut State Police, Detective Szamocki was himself no slouch of a man. A bit lanky at six feet three inches, Szamocki was solid and strong. He carried himself with confidence and spoke like a well-trained cop. He knew which questions to ask Dick and which to leave back at the station for watercooler talk. He couldn't step into the Carpenters' home and begin accusing Dick of murder without any solid evidence.

Szamocki and Graham were on the hunt for information. The theorizing would come later, when all the interviews had been conducted and the detectives could sift through the facts.

"Come on in," Dick said as he opened the door. "This is my wife, Cynthia."

They retreated to the living room, which was just up at the top of the stairs. Cynthia, with her curly red hair and slim figure, looked academic and bookish, but she managed to hold on to an air of intrigue and secrecy. She was a thinker—it was easy to tell right away—not a talker.

"We're here," Szamocki said, "to investigate the apparent homicide of Buzz Clinton, your son-in-law. We need any information you may have that might help us investigate the case."

As Dick and Cynthia became acquainted with the detectives, discussing routine matters, Richard Carpenter, Cynthia and Dick's son, showed up. Rather skinny, with a long, detailed, pudgy face, Richard mostly resembled his mother. The only hint that Dick was Richard's father was the receding hairline.

About thirty minutes into the interview, Beth Ann, the couple's eldest daughter, thirty years old, came strolling in. She was with her boss, a local big-shot real estate attorney, Haiman Long Clein, who had, three weeks prior, turned fifty-three. Beth Ann had been working for Clein for about the past year and a half. It was her first real job as a lawyer. Clein was a big man, standing six feet two inches, weighing two hundred pounds. He had a full beard and mustache, and was dressed as one might expect a lawyer to be: snazzy pants, dress shirt, jacket.

Still, Szamocki and Graham noticed that Clein looked tired and beaten down, his shirt halfway sticking out of his pants, his face a bit jaundiced and sweaty.

When Beth Ann stood next to her mother, it wasn't hard to tell that if they were the same age, they could easily pass for sisters. Beth Ann's shoulder-length red hair was radiant and silky, like satin. Besides her apple red lipstick, she wore little makeup to accentuate her pale-white skin. She appeared stoic and serious, as if the weight of the situation had just hit her. She hadn't told anyone, but she was pregnant with Haiman Clein's child, and she was determined to have it—whatever the cost to Clein, who was married with four children, plus an adult child from a previous marriage.

Clein and Beth Ann walked in and sat down in the living room.

"I'm Detective Szamocki. This is my partner, Detective Graham," Szamocki said, extending his hand to Clein. "Have a seat."

As the two detectives questioned Cynthia and Dick, they occasionally asked Beth Ann and Clein if they had anything to add. Most of the discussion was geared toward Dick's rocky relationship with Buzz and his family.

Beth Ann and Clein watched and listened carefully to what was going on. Being lawyers, they knew the boundary lines. If any accusations had been made, the interview would be terminated immediately.

Dick said at one point that Rebecca had made comments such as, "Daddy beats my butt," referring to Buzz. He said they were concerned that Buzz had been abusing her. And an investigation for sexual assault had even been opened back in December 1993.

"Do you own any firearms?" Szamocki asked at that point.

"An old rifle and shotgun."

"What about a handgun?"

"Nope."

"Can we have a look at the guns?"

"Sure," Dick said, and left to go get them.

After a few more questions, Dick provided an alibi for March 10. Szamocki and Graham, however, were quick to note that the only person who could verify Dick's alibi was Cynthia. Being his wife, she was immune from testifying if it ever came down to it.

"If you think of anything else, please call us."

If there was one person with a motive to murder Buzz, detectives realized, it was *Scott Farmer*, Natalie Farmer's husband. When interviewed at his home in Old Lyme, just west of East Lyme, late in the day on March 11, Scott said that Buzz had been calling his house between three and four times a day looking for Natalie.

"I told her to stop talking to him. . . . I told her. . . ." Farmer said. "Buzz was becoming a pain in the ass!"

"Were you aware of an affair between them?"

"No. I don't think she was having an affair. But one can never be sure."

"Where were you Thursday night?"

"Home, here, watching my baby by myself."

"All night?"

Farmer hesitated, then ran his hand through his hair.

"Well, I left here about seven-thirty to go over to the firehouse in town. My mother came over to baby-sit."

"How long were you there?"

"Until eleven o'clock."

A second detective interviewed Natalie Farmer in another room while Scott was being questioned.

Natalie admitted that she'd had a "brief sexual affair with Buzz." They'd had sex twice, she said, but recently ended the affair to save her marriage. She remained friends with Buzz, though, she claimed, and she had spoken to him often on the phone.

"What would he tell you?"

"He was having problems with Rob Ferguson," Natalie said.

"Do you know anything about Mr. Ferguson?"

"He has a bad temper . . . and, in my opinion, is capable of shooting someone."

Chapter 6

Christopher George, a twenty-four-year-old local man who worked at Foxwoods casino, was the person who had told Rob Ferguson there was a dead guy on the Rocky Neck connector on the night Buzz had been murdered. Chris had stopped at the Lyme Tavern for a beer and had run into Rob. As soon as Rob heard about the shooting, he drove over to Kim's apartment and told her.

There were a few things, however, Rob had said to Chris that led detectives to begin focusing not on Rob, but more on Charlie Snyder.

For example, Rob had told Chris that Buzz was in debt for "a lot of money" to Charlie—which, of course, was one of the oldest motives in the world for murder.

When Marty Graham and John Szamocki arrived at Blonders on Saturday, March 12, the front-desk clerk, Kevin Albrecht, told them that Charlie had left town.

Szamocki and Graham were puzzled. "Where did he go?"

"Skiing. He's in New York. He left this morning. I don't know exactly where."

"When will he be back?"

"Monday maybe? I'm not too sure."

Kevin eventually, after a bit of prodding, told them that Buzz had owed Charlie a lot of money, in the neighborhood of $500 to $600. Then, "What I know of Buzz is that he's a bullshitter!"

"You have Charlie call us when he gets back," Graham said, handing Kevin his business card.

Reggie Wardell was a crack investigator. He had worked for the Organized Crime Unit of the state police for many years before joining the ED-MCS. With the help of his colleagues, Wardell had busted two of Connecticut's most reputed mobsters after a long and tedious investigation. But the murder of Buzz Clinton, Wardell explained later, even in its early stage, was turning into a textbook whodunit case.

"People can be temporarily eliminated as suspects," Wardell recalled, "until they are brought back into the picture by some piece of evidence or witness."

Charlie Snyder was one of those people.

Canvassing the neighborhood near Blonders on March 14, Wardell walked into Flanders's Shell, in East Lyme, only miles down the road from Blonders. The manager, Mike Magliano, worked the day shift and had known Snyder as someone who came in every morning to get his daily dose of caffeine. The last time Mike had seen Charlie, he explained to Wardell, they had a conversation that he thought he ought to relay to the cops after reading about Buzz's murder in the newspaper.

According to Magliano, on March 10, Charlie had walked into the Shell station at about 9:00 A.M., and Mike noticed almost immediately that he "looked a bit pissed" at something.

"What's wrong?" Mike said he asked Charlie when he saw how upset he looked.

"Ah . . . someone called the DEP on me for dumping chemicals on the ground at Blonders." Charlie was

frowning. His teeth clenched. Not paying attention to
what was going on around him.

"Really," Mike said.

"Yeah. But I know who the motherfucker is! I caught
him stealing once. Instead of calling the cops, I beat the
shit out of him and fired him."

Charlie then collected his change and began walking
toward the door.

"What are you going to do?" Mike asked.

"Now that fucker is dead!" Charlie said as he walked out.

Laurence Myers was an employee at Blonders who
had heard about Buzz's murder and phoned the state
police with information he thought might be useful.
Myers, who had worked for Charlie since 1993, told a
trooper he thought Buzz owed Charlie about $800 or
$900. On Wednesday, March 9, Myers said he was stand-
ing next to Charlie when Charlie phoned Buzz and told
him that "if he didn't get his money, he was going to get
taken out."

On Thursday morning, the Department of Environ-
mental Protection (DEP) called Blonders at 8:30 A.M.
and said that they would be showing up later that day.

"Charlie was very upset," Myers recalled to police. "He
said he was tired of people playing with him." When
Myers asked Charlie who he thought had made the complaint to the DEP, Charlie muttered, "Buzz made the
complaint."

After speaking to Mike Magliano and Laurence Myers,
John Turner and Reggie Wardell drove over to Blonders
early in the morning on Monday, March 14, and informed Susan Nance, one of Charlie's employees, that
they needed to speak to Charlie right away.

Forty-year-old Nance, a loyal friend to Charlie for years,
who had also known Buzz pretty well, said, "He's not
here."

"We need to talk to him," Turner said. He didn't actually say that Charlie was a suspect, but Susan clearly got the impression that Turner and Wardell weren't there to buy a refurbished alternator for one of their cruisers.

"I'll tell him when he gets back."

Susan was Charlie's eyes and ears when he wasn't around. Not only did she wait on customers, but she answered phones and kept things honest when Charlie took time off.

Charlie hadn't left for his skiing trip on Saturday, as many had originally thought. He left early on Friday morning. He and his wife had spent the day driving to Lake Placid, New York.

After Turner and Wardell left Blonders, Susan Nance phoned Charlie at the condo he'd rented and told him what was going on.

"Buzz is dead, you know?" Nance said.

There was a brief pause.

"Get the fuck out of town," Charlie said. "No fucking way."

When Charlie hung up, he turned to his wife and stared at her in quiet disbelief.

"What's wrong?" she asked.

"Buzz Clinton is dead."

"*What?*"

"Can you believe it?"

For perhaps the first time in his life, Charlie Snyder was fully satisfied with the person he had become. He lived simply now: New England Patriot games on Sundays and shooting darts with his pals at the local pub after work during the week. With his boyhood red hair grown out into a hue of blond, halfway down his back, Snyder kept it pulled back in a ponytail these days. He wore reading glasses and crunched numbers for his business and waited on customers most of the time. His voice was scratchy and a bit hoarse. When his employees spoke to him, they addressed him with the respect and authority he had earned throughout the years. What had once been a place where every derelict and drug addict in town came to loiter and get high, Charlie said later, Blonders had become a sort of a safe haven in recent years. Ever since Charlie had entered into recovery himself sometime ago, he'd turned Blonders into a place where people could hang out and feel safe.

"We always had a pot of coffee on," he recalled. "People could come in and just sit and talk about what was going on in their life."

Before he was murdered, Buzz was one of those people.

Charlie had not only hired Buzz to work for him, but he'd gotten to know Kim and the kids. He felt bad for Buzz when things didn't go his way and was friendly with Buzz's mother, Dee Clinton. Over the years, Charlie noticed how Dee had always gone out of her way for Buzz, helping him wherever she could. But when Buzz failed to follow her rules, she'd cut him off. Tough love. Being in recovery, Charlie understood that it was the only way to reach someone sometimes—especially a family member.

"She wanted to see Buzz do the right thing, and it hurt her when he didn't. I was, in a way, her eyes and ears when she wasn't around. I, too, wanted Buzz to make something of himself." Furthermore, Charlie said, Buzz wasn't someone who had to watch his back. "If someone would have asked me to make a list of twenty people to possibly be murdered, Buzz's name would *not* have been on that list. Not even close. He was a hustler, sure. But he didn't rip people off. He had people who cared about him, and he cared about people. The kid tried to put food on his table, and he didn't have a full-time job. His mother and father helped out where they could. But he did what he had to do."

Driving back from Lake Placid with his wife, Charlie contemplated the next few days ahead. It was odd to him that he was now a prime suspect in Buzz's murder. He had an alibi for the night in question, but he still wondered how far the cops were going to pressure him.

Charlie Snyder was the first to admit that he, at least for the past year or so, had been supporting Buzz and had been angry with him at times. Charlie gave Buzz work and advice. He loaned him money. Fronted him parts for his tow truck. But there were times, Charlie later confessed, when it seemed that Buzz was ungrateful.

"I shared in a lot of Buzz's life those last few months. He told me about his desire to become a nurse. It was his ticket out of Connecticut. I encouraged him to go for it. He wanted so bad to do better for himself and his kids. He talked all the time about getting help for his drinking. He wanted to stop. Buzz knew that he could come to Blonders and talk to someone about his problems. People—good people—were always around. That wrecker he owned, it was his life. He relied on it to earn a living. He loved that truck. He paid off most of his debts to me by towing cars. I called him all the time. I would say, 'Hey, asshole, you owe me money, get your ass down here and tow some cars. Don't give me any bullshit. This isn't anybody else you're talking to.'

"He'd show up and work for a couple of days, and then I wouldn't see him again for a while."

Now all of those conversations and seemingly baseless remarks of "You better pay me, or else" would be looked at under a microscope. Anything Charlie had ever said to or about Buzz, especially over the past week or so, would come into question now that Buzz had been murdered.

When Charlie returned to work on Tuesday, March 15, he called the Westbrook state police barracks and informed them that two detectives had been looking for him in connection with Buzz's murder.

Dispatch informed him that someone would be out to see him soon.

An hour later, at 9:55 A.M., Reggie Wardell and John

Turner showed up. When they walked in, Charlie was behind the counter, flipping through an auto parts manual looking for an item.

"Hold on," Charlie said when he looked up and saw who it was. "Let's go outside. I've got customers here. This is private."

As the three men walked outside, Charlie's employees looked on with curiosity. They knew what was going on and recognized that Charlie had been acting a bit strange the past few days: nervous, fidgety, not himself.

Leaning against a fence out in the yard, Wardell began the interview.

"Can you tell us about Buzz Clinton?"

"What do you want to know?"

"Start with how you heard about his murder."

"Well, Ray Myers, an older customer of mine, told one of my employees last Saturday that I was considered a suspect in the murder. I should add that Kevin Myers, Ray Myers's son, used to work here, but he's been *excused* for using cocaine and stealing."

Charlie then explained that when he returned from New York, he called the Westbrook barracks first thing in the morning. He then spoke of his relationship with Kim and the kids; how they used to come into Blonders with Buzz and sometimes hang out in the office while Buzz was out on the road working. Charlie said he liked Kim. "She was quiet, friendly. Buzz loved her."

"When was the last time you saw him?"

"I gave him a transmission for his tow truck about a month ago. He never paid me. He said he was going to open up a shop called Finishing Touch, cleaning cars, bodywork. Whatever work he could get."

"Did you ever go down there?"

"Nope."

As Wardell and Turner continued their questioning, Charlie noticed a change in their approach and demeanor. It had gone from a relaxed cadence, just talking back and forth, to more of a hostile, Joe Friday–like interrogation. Charlie didn't want any part of the good cop/bad cop routine. As he saw it, he had nothing to hide.

It became apparent to Wardell and Turner that on some days Buzz would treat Charlie like the long-lost big brother he'd never had, and on others he would avoid Charlie like the plague.

"How did you meet him?"

"Buzz just walked in off the street and asked for some work. So I gave it to him."

It was about a year and a half ago, Charlie explained.

"What about money—he owed you money?"

"Buzz's parents had thrown him and Kim out of their house, and Buzz needed money," Charlie said. "He also needed some parts for his tow truck. I gave them to him. I told him to pay me back when he got it."

Wardell explained that it was possible that Buzz had been trying to sell his tow truck on the night he was killed. Charlie said the tow truck had broken down last summer. Since then, he really hadn't seen Buzz much. When Charlie became worried about the money, he said he called Big Jim's Junk Yard in Essex. He'd heard that Buzz was doing some work for Big Jim.

Then the subject moved to Charlie himself. Wardell and Turner wanted to know if he hung around area bars.

"I'm a reformed substance abuser—I don't hang around bars!"

"What about Buzz?"

"Buzz, as far as I know, was involved with dope through association."

"Let's talk about last Thursday night, Charlie."

Customers had been coming and going as the three men stood and talked outside. Curious and snoopy, every once in a while, one of Charlie's employees would look out through the blinds in the window to try to get a handle on what was being said. Charlie was beginning to feel like a lab rat, he later recalled. The questions were getting uncomfortable.

"I drove by Exit 72 at about . . . I was traveling, I believe, east bound, at about eight-thirty, maybe eight forty-five. The entrance ramp was closed."

"Where were you coming from?"

"My therapist's office in Southington." Southington, north of New Haven, was about an hour's drive from Blonders.

"What time did you leave for Southington?"

"I worked all day Thursday. I went home after work, maybe five. Changed my shirt. And left. I stopped at Shell in town to get gas and—"

"What is your therapist's name?"

"As I was saying, I bought a bag of peanuts at the Shell station."

"The name, Charlie?"

"Henry Schliser. My appointment was at six. I left his office about seven."

If Charlie was telling the truth, he really didn't have time to kill Buzz. Christine and Steven Roy had found Buzz's body at about 7:30 P.M. No one knew the exact time of death as of yet, but by all accounts, it was between 6:30 and 7:30 P.M.

"Where did you go after you left your therapist's?"

"I stopped in Old Saybrook to attend a recovery meeting, but then changed my mind, and went home to talk to my wife about what had happened during my therapy session."

Before they asked, Charlie thought he'd better own up to something that might be important.

"I own five rifles and a thirty-eight-caliber handgun," he said.

Silence.

Not much was known about the crime, but investigators

were certain that Buzz had been killed with a .38. More important, though, was that they believed he had not only been killed by someone he knew, but by the hand of an expert shot—like a hunter or marksman.

"Where are the weapons?"

"My handgun is at home. My rifles are in my office."

"Would any of your employees know anything about Buzz?"

"Maybe. I'm not sure."

"We need a list of names. We also need a list of names of the people at your recovery meeting, people who can back up the fact that you were there. They may need to sign statements. . . ."

"No way. Recovery is all about anonymity. I can't do that."

It was getting to the point where Charlie felt as if he had already said too much.

"I have to get back to work."

"We may be back to talk to you, Charlie," Wardell warned.

As they started to walk away, Charlie said, "Let me ask you something, Detectives. Did Buzz have his tow truck with him when he was killed?"

"No. Why do you ask?"

"What car was he driving?"

"His car. The Firebird."

"I don't buy the tow truck scenario," Charlie said. "If Buzz was going to sell his truck, I know him well enough to know that he would have had the truck with him."

It had been a long morning for Charlie Snyder. He had been asked questions he thought were way out of line and had given answers, he now thought, that maybe he shouldn't have. After all, the ED-MCS didn't have a warrant.

At 4:45 P.M. that same day, Wardell and Turner returned to Blonders. Charlie walked them outside again.

"What do you want now?"

"Had you spoken to Buzz over the phone lately?"

"No. I told you I hadn't seen him in a while."

"Tell us again why you didn't go to that recovery meeting?"

"Listen, I'm cooperating with you guys. Don't push it."

"We need to know who was at the meeting, Charlie."

"It's none of your fucking business who was at that meeting."

"Listen, we just—"

"No," Charlie interrupted, "you listen to me. If you want me to talk to you, you had better change your fucking tone with me. There's nothing that says I *have* to talk to you. I have an alibi. It's locked. Do your fucking jobs."

Charlie felt that if they had gone out and done their jobs, they would have exonerated him by now. It was a matter of doing the footwork. Charlie Snyder had no patience for lazy people, especially lazy cops, he said later. What was more, he was overwhelmed that he had told them about his guns, yet they dropped the subject as quick as they brought it up. Charlie didn't know Buzz had been killed with a .38. Still, he wondered why they hadn't come back with a warrant for his guns. Or even ask to smell the chambers.

Chapter 7

The ED-MCS held an 8:00 A.M. informal meeting every day. It was a time for detectives to get together before the workday began and discuss cases. Toss out ideas. Brainstorm. Confer about cases as a unit. "Gossip chat." What each detective thought about a particular witness. Evidence. Hunches. Gut feelings. They were a team. They respected one another's opinions. No idea was a bad idea. Homicide is an irrational act, and cops have to think irrationally to solve a case. The 8:00 A.M. meetings were a time for that. No two crimes were ever the same; no two criminals were alike.

"How did we know," Reggie Wardell said later, "that Buzz didn't just piss someone off on the highway, and that guy decided to take out his anger by shooting him? We had to keep an open mind. It seemed that everyone we spoke to early on opened another door."

The two most prominent suspects were Charlie Snyder and Rob Ferguson. And by March 15, each witness that detectives had spoken to seemed to bolster further the theory that one of the two had killed Buzz.

Marty Graham spoke to another former employee of Blonders who had some negative things to say about Charlie. It turned out that it wasn't Buzz who had called the DEP on Charlie, but a guy named *Brad Riggs,* who claimed that Charlie not only had threatened his family when he found out he had made the DEP call, but also said he thought Buzz owed Charlie a lot more money than people were saying.

Kim Clinton, when she was reinterviewed on March 15, put Rob Ferguson's feet closer to the fire by saying that Rob had called Buzz back in February looking for his rent money, and when Kim said that Buzz wasn't around, Rob told her that "he will have more fucking problems unless he calls me back." Then she indicated that she was positive someone had called on the night Buzz was murdered and wanted information about a "Toyota" or "Mustang" that Buzz had had for sale. There was even the chance, she said, that Buzz had gone off to meet the person who had called so he could show him the cars.

Buzz's body had been released by the medical examiner's office on March 16. The Clintons, nearly a week after Buzz had been killed, could finally put him to rest. Dee Clinton had already said good-bye to her son on the day he was murdered. The funeral, she later said, was just a way to say good-bye to his body.

Dee and her family were, of course, devastated by the loss. In many ways, Buzz had been the center of the Clinton family. Now he was gone. Just like that: one minute he was here; the next he wasn't.

Interviewed by a local newspaper, Dee told a reporter that Buzz had visited her on the day of his murder only moments before he was killed. She claimed his "mood was upbeat" when he walked out of the house. He was especially happy, Dee noted, "about his wife's pregnancy and a new job he was due to begin at a Groton convalescent home.

"Everything was wonderful. He was thrilled. His life was fine."

On March 17, St. Patrick's Day, as a slight rain fell and a cool breeze blew umbrellas out of people's hands, a service was held at the Clintons' parish, Christ the King Roman Catholic Church.

Earlier that morning, Cynthia Carpenter had called with some rather disturbing news. Dick had been in an accident. His car had slid off the road. Dick escaped without serious injury, but his car was totaled and he was shaken up a bit. Cynthia said she'd watch the children while Dee and the rest of the Clintons buried Buzz. On the surface, it seemed like a noble gesture.

Before family and friends headed off to the cemetery, near the end of the short church ceremony, Dee stood up and read from a eulogy she had spent days composing. Buck Clinton had been a staple on the wrestling circuit in state for years. He coached high-school wrestling and held on to a passion for the sport. When the Clintons showed up at the wake the previous night, it was a comforting feeling to see that Buck's entire wrestling team, wearing their wrestling jackets, had been bused in to support the family.

Garbed in a black dress, Dee first addressed the crowd by stating that she was the person who likely knew Buzz best. A spiritual woman, Dee closed her opening by saying, "I believe God picks out special children to send to us so we can learn something."

Attendees, drying eyes and whimpering softly, were captivated by Dee's remarkable strength and candid demeanor. When she spoke, it was easy to tell where Buzz had gotten his strong disposition. Dee was a powerful person, not afraid of anyone. She was going to speak her mind today—regardless of what anyone thought.

This was Buzz's day.

"I don't think there is one person who has crossed Buzz's path who doesn't have a story to tell about him," Dee said.

Some people nodded. Others broke into half smiles through their anguish.

"God has carried me over some bumpy roads, and He has granted my family with more miracles than we probably deserve."

People who knew Dee weren't shocked by her display of gratitude. She had always been a person who never took anything for granted. Here was a woman who had just lost a son to the hand of a violent murderer, and she was speaking of how lucky she and her family were. Her strength was astonishing.

Years ago, it was discovered that Suzanne, Dee's middle child, had a bone tumor. The prayers from friends and family, Dee explained, had apparently helped "make another miracle possible." Suzanne beat it. She was fine now. "Buzz would have given his life to save his sister," Dee recalled later. "He was overwhelmed by Suzanne's pain."

Buzz had married and divorced before he met Kim. His first wife, Lisa, had bore him a son, Michael.

"The marriage ended," Dee explained to the crowd, "but not our relationship—and Lisa is wonderful [for] letting us share in the joy of Michael."

She second-guessed herself for having scolded Buzz for getting Kim pregnant shortly before he was killed.

"I read him the riot act," she said somberly, looking down at her notes. When she looked back up, she revealed, "Now I wish I [had] kept my mouth shut."

Then she tilted her hat to Kim, her daughter-in-law, a woman with whom she had just begun to bond. Since Buzz's death, Kim had moved back into the Clintons' house. Dee promised to build her a home of her own on a part of their fifty acres. There would be insurance money from a policy Dee had on Buzz. Dee wanted to be sure her grandchildren were taken care of with the money.

"Kim was his strength, giving him the will and desire to change his life. A quiet and gentle woman with unbelievable courage, whom I thank for loving my son."

Dee finished by saying that she had confidence that

Buzz was "in God's presence and light. . . . I have to say good-bye to our son." She ended with ". . . we'll miss you."

When the Clintons returned home after Buzz's funeral, reminders of him were everywhere. His clothes were still hanging around the house. His shoes and sneakers lay in the hallway. His hat hung on the rack by the door. His smell lingered in the air, on his clothes. His favorite chair was empty. Indeed, everything was still the same as it had been on March 9, but Buzz was gone. It was as if he'd gone off to work, or gone out for the night . . . and just hadn't come home yet.

Later, Dee Clinton, standing in her driveway next to a stone wall that Buzz had built years ago, remembered him.

"I can still see the sweat rolling off his back as he lifted each stone and placed it carefully next to one he had just put down. The sun was shining that day on his back. The glare. I can still see him. . . ."

There was a tree to the left of the driveway that Buzz had planted. When he put it in the ground, it was about the size of a houseplant. Now it stood fifteen feet tall. It was a subtle reminder to Dee that life still went on, even though part of her world had been shattered.

Throughout the weekend of March 19 and 20, detectives laid out a plan for the next few days. It included visits to several of Buzz's former friends, his ex-wife and a number of people he'd worked with throughout the years. Something was missing. Someone had it out for Buzz. There wasn't really much more to it than that. The hard part was tracking down that one nugget of information that would eventually open up the floodgates.

Before detectives began interviewing people, they decided to visit Dee again. Some time had passed. Maybe she could remember something significant?

The basic premise of the second interview was to find out what she "thought," Dee later speculated. They wanted to know how she felt about who murdered her son, and if she had any idea who it could have been.

Dee was adamant this time. She suspected that the Carpenters had had something to do with Buzz's death. She didn't believe anymore that a state trooper was responsible. It was after Buzz's funeral, Dee said, that she began to develop her suspicions. When Cynthia brought the kids back after the funeral, Dee had said, "Thank you. You've been so kind to my family."

Cynthia, befuddled and a bit disconcerted, said, "No, I haven't."

That was when Dee began to have a feeling of "discontent." Something, she thought, was askew.

"I told those detectives when they came back," Dee later recalled, "about the signs. They were there, especially since the last time I had spoken to them."

Dee was referring to Dick Carpenter's accident on the day of Buzz's funeral and the fact that he had also lost a fight with his chain saw some days later when he fell off a ladder and cut off one of his fingers.

"There's no way," one of the detectives chimed in when Dee began insisting that one of the Carpenters had killed her son, "that Dick Carpenter had anything to do with your son's murder."

"Whatever," Dee said. "But I told you last time to watch the signs. Buzz will lead you to his murderer."

The way Dee saw it, her job was to keep her family intact and be the force of strength that held them together through their horrible tragedy.

"[The detectives'] job," Dee later said, "was to find my son's killer."

If Charlie Snyder thought his days of being interrogated by the ED-MCS were behind him, he thought wrong. On the afternoon of March 23, Snyder looked out the cracked front windowpane of his office and saw Reggie Wardell and another detective walking from their state-issued blue Crown Victoria into Blonders for a third time.

As they walked in, Charlie once again stopped them at the door and led them outside, thinking, *What the fuck is this?*

Standing atop of the hood of an old Chevy Caprice lying on the ground in the parking lot, Wardell looked Charlie squarely in the eyes and said, "We want you to take a lie detector test."

Charlie became incensed, but he kept his anger in check, smiled coyly, then started walking toward his office door without saying anything. Then, "Come with me," he said, gesturing with his hand as he opened the door. "Come on. Let's go!"

The office Charlie kept was a tomb of stacked books on car parts and old customer files piled anywhere there was available space. There were alternators and distributor caps, old air cleaners and carburetors lying on chairs and filing cabinets. It was hard to tell what color the carpet had been because it was black and soiled with grime, oil and dirt. On the wall there was a gun rack with one shotgun set up in it. Charlie kept his .38 revolver in his top, center desk drawer, right next to a stack of cash, counted and banded.

Sifting through the rubble, he found the phone.

"Hold on one minute, gentlemen," he said.

Wardell, undoubtedly knowing what was going on, just looked at his partner without saying anything.

After a few brief pleasantries to his lawyer, Charlie said, "Listen, this is the third time these cops have been here and they're questioning me on a murder. What are my rights?"

"You don't have to tell them a fucking thing! Hand the phone to one of them."

Charlie gave Wardell the phone.

"Unless you have a warrant, leave the premises right away."

Wardell motioned to the other detective and they left without another word.

Later, Charlie remembered how he felt that day.

"After two meetings with them, they still didn't ask to do forensics on my thirty-eight, when they knew damn well it was the same caliber that had killed Buzz. They knew I didn't have anything to do with his murder. They were just seeing what they could get away with. After that day, I never heard from them again."

"The questioning of Charlie Snyder," Reggie Wardell said later, "became more intense every time we spoke to him. We looked at Charlie as someone who was possibly involved in the murder of Buzz. We're not just working on one case. We're always worried that something will slip through the cracks. So it makes us be more thorough in our investigation. That's why we interview so many people. We had to scratch people off our list. When Mrs. Clinton said she thought it might have been the state trooper who Buzz got into a skirmish with, even though he was one of us, we had to check it out. When people told us Charlie Snyder had threatened Buzz, we had to look at it."

Asked if his final interview with Snyder had gone the way Charlie later described it, Wardell said, "Not quite." Wardell had a smile on his face. "Charlie was much more cooperative."

Days later, however, after talking with Charlie's therapist and getting a statement that proved his alibi, the ED-MCS steered away from Charlie and set its sights on two other suspects who had recently been put on their radar screen.

Chapter 8

Deep River, Essex, Old Saybrook, Old Lyme and East Lyme are located at the tail end of Route 9, a two-lane highway system that begins in Elmwood, Connecticut, a suburb of Hartford, and ends at Interstate 95 in Old Saybrook. On the Old Saybrook end, the Route 9 and I-95 interchange is shaped like the eye end of a fishhook, with arteries jetting out north and south, as well as into downtown Old Saybrook. These are small seaside communities. Everybody knows everybody.

As the interviews piled up, it was beginning to look more like Buzz wasn't the likable life of the party his family and some of his friends had been trumpeting. There were people who didn't like Buzz. There were people who had some pretty bad things to say about him. And, notably, there were people who had motives to kill him.

Mark Marion, the assistant manager of the National Automotive Parts Association (NAPA), in Old Saybrook, had known Buzz for ten years. At one time, the two used to see each other at the local bowling alley in Old Saybrook. But other than a bit of casual conversation, and the fact that Buzz had used NAPA as one of his parts suppliers, they really hadn't hung around together much.

When Reggie Wardell showed up at NAPA to talk to Mark Marion on March 23, his goal was to find out about the other side of Buzz. Wardell had gotten several bits of information leading him to believe that NAPA was one of Buzz's hangouts. He'd even order parts from NAPA from time to time and charged them to Blonders's account.

After Wardell explained to Marion that Buzz had been murdered, the thirty-year-old manager said it was the first time he'd heard about it. The last time Buzz had been in the store, Marion said, was about one month ago.

"He had called one day around the same time period to ask a question about a distributor cap. But that's it."

Wardell wanted to know what Marion thought of Buzz.

"He was a pain. I think he not only used drugs, but *dealt* drugs."

"What about Kim and the kids?"

"He generally ignored them when they came into the store with him."

Marion then said he remembered how Buzz used to come into the store dressed in his white nurse's uniform and complain about all the bedpans he had to change during his shift at Pettipaug Manor. Buzz had worked at this convalescent home in Essex shortly after graduating from nursing school up until about one month prior to his death.

"Tell me about the tow truck."

Marion didn't know Buzz was selling the truck. But there was someone by the name of Marc Stevenson, Marion added, whom he thought Buzz had started working for recently. Stevenson ran a service for exotic dancers called Dance Club. Buzz, Marion added, used to dance for Stevenson's service once in a while.

It was a totally different portrait than what had surfaced during the past two weeks. But that's how these types of investigations went: there were always two sides to a story. And as more information poured in over the next few weeks, yet another portrait of Buzz emerged.

The first bit of disconcerting information came from Susan Murphy, a forty-year-old former classmate of

Buzz's at Vinal Tech, in Middletown, where Buzz had studied for his CNA. Murphy and Buzz had attended classes together. She said Buzz used to "brag" about using prescription drugs he'd obtained from a "male relative . . . an uncle or cousin," and thought the drugs might have been "Xanax and codeine-Tylenol."

Buzz was seen as a loudmouth in class, Murphy explained. A class clown. He would bring in photographs of himself, ranting and raving about his life as a male exotic dancer. She said she'd stopped riding to school with him because he liked to drink beers while he drove.

The next logical place for detectives to visit was Pettipaug Manor. It had been Buzz's first job as a CNA after graduation and his last-known place of employment.

John Turner and Marty Graham interviewed Louroy Manning, the maintenance supervisor at Pettipaug. Manning had been working at Pettipaug for about ten years. He said he had met Buzz at another nursing home in New London about ten years prior to Buzz's working at Pettipaug, but Manning couldn't remember the name of the place. This was highly unlikely, considering that Buzz would've been only seventeen or eighteen at the time and just out of high school.

"Buzz was a bragger and liar," Manning asserted. "The last time I spoke to him was shortly before he was fired."

Fired? No one had mentioned up to now that Buzz had been fired from Pettipaug?

There had been many women in Buzz's short life. And they all had a story to tell. The big difference, however, was that the stories detectives were getting now weren't peppered with saccharine anecdotes of hiking trips and walks along the beach. They were filled with violence, threats and dysfunction—a trio of ingredients that when, coupled with rage, anger, marital jealousy, could lead to murder.

Richard Silva, a fifty-three-year-old warehouseman, was next on a long list of people with whom detectives wanted to talk. When Wardell and Szamocki tracked him down on April 8, 1994, at his house in Clinton, their purpose was to see if Silva could put them in contact with his daughter, Tina, whom they knew to be one of Buzz's many ex-girlfriends.

The town of Clinton is about ten miles south of Old Lyme. The Westbrook state police barracks is nearby. When Turner and Wardell showed up on that Friday afternoon, Silva told them that his daughter now lived in Ivoryton, a small, rural town just on the outskirts of Essex, with her new boyfriend, Chris Rook. It had been years since she'd dated Buzz, Silva said. And he hadn't heard from him since.

"What can you tell us about him?" Turner asked.

"Tina and Buzz lived together in Lyme. They argued a lot. I believe Tina told me that Buzz had hit her once. After they broke up, Buzz called me a couple of times looking for her. . . ."

"What is it?"

Silva hesitated.

"Well, I remember that Buzz called one time and threatened to kill himself. He even threatened to bring a bomb over to my house so it would explode and kill Tina."

Young love. Romeo and Juliet. It meant nothing.

Presumably, Buzz was probably drunk and stupid at the time he made the threat, bitter over the breakup and just wanted to get back at Tina and her family by making idle threats. Nonetheless, it was a frightening thought to Silva: someone calling his home and threatening to blow it up to get back at his daughter.

Tina Silva lived in Ivoryton, but she wanted to be interviewed at Jon's Brickoven Pizza, in Old Saybrook, her financé's restaurant. Attractive and slim, twenty-five-year-old Tina Silva was an unemployed hairdresser, pregnant with Rook's child. She remembered the last time she saw Buzz was at the Variety Bar, in Old Saybrook. "He introduced me to a blond-haired female that he said was his wife."

If it was Kim with Buzz that night, he and Kim hadn't gotten married until January 17, 1993, about eight months before they ran into Tina.

Why would he lie?

Tina and Buzz had met in high school. They had moved into an apartment together back in 1991 for about six months. Before that, Tina explained, Buzz had lived at the Baldwin Bridge Hotel, in Old Saybrook, which had recently been turned into a Howard Johnson's.

"He punched me in the face one night when he lived there," Tina offered.

"Did you fill out a complaint?"

"No."

Still, Tina Silva said she wasn't taking it. So she moved back with her parents after the incident, she said. And that's when Buzz, she claimed, threatened to kill her and her family if she wouldn't see him again. He had even entered Stonington Institute, in North Stonington, she claimed, to get help with what she said was a "substance abuse problem." The threats continued even while Buzz was in Stonington. At one point, Tina said, she made a complaint to the Clinton Police Department, but Buzz was never arrested. The threats finally stopped, she added, but not until a year later.

So, Buzz wasn't a member of the 4-H club. His own mother was the first to admit that. He had run with some shady people at certain points in his life. But as far as all the other accusations against him, detectives knew they had to be looked at through a cautious lens. A dead man, after all, had a hard time defending himself.

"If my son was doing the things he was being accused of . . . I would have killed him myself," Dee Clinton later said.

At about 1:30 P.M., on April 12, Reggie Wardell and Marty Graham drove to Wallingford, Connecticut, a small industrial town just north of New Haven, to interview Buzz's ex-wife.

At twenty-eight, Lisa Chenard had already been through the wringer. Her short-lived marriage to Buzz, as Graham and Wardell were about to find out, had been riddled with dysfunction, violence and accusations of the worst kind.

When Lisa met Buzz, she was living in West Haven, in an apartment below Buzz's cousins. When Buzz had attended school in New Haven, he usually stayed at his cousins' apartment. Old Lyme wasn't far from New Haven, about a twenty-minute ride, but Buzz was always having problems with his vehicles. Staying at his cousins' apartment assured him that he would always make it to class.

In March 1989, after courting her for a while, Buzz moved into Lisa's West Haven apartment. Three months later, in June, they took off to Las Vegas and got married. When they came back to Connecticut, they moved into Lisa's parents' house in Wallingford.

Following the construction boom during the late 1980s, Buzz and his new bride moved to Phoenix, Arizona, where Buzz had family and friends. Like his father before him, Buzz soon found work as a union ironworker.

From almost the first day, the marriage was doomed, Lisa explained to Graham and Wardell.

"I had Buzz arrested three times while we lived in Phoenix for beating and threatening to kill me. Two months and five days after we were married, he raped me and dumped me at the airport."

Graham and Wardell were silent for the moment. *Rape? Threats?* They took notes like college freshmen.

In August 1989, Lisa arrived back in Connecticut and moved into her parents' house. Weeks later, she said, Buzz returned to the state and, surprisingly, Lisa's parents allowed him to move back into their house.

"He returned from Phoenix," Lisa recalled, "with a venereal disease. In October, he choked me."

"Did you have him arrested?"

"No."

According to Lisa, Buzz used cocaine, alcohol and pot. She'd even gone with him on occasion to buy drugs, she said. It didn't matter if Buzz was high, drunk or sober, Lisa insisted he liked to beat on her. And if he wasn't physically abusing her, he just wasn't available emotionally. When she gave birth to their son, Michael, on February 8, 1990, she said Buzz had taken off for four days with a married woman.

The divorce was finalized on October 7, 1990. Four years later, a few weeks before Buzz was murdered, Lisa Clinton married Dan Chenard.

"Michael calls Dan 'Dad.' And he's done it in front of Buzz," Lisa said after Wardell and Graham asked how the relationship between Buzz and Dan had been. "He handled it well and got along great with Dan. Within the past year, actually, Buzz seemed to be much more civil to us and Michael."

"When was the last time you saw him?"

"Christmastime last year. We were all at Buzz's parents' house."

The relationship between Buzz, Lisa and Dan was a no-win situation for Buzz, Dee Clinton later said. Lisa was going to sour Michael on Buzz no matter what Buzz did. Lisa wanted Buzz to give up full custody of Michael, which Buzz gladly did. Michael never even knew that Buzz was his father. Lisa wanted it that way. Buzz didn't argue.

Wardell asked Lisa why she didn't attend Buzz's funeral. "I didn't want to be a hypocrite." Showing up would seem like false sympathy on her part. Her mother, she added, and her husband, Dan, did go, however.

Lisa's attitude and accusations against Buzz riled Dee Clinton. For one, Lisa had told Dee that the reason she didn't attend Buzz's funeral was because she was in the hospital with pneumonia. On top of that,

the rape allegations against Buzz made little sense to
Dee. Why would Lisa's parents allow a man who had
purportedly just raped and beaten their daughter to
move back into their house right after the incident?
What kind of mother would go along with such a thing?

It was a fair question. Lisa's mother, according to Dee,
had been on the phone with Lisa as Buzz had been al-
legedly abusing her that night. Later, she had told
several people that, on top of everything else, Buzz had
also thrown her daughter down the stairs that evening.

Would any mother allow this kind of monster to sleep
in her home?

These were strong allegations and put Buzz in a much
different light as far as law enforcement was concerned. If
he had done to his ex-wife, who was pregnant at the time
of the incident, what she had claimed, a good question
might be: what had Buzz done that no one knew about?

Was it possible that Buzz could have enraged someone
so much to cause him to commit murder as an act of revenge?

Graham and Wardell were beginning to think so.

In regards to Lisa and the Clintons, here were two
conflicting stories, each family undoubtedly protecting
his or her own interests. But regardless of who was right
and who was wrong, why would Lisa lie about such a horrible thing? What could be her motive—to smear the
memory of a dead man, or to cover up a murder?

The ED-MCS would have to look at it all. They would
make a few calls to Phoenix and see what—if any—police reports existed.

After a careful check, there were no reports of Buzz's
having been arrested.

It would be the beginning of a set of new questions
that—while puzzling investigators—would eventually
have little, if nothing, to do with Buzz's murder. At this
point, however, after about five weeks of what seemed

like never-ending interviews leading nowhere, detectives were no closer to solving Buzz's murder. They'd zero in on someone, and then exonerate him. They'd think they had it all figured out, then talk to someone and realize how much they *didn't* know about the case. It was frustrating. Confusing. Time-consuming.

And going nowhere.

With all police work, however, came luck—and Lady Luck was about to shine her bright light on the investigation, and in the process, she would bust the case wide open.

Chapter 9

Spring couldn't have come any sooner for Connecticut residents in 1994. The past winter had produced so much snow that by the time April had come and gone, many wondered if the snow would ever melt.

Nothing could stop the inevitable, however: warm air, shorts, tank tops, the schools of bluefish and flounder that would eventually draw thousands of fishermen to the Long Island Sound, golf courses overflowing with loudly dressed weekend hackers, beaches packed with tourists and townies, barbecues, weddings, graduations.

For the ED-MCS, the changing seasons were abstract parts of the year. Their job was crime. It didn't matter what time of the year it was. The more time that went by, the more frustrating and confusing things became. Here it was the first week of May, and any new leads in Buzz's murder appeared to be at a standstill. There were countless people saying that Buzz wasn't the most well-liked person in the world and others who claimed he was the salt of the earth. There were scores of interviews that still hadn't produced a single tangible suspect—someone whom investigators could focus on exclusively. Rob Ferguson and Charlie Snyder had long been scratched off the list and were cleared of any wrongdoing. Detectives now thought that Buzz might have been killed by a jealous husband or boyfriend, but they were no closer to finding out exactly who that person was.

On May 5, 1994, Shawn Butterfield, a twenty-seven-year-old hotel manager and former friend of Buzz's, was driving to his parents' house in East Lyme for a dinner party. Shawn lived only about two miles away, on the other end of town.

As he crawled up to a stop sign right down the street from his parents' house, easing his way through, he noticed a cop car on the other side of the street.

At first, Shawn thought nothing of it, but then the cop began tailing him.

When Shawn pulled into his parents' driveway, the cop pulled up right behind him, blocking his car.

What the hell?

"Sir," the unassuming cop said, "you didn't come to a complete stop back at that stop sign. . . ."

"What . . . are you kidding me? You followed me for *that?*"

"Listen," the cop said, taking a step closer, "what can you tell me about Buzz Clinton?" He sounded overly intimidating, as if he were trying to be tough. Shawn, a big guy himself at about five feet nine inches, a solid 180 pounds, wasn't falling for it, however.

"Look," Shawn said, "I'm not going to murder anyone over a hundred dollars, if that's what you're thinking."

After taking Shawn's name and address, the cop took off.

A week later, on May 12, ED-MCS detective Diane Morianos showed up unexpectedly at Shawn's work, the Days Inn, in Mystic, Connecticut.

"We need to talk somewhere alone," Morianos explained.

"Over here," Shawn said, pointing to an empty room.

Morianos said her visit was routine. There was no reason to be alarmed. They were just connecting the dots.

Since Shawn and Buzz had known each other at one point, Morianos explained, Shawn might know something without realizing it. Yet the first thing Morianos wanted to know was what Shawn had meant the previous week when he told the cop he wasn't going to murder someone over $100.

Butterfield explained that he and Buzz were former high-school classmates and had worked together for about a year, in 1990 through 1991, but he hadn't seen him since.

After Morianos asked a few more questions, Butterfield said there was an incident that had taken place sometime ago with Officer Joe Dunn, the Old Lyme police officer who had made an identification of Buzz's body.

Buzz and Shawn had hooked up together shortly after Buzz and Lisa got divorced. Back in high school, they'd been on the gymnastics team together, but that was the extent of their relationship. After Buzz split with Lisa, he ran into Shawn at a local bar, and the two began talking about old times. Before the night was over, Buzz said he was working for a guy in Newington, Connecticut, installing pools, and he asked Shawn if he wanted a job.

The next day, they were working together.

Shawn saw Buzz as someone who never followed through with anything in his life. He viewed Buzz as a "bullshitter," someone who was always playing himself up as someone he wasn't. "He talked a lot about doing this and doing that," Butterfield recalled, "but he never did *anything*."

One night, after drinking for most of the evening at a local bar, Shawn drove Buzz back to Buzz's apartment in East Lyme. Shawn had lived nearby with his parents. So dropping Buzz off had become a routine after-work chore.

On that particular night, though, they'd both gotten pretty drunk, and Shawn later admitted that he probably shouldn't have been driving a car, but he was young and naive.

When they approached Buzz's apartment, Shawn got pulled over by a cop who had been following them for a while. He didn't know it, but he had a taillight out.

When the cop came to the window, Shawn recognized him as Joe Dunn. Shawn pulled out his wallet, took out his license and handed it to Dunn, then placed the wallet on the console between him and Buzz and refocused his attention back on Dunn.

Dunn, who had known Shawn from around town and had watched him grow up, leaned into the car after a moment and said, "Pull over to the side of the road."

Shawn then looked over at Buzz and thought, *Oh, shit! We're fucked now.*

After getting out of the car and talking to Dunn for a few minutes while Buzz waited in the car, Shawn came back and told Buzz that Dunn was going to let them walk to Buzz's apartment and come back in the morning to get the car. It was an odd thing for Dunn to do, Butterfield later said, because Dunn had always been a "ball buster of a cop."

When they got back to Buzz's place, Shawn realized that he'd left his wallet back in the car.

"Thank God [that] Joe Dunn made me lock the car up, huh, Buzz?"

"Yeah," Buzz said. "It'll be all right for the night."

"I'm going back to get it now. Come with me."

"Whoa, whoa, whoa!" Buzz said. "Get it tomorrow. Don't even worry about it right now." Buzz seemed inflexible for some reason, Shawn later remembered, and made it clear that he didn't want Shawn to go back to the car until morning.

After they argued a bit, they ended up walking back to the car. But after scouring the car for about fifteen minutes, Shawn couldn't find his wallet.

"It's gone. I don't believe it. It's fucking gone. It was right here on the console."

The car had been locked, yet there was no sign of the wallet. Shawn looked at Buzz, who was hanging around outside the car. *I know you took it, you son of a bitch. You were the only one who could have.* There was about $100 in the wallet.

"But it wasn't about the money," Shawn later said. "It was about friendship and trust."

The following day, Shawn called the Old Lyme Police Department. "Where's my wallet?" he asked Joe Dunn.

"I watched you place it on the console," Dunn confirmed. "The car was locked."

Later that night, Shawn drove over to Buzz's. "I want my wallet," he said when Buzz answered the door.

"What?"

"Come on, man. Where else could it be? You were the last one near it!"

"I don't know what you're talking about, Shawn."

Buzz never admitted taking the wallet, and there was no way to prove it. But Shawn, even years later, never doubted Buzz was the thief.

"Buzz only cared about himself," Butterfield later said, shaking his head in disbelief about what he was saying. "That's the way he was. That's the way I remember him. He ruined a friendship—a *good* friendship—over a lousy one hundred dollars. He used to get kicked out of his house all the time. My parents even let him sleep over whenever he was homeless. I don't understand how he could have done that to me.

"When I first heard that he had been murdered, the first thing that I thought was 'He must have ripped somebody off.'"

Butterfield considered Dee Clinton a "sweetheart," he added. She'd always been hospitable and extremely friendly to him.

"There was something strange there, though, at the Clinton home. Buzz was always a mama's boy around Dee. He was her baby, for sure. But when Buzz was away from her, he was a totally different person. *Completely.* He was a little angel at home . . . but when we went out, he was wild. His entire character changed."

The interview Morianos conducted with Shawn at the Days Inn offered nothing in the form of a lead. If anything, it was just more anecdotal evidence that lent itself to the fact that there were people in Buzz's life who had motive to kill him. As far as finding the person responsible for his murder, it was still a situation that needed some sort of intervention from the public—someone who had seen something or heard something, but had been afraid to come forward for some reason.

Chapter 10

The ED-MCS building is at the top of a long stretch of road off West Thames Street, near downtown Norwich. It is an archaic-looking structure, about the size of a century-old schoolhouse. Its outside finish is made up of cement-colored brick and mortar, faded and coarse. With its stone steps leading up to the main entrance and its large, life-size windowpanes off to the right and left, it looks more like a historical library than a meeting-house for cops who track down eastern Connecticut's "most wanted."

Detective John Turner was assigned to the ED-MCS as a member of the Major Crime Squad back in 1987; he joined the force in 1982. Since becoming a detective, Turner had investigated murders, rapes, child abuse cases and violent crimes of all kinds.

The Buzz Clinton murder investigation, however, had Turner baffled. He knew the answer—or at least some of the answers—was right in front of his face, if only he could put his arms around the motive. Every murder has a cause: jealousy, revenge, robbery, money, drugs, hate. The reasons are endless.

In Buzz's case, though, something seemed to be missing.

Then it happened—that "break" they'd been waiting

on all along came in the form of a phone call that would change everything eventually.

Turner received a message on May 25, 1994, that a woman had called the state police barracks in Montville and stated that she knew who "killed the man on the Rocky Neck connector in East Lyme."

It was heaven-sent. The detectives had exhausted just about every single lead, and now a potential killer was going to be delivered on a silver platter?

It seemed too good to be true.

While waiting on the line to be transferred to where Turner and the rest of the ED-MCS were attending a meeting, dispatch lost the caller. For the next ten minutes, Turner and the ED-MCS waited nervously for their new witness to call back. Finally the phone rang. After trying to be cryptic, hiding who she was, the woman identified herself as Catherine White.

Thus far, this was a name unconnected to Buzz's murder in any way.

White told Turner she was scared that her boyfriend, who was involved in the murder, would find out about the call. She had called Troop F because it was the closest station to her apartment. No long-distance charges would show up on her phone bill.

After running a background check on White, Turner's initial jubilation was short-lived. Catherine White was a convicted prostitute. A rather well-known "lady of the evening" around town, she was also a heavy drug user.

Nevertheless, she might know something.

After sending a few troopers to fetch her, John Turner and Marty Graham sat down with White and began to hear a story that made little sense at first blush.

"It was my boyfriend, Joe Fremut," White explained, "and his friend Mark Despres who planned and committed the murder."

Turner was curious about why White had waited so long to come forward.

"I can deal with a lot of things in my life," she said, tears falling, "and I have done a lot of things I'm not proud of—but I can't be part of a murder. Just knowing about it, well, I can't sleep at night."

At thirty-three, Joe Fremut had followed in the footsteps of his father, James, who had owned and operated Fremut Texaco Service Station on South Main Street in Deep River for most of his life. Fremut, at five feet eight inches, 160 pounds, had worked at the Texaco station, it seemed, since he was a child. In recent years, Fremut Texaco had also gotten into the used-car market and had a parking lot full of used cars. Former customers viewed Fremut as nothing more than "the guy you went to in town to buy a used car."

Others, however, remembered him differently.

One former acquaintance said he was the kind of guy you left alone. In pretty good physical shape, slim, but built solid, Fremut had a look about him that spoke of a hard life. With his short-cropped black hair and cocky grin, he resembled actor Robert Blake during his *Baretta* days. He always seemed intense, as if on edge.

"No one went out of their way to mess with Joey Fremut," a former friend said. "That's for damn sure."

Some said he was a quiet guy who liked to shoot darts at the local pub. He fixed cars, kept to himself and never really bothered anyone. In fact, if someone brought trouble to him, he usually walked away without incident, or insisted the guy drop it.

"There was respect there for Joe. Joe never went out and looked for trouble. But let me tell you something: if you shit on Joey Fremut's front lawn, you'd end up eating your own shit. He didn't run from trouble. And if you brought it to him, well, you had better be ready."

The ED-MCS now had a key suspect. Still, what was Fremut's connection to Buzz? Deep River, although it wasn't too far from Old Lyme, wasn't exactly part of Buzz's stomping grounds. Besides working in town at Pettipaug Manor for a few months, Buzz had rarely gone into Deep River.

Could Buzz have screwed over Fremut on some unpaid vehicle repair bills, or maybe a bad drug deal? Fremut, it was soon learned, had been dealing cocaine; plus, the drug-deal-gone-bad theory was on the ED-MCS's shortlist of possible motives. Furthermore, how did Mark Despres, a second name White had given the ED-MCS, fit into things? Despres, a local man, had known Joe Fremut for about twenty-five years and had worked for him at Fremut Texaco. Catherine White said Despres worked as a used-car salesman—at least that was his job title. But Turner and Graham soon learned that Depres also had a few side businesses. Not only was Despres a paid confidential informant for the state police, but he, too, sold cocaine.

Despres usually dealt drugs, many claimed, out of a local bar in Ivoryton and hung around with Fremut at the Texaco station. In a sense, selling used cars was a front.

So how did Catherine White find out that her boyfriend, Joe Fremut, with whom she said she'd been living for some time now, and his best friend, Mark Despres, killed Buzz? Where was White getting her information? And why would two tough guys who had no connection to Buzz want him dead, anyway?

Detective Pete Cleary drove over to Fremut Texaco with another detective on May 26. He hoped Fremut could give him a few answers.

Fremut immediately turned over on Despres.

At a car auction in January, Fremut explained, he saw

Despres wearing an "odd-looking ring and pendant necklace," so he asked him about it.

"It has something to do with Satan," Despres said. "Anything can be done for a price. I know people that would beat up, break legs or kill someone."

A few weeks later, Fremut said, Despres told him he had been offered between $5,000 and $10,000 to "take care of someone."

Then Fremut explained the mechanics of the contract and how Despres had shown him several guns—including a .38. He said after he'd heard that someone had been killed on the connector in East Lyme, he remembered that Despres had told him the contract was for a guy from East Lyme.

One and one made two.

"It was back in February," Catherine White explained to John Turner. "While I was at Fremut Texaco, on or about the last week of February, I overheard Joe and Mark talking about how Mark was following a guy around but never had the opportune moment to 'do him' because someone was always around."

Turner was astonished, but at the same time elated. From a source, cops listen for details of a particular crime that haven't been reported in the newspapers— details that only someone who had inside information about the crime could know.

White, it was easy to tell right away, appeared to have known more than the local reporters covering the case.

"I heard Joe tell Mark that he should continue following the guy around, and the moment will present itself."

Joe Fremut, Turner learned next, had even sold Despres out to White at one point.

"Later that evening," White continued, "Joe told me that Mark had picked up a contract for eight thousand dollars to 'do this guy.'"

It was obvious that Fremut and Despres hadn't read

any how-to books on murder, and they probably had never killed anyone before. Any armchair criminalist knows the first rule of getting away with murder: never tell anybody what you're about to do. From what White was saying, it appeared as though Despres and Fremut had been discussing the murder at length within earshot of anybody who happened to be around.

White's statement, however, added another facet to the investigation, an element that ED-MCS had speculated on earlier: there was obviously some sort of mastermind behind the crime—someone else, who was involved at a higher level, had paid Despres and Fremut to commit the murder. In other words, they were nothing more than hired hands.

As White continued, a pretty good portrait of Buzz's final hours—hours detectives had been looking to make sense of for about the past ten weeks—began to emerge with lucid accuracy. There were things White knew that only a person involved in the murder could have known. She was stating particulars: times, dates, names.

Answers.

According to White, on the day after Buzz's murder, she heard Fremut and Despres discussing a trip to Florida. At one point, White said, Despres backed out of the trip.

"I can't go," Despres told Fremut, "because I have not received my money yet."

Apparently, whoever had hired Despres to kill Buzz hadn't finished paying him.

Later that same night, March 11, White went to Fremut and asked him about the conversation she'd overheard earlier that day.

"Mark went through with it!" Fremut roared. He seemed happy about it.

"With what?"

"Mark called the man he was going to hit and expressed

an interest in a tow truck he was selling in order to lure him away," Fremut explained.

"*What?*"

"Mark made arrangements to meet the guy, then followed him up onto the connector in Niantic. Once they got on the connector, the guy stopped his car and approached Mark, who had stopped behind him."

"Yeah . . ."

"When the guy got out of his car, Mark shot him six times with a thirty-eight!"

White then stated that when Despres saw a set of headlights coming over the crest of the connector, he got back into his car and "drove over the body and fled the scene."

White insisted Fremut had even encouraged Despres to commit the murder, and helped plan it. And when Despres came back the following day, explaining how he'd gone through with it, Fremut "praised" his efforts.

After taking a break and getting a glass of water, White sat back down and continued.

"There's more?" Turner asked.

"Plenty."

Days after the murder, Despres went to Fremut and told him he was having trouble sleeping.

Fremut, perhaps more heartless than Despres, couldn't understand why—especially since Despres, White said, had cut up the gun he used in the murder, buried it and sold the car he'd driven that night.

Then came perhaps one of the most unbelievable aspects of the murder thus far. According to White, Despres had brought along his fifteen-year-old son, Chris, when he killed Buzz.

In January 1994, about ten weeks before Buzz's murder, Chris Despres moved in with his dad. Chris was a scrawny kid, with long, hippie-style hair. Living with his mother, Diana Trevethan, in Newington, Connecticut, just south of Hartford, Chris had been having the same problems at home every teenager faced at some point in his or her life. Trevethan was working for the phone company at the time and had remarried. Ever since her split from Despres, life seemed to be going well for Trevethan.

Chris, however, didn't quite see it that way.

"Mark Despres, when he and Diana were married, wasn't very settled," a former family friend later recalled. "There was infidelity on Mark's part. Diana is a great person . . . the sweetest person in the world. She would do anything for anyone. She got married to Mark and became pregnant when she was young. She knew she needed to provide for Chris. She managed to scrape up enough money to buy a house, worked full-time, and raised Chris while Mark was out and about, not working, racing cars and hustling. As much as she loved Mark, she did the best thing for Chris and let go."

When the divorce was finalized, Chris was about three years old. Ever since the divorce, Mark had not really paid much attention to his son. As he grew older, Chris developed an urge to hang around with his dad and had always wanted to be part of his life. But Mark wanted little to do with being a father and always let Chris down.

"Mark paid no attention to Chris throughout the years. He was gone all the time. He would say he was coming for a visit, or a birthday, and he wouldn't."

Two months prior to the murder, Catherine White, who, Turner noticed, was obviously getting tired and worn out from talking about such horrible memories that had overrun her recently, said she was with Fremut and Despres at Fremut Texaco when she saw something disturbing.

It was a Sunday. Business was slow. Fremut and

Despres were just hanging around the station, passing time.

At one point during the day, Fremut and Despres went out to the back of the garage and began test-firing different weapons, as if they were pumping themselves up for the murder. From afar, White said, she watched as Fremut slipped inside a beige-colored station wagon, and Despres fired a gun just outside the window of the car.

After a few rounds, Fremut would get out of the car and the two men would discuss how loud the shot sounded from inside the car. Then they would get a different gun and, with the radio in the car turned up loud and then turned down soft, test-fire the new gun. It went on for some time, White explained.

Obvious to John Turner at this point was that Buzz's murder was, most likely, a partially thought-out crime, a merciless killing, committed by a couple of misfit criminals, who really didn't know what the hell they were doing. Others were definitely involved, Turner knew. Despres and Fremut both spoke of a third party who was responsible for paying them. Two guys like Fremut and Despres wouldn't just kill some guy from Old Lyme for sport—especially someone they had no connection to.

So the detectives from the ED-MCS had some information as to what had happened to Buzz on the night of March 10, 1994, and, perhaps, who had pulled the trigger on the gun that had killed him. They knew Charlie Snyder and Rob Ferguson didn't have anything to do with Buzz's murder, and they officially dropped both men as suspects. Still, it wasn't enough. What they needed to know next was who had hired Despres—or, better yet, why?

Answers would come, but not until the ED-MCS began unraveling Buzz's brief marriage to Kim Carpenter Clinton. There had to be a connection with Despres, Fremut or both. The task now was to find out what it was. In addition, who was the *real* Buzz Clinton? Cops had put together a file as thick as an encyclopedia on him with allegations of everything from rape to theft to drug abuse. But that was it: they were "allegations." Former friends, girlfriends and an ex-wife, who had all been scorned by Buzz at some point, had made claims against him, but were they true?

The time had come to find out exactly what had been going on in Buzz's life around the time of his murder, where detectives assumed they'd find a connection to Despres and Fremut. And as a portrait of Buzz's life the past few years emerged, a disturbing and sinister murder-for-hire plot rose to the surface—one that detectives themselves could never have imagined.

Buzz

Chapter 11

For anyone who had known Anson Clinton Jr., or crossed his path throughout his twenty-eight years, he was called Buzz. Many assumed the name was given to him because of a hearty appetite for booze and drugs. "He *was* always buzzed," Shawn Butterfield later recalled. "That's how he got the name."

Actually, the nickname Buzz wasn't given during some keg party in the woods one night by a bunch of hoodlums sitting around a campfire funneling beers. Nor did a drinking buddy lean over one night at a bar and say, "You're buzzed all the time. We'll call you Buzz!"

No. The truth of the matter was much more innocent.

Buck Clinton was in Arizona on a wrestling scholarship when his blue-eyed, blond-haired son Anson was born on January 7, 1966. Buck and Dee had been married a year. Dee, at twenty, couldn't afford to make the trip after she'd given birth, so she stayed in Connecticut, where she lived with Buck's parents. A few days after the birth, Dee sent Buck some photographs of little Anson, along with a note: "I'll call you in a few days."

"Think of a nickname," Dee told Buck a few days later. He was sitting around with three of his buddies envying the photographs Dee had sent. "We need a nickname," Dee urged, "because I am *not* calling him *Anson*."

It was her husband's name. His father's name. A

Clinton family name that had been passed down. And Dee hated it.

"We'll come up with something," Buck promised.

A few more days passed, and Buck sent Dee three names.

"The other two names I cannot even remember to this day," Dee said later. "I picked Buzz because it was one of the names on the list."

The Clintons moved to Old Lyme when Buzz was in the fourth grade. He was diagnosed with dyslexia shortly thereafter and participated in a Connecticut learning-disabled program for six years, where he overcame his disability. In 1985, six weeks before graduation, Buzz dropped out of East Lyme High School, but he took his GED and passed the test sometime later. Despite having a promising future ahead of him in wrestling, he followed in his father's footsteps and became an ironworker.

During his high-school years, Buzz was scrawny. Very petite. And generally stayed to himself. "He was a loner," a friend recalled. Because of his size and build, Buzz was pushed into joining the gymnastics team, where he excelled. But it was wrestling he loved most. Buck was a well-respected wrestling coach of Wethersfield High School at the time Buzz had dropped out of school, and he had been an all-American himself.

After the realization that he couldn't make a career out of wrestling, Buzz began taking seriously his passion for spinning records. Soon he was getting jobs around town under the name Rent-A-Buzz-Entertainment. While doing that, he worked hard on getting his iron-worker's union book. By the time he was twenty, in 1986, Buzz was working with his father, who had been an iron-worker since 1967.

He worked in Waterbury, Hartford, Bridgeport, Connecticut, and even in Iowa. Wherever there was work, Buzz went. But when the bottom fell out of the steel industry, Buzz always returned to the Old Stagecoach Road home of his mom and dad.

Some friends recalled that Buzz didn't seem to have a problem with alcohol or drugs at this time. He more or less had a few drinks and took a hit of a joint at a party once in a while. He wasn't bouncing off the walls or crashing cars. He was just Buzz: seemingly happy all the time and always working on some sort of "deal" that would better his life.

"He had no big reputation for being a tough guy," one friend remembered. "He thought he was tough, but he never really gave anyone any trouble. More talk than anything else."

To others, Buzz was someone who liked to exaggerate the truth. "A bullshitter," Shawn Butterfield later said, "to be exact."

One day, however, Buzz proved that his tall tales held some truth.

While Buzz and Shawn were installing pools one afternoon, Buzz took Shawn aside; knowing that Shawn was an avid music lover and guitar player, Buzz said, "Would you like to meet Ritchie Blackmore?"

Ritchie Blackmore was the lead guitar player and one of the founders of Deep Purple, one of the largest-selling rock acts in the world. There wasn't a budding guitar player alive who hadn't asked his guitar teacher to show him "Smoke on the Water," Deep Purple's first big international hit.

Shawn looked at Buzz and thought, *You're so full of shit.* Then, figuring he'd call Buzz on his lie, he said, "Sure. Just tell me when and where."

"Great!" Buzz said. "Meet me in Redding tomorrow at the soccer field."

That Friday, Shawn showed up at a Redding soccer field and was amazed to see Buzz running around the field playing soccer with several men Shawn couldn't recognize from a distance—but all of whom had waist-long hair.

"I told you, you son of a bitch," Buzz said when he greeted Shawn.

Butterfield was speechless. Here was Buzz playing soccer with Ritchie Blackmore and several of Blackmore's friends and roadies. It was remarkable. Not only because Shawn was meeting Ritchie Blackmore, one of his idols, but that Buzz had been telling the truth all along.

Buzz became involved heavily with alcohol and drugs in the early 1990s. His mother and father knew it. His friends knew it. And most around him knew it. Alcohol became a friend to Buzz. He had been hanging around area bars and nightclubs and, perhaps like a lot of people, got caught up in the moment. The late '80s were a maze of clubhopping, dance music and booze. Cocaine flowed like talcum powder. The drug made it out into the suburbs and became somewhat of a social statement for the middle class. Everybody, it seemed, was doing it.

Now in his early twenties, Buzz would live out on his own for a while, then go crawling back to his mother and father when the money ran out. Even though the Clintons now had two young children in the house—Suzanne, who was seventeen years younger than Buzz, and Billy, nineteen years younger—they always found room for Buzz.

But Dee wasn't naive or easily fooled. The deal had always been: As long as Buzz stayed in the house, he would live under her rules. If he couldn't, Dee would throw him out.

One night, Buzz had come home complaining of severe abdominal pain. "I'm sick, Ma," he said, holding his stomach as if he'd been punched.

Dee had had it by this point. Buzz hadn't paid his rent for some time. But as Dee carried on about how irresponsible Buzz was, he fell to the floor, still holding his stomach. Then he began vomiting.

"See!" Dee fumed. "That's what you get for drinking all night long."

"Ma, you have to believe me. I haven't been drinking."

"Yeah, Buzz. Right. That's what all the drunks say," Dee said as she made her way to her bedroom, closed the door and went to bed.

Around 2:00 A.M., Buck woke Dee out of a dead sleep and said, "Buzz is still up. He needs you," adding, "He's calling out your name. Something's wrong."

When Dee entered Buzz's room, she saw him stretched out on the floor in a fetal position. "He was crying," she recalled. "Not loud, but softly, as if he was in too much pain to cry any louder."

Dee then walked over and put her hand on his head.

"I'm dying," Buzz whispered.

Something is dreadfully wrong, Dee thought—and it had nothing to do with alcohol.

"I'll take you to the hospital, Buzz," Dee said, caressing his forehead and tearstained face. "It's going to be okay, honey."

"I can't move, Ma."

Dee tried dressing him. Then, *Forget this shit*, she thought after several failed attempts to get his pants on, *I'm calling an ambulance*.

Sometime later, doctors diagnosed Buzz with peritonitis, which meant "an inflammation of the membrane lining the cavity of the abdomen." There was a good chance, doctors added, that his appendix was swollen and, possibly, had ruptured.

If that was the case, Buzz was in big trouble.

When Dee showed up at the hospital, doctors informed her that if he hadn't gotten help when he did, he would have been dead within a few hours. His appendix, they said, would have exploded inside his body.

The morning after emergency surgery, Buzz called home.

"Ma, bring my cigarettes, lighter and my special blanket when you come in today."

"Sure," Dee said. "How are you feeling?"

"I'm okay. Sore, but okay."

When Dee spoke to Buzz's doctors later that day, one of them blasted her. "Do you realize, Mrs. Clinton, that you should have had this young man in here two days ago?"

"Young man? He's twenty-three years old! He can take care of himself."

"Do you understand that he's really not out of the woods yet?"

Dee was surprised. She had assumed everything was okay. The operation went well. Buzz was recuperating just fine.

"What do you mean?"

"If he makes it through the next forty-eight hours, he'll live. But he's not anywhere near 'okay' just yet."

Dee had beaten herself up enough already for not believing Buzz when he came home and said he was sick. She didn't need some doctor who looked young enough to be her son making her feel even worse.

When she entered Buzz's room, he was, she said later, "pretty doped up on morphine."

"Mom," Buzz said softly, "I can't even die of natural causes."

Buzz had been at a low point in his life. He was unemployed and had no future. He wasn't really sure of what he wanted to do with his life. With everything that had happened the past few days, Buzz had had some time to reflect. The morphine—a narcotic named after the Greek god Morpheus, "the god of dreams"—surely didn't help. A pain reliever and sleep inducer, the drug, sometimes compared to heroin, caused depression and anxiety. It was obvious to Dee that Buzz was disappointed that he'd let her down. He should've been somebody by now. He should have made Dee and Buck proud of him.

Dee began gently pushing Buzz's sweaty hair away from his eyes. It was quiet in the room. Peaceful.

"Listen to me, Buzz Clinton," Dee said, "you were sent here to so something special. You can't get out of this world until you get it done. Just remember that God has a plan for you."

It was a moment between mother and son that would stay with Dee forever. She said later that Buzz just looked up at her and nodded when she said it.

"He understood what I meant."

Even with rising unemployment rates and downturns in business, there are three types of parking lots jammed with cars: casinos, bars and strip clubs. People always seem to find extra money when it comes to gambling, drinking and sex.

Male exotic-revue dance nights became the craze during the latter part of the 1980s and beginning of the '90s. Bars and nightclubs, on certain nights during the week, were inundated with magazine-ad-looking males with chiseled arms, legs and six-pack abs, wearing as little clothing as possible. Women went wild. What had been a "men's only" type of extracurricular activity became watercooler conversations of soccer moms and females everywhere.

By the time Buzz entered his early twenties, he'd grown into an attractive man. He wasn't the scrawny DJ from Old Lyme anymore; he was the handsome, gruff guy with just the right amount of stubble on his face who drove around town in his tow truck. "He reminded me of Charles Bronson," Dee later said.

When the opportunity to dance came along, Buzz saw it as merely one more way to make a buck. He was an ironworker and a pool man. He sold firewood, did bodywork and mechanic work on cars. He towed cars. Why not try dancing?

It wasn't as though he'd had a dream of becoming a Chippendale, touring up and down the East Coast. It was that the opportunity presented itself one day, and Buzz went for it. He saw dollar signs, plain and simple. An old friend was running a service for male dancers and asked Buzz one night if he wanted to dance. Buzz took him up on the offer. It was a few times a month at the local watering hole. Shake your ass. Take some clothes off. And let the ladies slip cash into your G-string. Most men who had the looks and body that Buzz had would have jumped at the chance.

Almost everyone in Old Lyme and East Lyme knew Buzz, for good or bad. He was that kind of memorable person. Still, with all that was being learned about Buzz by the ED-MCS during the weeks and months following his murder, there was a part of him that didn't quite fit into the portrait detectives had developed. To those who had been scorned or ripped off by Buzz, he was a selfish liar who cared only about himself.

Nonetheless, there were times when Buzz's unselfish acts of pure love revealed a totally different person.

One night, Dee got a phone call in the wee hours of the morning. It had woken everyone in the house up—including Buzz. A friend of the family had gotten into a fight with her boyfriend and was calling for a ride. Apparently, the young girl had been at home with her live-in boyfriend. While they were drinking, they had gotten into a fight that was teetering on becoming violent.

The woman told Dee she'd taken off from the house and just started walking. Hours later, she was far away from home, lost and scared.

Buzz stood up as Dee talked to the woman. "I'm going to get her," he said, rubbing sleep from his eyes.

"Sit down," Dee said. "You just relax."

Dee had little tolerance for the drunk and disorderly. Her disgust of her own son's behavior at times was a testament to that fact. And after considering the woman's predicament, Dee surmised she was in no real immediate danger. Her problem, Dee thought, was that she was intoxicated and had likely overreacted to the situation she was in. To Dee, it was the same old story with people who drank.

"I'm going to get her," Buzz repeated while slipping on his shoes.

"Are you crazy? It's two in the morning. She'll be fine. Let her walk home. It'll do her some good."

"I don't care, Ma," Buzz snapped. "I don't leave ladies out in the cold in the middle of the night."

"Well, she's not a lady," Dee said. "She's a *drunk!*"

"So what? She had too much to drink. I'm going. . . ."

Years later, recalling this episode, Dee said, "Buzz could never say a bad word about anybody. It wasn't in him. He knew this girl needed help. That's all he cared about. It didn't matter to him—as it had to me—what she had done or how much she'd had to drink. What mattered was getting her home safely."

It was a side of Buzz, Dee added, that many never knew. He was a delicate person, misunderstood by many. He liked to play with his siblings, for example, and often spent hours outside in the Clintons' woodsy yard— swinging, playing ball and just being a big brother. He took Suzanne for rides in his tow truck. She loved it. Sometimes he'd just sit around and talk to the kids, telling them stories. There were even times when Buzz spent time with some of the elderly in town, playing cards, being a friend.

Indeed, there were many different aspects of Buzz Clinton—and as time went on, his future in-laws, the Carpenters, came up against a person not many knew existed.

Chapter 12

South central Connecticut—New London, Old Lyme, Waterford, East Lyme, Groton—in the late 1980s and early 1990s had always been a haven for hardworking American families. The U.S. Naval Submarine Base, the Global Research and Development Center of Pfizer, Inc., and Electric Boat Division of General Dynamics, where submarines were built, had provided jobs for area residents for decades. The Subway sandwich shop corporation had even opened its first restaurant in nearby Bridgeport in 1965.

But as the manufacturing boom subsided, residents felt the cut. People were being laid off by the thousands. Jobs were scarce.

Route 156 runs parallel to Interstate 95 and, in several of the larger coastal towns, intersects with Route 1, a major thoroughfare that hugs the scenic Long Island Sound. From Waterford to East Lyme, Route 156 has always been a homey, comforting path to travelers. Small-town ambience. Local bars. Diners. One-pump gas stations.

The Café Del Mar wasn't the classiest nightspot in town. It was a "gin mill," filled with locals and passersby who stopped in for a couple of beers and went home.

In early 1992, Buzz had been dancing at the Café Del Mar on a somewhat regular basis on ladies' nights. One evening, Kim Carpenter wandered into the bar with some friends. Buzz happened to be dancing that night.

Spotting her from where he stood onstage, after his set, Buzz went over to Kim and struck up a conversation. She seemed unassuming and withdrawn, but pleasant to be around.

Buzz, of course, didn't know it then, but Kim had been easily tamed by the men she'd dated throughout her life. She had married right out of high school, and many of Kim's relationships had ended sourly. Her first husband, who was in and out of jail throughout their relationship, had scarred Kim. In one way, she was broken and despondent when she met Buzz. They were the same age, twenty-six, born about one month apart, and they seemingly had a lot in common.

It didn't take long for Buzz to become infatuated with Kim. They fell in love almost immediately.

"He must have loved that woman," Charlie Snyder recalled. "Because Buzz was a decent-looking guy. Being a dancer, he could have had any number of women. But he chose Kim for some strange reason."

"When she was with my son," Dee recalled, "[Kim] was a good wife, good mother. Buzz loved her dearly."

But Kim's upbringing and family life, according to some, had been anything but pleasant. One person close to the family likened Kim's upbringing to that of Cinderella's: Kim was treated like the unwanted stepdaughter, while her older sister, Beth Ann, had the luxuries of royalty.

"Kim could do no right; Beth could do no wrong!"

In the short time that Buzz and Kim had been together before Buzz was murdered, this parallel would play itself out almost as if it were scripted—with Buzz, Kim, Cynthia and Beth Ann playing the leading roles.

* * *

Kim Carpenter had grown up in a socially mixed family of academics and blue-collar men. Her mother, Cynthia, was a college graduate with several degrees, while her father, Dick, was a military brat who later owned and operated a landscaping business. He was gone for most of her formative years, so when Dick returned from the navy, Kim later said, "they all had to adjust to the fact that he would be around permanently."

Beth Ann had dreams of becoming a doctor, while Kim graduated from high school, waited tables at a local restaurant, married a "heavy drinker [who] was physically abusive," then began a career at Stop & Shop. Afraid to leave her husband while he was around, Kim filed for divorce when he went to jail.

After dating a local Groton man for a time in late 1989, Kim became pregnant. She wanted to keep the baby, she told the guy after she found out. But he didn't like the idea of being a father at such a young age, and asked Kim to have an abortion. He said he would kill himself if she didn't.

Not sure of what she was going to do, the man left Kim before she made a decision. But in August 1990, Kim gave birth to a blond-haired, blue-eyed angel, Rebecca Ann Carpenter.

With no man around, after giving birth, Kim began raising the girl, she said later, "with the support of her family."

Beth Ann Carpenter was born on Saturday, November 23, 1963. For most of America, it was probably the second most tragic day in history. On November 22, a balmy Friday afternoon in Texas, President John F. Kennedy was gunned down in broad daylight as millions watched in horror.

Yet for Cynthia and Dick Carpenter, cute little Beth Ann, their first child, came on like a blessing—a fleeting relief from the collective grief that had gripped the country that week over the death of one of its most beloved leaders.

From day one, Beth Ann was adorable: blue eyes, pale white skin, dark red hair and the rosiest red cheeks of any kid in the nursery.

When she graduated in 1981 from Ledyard High School, Beth Ann looked more tomboyish than many of the girls in her class. Her rust red hair, freckles and boyish manner made her a prime target for her schoolmates to call her "Red." In photos from that era, Beth Ann looked like a female version of Opie, Ron Howard's straitlaced redheaded character from the popular TV program *The Andy Griffith Show*. She sported bony wrists, twig arms, thin legs and lips, and an awkward, stubborn smile that appeared forced. Her straight, fine hair was cut ultraconservatively—butchlike—just above her ears, and parted to the right side like a child on his first day of kindergarten. She was petite, much shorter than her fellows, and wore little makeup. She was sometimes called "Turtle." Her favorite sayings were "Tell me about it" and "Really." She liked to ski and swim.

Throughout high school, Beth Ann dreamed of only one occupation: medicine. She wanted to help people. But more than anything, perhaps, becoming a doctor would allow her a chance to get out of Ledyard. There wasn't much Ledyard could offer a child who had dreamed of anything else besides agriculture.

Born in 1966, Kim was a couple of years behind Beth Ann. She was more girlish and prissy than her more masculine sister. Always smiling, she dreamed of hairdressing school and moving out of Ledyard. Like Beth Ann, Kim loved the water and went swimming with friends whenever she could. She liked to play tennis and ride horses, developing decent skills for both.

Kim smiled in her high-school yearbook photograph. She appeared happy and certain. Almost content. In stark contrast to big sister Beth Ann, Kim styled her hair appropriately to the times and wore plenty of eye shadow, blush and other kinds of makeup.

The Carpenter sisters, it would turn out, were as different as a snake and a bird.

As fifteen-year-old Kim entered her sophomore year at Ledyard High School in 1981, Beth Ann was off to the nation's capital to attend the prestigious George Washington University. Admitted as a botany major, hoping to accrue enough knowledge and accreditation to further her studies in medicine, Beth Ann went through her George Washington years doubting her decision to go into medicine after graduation.

After graduating in 1986 with a bachelor's degree in botany, the ideal next step for Beth Ann would've been medical school. Among the requirements for admission to medical school were fifteen hours of botany, fifteen hours of biology (genetics and biochemistry), one year of math, two years of chemistry and one year of physics.

Beth Ann had done it all.

But instead of taking the expected route, Beth Ann abruptly decided to take a year off. She was a woman now, much more feminine and removed from that young and naive girl back in Ledyard. Suddenly, being a doctor didn't seem appealing any longer.

With nothing but time on her hands, Beth Ann decided to take the LSAT, "a one-hundred-question, three hour and twenty-five minute exam consisting of five multiple choice sections followed by a thirty-minute writing sample." There is no other test more important in preparation for law school than the LSAT. Seventy percent of the admission process is based on one's LSAT score. Beth Ann now wanted to become a lawyer—not a doctor. It was a total flip-flop in professions. She had studied for four years to go into medicine, but had thrown it all away to go into law inside of a year.

It was an odd change, indeed. But Beth Ann was a smart kid; she could have done anything she wanted to, and her family would've likely supported her proudly.

On the first try, she did exceptionally well on the LSAT. And because of that, her next decision wasn't hard. Beth Ann later said, ". . . I thought [law] was a proper profession for me."

Armed with an unquestionable understanding of prelaw, Beth Ann applied to the Catholic University School of Law, also in Washington, DC, in May 1987. Because of her clear understanding of the law and subsequent high score on the LSAT, she was accepted with open arms.

Quickly, though, any dreams of studying criminal and corporate law that she might have harbored were replaced by a desire to go into real estate, divorce and contractual law. Guardianship and conservatorship was another option. A paper lawyer. Beth Ann later said that the idea of working in a court of law seemed "very intimidating." She wanted no part of arguing cases before judges, but instead wanted to work with people behind the scenes.

After three years at Catholic University, she graduated in 1990 and decided to take the bar exam immediately. Back home in Connecticut, the housing boom was in full swing. She thought she would have no trouble returning, passing the bar exam and finding a job as a real estate attorney or divorce lawyer.

Not only was she in debt for more than $150,000 in student loans, but after going out to Los Angeles during the summer of 1990 to study for the New York bar, Beth Ann returned and failed the New York test horribly.

While at Catholic University, Beth Ann would take her breaks from school and return home to Ledyard. One night, in 1987, while on a break from studies, she went to a local disco. Sitting at the bar was an olive-skinned man about thirty-one years old. Classy-looking, he had dark hair, cropped tightly back like Dean Martin, and was in good physical shape.

Dressed fashionably, the man soon noticed Beth Ann, walked over and struck up a conversation. "My name is Joseph," he said with a strong Middle Eastern accent. "Joseph Jebran."

Jebran was a bit older than Beth Ann. He had been a successful architect for about four years when they met. A man of the world, he'd grown up and attended high school in Lebanon. After that, he and his family moved to Paris. It was the mid-1970s. By 1984, Jebran had graduated from one of the most prestigious schools in Europe, the Beaux-Arts School of Art and Architecture. From there, he bounced back and forth between Rome and Beirut working for a local contractor. In 1986, Jebran moved into his cousin's house in New London, Connecticut, and became an American citizen shortly thereafter.

A GQ-looking guy, Jebran had no trouble finding women. But Beth Ann, from that first night, seemed different. She had a peculiar way about her, almost alluring. By this time, Beth Ann had grown from a rather plain-Jane schoolgirl into a beautiful woman of five feet three inches, 110 pounds. She was fit and trim, with a nice shape. Men were all over her. Her bronze red hair flowed halfway down her shoulders. Redheads were always noticed, and Beth Ann, one would expect, liked the attention. She didn't look anything like the tomboy she had been back in high school. She was stylish and smart-looking now, determined to become a lawyer.

Joseph Jebran—with his heavy foreign accent, well-dressed appearance, old-fashioned manners and playboy looks—undoubtedly fulfilled her blueprint for the man she saw as being fit to be with her. Since moving to the States, Jebran had hooked up with a local architectural firm in nearby Norwich, and he was working for Richard Sharpe, a respected architect who had taken Jebran under his wing and sponsored his American citizenship.

As Beth Ann and Joseph talked that first night, they ended up exchanging phone numbers.

The next week, after Jebran had thought about the night many times, he called Beth Ann a couple of times to hook up, but she never answered her phone or called him back.

Maybe she'd changed her mind? Perhaps she was out of town? Either way, Joseph wrote her off.

A week or so later, however, while back in Washington studying, Beth Ann called Joseph out of the blue.

"Would you like to come to Washington?"

It was an odd request. They'd just met. Jebran had thought he'd never hear from her again. But at the same time, he felt something. So he packed up his car, and off he went to the nation's capital.

In the end, Joseph spent the weekend and, just like that, found himself involved in an intimate relationship with a woman he had known for only about two weeks. As time went on, he made the five-hour trek to Washington about once a month.

On paper, they were made for each other: Beth Ann studying to become a lawyer and Joseph already an established architect—two professionals on their way up the socioeconomic ladder.

Both were going places. It seemed like the perfect match.

After Beth Ann finished law school in 1990 and spent that summer in California studying for the bar exam, she moved back home to her parents' Ledyard home. Joseph Jebran, who was now working for a high-brow architectural firm in New York City, began spending more and more time with her. Beth Ann had gone to Europe with her brother, Richard, for about eight weeks after taking the bar exam, but now she was back, settling into life.

Because of his job, Joseph began living in New York City with four other men during the week and commuting to New London on weekends. For the most part, Jebran would hang around the Carpenter home when he was in town. But even though it was just weekend visits and telephone calls during the week, Joseph fell hard for Beth Ann. When the weekend visits were over, Beth Ann would drive Joseph to the train station in downtown New London, see him off until the next weekend and go about her life.

For Jebran, he would count the days until they saw each other again.

Soon after Kim gave birth to Rebecca in 1990, the child became the main topic of conversation around the Carpenter house. One of the things Joseph Jebran would later recall in vivid detail about being at the Carpenter house during this time was how Rebecca was all anyone—especially Beth Ann—ever talked about. *How was she doing? How was Kim treating her? What have the doctors said recently?* It was as if the entire ebb and flow of the house were driven by Rebecca and her needs.

Shortly after birth, Rebecca had been diagnosed with several problems. Most prominently, she was having trouble with speech and motor skills. Kim had been diagnosed years earlier with phenylketonuria (PKU) disease, a genetic blood disorder that required a strict diet. The family was worried that Rebecca would end up with it, too. She was constantly fidgeting with her fingers, putting them in her mouth, chewing on them, and she seemed not to be able to concentrate entirely on what she was doing.

By this time, Beth Ann had a bigger problem on her hands that had little to do with her niece, however. By the end of the summer, after failing the New York bar exam, she was forced to make a decision. If she wanted to become a lawyer, she would have to hunker down, study and take the exam again. There would be no time to spend with Rebecca.

So beginning in October 1990, for four months, Beth Ann studied between twelve and thirteen hours a day, mostly at the Connecticut College Law Library, in New Haven, and the local Ledyard Dunkin' Donuts when the library was closed. This time around, she vowed not only to pass the New York bar exam, but Connecticut's, too.

By February 1991, she made good on her promise and passed both exams.

Passing the bar exam in two states was one thing, but finding a job in what had become a tight job market since she'd graduated was another. Armed with excellent scores from the bar exam, Beth Ann began sending out hundreds of applications and answered ads in all the local law publications. After about a month, she realized that test scores and determination weren't necessarily enough to secure a job as a lawyer. In the course of about two months, she could schedule only three interviews.

Nobody seemed to want someone fresh out of law school, with little experience.

By the end of 1991, Beth Ann had such a stranglehold on Joseph Jebran and his feelings that he was signing over his paychecks to her and sending them back to Connecticut. When she got her hands on the money, she would pay his bills, pay her bills and send Joseph a stipend to live off while he worked in the city during the week. As for the rest of the money, Joseph and others later claimed, she used it to live in the lap of luxury, driving around town in a BMW, a car for which, in fact, Joseph had traded in his own vehicle as a down payment.

Nevertheless, Joseph was still in the dark as to how Beth Ann viewed the relationship. Yes, he would take her on expensive cruises and out to elaborate downtown dinners, buying her anything she wanted. But he still wasn't sure how she felt about him. It seemed hot and cold. In one of the many cards Jebran sent Beth Ann throughout the years, his confusion over how the relationship progressed was evident.

"You're the one I want to turn to," he wrote, "when I want to talk about my most important joys and my most private problems." He went on to say that he didn't really know if they were "in the same place . . . emotionally and physically. . . ." Ending the brief card, Jebran wrote that he loved her and knew they were always together, if nothing else, in "spirit."

Later, in a card Joseph gave Beth Ann for her graduation, he wrote in a large font: "I LOVE YOU." He called her "beautiful, elegant, honest." He wrote her poems: "When things are chaotic, I wish you inner silence / When things look empty, I wish you hope / When pockets are empty, I wish you win the <u>LOTTO</u> . . ." He had underlined Lotto, and, perhaps developing an understanding of how Beth Ann was using him for his money, he finished the Lotto line with, "So you don't buther [sic] me."

Chapter 13

According to Cynthia and Beth Ann Carpenter, Kim was anything but an ideal mother, daughter or sibling. Since the latter part of her high-school years, Kim's life proceeded in a downward spiral that seemed to get worse around every corner. The only difference now was that Kim had a child to care for, Rebecca, who had turned two shortly after Kim had met Buzz in 1992.

By the time Kim had met Buzz, the Carpenters were saying that Rebecca was being neglected horribly. Kim would have to make some changes, or the family was going to have to step up and take charge. They were tired of Kim's lack of responsibility. Rebecca needed a mother, she needed special attention. Kim just wasn't giving it to her.

"[My parents]," Beth Ann later said, "had problems with my sister her whole life. She has PKU. It's phenylketonuria. It's a genetic disorder disease where you lack the enzyme in your blood to digest protein. It leads to mental retardation, cognitive problems and sexual promiscuity. Because she came off the diet, her IQ was lowered to seventy. . . . She was a constant source of problems for my parents through her life [and] high school."

PKU is an inherited disease. It can, if left untreated, cause mental retardation in adults. Kim was at risk, certainly. A person with PKU, however, can lead an otherwise normal life as long as she takes proper care of herself—obviously something the Carpenters felt Kim wasn't doing. The best treatment is a diet devoid of high protein foods: meat, fish, poultry, etc. Victims of the disease generally take an expensive synthetic formula to replace the food products they can't eat. With Kim working part-time at the local Stop & Shop, having moved back home after her divorce, and then the birth of Rebecca, it was likely she didn't adhere to a strict diet.

But Kim's "sexual promiscuity," if indeed she was sleeping around, wasn't brought on by her PKU, as Beth Ann had suggested. It couldn't have been. Sexual promiscuity was not among the known symptoms of the disease. In fact, when asked, people who suffer from PKU get upset at the common, misinterpreted correlation. "There is no connection whatsoever between PKU and sexual promiscuity," one woman who has suffered from the disease for years opined. "Absolutely not!"

On July 14, 1992, Buzz returned home from his job at the Café Del Mar. Like a seventh grader who had just gotten home from his first date, be babbled on and on about how he'd just met the girl of his dreams.

"I'm all finished with it, Ma," Buzz said the following morning. "I met a really nice girl last night, and I'm not dancing anymore."

"That's good, Buzz—but don't bring her home until you've been married for five years."

Dee had seen her son go through women as if they were cars. It seemed that every day brought a new woman for Buzz, and Dee wasn't buying any of the "this is it!" crap she'd heard Buzz say more times than she could remember.

"By the time he was fourteen, Buzz had girls all over him—and he never really ever slowed down," Dee later said. "He wasn't an angel . . . but then who is? He was a guy, and like any guy his age, he was always looking for women."

Indeed, it wasn't hard for Buzz to hook up with many different women, often at the same time. But the girl he had met on July 14 was different from all the rest, he insisted.

About five feet four inches, 120 pounds, strawberry blond hair running down past her shoulders, Kim seemed to be everything Buzz had been waiting for. She was fragile and shy. He liked that. She wasn't overbearing. He liked that, too.

Kim had been out of school for about six years, already married, had a child and was now single for the first time since she'd started dating back in junior high. Going out on the town was something Kim had never really done before. She had been tied down ever since childhood.

If nothing else, Kim was naive, perhaps even codependent. She spoke only when she was spoken to. Part of it had to do with her PKU disease. Part of it was her character. Being single, she liked to go out with friends. The Carpenters, however, viewed this as neglect on her part. To Beth Ann, Cynthia, Dick and Richard, Kim was a mother. It had been her decision to have the child. If she wasn't going to take care of Rebecca, they would have to do it for her.

When the Carpenters found out that Kim had met Buzz, it just added to their concern. Kim was out of control. Now she was going to bring an exotic dancer into the picture?

Buzz was outgoing, energetic and not afraid to speak his mind. He was a hustler, talking his way in and out of trouble whenever he had to. Unbeknownst to Buzz and Kim during the first weeks of their relationship, this posed a major problem where the Carpenters were concerned: Kim would now have a voice in her corner speaking up for her. Before Buzz, the Carpenters could manage Kim with little opposition.

From Kim's point of view, Buzz wasn't John Wayne, but he was nothing like her first husband. Sure, Buzz had had his share of run-ins with the law, but he wasn't a jailbird.

Buzz had learned his strong will from his parents. Growing up, he watched Buck and Dee fight the town of Old Lyme for ten years for a permit to build and open a kennel on their property.

"We taught Buzz," Dee said later, "to fight for what he believed in. But fight issues, not people. Never make it personal. Fight for your beliefs!"

Indeed, principles, not personalities.

To many people who knew them, Buzz and Kim were far from winning any couple-of-the-year awards. But they still meshed well together and got along. It was a match. And there wasn't much anyone—including the Carpenters—could do to stop the relationship.

A week or so after they met, Buzz brought Kim home and introduced her to Suzanne, who was eight years old then.

When Buzz and Kim left, Suzanne went running into the kennel where Dee was working. Dee could tell Suzanne was excited about meeting Kim. She could see it on her face. Buzz and his first wife, Lisa, hadn't ended their relationship on good terms, and Buzz hadn't really met anyone in some time that the family felt serious about. Buzz had recently turned over parental rights for his son, Michael, to Lisa and her new husband, Dan. It wasn't an easy decision, of course, but something Buzz knew would make a better life for Michael. As it was, Buzz hadn't really seen the child much because Lisa had moved away and, for no malicious reason, had kept the child from him.

It wasn't hard for Dee to tell that Suzanne was drawn

to Kim in a big-sister way. It was a good sign that maybe things were looking up for Buzz—that he had finally met someone who cared about him, that he could care about, plus the family approved of her.

"Mom, she's really nice. I just met her," Suzanne said excitedly.

"They're *all* nice, Suzanne."

At first, Dee thought it was just one more bimbo to add to a long list Buzz had accumulated throughout the years. But weeks later, when Dee finally got a chance to sit down and chat with Kim, she realized she might have been wrong.

They sat and talked for hours, Dee recalled. Kim showed Dee photographs of Rebecca. Then she told her that Rebecca was sick and needed to have an operation. Dee later said Kim was very "articulate and knowledge-able about [Rebecca]," her condition and the treatment she needed.

That impressed Dee.

"When can I meet Rebecca?" Dee asked.

"I don't know. . . ."

"You don't know?"

"I'll have to ask my mother," Kim said, looking down.

It was a strange answer, Dee thought. But she didn't press Kim. She could tell by Kim's voice that there was something going on, yet it wasn't any of her business. Dee had no idea, of course, that the Carpenters had had total control over Rebecca by this point, including how often Kim could see her.

The reality of the situation, however, was much more difficult. Because once Buzz came into the picture, the Carpenters made it their number one priority to gain legal custody of Rebecca. Time had run out for Kim. Even though she was falling in love with Buzz—and, perhaps, for the first time in her life was going to have a stable environment to raise Rebecca in—the Carpenters didn't want to hear about it anymore. They wanted Rebecca to live with them, no matter where Kim's life was heading—and they routinely made it known that they were prepared to do anything to get their way.

Only a few weeks into Buzz and Kim's relationship, Dee, seeing Kim and talking to her several times since they'd first met, began to realize something was incredibly askew regarding Kim, Rebecca and the Carpenters. Kim would tell Dee stories about Rebecca and how her mother, father, sister and brother viewed her relationship with Buzz. Kim was fraught over the entire ordeal. Here she was falling in love and losing her child at the same time.

It wasn't fair.

There was one night when Cynthia and Beth Ann approached Kim to sign a document that would legally hand over all medical rights of Rebecca. By signing it, Kim would be passing over to the family the right to make any medical decisions on Rebecca's part without Kim's consent.

Kim refused.

Still living in the Carpenters' Ledyard home with Rebecca, Kim came home the following night after refusing to sign the document to find the doors locked. Looking in through the picture window, Kim could see a flickering glow of the television visible from where she was standing on the porch. So she peeked through the shades and looked inside.

There was Beth Ann sitting on the couch, watching television, paying no mind to Kim's banging on the door.

So Kim knocked harder.

Beth Ann came up to the window, looked at her, then sat back down without answering the door or saying anything.

It was a slap in the face. *If you don't sign the papers, you don't live here.* The Carpenters, apparently, were playing hardball now.

When Kim returned to Buzz's house in Old Lyme and told him what had happened, Buzz insisted it meant only one thing: Kim had been kicked out of her house.

"Great, now what am I going to do?"

"You'll move in here with us. I'll talk to my mother."

The following day, Kim and Buzz went to the Ledyard Police Department (LPD) and filed a police report. Buzz wanted to be sure to document everything that was going on. Beth Ann, whether she had a job or not, was a lawyer who had, in fact, been studying this very type of litigation. She knew the ins and outs. Buzz wasn't educated in law, but he wasn't stupid. He knew what they had to do to protect themselves; like the Carpenters, he was prepared to fight.

While Buzz and Kim were at the LPD filing the report, they found out that Beth Ann and Cynthia had filed a ten-day temporary-custody order for Rebecca.

It was the beginning of what would amount to a battle between the Clintons and Carpenters that would escalate with each passing day. It was the first strike—the beginning of a war that would last for the next year and a half and end with Buzz's murder.

By midsummer 1992, the Carpenters had had it. As they saw it, they were raising Rebecca themselves, while Kim and Buzz were always off doing their own thing.

Moving back home after her first husband had gone to jail seemed like the best thing to do for Kim at the time. For Rebecca, moving into the Carpenter home wasn't that big a change. Cynthia claimed Kim had been dropping Rebecca off at least three times a week prior to Kim's moving in, anyway, and that the Carpenters had developed a rather close relationship with the child because of that. Rebecca's moving in really didn't change anything in that respect; it just made the bond between the Carpenters and Rebecca that much deeper.

A bond the Carpenters, apparently, weren't prepared to sever.

But Kim's lack of care and concern for Rebecca's well-being after moving back home only got worse, not better, Cynthia later wrote in an affidavit to the family court.

Things reached a crescendo on July 6, 1992, shortly before Kim had met Buzz. Kim went out that night, never returned, and it was the last time the Carpenters "saw her on a regular basis," Cynthia wrote. In fact, for four days, while the Carpenters took care of Rebecca, they claimed they didn't even know where Kim was. And when she did finally reappear on July 10, she sneaked into the house in the middle of the night, retreated downstairs and closed the door so no one, including Rebecca, would bother her as she slept in the next morning. When she did wake up, Cynthia and Dick asked her where she was going, but Kim failed to answer. So they asked her for a phone number, just in case something—God forbid—happened to Rebecca in her absence.

But on her way out the door, Kim would only say, "Call me at work if you need me."

Not having a phone number to reach Kim wasn't necessarily the end of the world, but things only got worse from there, Cynthia insisted.

When Kim did come home, for example, and stay for a night or two, she would "ignore Rebecca" and expect Beth Ann and Cynthia to care for the child, which they gladly did without reservation. It was obvious to the Carpenters that Kim was just coming home to sleep, rejuvenate and prepare for the next night out—and they were tired of it.

On July 21, Rebecca had an appointment at Boston Children's Hospital, a two-hour drive from Ledyard. She needed to be tested for several different things. There was plenty of evidence that she had some sort of learning disability; she hadn't been communicating like other kids her own age and was still lacking appropriate motor skills. The family also wanted to have her tested for PKU. It was possible, doctors were saying, Rebecca had it. The sooner they found out, the better off she'd be.

The appointment was scheduled for 11:30 A.M. Cynthia had even gone to Kim's work to remind her about the appointment earlier that week.

Kim promised she'd be there.

By the time Kim had shown up at 10:30 A.M., however, Richard and Dick had already left with Rebecca for the appointment. They said later they were worried they'd miss it.

"I overslept, Ma," Kim said when she arrived.

The hospital ended up verifying what mostly everyone suspected: Rebecca had "slowness in the development of fine motor skills and speech development." Results on the more intricate tests to see if she had PKU would take weeks, maybe months. But it was enough to indicate that Rebecca needed special attention, which, according to the Carpenters, she wasn't getting from Kim.

If missing the appointment, showing up late and not driving Rebecca to Boston weren't bad enough, the part of the day that troubled the Carpenters most, Cynthia said, was that Kim never called that night to find out what had happened in Boston. After she left the house at 10:30 A.M., the Carpenters claimed they never heard back from her.

It was one more brick added to a foundation of missed appointments, neglect and a total lack of responsibility on Kim's part. The Carpenters weren't going to hear any more of it. It was evident that Kim wasn't about to change anytime soon, and with Buzz now in the picture, her chances of giving Rebecca the common life the Carpenters thought she deserved were even less than they had been. Added to this was the fact that the more information the Carpenters found out about Buzz, the less they saw him as someone who could be a future role model for Rebecca.

The Carpenters viewed Buzz as a male-revue dancer. They had no idea he was planning on going to school to become a visiting nurse's aide or, like his father, had been a member in the ironworkers union for years but just couldn't find work.

There was a major conflict now. Because as Kim and Buzz's relationship blossomed throughout the summer, Kim began to see an opportunity to involve Rebecca in the new union. It was the closest family environment she could offer Rebecca personally. Other than what the Carpenters, as grandparents, had given her, Rebecca had never really experienced that situation.

The Carpenters, though, didn't quite see it that way—and were now beginning to line up their troops to do everything possible to take (and keep) Rebecca away from Buzz and Kim.

Chapter 14

In Hollywood, there was a child custody fight heating up in August 1992. Mia Farrow and Woody Allen were locking horns in what would later prove to be a scandal that would brand actor-director Allen, many agreed, as the worst scourge on the planet: a child molester. Buzz Clinton didn't know it at the time, but he and Woody Allen had more in common than merely living on the East Coast.

Late in the day on August 20, Kim approached Dee with what turned out to be a rather odd document.

Buzz wanted Kim to sign a prenuptial agreement. It wasn't, Dee said later, that the two lovebirds had only known each other for a month and were already planning on getting married. Still, Dee wondered why Kim would even consider signing such a ridiculous document. Was she *that* intimidated by men?

Dee knew her son better than most. He was always coming up with quirky ideas that made little sense to many of the people around him. But this prenuptial agreement was different. It was an odd thing to ask of a woman after knowing her for only one month. Yet as Dee considered it later, she began to understand Buzz's trepidation toward marriage. He had been burned by his former wife, Lisa, and, Dee suggested, had been screwed over by most of the women he'd dated. To insure that it wouldn't happen again, before dipping his toes farther into what was becoming a very serious relationship, Buzz wanted something down on paper to protect himself. He wanted security.

It was an outrageous document, etched in poor grammar, yet extremely matter of fact. Buzz wasn't a Rhodes scholar—and the writing in the prenup pretty much proved that.

On the other hand, however, Buzz surely knew what to say as it pertained to his future with Kim.

The one-page document began by having Kim insist that she had not been "forced" or "threatened" to sign the contract. By signing it, however, she would be releasing Buzz from "all financial responsibility" to her, including any future "child support payments, alimony, any inheritances, real estate, motor vehicles, personal property, bank accounts, stocks, bonds, mutual funds, pensions, retirement plans . . . or any other assets. . . ."

Even more bizarre was that by signing the contract Kim would have to agree that Buzz was a "good parent for any and all children [they] may have in the future and . . . [agree to] give up all parental rights and . . . custody to [Buzz] . . . [and to] let [him] set all, if any, visitation times and dates."

Ending the document, Kim was also admitting that the "contract means I have no control over any and all children. . . ."

Apparently, Buzz had learned a few things being involved in the fiasco that had ensued between Kim and her family the past few weeks.

But there was something else tugging at Buzz's heartstrings. He had been torn apart, according to Dee, by his divorce from Lisa; in the process, he had lost contact with Michael. He wasn't about to let that happen again.

Kim had gone to Dee and showed her the contract after she signed it.

After hearing Kim out, Dee looked at her for a moment and fell silent. Then, "Are you nuts?"

"Oh, it's nothing, Mrs. Clinton," Kim replied. "It'll never hold up in court."

"How do you know *that?*"

"My sister's a lawyer. I showed it to her. She told me not to worry about it."

It was the first time Dee had heard that Kim's sister, Beth Ann, was a lawyer.

After Beth Ann passed the New York and Connecticut bar exams, she began looking for work right away.

With her prospects grim, she volunteered at the public defender's office in Norwich and began logging some hours working on probate cases. It was paper-pushing work for the most part, but legal experience nonetheless. Once in a while, she was even asked to show up in court and work a motion or represent a client.

Working probate cases, however—guardianships and conservatorships—was an interesting choice. One, Beth Ann could acquire that much-needed experience her prospective employers craved from law school graduates; and, two, perhaps most important, she could study the law as it pertained to Rebecca's situation.

By the end of summer, Beth Ann had settled into a position with the public defender's office, sharing an office in New London with another promising young lawyer, Michael Hasse.

While working in New London with Hasse, Beth Ann continued to send out job applications. Still, nothing materialized. Then one day after work, she walked into the law offices of Haiman Long Clein, a real estate attorney from Old Saybrook with a small satellite office in downtown New London, on State Street, directly across

the street from the New London Superior Courthouse—
and her life changed.

Haiman Long Clein had been known to many people
as somewhat of a high-powered attorney who drove expensive cars and owned mansion-size homes, took friends
and clients out to extravagant dinners, held wild stag parties and made good investments in real estate. When
someone in the area needed a lawyer who knew the ins
and outs of real estate transactions, Clein's name always
came up. He was well respected around town by some and
revered as the go-to lawyer for the wealthy in communities
like Waterford, New London, Old Lyme, Old Saybrook,
Essex and a few surrounding boroughs. Clein had dabbled
in a few criminal cases throughout the years, but his main
focus and chief source of income came from real estate
transactions, fiduciary cases and investment banking.

Others, however, painted Clein as being fake and
phony.

"He never impressed the shit out of me, or I would
have hired him myself," a local businessman later said. "I
have lived in Waterford since 1984. I'm pretty well
known. [Clein] never ran with people who impressed
me all that much. He wasn't known as a high roller in
the circles where it really mattered. To some people,
maybe he was this big-time lawyer living in a big house
up on the hill. But to me, he was nothing. Just another
lawyer. There were some big-time lawyers around town
that everyone knew—but Clein wasn't one of them."

When Beth Ann met Clein in August 1992, Clein had
hit rock bottom. With the real estate market trying to gain
back its legs, but still not anywhere near where it had been
in the early 1980s, many of his investments had dried up.

Most of the property he owned depended on borrowed monies. Recently he found himself for the first time not being able to meet loan payments. At one time, Clein had owned three office complexes in Old Saybrook and one in Essex. He was collecting rents, spending big and living large.

Lately, though, he was having trouble sleeping. He suffered mood swings. And it was the anxiety of losing everything he'd worked for that sent him running to psychotherapy—where he was quickly diagnosed with severe depression and, like millions of others, was prescribed Prozac.

Born on March 25, 1941, the brutish-looking lawyer had just turned fifty-one when the beautiful redhead Beth Ann Carpenter came bouncing into his New London office. Clein sported a salt-and-pepper beard and mustache, potbelly and a six-foot frame. Stick a shotgun in his hand and he could have doubled for 1970s television star Dan Haggerty, who played the country-bumpkinish character Grizzly Adams on a show of the same name.

Unlike many of his contemporaries, Clein didn't play the part of the high-powered attorney in public: crass and sharklike. He never wore expensive suits or Bruno Magli shoes, and he hardly came across as all that tough. When he was working around the office, he usually dressed in plaid lumberjack shirts and jeans. He was unpretentious and soft-spoken, and his clients, who liked him that way, ran the gamut—from low-life hoodlums and thieves to drug dealers to two-bit criminals to millionaire businessmen. But it didn't matter who it was, like Beth Ann during that first encounter, those who met Clein usually fell victim to his down-home charm. It was a spell. He appeared trustworthy. People felt comfortable around him.

Clein's magnetism and charming personality, undoubtedly, were somewhat built around his upbringing in Miami, Florida, where he attended the University of

Miami in 1959. Forming an interest in law while there, he transferred to the University of Florida in 1961. Entering the University of Miami Law School in 1963, six years later, Clein found himself practicing law in the fast-paced world of Miami, where cocaine ran through the city like rainwater and beautiful women were everywhere.

Later, Clein would tell people he was "the black sheep of [his] family," expressing it in a way that led many to believe he wasn't the least bit sorry about admitting it. In fact, when questioned about what made him decide to go into law, Clein told several people that he had become a lawyer to "know the laws so I could get around them without being caught or penalized."

While in Florida going to school, Clein met his first wife, a woman from Niantic, Connecticut, and by 1977, the happy couple was on a plane back to the Northeast to begin a life together.

By 1978, now a permanent resident of Connecticut, Clein was licensed in the state. Connecticut was, in many ways, the yin to the yang lifestyle Clein had grown accustomed to in Florida. Connecticut was slower paced and more of a playground for the artistic, academic and political. There was the famed Yale University in New Haven and Trinity College in Hartford; Katharine Hepburn was a state resident; *Saturday Night Live* onetime executive producer Dick Ebersol lived in Litchfield with his actress-wife Susan Saint James; David Letterman and Martha Stewart had homes in state; authors, lawyers and doctors had been buying up real estate in and around the Greenwich and Stamford areas for decades; the Kennedys even had blood in the state.

Indeed, Connecticut wasn't West Palm Beach or Ft. Lauderdale, but it was brimming with potential wealth for Clein to take advantage of.

A few years after Clein and his new bride set up a home in Old Saybrook and had a daughter, the marriage dissolved. But Clein was never one to be without a woman. Some even said later that the divorce was based in part on a relationship Clein had begun with Bonnie MacHaffie, a local woman who had grown up in Gilford, New Hampshire, under the guidance of a family heavily influenced by the church.

In 1981, shortly after Clein closed his practice in Florida and dedicated himself exclusively to his Connecticut practice—he had been going back and forth between his offices—he ended up marrying MacHaffie. As the years passed, the couple found themselves raising four kids.

Finally, it seemed, Clein had met a woman who viewed the world the same way he did. Bonnie, a bit on the homely side, was her own person. On the other hand, like a Stepford wife, she listened attentively when Clein spoke, and some said, she never caused any problems for him when they were in public, playing the role of the happy homemaker well. During dinner parties, Bonnie would sit quietly, nodding at the appropriate times, schmoozing with her dinner guests, drinking expensive bottles of Cabernet and speaking when she thought it was the proper time.

"She was a pleasant woman who didn't talk much," one former acquaintance said.

Things were going okay for the Cleins. Haiman had a practice in Old Saybrook and was talking about opening up a satellite office in New London. The stock market had taken a dive in 1980, and its impact on Clein's business had been substantial. But he had spent the remainder of the 1980s rebuilding his practice. By the mid-1980s, the Cleins had money again—lots of it. They had friends in high places. Cars. Two homes: one in Old Saybrook in a gated community overlooking the Atlantic Ocean and a second in Waterford. And although Bonnie had grown up in somewhat of a strict, religious-based home, she had no trouble converting to Judaism after

144 M. William Phelps

marrying Clein, who himself wasn't an Orthodox Jew, but practiced the faith nonetheless.

When the 1990s hit, however, things went bad. It was brewing up to be perhaps the worst time to own real estate in the past sixty years. If experts were right, the monies people were going to lose would dwarf any losses from the '80s. Investments were going bust left and right. Unemployment rates soared. People were losing their homes. Pensions were being sucked dry by bad investments.

To Clein, it was a devastating blow to his ego. He had migrated to Connecticut with his first wife in the late 1970s and began almost immediately reaping the benefits of stepping on a fast-moving bandwagon of wealth. Sure, the 1980s were tough, but he got through it unscathed. It was nothing compared to what was happening now—or what was about to happen.

It had taken years, but what had begun as a small operation on Main Street, in downtown Old Saybrook, in an old run-down and rustic one-family house, grew into a full-fledged law firm specializing in real estate transactions.

As the years passed and business slowed after the boom of the 1980s, Clein's new friends began to see a different person emerge—someone, many later said, who couldn't handle the stress of a waning economy.

One of Clein's closest friends throughout the years had been Matthew Elgart, an optometrist in town who ran a practice near Clein's Old Saybrook office. Married, in his early thirties when he met Clein in 1973, Dr. Elgart had graduated from the New England College of Optometry, in Boston, around the same time Clein had entered law school in 1963. In 1972, a second doctor joined Elgart's practice, and he soon began building what would eventually become a successful and distinguished practice. When asked about him, a man in the area later said, "Anybody who lives in the

Old Saybrook area knows Dr. Elgart; he's the guy on those huge billboards all over town."

Walking into Clein's law practice one day in the early 1970s, Elgart needed some legal work done and struck up a friendship. A hairdresser in town had initially referred Elgart to Clein. Since both men were Jewish, not to mention professionals and neighbors, the woman assumed they'd get along.

And they did.

Near the end of the 1980s, however, Clein's world took a turn. His business life became more about recruiting new clients than tending to the legal matters of the client base he'd already built up. According to his psychiatrist, Vittorio Ferrero, Clein had "[h]is wife [Bonnie have] sex with friends . . . several different friends . . . and he watched it. Part of his rationalization . . . is that these people were business partners and he needed their support."

Ferrero then added "that [Clein] was having his wife have intercourse with other partners, with other—not business partners, but other men in his presence or—and/or having parties where couples would swap, change, change partners."

Throughout the years, Dr. Elgart later recalled, he began to notice that Clein had a rather insatiable appetite for hard liquor. Elgart, not too much of a drinker himself, had a glass of wine once in a while, but that was the extent of his alcohol intake.

"Well, it was prodigious, I would say," Elgart said later, recalling Clein's drinking habits. "He drank very, very heavily . . . and pretty much by the glassful."

Be it his favorite, Bombay Sapphire gin, or Stolichnaya, a popular Russian vodka, Clein seemingly had a drink in his hand whenever Elgart saw him, whether it was at a local bar, Clein's office or at his home.

Around this same time, Elgart began to notice that

Clein dealt with the stress of his failures in other ways, too. Based on their conversations throughout the years, Elgart later put it together that Clein not only acquired a robust appetite for booze, but also for women—lots of them. In all, Elgart recalled that Clein had admitted to him no less than ten affairs over the years.

Not one or two, but *ten*. When asked by friends why he was having so many affairs, Clein would say, "I can't have sex with Bonnie"—the same woman, by the way, who had bore him four children—"because she is old and wrinkly."

Becoming a regular fixture at the extravagant parties Clein would throw from time to time, Elgart noticed during the latter years of their friendship that Clein added another element to an elixir that now consisted of booze, wife-swapping parties, Prozac and women: cocaine. Clein loved it. It kept him going and allowed him to sustain a social stamina he'd built up throughout the years. His job forced him to carry a smile-on-your-face attitude all the time. He always had to be "on." And cocaine worked like fuel. With his investments tanking, his marriage defining the term dysfunctional, and his law practice slipping, Clein found solace in cocaine. It helped him forget about reality and concentrate on a fantasy world he'd created.

A fictional character living in a nonfiction world.

Clein wasn't shy about his drug use during office parties, or even selfish about it, and had no qualms about passing the drug around to anyone who wanted to try it. Dr. Elgart, the same book-smart, owlish-looking respected doctor who smiled for billboard photos, later admitted that he, too, had even gotten caught up in the moment and used cocaine sparingly with Clein.

As time passed and the pressure on him to succeed mounted, Clein's cocaine use escalated sharply. The optometrist might stop by unexpectedly on a Friday night, Elgart later recalled, after he got out of work to say hello, and there was Clein laying out lines on his oak desk. The packets of cocaine went from tiny envelopes half the size of a matchbook to, Elgart said, "a fistful, a bagful of it. . . ."

Ironically, Clein's drug dealer was Mark Despres, one of the chief suspects in Buzz's murder. Clein had met Despres back in 1977 when Despres was eighteen. Despres had been working for Clein's brother-in-law at the time, painting his Old Saybrook home. Clein had even hired Despres one time to build a dollhouse for Bonnie.

Throughout the years, Clein represented Despres in court several times on a wide variety of petty crimes, divorce and anything else Despres needed legal advice on. When Clein decided to use cocaine, he knew what guy to call.

As his supplier, Despres saw Clein's cocaine use from a much clearer perspective. Despres later claimed Clein was buying about "an ounce and a half" per week. Clein would conduct the deals with Despres in his Old Saybrook law office, always paying him in cash. Sometimes they'd meet at a Dunkin' Donuts. If for some reason Clein wasn't going to be around, Clein would leave the money outside in back of the office in an envelope next to the air conditioner, and Despres would drop by and exchange the envelope for a bag of cocaine wrapped in plastic.

Clein told Despres that the bulk of the drugs were "for a doctor friend of his," perhaps meaning Matthew Elgart. But Despres said later he found out that the drugs were mainly for Clein and his brother. Clein was laughing one day, Despres later said, when he told Despres that his brother couldn't stop talking when he snorted cocaine. Clein thought it was the funniest thing in the world that his brother, an otherwise quiet guy, became this chatterbox, rambling on about everything from sports to politics, making no sense at all.

In 1991, Clein had claimed a loss of $2.25 million on his tax return. The bulk of the losses came from property he owned in and around New London, Old Saybrook and Chester. By 1992, with Clein now splitting his time between his two law practices, he was in debt for more money than he had ever been, and his personal life was spiraling out of control. He had lost his extravagant home in Old Saybrook in 1991, and he was on the verge of losing his house in Waterford.

Yet the question remained: if he was broke, where was he getting the money to sustain such an active life of drugs, booze and women?

The answer would come later.

Clein had been stealing clients' funds for years, embezzling monies put in escrow for any contingency fees that might arise while doing legal work for clients. If there was no money in *those* accounts, he would steal from his clients' personal accounts, credit cards and trust funds.

Chapter 15

When Beth Ann Carpenter—young, eager and ready to begin her life as an attorney—walked into Haiman Clein's New London office in August 1992, she had no idea she was marching into a world that was about to crumble.

Despite his failures and addictions, Clein was still living in a rather large colonial house in an upscale Waterford community, just west of New London. Built on a man-made pond, the house was an immense piece of real estate. He'd built an in-ground pool that dwarfed any YMCA pool in the area. He'd thrown holiday parties with hundreds of people, bar mitzvahs for his kids, dinners and cocktail parties. Things appeared—on the outside, anyway—to be going well for Clein. But it was all part of his perfectly manicured image. Underneath the facade was a businessman in dire straits. He'd even stooped as low as having business cards made up to say that he was a travel agent so he could get deals on rooms when he traveled.

If all that weren't enough, Clein had taken off on a binge one day to England because, he later said, he "could not pass up the opportunity to fly on the Concorde" after a friend offered.

With all the chaos going on in his life, in walked Beth Ann. Here she was: young—just twenty-eight—pretty, hungry to begin her legal career and seemingly ready to do anything to land that ultimate job in law that had eluded her since graduation.

Leaving Clein's office after they first met, Beth Ann had a good feeling. The receptionist had told her she would hear something soon. She had even met Clein himself and gotten good vibes from the meeting.

A short time later, Clein called and told her to come in for an interview. After two more additional interviews, Clein called one day and said, "You can start in November. We'll give you your own office."

Beth Ann was ecstatic. She had finally scored what appeared to be the job of her dreams.

Back in the spring of 1992, twenty-five-year-old John Gaul, a well-liked, hardworking, blue-collar man from Groton, asked his girlfriend of many years, Tricia Baker, a slightly overweight but stunningly attractive blonde who had grown up in Waterford, to marry him. Friends before they started dating, Tricia had known Gaul since 1986, and for the past few years, they had been living together. Noticeably taller than Tricia, John had short-cropped brown hair, militarylike, and a bit of a mustache. He was skinny. They resembled a plastic couple on top of a wedding cake—the perfect pair.

Excited, Tricia said yes to John's marriage proposal.

Like many happy couples, John and Tricia announced their engagement in the local newspaper. Shortly afterward, while they were at home one day, a Honda Accord pulled into their driveway.

"There were two women in the front seat and a baby in the back," Tricia later said. "John went out to see what they wanted."

Returning after a moment, John came back into the house and told Tricia that it was Kim Carpenter and her sister, Beth Ann. The baby's name was Rebecca.

"They say I'm Rebecca's father."

At first, John and Tricia didn't quite believe it. Gaul hadn't seen or heard from Kim in several years and had only dated her briefly. The last time they had spoken, Kim had informed him that she was pregnant and getting an abortion. She had been married when they had the fling. Now John was supposed to believe he was the father of a child he'd never met?

After the introductions, Kim and Beth Ann left without incident. It was more or less a trip to inform.

A short time later, John was served with papers. Kim, insisting he was Rebecca's father, was coming after some long-overdue child support.

Kim's legal action had actually begun back in January 1992. Six months later, on June 26, a few weeks before she met Buzz, Kim filed a petition with the New London Superior Court seeking to "establish paternity of [Rebecca] by finding that John Gaul is the father . . . and order him to stand charged with the support and maintenance thereof. . . ."

A hearing had been scheduled to take place on July 31, 1992. Beth Ann and Kim were letting John know that they were going to find out, one way or another, if he was the father.

Something didn't seem right, though. It wasn't as if John had disappeared. He had stayed in town and could've been reached by a simple phone call anytime. Why now? Why was Kim hell-bent on coming to him for money now?

A number of factors were involved. For one, Kim was single at the time she filed the paperwork. She needed the money to support herself and Rebecca. Second, since Beth Ann and her mother had made up their minds to fight Kim for custody, she was obviously pushing Kim to take action wherever she could—but only if that action later benefited Beth Ann and her mother's cause.

Everyone was about to find out that getting John involved would serve several different purposes for the Carpenters.

The fleeting relationship John and Kim had had was anything but sunset cruises on the Long Island Sound and candlelit dinners.

John said later that while he had been dating Kim, he was driving around town one night in Kim's Trans Am with a friend of his. As they pulled up to a local hangout, Kim's husband came running up to the car.

"What the hell are you doing?" he demanded.

"Who are you?" John asked, having no idea who the man was or that Kim had been married.

Without answering, the man grabbed John by the throat and began choking him. "You're driving my wife's car, asshole."

Later that night, John went to Kim and broke off the relationship. That was the last time he had seen her, until she and Beth Ann showed up in his driveway with Rebecca.

As Tricia and John discussed the situation, deciding how to cope with the fact that John might be Rebecca's father, Beth Ann sent John a letter, adding yet another element to an already confusing situation.

Tricia had always opened John's mail because she generally took care of the household bills. They were partners. They trusted each other. When she opened the letter from Beth Ann, Tricia couldn't believe what it said.

After explaining that she was Kim's sister and an attorney, Beth Ann wanted to make it clear that she thought Rebecca had been living in a "deplorable situation" with Buzz and Kim.

Tricia's interest was piqued.

Working at a hospital for most of her life and seeing how bad kids could be treated, Tricia had developed a soft spot for abused children. Her heart sank as she read on. Beth Ann described that there was a good chance Rebecca was being "abused." She didn't spell out if it was sexual or physical abuse, but it really didn't matter to Tricia.

Reading the letter, Tricia realized how different the stakes were now. She and John could possibly make a difference in Rebecca's life. With that, how could she turn her back on the child?

Ending the letter, Beth Ann left a phone number and asked Tricia to call her right away.

The next morning, Tricia phoned Beth Ann.

"I'm John's fiancée. This letter . . . Why are you sending us this letter? What is going on?"

"We," Beth Ann said, "think John is Rebecca's father. . . ."

"Yes, and?"

"Well, Rebecca lives in a shed, you know, with Kim and her boyfriend. She's being abused by [Buzz.] The conditions she's living in are horrible." Then, after talking a bit more about Buzz, she added, "He's not a nice person."

"What do you mean 'horrible conditions'?"

"They live in a shed! There's no electricity. It's, basically, like a dog kennel."

Beth Ann was either exaggerating the facts, lying or was confused. Dee owned a dog kennel, true. But Buzz and Kim didn't live inside it. Their in-law apartment was to the right of the kennel, on the same side of the property, about fifty yards away. The buildings weren't connected.

Beth Ann then said, "Can you meet me at the town hall in Groton? Me and my parents have to go down there tomorrow. We have a custody case pending against Kim for Rebecca."

It was the first time Tricia had heard that Kim was being sued for custody.

"What custody . . . what do you mean?" Tricia wanted to know.

"My parents are taking Kim to court for custody of

Rebecca because of the abuse, and Kim and Buzz being unfit parents."

Tricia had heard enough—one five-minute phone conversation with Beth Ann, and she was worried sick for a child she didn't even know.

"Yes. Of course, we'll meet you."

As Beth Ann got used to her new job at Haiman Clein's law firm, Kim and Buzz began spending nearly every moment they could together. They had been living as a couple now for a few months at Buzz's house. Aside from the custody battle, Buzz and Kim's life seemed ideal.

With Rebecca living with the Carpenters, it was time, Buzz and Kim decided, that they brought her home where she belonged. As it was, when Kim wanted to see Rebecca, or spend any time with her, she would have to call the Carpenters and say she was coming to get her. It was getting old. Buzz was fed up with having to watch his girlfriend ask her parents for permission to see her *own* daughter. He couldn't understand how family members could treat one another so despicably.

"I want to take Rebecca to Riverside Park," Kim said one night in late August when she called home.

Cynthia later said the trip to Riverside would have generally been a good idea. But, she claimed, the company Kim was keeping at the time—"Buzz and his friends at the Café Del Mar"—were not the kind of people the Carpenters wanted Rebecca to be around. Riverside Park was a popular amusement park in Agawam, Massachusetts. Rebecca was only two years old. How much was she going to get out of a day at an amusement park?

When the Carpenters found out Kim was going to Riverside with Buzz and a few friends from the Café Del Mar, they told Kim they were against the trip. But it wasn't so much the company, Cynthia now claimed; it was that after the amusement park, Kim said she wanted to take Rebecca to a rock concert.

"That's an inappropriate place to take a two-year-old, Kim," Cynthia said she told her daughter. "Rebecca's not going!"

By the Sunday of the long Labor Day weekend, 1992, Dee had pretty much accepted the fact that Kim, with all her baggage, was going to be part of Buzz's future, like it or not. Dee had grown quite close to Kim over the past six weeks and thought she might be good for Buzz. But she still hadn't met Rebecca. It was time, Dee insisted, that the Clinton family got a chance to meet this child they had heard so much about.

"Bring Rebecca over to meet the family," Dee suggested one afternoon.

"Let me give my mother a call."

After the phone call, Kim came back to Dee and, beaming, told Dee her mother, surprisingly, had said it would be "all right" for Rebecca to visit.

So Kim took off to Ledyard to pick her up.

A few hours later, when she returned empty-handed, a puzzled Dee asked what had happened.

"My mother changed her mind and wouldn't let me take her."

Dee thought the situation was highly unusual. Here was a woman who couldn't even take her own child to meet a family she had been spending a great deal of time with lately. Maybe Cynthia was being a little overprotective because she really didn't know the Clintons?

The Carpenters, Dee claimed, never took the time to get to know the her family; the Carpenters just assumed they were bad people, or people with whom they were too good to associate.

Thinking about it, Dee suggested to Kim that perhaps she should take Suzanne on a second trip. She speculated that Suzanne's presence would ease some of Cynthia's trepidation about Rebecca's spending the day with the Clintons.

In the end, Cynthia decided it was okay to let her go, but only under one condition: she would go along, too.

During the course of the day, Dee tried to make conversation with Cynthia several times, but figuratively speaking, Cynthia always pushed her away. She "kept Rebecca with her the entire time," Dee recalled later. "She had complete control over her. Kim tried to be loving with Rebecca without overstepping her bounds with Cynthia."

Even afterward, when they went out for ice cream, Cynthia wouldn't let Rebecca out of her grasp.

But what bothered Dee more than anything was that Rebecca had no verbal skills whatsoever. The child had a hard time communicating. She was passive, like Kim, but in a more profound way. On top of that, Rebecca had kept her head down the entire time they were together and twisted her hair with her fingers to the point of nearly ripping it out by the roots.

When they finished eating their ice cream, Cynthia stood up and abruptly said, as if something had gone wrong, "I'll take Rebecca home now." Then she left.

To say the least, Dee thought it was a bizarre outing.

By the first week of October, Kim and Buzz were officially living together, by themselves, on the Clintons' property in Old Lyme.

Back in early 1990, when Buzz returned home from Iowa after finding out that ironwork was just as hard to come by there as it was in Connecticut, he asked his mother if he could move back into the house. He had no money. No future.

"No," Dee said, "you're not living in this house, Buzz. We've been through this before."

Dee and Buzz fought a lot. They were always going at each other when they disagreed. Both being strong-willed people—bulls—when they butted heads, it often turned into a full-blown argument. Dee worked hard in her kennel. She didn't need the stress of Buzz around the house.

Buzz had an idea, he said, that would help them both: "What if I fix up the shed out back and turn it into an apartment?"

Dee loved her child dearly and disliked practicing tough love, but Buzz's idea seemed logical. It might just work out.

"Okay," Dee said.

Buzz broke out his tools and got to work.

"Ever since that day," Dee said later, "we just always called it 'the shed.'"

At about fifteen by twenty feet, it wouldn't be the largest apartment in town, but it would suffice. Buzz insulated the entire building and installed electric heat, lights and a smoke detector. He put in two windows, wall-to-wall carpeting and he painted the walls. Again, it wasn't the Ritz-Carlton, but it was a place to sleep.

When Buzz and Kim took over "the shed" it became a lot more, however. In a sense, it was affordable living for a couple in love who were just starting out. Dee agreed to $100 per week in rent. As far as accommodations for Rebecca were concerned, the Clintons already had a crib and playpen in the house for when Buzz's son, Michael, spent the night. Rebecca could use that until Buzz and Kim found a more spacious apartment in town. Dee had even given Kim bags of clothes she'd saved from when Suzanne was a toddler. They were hand-me-downs, sure. But again, the clothes, like the shed, would serve the purpose until Buzz could provide a better life.

As Buzz and Kim settled in, they decided to announce to Dee that they were planning to get married after the first of the year. It would be a simple ceremony, probably held right there at the house. Dee wasn't all that thrilled, but she knew she couldn't stop them, so she pledged her full support.

But it would be some time, Buzz and Kim decided, before they notified the Carpenters about their decision.

Chapter 16

Buzz Clinton was an extrovert. When he said he was going to do something, he did it, no matter what anybody else thought or said. For instance, when he said he was going to get a tattoo of a playing card on his left upper arm with roses on each side of it, he went out and got the ace of spades with an upside-down heart inside of it. When he said he was going to get another tattoo—a much larger one—he went out and came back with an enormous Bengal tiger inked on the entire section of his right shoulder blade. But the tattoo Buzz felt most proud of, one that he never got finished, was inscribed around the roses and ace of spades: DAY BY DAY WITH LOVE. It was a mantra Buzz learned from being in recovery from alcohol and drugs.

So when Buzz told Kim they were going to get Rebecca back and keep her, he wasn't just mincing words; he was making a promise he intended to keep.

Day by day with love.

With their living conditions in place, Buzz now pushed Kim to involve Rebecca in their relationship. He wanted to give Rebecca a life she'd never had. He wanted to be a father to her, perhaps because he and his son had never had that type of relationship.

The Carpenters were thwarting Buzz's efforts, however, at just about every opportunity. During the second week of October, Buzz and Kim went over to get Rebecca. When they came back, Dee recalled, they were "very upset" because the Carpenters had not allowed them to take her.

On October 17, Kim got permission from her parents to take Rebecca to a school fair in Old Lyme that Dee, Suzanne and Billy had already made plans to attend.

Buzz, who had given up dancing and decided to go into nursing, had just started applying for aid to go to school. He was towing cars and selling wood—anything he could do to earn a buck—but promised to turn his life around once he was finished with nursing school.

After agreeing to let Rebecca go, the Carpenters made it clear she was to be back in Ledyard by 4:00 P.M. No excuses. Legally, the Carpenters didn't have a leg to stand on. Nevertheless, Kim agreed so as not to cause any problems. After all, she desperately wanted to spend time with her own child. Buzz had promised Kim that she would soon have Rebecca back. If they needed to go along with the Carpenters' rules for visitation for a few more months, so be it. It would all be settled soon.

During the fair, one thing led to another; because they were having so much fun, Kim lost track of time. They didn't return to Old Lyme until after five. As soon as they walked in, Buck Clinton informed Kim that the phone had started ringing at about four and never stopped.

"Let me guess," Kim said. "My mother?"

"Actually, it's your sister, Beth. She's livid!" Buck said.

So Kim called the Carpenter house.

"I want to give Rebecca dinner over here," she said. "Then we want to put leaves into Halloween bags. . . . I'll have her home after that."

The Carpenters said it was okay.

At around seven o'clock, Kim realized that maybe it wasn't such a good idea for Rebecca to go back to Ledyard; the entire day and night had been a page out of *The Waltons*. Rebecca was having a ball with her new family. There had been lots of smiles, laughs and love. Why end it now?

So Dee made a suggestion.

"Look, it's cold, it's late. We're all tired. Why don't you call your mother and tell her that Rebecca is going to stay here? She can sleep with Billy or Suzanne. We have plenty of beds."

Kim agreed. So she called her mother and explained the idea.

"Bring Rebecca home in forty-five minutes, or I'll call the police!" Cynthia snapped.

Kim began to shake. Her eyes welled up with tears. She turned white.

Obviously, Cynthia was appalled that Kim would even bother to ask. What concerned Cynthia most, she later said, was that Suzanne had mentioned one day that Buzz and Kim were "living in a shed behind the house." So Cynthia assumed the worst, as one might imagine any mother would. Allowing her daughter to live in a shed with a male dancer was one thing; Kim was an adult. She could make up her own mind. Allowing her grandchild to sleep in a "shed" wasn't something Cynthia was interested in discussing. In addition, Rebecca had no clothes other than what she had been wearing, and Kim had only taken two diapers for the day. Rebecca could have stayed in the Clinton home, of course, but Cynthia speculated that the Clintons had no crib for her. Rebecca could get wild at night when she slept. An accident might occur.

Isn't anyone thinking of the child? she projected.

But Cynthia never asked about "the shed," or if the Clintons could accommodate Rebecca's needs for the night. She just assumed the worst.

When Kim hung up, she walked over to Dee, bowed her head and stood in front of her.

"What happened?" Dee asked.

"I have to bring Rebecca home."

"Who has legal custody of Rebecca?" Dee wanted to know. She was through with staying out of it. It was time to get to the bottom of things.

"I do," Kim said.

Not to make any trouble, Kim gathered Rebecca's things and brought her back to the Carpenters'.

When Buzz returned home and heard what had happened, he phoned Cynthia. At his breaking point, Buzz had heard enough. It was time he spoke up to Cynthia and Dick. No more games. Kim had custody of Rebecca, *not* the Carpenters.

"I'm not happy with the arrangements for Rebecca," Buzz said to Cynthia. "Kim and I are planning on getting married in a couple of months, and I am planning on adopting Rebecca."

"I am going to get Rebecca one way or another," Cynthia shouted back before she hung up.

The battle had begun. Mentioning the word "adoption" was akin to the Japanese strike on Pearl Harbor. Buzz had just awoken a sleeping giant. The fallout, Kim warned, was going to be endless.

Within days, the Carpenters had made it clear: Rebecca would not be allowed to go over to the Clintons' home any longer.

Kim had always had a tough time speaking up for herself. She later claimed her parents made her "nervous." It was obvious to anyone involved in the custody dispute directly that Kim was being told what to do by her parents and was easily intimidated by them as well. But as Buzz began to step up his presence and rally behind her cause, Kim became more of her own person. Buzz was resolute, tenacious. If he wanted something, he didn't wait for people to give it to him; he went out and took it. But at the same time, he was a fair man, willing to play by the rules. He had fallen "head over heels in love with

Kim" by this time, Dee later said. He was attracted to her "gentleness, kindness."

"He got serious about getting a new job. He was talking about going to school to be a CNA. He began to become responsible and vowed to do anything he had to do to support a family."

A family that, indeed, included Rebecca.

For the past few weeks, Buzz had been begging Dick Carpenter to sit down and talk to him "man to man." But Dick had always refused, saying, "Speak with my wife." This only heightened Kim's anxiety. She was finding herself always stuck in the middle. Buzz had just wanted to express to the Carpenters in a calm manner that he and Kim were getting married and that they wanted to take Rebecca and give her a life she had never had. Regardless of what Kim and Buzz had done up until that point in their lives, things were different for them now. They both had made mistakes in the past, but they were in the process of putting their lives back together. Buzz was going to be a certified nurse's aide soon. Once he got his certification, he could look for work anywhere. They could move off the Clintons' property, get their own place and live a normal life. But the Carpenters, some later claimed, either couldn't accept Buzz for who he was, or didn't want to give him a chance.

After the phone call, Cynthia became suspicious of Buzz's intentions toward Rebecca, she later said. She wondered what business Buzz had with Rebecca. Why, for instance, was he so "interested" in her? She also felt Buzz was talking for Kim. Kim wouldn't say such things, Cynthia maintained. Buzz was putting thoughts in her head and words in her mouth. Furthermore, what kind of relationship, Cynthia wondered, did Buzz have with his own family if they allowed him to live in a shed behind their home? Did he think for one minute that Rebecca was going to be living in a shed? He was a male stripper and his current employment was selling wood! What did he have to offer Kim and Rebecca?

These were the things Cynthia fretted over and spelled out in an affidavit she was preparing to bring into probate court so she could sue Kim for total control over Rebecca's life.

On the outside, it appeared as though Cynthia and Dick Carpenter were the driving force behind the fight to win custody of Rebecca, and Beth Ann was merely a concerned sibling, educated in the law, who could help out when needed.

But that was not true—and a letter Beth Ann wrote to John Gaul on October 19, 1992, was proof.

Beth Ann opened the letter by telling Gaul that "an application for Removal of yourself and Kim Carpenter as guardians of Rebecca has been filed in Ledyard Probate Court." For the first time, Beth Ann admitted her intimate involvement in the lawsuit: "Myself," the next sentence began, "and Mrs. Cynthia Carpenter have also applied for temporary custody and appointment as co-guardians." Then she went on to explain that a form she had included in the letter, if Gaul signed it, would act as a release so he could be notified of all "hearings, etc." Ending the letter, Beth Ann asked Gaul to contact her "ASAP" if he "consented to removal of guardianship."

The letter had been sent certified mail. Beth Ann wanted to be 100 percent sure Gaul received it, read it and completely understood it. The Carpenters—Beth Ann included—were preparing for war, and, at the same time, letting John Gaul know that there was indeed a reason behind Kim and Beth Ann's little visit a few months ago: the Carpenters and Beth Ann wanted Gaul on their side.

It was a team effort now. Together they could fight Kim and Buzz on Rebecca's behalf.

Together they could win.

Chapter 17

One day in late October, Kim showed up at the Clintons' house with a set of legal papers Cynthia had given her to sign the previous night. When Kim walked into the main house foyer, Dee was standing there talking on the phone to an old friend. Kim, Dee later remembered, looked disheveled and confused.

"I'll talk to you later," Dee told her friend. Then, turning toward Kim, she asked, "What's wrong, Kim? What's going on *now?*"

Kim handed Dee the document. If Kim had signed it, she would be agreeing legally to give up all parental rights to Rebecca.

"My sister, Beth, drew them up," Kim explained.

"You didn't sign this, did you?"

"No!"

"Thank God."

After a further reading of the papers, Dee realized the Carpenters wanted Kim to sign over *complete* parental rights of Rebecca.

"My mother said to sign these. . . . It will make things easier for me."

Things had calmed down somewhat since Buzz and Cynthia had had their little blowout over the phone, and the Carpenters had begun letting Rebecca spend some time at the Clintons' home. No sleepovers, of course.

But an afternoon here or there didn't seem to bother the Carpenters. It almost seemed as if they were giving in a little bit.

Later that day, Cynthia showed up at the Clintons' to drop off Rebecca for a few hours while she did some shopping nearby. When she pulled up, Dee and Kim came out to greet her.

As Cynthia took Rebecca out of the car, Dee could feel the tension in the air.

"Just sign the paper, Kim," Cynthia said before getting back into her car. "It's going to make it easier on you if you do."

Kim didn't say anything. "As usual," Dee later said, "she just shook. She was frightened to death of that family."

When Kim finally dredged up enough courage to speak, she said Buzz's reaction was going to be bad when he found out about the paper. "I'm not signing that."

Cynthia became incensed.

"This has *nothing* to do with Buzz. It has to do with you and me!"

When Buzz came home and learned about the paper, he didn't quite react in kind, but just saw it as another way for the Carpenters to try to control not only their granddaughter's life, but their daughter's life. Instead of butting heads, arguing and making idle threats, Buzz decided to make himself visible whenever there was going to be a visit with Rebecca. Whenever Kim took Rebecca, Buzz said he'd be there.

But it didn't make any difference. The Carpenters were steadfast now about their intentions. Buzz and Kim were not going to be taking Rebecca anymore. That was it. Absolutely no more visits. The court would decide when, where and whom Rebecca should be with. Until then, the Carpenters suggested, they were calling the shots.

A week or so later, for about three days, Kim and Buzz had no idea where Rebecca was. The Carpenters had re-

fused to answer their door or telephone, which only infu-
riated Buzz more.

Afraid for her granddaughter's well-being, on October
20, 1992, Cynthia filed an immediate temporary custody
order with the Ledyard Probate Court in hope of, first, obtaining temporary custody of Rebecca and, second,
gaining perhaps permanent custody later on. The Carpenters had seen enough. With Buzz and Kim living in
what they saw as a shack, Kim not really paying as much attention to Rebecca as the Carpenters had wanted, and
Buzz fumbling along as a tow truck driver, the Carpenters
saw no alternative other than letting a judge decide as to
who should legally care for the child.

When it came down to it, as blood relatives of Rebecca,
the Carpenters had every right to seek custody of the
child. By filing the paperwork, they were merely exercis-
ing that right.

In her four-page, single-spaced petition to the judge,
under the guise of anecdotal evidence collected
throughout the past six months, Cynthia accused Kim of
the most egregious parent-child violations imaginable.
She wrote that Rebecca had been "abandoned" by Kim
and that Kim had made no attempt to show any "interest" in her welfare. Rebecca needed "stability" in her life,
Cynthia wrote, especially since Kim had already been diagnosed with PKU. It was possible Rebecca, already
contending with several disabilities, could end up with
the disease.

Still, the bulk of Cynthia's argument centered on
Kim's new beau, Buzz, and Rebecca's attachment to
her "aunt Beth, who," Cynthia wrote, "takes her to gymnastics each Saturday." She also said that when Kim
was at the Carpenter home in Ledyard, Rebecca
"showed little interest" in her and "preferred going to
Beth or her grandpa." She insisted she was "saddened"
that things had turned out the way they had, "hoping

[Kim] would begin to put Rebecca's welfare ahead of her own."

Then came the attack on Buzz.

Cynthia said she was "very concerned about Rebecca's welfare" while she was under Buzz's care, because, "historically," Buzz had "shown no interest in children. . . ." It was an accusation based solely on Buzz's relationship with his son, Michael. Apparently, the Carpenters had taken the time to investigate Buzz's life as it pertained to his son, but not as it concerned Kim.

Nowhere in Cynthia's statement did she take into account that Buzz was studying to become a nurse's aide. She was only concerned with what Buzz *hadn't* done, not with what he was doing.

Yet it didn't end there. The final paragraph made reference to a notion that Buzz was Kim's puppeteer—that Kim wouldn't act unless Buzz snapped his fingers: "Being manipulated by him, she now expresses no ideas of her own." The petition concluded by stating that Kim was now more concerned with Buzz's priorities than Rebecca's.

If one piece of truth rose to the surface out of the petition, it was that Rebecca was in desperate need of a guardian who would love her unconditionally and care for her mounting health problems without concern for himself or herself. Caring for Rebecca was, indeed, a full-time job. Diagnosed with ptosis—a droopy eyelid—the child had just gotten surgery on her right eye within the past week so she could see better. Allergic to Enfamil (an infant formula) and regular cow's milk, it was a constant fight to make sure she had enough vitamins and calcium in her system. Her vocal quality, moreover, noted one speech therapist, was "breathy and raspy." She was still having trouble speaking like other children her own age.

Buzz and Kim were beginning to understand that Rebecca needed them desperately. A custody fight would only spread any dysfunction further. It was time for

Rebecca to have a permanent home—and Buzz insisted that he could provide it, if only given the chance.

A week after Cynthia filed the petition, the court agreed there was ample amount of evidence to—at least for the time being—award full temporary custody to Cynthia.

The Carpenters had won the first battle.

Buzz and Kim were upset, of course. Here they were engaged to be married, with Buzz beginning a new career, while getting his and Kim's life on track, and the Carpenters stepped in and took away the one stable thing they had in their lives: Rebecca. Now it would be court dates, pleadings, motions. Neither Kim nor Buzz had money or anything of worth to put up for collateral. They would have trouble getting a private attorney to represent them, whereas the Carpenters could hire anybody they chose— not to mention, perhaps, one of the most important factors to date: Beth Ann was an attorney who had studied this very type of litigation. She was even going to be starting a job at a highly regarded law office with a lawyer who had himself taken on child custody matters.

A full investigation into Kim's life was subsequently unleashed by the Department of Child and Youth Services (DCYS), a state agency charged to look into any allegations of child abuse and neglect made by family members, hospital personnel and law enforcement. The state would now decide if Kim was, in fact, the horrible mother her own family had been making her out to be.

Because of the pending investigation by DCYS, it was suggested by Judge Frederick Palm, on October 27, 1992, that Kim and Buzz attend parenting classes at a local church, and that Kim submit to a psychological evaluation and have supervised visits with Rebecca three times a week at the Carpenter home.

It seemed Buzz and Kim couldn't win. Suddenly, Kim wasn't the mother anymore; she was a "parent" being mandated by the court when and, more important, where she could see her own child.

Feeling helpless, Kim sat down one day with a copy of her mother's statement and began on paper to dispute the accusations against her.

Where Cynthia wrote that the Carpenters had been "babysitting Rebecca since birth," Kim fired back that her parents had always "offered" to baby-sit while she was at work. Where Cynthia claimed Kim had taken off on July 6 and it "was the last time [the Carpenters had seen] her on a regular basis," and that they didn't know where she was and didn't have a phone number to reach her, Kim said it had all been fabricated to make her look like a bad mother. Kim said she was "home that night and every night after." After she met Buzz, Kim insisted that the Carpenters had Buzz's "beeper number." Moreover, the reason she had been sleeping downstairs at the Carpenter home wasn't because she wanted to get away from Rebecca, but because Beth Ann's boyfriend, Joseph Jebran, needed a place to sleep when he was in town. Whenever Joseph stayed at the house, the Carpenters insisted that he sleep in Kim's room, while she was forced to sleep on the pull-out couch downstairs.

More important, though, Kim explained that every time she tried to care for Rebecca at home, Beth Ann or her parents would insist on tending to Rebecca's needs themselves, pushing her out of the picture.

The biggest discrepancy of all, however, was with conflicting stories surrounding the day Dick and son Richard had taken Rebecca to Boston Children's Hospital. In her statement, Cynthia blasted Kim, stating that Kim had shown up late.

According to Kim, it happened differently. She and Buzz had shown up at the Carpenter home that morning at 9:30, which would have given them plenty of time to make it to Boston. When they arrived, Kim was told that

Dick, Richard and Rebecca had left at the ungodly hour of 7:30 A.M., four hours before the appointment.

Near the end of Kim's rebuttal, she said she was confused. She felt scorned. Why was her own family so against her raising her own child?

"I am sad that things have reached this point," she wrote, "but it's my responsibility to raise Rebecca. It's not my parents' right . . . to take over a task I am capable of doing. Yes, I have to call and ask permission to be with my own child. . . . Rebecca loves me and I love her. I am afraid that if this is allowed to go on much longer she will forget about me."

She will forget about me.

Kim ended her statement by stating that her mother had met Buzz on only two occasions and "knows nothing about him." Buzz had been kind to her family, Kim explained, but they want nothing to do with him.

Dee then stepped in and wrote her own depiction of the events as she had seen them materialize.

"After knowing Kim for a few months," Dee wrote in a letter to the court, "it is my observation that Kim is a responsible adult capable of raising her child." Dee further maintained that Rebecca and Kim's relationship, as she saw it, was always "warm and loving." In addition, she went on to state that she had heard Kim ask the Carpenters on several occasions if she could take Rebecca for a visit and was repeatedly denied. Even before Kim lost temporary custody, Dee claimed, "Kim said that her mother and sister would not allow her to take the child."

Still, regardless of how Kim, Buzz or even Dee felt, the Carpenters had waged legal combat. By the simple process of filing a complaint, they had won the first skirmish in what was brewing to be one hell of a war between the two families.

With the first phase of the Carpenters' attack revealed, Cynthia and Beth Ann began aligning their troops for what Buzz had since promised was going to be the fight of their lives. It didn't matter, Buzz raged, how much money the Carpenters had and how much money Buzz and Kim didn't have; Buzz and Kim were not going to give up without a fight. They were going to get custody back one way or another, and when they did, Buzz promised, they were packing their bags and moving.

On top of everything else, Kim was now pregnant with Buzz's child. They were going to be a family—and nothing, Buzz promised, was going to stop it.

Chapter 18

With the blessing of his future wife, who was 100 percent behind him, by the end of November, John Gaul had accepted full responsibility of being Rebecca's biological father. A blood test had recently confirmed there was 99 percent chance that John was the father. A family man, John wasn't one to run away from things. If he was Rebecca's natural father, he and his wife-to-be would begin taking responsibility and accept her into their hearts and home—which was exactly what the Carpenters had been hoping for all along.

Tricia had never met Beth Ann—that is, before she and John had subsequently met her and the rest of the Carpenter clan at the Groton Town Hall before the first hearing on Cynthia's petition for custody. Both Tricia and John assumed the meeting and recent interest from Beth Ann and Cynthia in John's being involved in Rebecca's life was about child support payments. They had no idea that a fierce legal battle was mounting between families.

Tricia had undergone a hysterectomy sometime ago. It was a heartfelt blow to the couple, who had talked frequently about starting a family together. Tricia was a natural-born caretaker. Friends and family agreed she would make the ideal mother.

Not being able to bear children was something many

women feared. Yet John had fathered a child out of wedlock some years before, and Rebecca was now thrust into their lives.

At first, John and Tricia were a "little torn as to what to do," Tricia later said. They had been planning their wedding, and John now had a child in his life.

"It was scary and shocking, and you don't know what to do," Tricia recalled. "On the one hand, you know, [Rebecca was] just [two] years old . . . and we had not been in her life." On the other, Tricia continued, she and John were operating under the assumption that Rebecca was being abused by Buzz. "And I wouldn't leave any child in that situation."

In the end, it was an opportunity for Tricia to have a child she could not have naturally—a chance to love a child unconditionally.

Since that day at the Groton Town Hall, Tricia and John were under the impression that Rebecca's life with Buzz and Kim was "the most horrible situation you could imagine." They were good people. They cared. Of course, they weren't going to abandon Rebecca. If it meant setting aside their own plans, so be it. The child had to come first.

This naïveté, or perhaps just plain goodness, however, played right into the hand of the Carpenters.

When they arrived at town hall, Tricia and John saw Buzz, Kim, Beth Ann, Cynthia and Dick outside in the hallway. They weren't together, but they were waiting separately to enter the hearing room.

Buzz went right up to John and asked him straight out to "terminate rights." Buzz was having enough trouble fighting the Carpenters; he didn't need John in the picture now.

"I want to adopt Rebecca," Buzz said.

John didn't answer one way or the other; he just took it in. After he talked with Buzz, Cynthia and Beth Ann and Dick sat down with John and Tricia and, after introducing themselves, began laying out their case.

Beth Ann specifically asked Tricia to make sure John didn't terminate his rights.

"Why?" Tricia wanted to know.

"Because Buzz wants to adopt her!"

"Yeah, he told us that."

"We're trying to get custody. That's why we're here. You guys shouldn't terminate rights."

"That's what we hear. But why?"

"Because Rebecca is being abused."

As the hearing began, Tricia and John had to leave because they were not allowed in. Beth Ann, however, before walking into the hearing room, pledged to Tricia that she would be calling her soon. She had plenty more to talk about.

As the weeks passed, Beth Ann and Tricia began calling each other on a regular basis. For the most part, their conversations were about Rebecca. Beth Ann would continue to beat the drum for custody, alluding to the fact on each occasion that Rebecca was being abused by Buzz. Whenever something happened with the custody battle, Beth Ann would call and fill Tricia in. With all the ups and downs the case was bringing, Beth Ann used Tricia as a sounding board, bouncing things off her. By this time, Tricia had confided in Beth Ann that she couldn't have kids of her own—and Beth Ann wasted little time using that to her advantage.

"Wouldn't it be great if we got Rebecca, because you would have a child that was half John's?" Beth Ann asked one day.

On another occasion, Beth Ann mentioned that if John and Tricia petitioned for "partial custody," the Carpenters would "be able to see Rebecca more, and John and Tricia would be able to see her more.

"It would work out great for both of us," Beth Ann insisted. "Because we would all get to spend more time with Rebecca and get her out of the situation she's in."

From almost her first day on the job at Haiman Clein's law practice, Beth Ann began pleading her case incessantly regarding the custody battle her family had waged against Buzz and Kim. By the end of November, merely weeks after she had started working, there wasn't a person in the office who hadn't heard the entire story.

"My sister has a child," Beth Ann explained to Clein one day. "My parents had gotten custody of her in the Ledyard Probate Court. There is some friction over the child between us and my sister's future husband. His name is Buzz. Buzz Clinton."

Clein, after that first conversation, said later he was under the impression that Beth Ann had custody of the child, not her parents.

"She was passionate. A bit overly concerned. Perhaps more than a sibling should be," Clein thought then.

"My sister is even living over [at the Clintons'] now," Beth Ann continued. "Buzz Clinton says they're going to get married."

"How is this Buzz?" Clein wanted to know.

"I'm afraid of his influence on my sister. She won't be able to stand up to him and properly mother Rebecca."

Her emotional state began to fluctuate. Some days, Beth Ann would come to work and tell Clein she had no idea what to do. She was scared that Buzz and Kim would gain permanent custody. At this time, the Carpenters didn't have an attorney, and Beth Ann said she was handling all the legal matters for the family herself.

Clein thought it was odd. A conflict of interest was one thing, but the family—if conditions were as bad as Beth Ann had described—should have the best legal representation they could afford.

When Clein offered Beth Ann the job, he saw an eager, young law school graduate whom he could perhaps take under his wing and mentor. She lived nearby. She had good credentials.

She had no idea, of course, how corrupt and misguided Clein's career in law had become. She saw a larger-than-life figure—someone she wanted to become herself, perhaps.

"She seemed like a good candidate for the job," Clein later said. "She was licensed in New York and Connecticut and had been a merit finalist."

By November, Beth Ann had her own office inside Clein's stone building on State Street in New London— a place that was quickly becoming the epicenter of the fight for custody of Rebecca.

On November 18, a "Social Study for Removal of Guardianship" was prepared by Teresa Jenkins, a social worker for DCYS, and was issued to everyone involved. Basically, it was a family history for both sides, along with detailed legal matters pertaining to the case up until that point.

"To date, Kim has followed through with all of the aforementioned recommendations," the report read.

Kim had kept her end of the bargain and attended all of the parental classes suggested by Judge Palm. The woman wanted her child back. She may not have been Carol Brady, but Kim was taking things seriously now. She was going to do whatever she had to do to get Rebecca back, and Buzz was right behind her every step of the way.

Still, the state recommended that "temporary custody [should] remain with [Cynthia Carpenter] for [an] additional thirty days [and that] Kim be involved in individual counseling on a regular basis [and that] Kim have full responsibility of Rebecca while in her care.

"Early intervention," Jenkins wrote, "to be held at Kim's residence. Visits between Kim and Rebecca to increase and to include weekends at Kim's residence."

Jenkins had visited the Clinton home and interviewed Buzz, Kim, Dee and Buck. She found no evidence that led her to believe Rebecca was being treated improperly or that the housing accommodations Buzz and Kim were living in were as bad as the Carpenters had described. Sure, they weren't living in a ten-room estate, but Kim and Buzz were making a go of it, doing the best they could.

Jenkins was impartial. She could look at things from a bystander's point of view and judge things on how they were, not on how Cynthia and Beth Ann or Kim had explained them. She had even visited the Carpenter home and interviewed Cynthia, Dick and Beth Ann and recalled later how Beth Ann "seemed to be the spokesperson for the family" during that interview. So it wasn't just Buzz, Dee and Kim claiming that Beth Ann was taking control. In many ways, the state of Connecticut thought it to be true also.

The DCYS report allowed the Carpenters, for the first time, to get a complete look at Buzz's plans. He had been enrolled at Vinal Tech, in Middletown, studying for his certification as a CNA, and according to what he had told Jenkins, he had expected to graduate in January 1993.

Buzz wasn't going to be driving a tow truck much longer. He was going to be a nurse's aide, something he had talked about for years.

What Buzz didn't tell anybody at this time, however, was that he was planning on moving not just off the Clinton property after graduating and getting married, but he was shipping out to Arizona, where the Clintons had family, and Buzz had already set up a job for himself.

Buzz had done some research and found out that Arizona was one of the toughest states in the country for a grandparent to sue for custody of a grandchild. As Buzz and Kim saw it, they were going to get back custody of

Rebecca, pack their bags and get as far away from the
Carpenters as they could. And *nothing,* Buzz repeatedly
told friends and family, was going to stop him from
doing it.

By Thanksgiving, Judge Palm, now a bit more informed about the situation, laid out a detailed visitation
schedule. The judge ordered dates and times for when
Kim could pick Rebecca up and drop her off. The Carpenters were even instructed by the court that they, too,
would have to drop Rebecca off at the Clinton house on
certain dates—something they surely hadn't planned on
and were probably not looking forward to.

What was clear from the judge's order was that, one
way or another, the two families were going to have to
make an effort to get along, if only for the sake of the
child.

This would prove to be wishful thinking on the judge's
part. Because the Carpenters, perhaps fearing now that
the court was leaning more toward giving Rebecca back
to Kim and Buzz, were even harder to get along with.
Plus, it was soon obvious that they were going to stop at
nothing to smear Kim's reputation.

On one occasion shortly after the court-ordered visitations began, Beth Ann and brother Richard called
Dee and asked if they could come over for a chat.

According to Dee, when Beth Ann and Richard got to
the door, Beth Ann asked Dee if they could come in for
a moment. There were some things about Kim they
wanted Dee to know—things no one had heard before.

A bit apprehensive, Dee agreed. Then she called Buck
into the kitchen so they could all sit down and chat. Kim
and Buzz knew about the meeting with Beth Ann and
Richard, but Dee and Buck had asked them to leave so
they wouldn't be around when Beth Ann and Richard
showed up.

"Kim is an unfit mother," Dee remembered Beth Ann

saying right away as the meeting got under way. "She's a slut and whore . . . a negligent mother!"

Taken aback, but hardly surprised, Dee and Buck said nothing.

"She was in love with a sailor before Buzz," Richard added, as if it were some sort of crime. "Did you know that?"

"She sleeps with everyone," Beth Ann said. "Do all in your power to stop the relationship."

The Clintons didn't react one way or another as Beth Ann and Richard continued to rattle on about how bad a person Kim was. *So what*, Dee thought, *Kim and a sailor. Big deal. Buzz is no Prince Charming.*

"I'm not going to get involved," Dee finally said. She wasn't about to begin telling her twenty-seven-year-old son how to manage his love life. "It was his business who he dated."

"Come on, Richard," Beth Ann said, grabbing him by the arm. "Let's go! We are not going to get anywhere here."

In a surprising move, during a December 15 hearing regarding which family would get custody of Rebecca, Kim and Buzz were awarded full custody. It wasn't time to celebrate just yet, though. There were a few stipulations that went along with the order. Kim needed to continue to attend parenting classes and individual counseling, and she had to apply for parental aid. The state had certain programs set up to help single mothers, both financially and emotionally. It was strongly urged that Kim take advantage of them.

Kim had little trouble accepting the judge's orders. After all, she was going to get her child back. It was time to rejoice and celebrate.

But there was one last stipulation that somewhat shocked Kim, Buzz and the Clintons. The judge made it a point to say that a visitation schedule needed to be set up between Rebecca and her "maternal grandparents." Buzz and Kim would have to let the Carpenters see Rebecca one weekend a month. There was no way of getting around it. Cynthia and Dick were Rebecca's grandparents. The court, understandably, agreed that no one should deny them the right to see her.

Regardless of what amounted to a minor setback, things were back on track. Point in fact: the state wouldn't have given custody back to Kim if it wasn't sure she could handle it, or thoroughly checked Buzz out. With all the talk of abuse on the Carpenters' part, if the state had even an inkling that Buzz was a threat to Rebecca—physically, sexually or emotionally—Buzz and Kim likely would not have gotten custody back.

At first, Teresa Jenkins had recommended that Kim get temporary custody. After several more meetings with Kim and Buzz, she changed her mind.

Why?

"[Kim] took responsibility for her role as a parent."

Joseph Jebran had been put through the mill since he and Beth Ann had become romantically involved. Handing over his paycheck and letting her take care of his finances turned out to be one of the biggest mistakes Jebran had made. While Beth Ann was cruising around town in her BMW, Jebran brown-bagged it in New York City and lived with four other guys. Ignorant of what Beth Ann was doing with his money, by the end of 1991, with about $40,000 in debt, Joseph filed for bankruptcy.

It wasn't all Beth Ann's doing, Jebran later said. For his part, Joseph said he "allowed" it to happen.

Jebran must have considered it a contingency of love. He was a young, highly skilled architect who could earn back the money he lost. But love, well . . . love was something different. One couldn't just find it anywhere.

By the beginning of December, the battle between the Clintons and the Carpenters was so heated it became the focus of, Jebran later said, about 90 percent of the conversations around the Carpenter home.

"Nothing against . . . Rebecca," Joseph recalled later, "the poor kid, but, you know, the conversation was Rebecca, Rebecca, Rebecca. And I go back to New York— and *still* Rebecca!"

Good or bad times, Beth Ann would call Jebran when he was working in New York and brief him on the situation. "We got custody," she'd say one day, beaming with excitement. Yet when things went bad, she'd call and spend much of her time sulking, crying and moping.

"She loved Rebecca," Joseph added. "Beth was very attached to her."

Beth Ann and Joseph, on his dime, had always gone on elaborate vacations to exotic locations. Jebran spared no expense. But when the custody battle heated up during the latter part of 1992, not only did the vacations stop, but Beth Ann found it hard to discuss anything else. She became obsessed with losing custody to Kim and Buzz, Jebran claimed.

One day near the middle of December, while Beth Ann was in the basement of her parents' home working at the computer, Joseph approached her. He wanted to talk about their relationship. Their life together. Where it was headed.

Beth Ann ignored the subject, but she said she had something she'd been meaning to ask him about.

"Go ahead."

"Would you run away if I asked you . . . [to] take Rebecca and me and go somewhere, leave?"

"No," he said vehemently. "Absolutely not!"

They began fighting, yelling and screaming, throwing verbal insults back and forth.

"You would do it if you love me," Beth Ann lashed out.

"This is beyond love, Beth."

Joseph was correct. It was called kidnapping. A lawyer, if no one else, should have known that.

"Ah," Beth Ann said, throwing up her hands.

She was looking for any avenue she could find to get Rebecca out of what she sincerely thought to be a dire situation with Buzz.

"Why are you asking *me*? What is her father?" Jebran asked in his broken English. He didn't know that John Gaul had been brought into the picture by this point. "Why don't you ask her father?"

"Why don't you do it?" Beth Ann wanted to know. Then, "You don't love *me*."

"This is beyond love," Jebran said again.

The fight lasted for about a half hour. After that, the subject was rarely brought up again.

Because the visitations were on weekends, and Jebran was only home on weekends, he often found himself being Rebecca's escort. On December 20, 1992, a Sunday, at about 5:25 P.M., the Carpenters were so distraught over Rebecca's having to go back to the Clinton family that, Jebran later said, no one in the house was able to drive a car. They were all huddled up together as if they were never going to see her again, crying hysterically. Beth Ann, especially, was devastated. She just sat there: shaking, trembling and crying softly.

"I mean, they were really destroyed by, you know, Rebecca leaving the house," Joseph later said.

So someone suggested that Jebran drive Rebecca back because none of them were in any condition to drive.

Jebran obliged.

Rebecca, now two and a half years old, was also upset. She was crying and visibly shaken by the mere thought of just having to leave. "Ba," Rebecca began to say as Jebran prepared her bag. "Ba. Ba. Ba," she kept repeating, reaching out for Beth Ann.

"Ba" was what Rebecca called Beth Ann. Rebecca's speech impediment was never more pronounced than when she was under duress. Clearly, the thought of leaving what amounted to her surrogate family had thrown the child into a fit.

"Ba . . ."

Beth couldn't handle it. She had to leave the room.

Jebran took Richard's Jeep and arrived at the Clinton home about thirty minutes after he left Ledyard. With the exception of Rebecca, Joseph was alone.

Kim was waiting at the door, while Buzz was in the living room.

Little was said, and Jebran was soon on his way back to the Carpenters', where Beth Ann was waiting to take him to the train station so he could return to New York City.

When Kim got Rebecca into the house, she immediately noticed that her diaper looked as though it hadn't been changed in some time. It was waterlogged, yellow in color. This bothered Kim, of course, but then she noticed a gash underneath Rebecca's right eye. Her left cheek was also bruised.

This bothered her even more.

Buzz was in the living room watching television.

When Kim took Rebecca's diaper off, she glanced down at her vagina. What she found next would open a Pandora's box of accusations, insults and threats.

Chapter 19

At about 6:00 P.M., Buzz and Dee were in the living room when Kim shouted for them to come into the bedroom, where she was changing Rebecca's diaper. "Look," Kim said, placing one hand over her mouth, the other pointing down.

"What?" Buzz asked. "What's wrong?"

"Kim, what's wrong?" Dee wanted to know.

Rebecca's vaginal walls were swollen and shriveled.

"Take a look, Buzz," Kim said, breaking down.

When Buzz leaned down and looked, he couldn't believe what he was seeing. "Ma, look at this!" he shouted.

"Oh. My. God."

"Should we take a picture?" Buzz asked.

Hearing the chaos, Buck had walked into the room. After quickly discussing it with Dee, he told Kim to take Rebecca straight down to the hospital for a full examination. To everyone in that room—at that moment—it appeared as though Rebecca had been abused sexually.

They were devastated.

Kim and Buzz packed up some of Rebecca's belongings and hurried off to Lawrence & Memorial Hospital in Waterford. They wanted a complete evaluation done. When they got there, Kim told intake workers that Rebecca had been "sexually molested," but the alleged perpetrator, Kim added, was "unknown" at that time.

Buzz returned home sometime later and told his parents one of the doctors had said Rebecca's "liver wasn't damaged." Apparently, the hospital had done a complete assessment of the child to see if she had been violated in any way. Because she was so small, if a male had entered her, doctors maintained, there would be some sort of damage done to her internal organs, types of injuries that were common in victims of sexual assault.

But according to what Buzz had heard from the doctors before he left the hospital, Rebecca was okay. She hadn't been assaulted sexually. In fact, the doctors' initial assessment failed to find any assault whatsoever. The bumps and bruises on her were normal licks a kid takes during the course of a day.

Were Buzz and Kim merely overreacting?

Rebecca had been in a saturated diaper for quite some time. And because of that, the moisture created an environment that allowed her vagina to become, as Kim and Dee had earlier suggested, "shriveled and swollen." There was a good chance that nothing sexual had been done to the child. One of the doctors involved had even written in one of his reports that there was "no medical emergency."

Whenever a report is filed at a hospital involving allegations of abuse of any kind toward a child, however, DCYS is notified by law.

So the following day, December 21, an intake worker from the Middletown office of DCYS was dispatched to investigate the allegations made by Kim and Buzz. It would be the seed from which the disdain the Carpenters already felt for Buzz would blossom into a full-grown tree of hatred.

While working late one night at the New London office, Beth Ann received a call from her mother's attorney, Barbara Quinn. It was important, Quinn said. "I've been unable to reach your parents. I have a message to give them."

After a bit of small talk, Quinn told Beth Ann about what had happened to Rebecca. There were claims of sexual molestation, Quinn explained.

Beth Ann gasped. "What?"

"The ER checked her out, though, and everything's fine," Quinn said before hanging up. "Don't worry."

Beth Ann later recalled that she and her family were "very upset," not only about the allegations, but by the entire ordeal Rebecca had undergone at the hospital and the days that followed. Being checked for sexual abuse is a rigorous set of tests and procedures. For a two-and-a-half-year-old child, it can be life altering. Rebecca had gone through enough trauma in her life already. Now this. She was being treated like a piece of property.

The next day, Beth Ann called Joseph Jebran, who was in New York City working. "Rebecca was admitted to the hospital the other night," she said. "You are being accused of sexual abuse."

Jebran became outraged.

"I spoke to Haiman. We both think you should get home right away."

"I can't believe what's happening, Beth," Jebran said. He was astonished, he later recalled, not only by the allegations, but by the fact that the Carpenters now would see him as someone who had let them down. He was in love with Beth Ann. What would this do to their relationship? Would Dick and Cynthia think differently of him—especially if they lost their bid for custody because of the allegations?

The next morning, Beth Ann picked Joseph up at his cousin's house in Norwich. She had already made plans with Clein and her parents to meet at Clein's Old Saybrook office to discuss what to do next.

Beth Ann didn't believe for one minute that Joseph was capable of what Buzz and Kim were saying. She had dated him now for nearly four-and-a-half years and couldn't see how anyone could accuse him of such a violent and evil act against a child. It just wasn't possible. At the same time, however, she was also scared—mostly, that they would now have little chance of ever gaining custody of Rebecca.

As they talked in Clein's office, Clein told everyone to reserve judgment until he received the police reports, which he had sent someone from the office to retrieve. The police reports would spell everything out clearly. Only then, Clein added, would he know what to do.

"If anyone," Beth Ann said at one point, "had abused Rebecca, it was *Buzz*."

While they waited, Clein spoke with an old friend, a local child custody lawyer, and was convinced that Jebran should write up some sort of affidavit. Clein's lawyer friend said he could have it typed up and certified later, but Jebran, while everything was still fresh in his mind, should write out his version of the events.

"Since prior to August 12, 1990," Joseph Jebran wrote, "I have resided weekends, holidays and vacations at the Carpenter residence. I also spent almost every evening at the same residence during the summer of 1992."

The remainder of the affidavit seemed to back up what Cynthia had written in hers. Joseph said Kim would leave Rebecca with her parents and just take off. When she was there, "she would isolate herself from her daughter."

Ending the two-page statement, Jebran made a point to say that Rebecca hadn't been harmed "in any manner whatsoever" when he dropped her off at the Clintons on December 20. "At the time of such delivery, Rebecca had no marks or bruises of any kind or nature on her body. . . ."

This was in total contrast to what Cynthia would lay claim to just days later when she met with Kim, however.

Kim asked Cynthia about Rebecca's lip and the mark she found on her cheek.

"Her cheek was like that when we got her, Kim. Do you think we'd do something like that to Rebecca?"

After two additional physical examinations and subsequent meetings with the doctors involved, the social worker who had been working on the case for DCYS couldn't validate any of Kim and Buzz's allegations. As far as the state of Connecticut was concerned, Rebecca hadn't been abused in any way. With that, no charges were filed. Sometime later, DCYS closed the case at the intake level and took it no further.

Regardless of what DCYS thought, Kim and Buzz decided they would not allow the Carpenters to visit with Rebecca unless it was supervised at a centralized location. They were afraid to let anyone at the Carpenter home go near Rebecca. It hadn't mattered what the evidence showed. Kim and Buzz were there. They had seen Rebecca's vagina. They had seen her eye and the bruises on her cheek.

Of course, this didn't sit well with the Carpenters. With everything that had gone on during the past few months, now they were being looked at as if they were child predators. It was an outrage. Kim had completely lost it. Buzz was controlling her every move. The Carpenters weren't about to lie down like scorned animals and forget about everything. They, too, were fighters, and they believed they were doing the right thing for Rebecca.

Beth Ann's continuing complaints regarding Rebecca and the custody battle had dominated nearly every hour she logged at Clein's law firm. During work, Beth Ann was having trouble staying focused on even the most basic tasks. Whenever she and Clein got together in the office to discuss work, the conversation always turned to Kim, Buzz and Rebecca.

"Kim shouldn't have custody," she told Clein one day before the incident involving Joseph Jebran. "Rebecca should be with her family. My sister can't take care of her. I'm afraid of Buzz's influence on my sister. My sister won't be able to stand up to Buzz. She won't be able to be a proper mother for Rebecca."

The same song and dance, over and over and over. Clein had known Beth Ann for only a brief spell, and he couldn't remember a day where she hadn't mentioned the custody fight. He decided he was going to have to face facts and deal with the custody issue himself, tell Beth Ann to drop it altogether and concentrate on her work, or find another job.

"I'm shaken. My whole family is shaken," Beth Ann said one day.

"She was very upset," Clein recalled years later. "She cried all the time."

They couldn't have a normal conversation about the issue of custody without, Clein added later, Beth Ann's breaking down in tears. The entire situation began to disrupt not only her work, but everyone else's work in the office.

"There were flurries of phone calls back and forth between her and her family," Clein recalled.

Realizing something had to be done, Clein had sent his new protégée a memo sometime before the incident involving Joseph Jebran. In writing, he explained that she was going to have to begin taking her responsibility as a lawyer more seriously, or there would be consequences.

"Explain to me what's going on in your personal life that's keeping you from completing assignments?" Clein asked in the memo.

Clein expected Beth Ann, as a young lawyer, to stay up nights and, if necessary, take work home with her until it was completed. That wasn't happening. She was focused exclusively on Rebecca, Buzz, Kim and gaining custody of the child. It became, Clein thought, an obsession. Her entire life revolved around Rebecca.

After Beth Ann received the memo, she went into Clein's office. "It's distracting me," she pleaded through tears.

"Well, then, I'll work more closely with you. How's that sound?"

Beth Ann nodded.

"Everything will be okay. Don't worry."

As they talked, Clein was shocked to learn that the Carpenters hadn't really hired an attorney who specialized in child custody matters and had been, basically, doing everything themselves. Barbara Quinn was the Carpenter family attorney. Beth Ann, of course, also acted as the "family" lawyer and helped out wherever she could, but Clein worried that there was no third-party attorney involved who knew child custody matters.

"It's time you guys hired a lawyer. Someone who knows this type of litigation," Clein suggested.

Clein surmised that referring the matter out of the office might free Beth Ann up to do the things she was supposed to be doing. As Clein saw it, it was a win-win situation.

Shortly after the allegations were made against Joseph Jebran, Haiman Clein suggested Thomas Cloutier, a rather well-known and highly respected family attorney, who was also a board-certified trial lawyer. Clein had known Cloutier for years. They were friends. Cloutier was a fine lawyer, Clein said.

For Kim and Buzz, once word spread that the Carpenters had hired counsel, they immediately applied for a public defender, which, being on public assistance already, they were entitled to. Carolyn Brotherton, a partner in a local New London law firm of Mariani, Brotherton and LeClair, was assigned the Clinton case. Soon after, a second attorney, Linda Kidder, became involved.

Thomas Cloutier didn't waste any time. On January 4,

1993, he sent a letter to Brotherton and Kidder, noting that the Carpenters had made several attempts to seek visitation with Rebecca, but Kim and Buzz had routinely denied them.

What sparked the letter was a phone call made by Cynthia the previous week. She had called the Clinton house to set up visitation for the coming weekend. While she was discussing the matter with Kim, Buzz had grabbed the phone from Kim's hand, Cloutier wrote, and "monopolized the conversation. . . ."

"The judge," Buzz shouted at Cynthia, "had no authority to issue any order regarding visitation!"

Then Kim got back on the phone.

"My attorney, Ma, indicated that I have the right to deny visitation."

This was a different side of Kim. She had been with Buzz now for about six months. His resolve was, obviously, rubbing off on her, and she was finally beginning to tell her mother how she felt.

Thomas Cloutier, however, wasn't concerned with Kim's recent foray into building self-esteem, vis-à-vis using Buzz as her mentor. Instead, Cloutier was overwhelmed—maybe even outraged, too—by Kim's suggestion that she could deny the Carpenters visitation.

In the same letter, Cloutier wrote that he "certainly [did] not think that any attorney would give that type of advice[,] given the outstanding Court order," which had clearly spelled out the Carpenters' right to visit Rebecca. Essentially, Buzz and Kim were defying that order and breaking the law. There hadn't been any proof of sexual molestation. They had no right to deny Rebecca's family the chance to see her.

It didn't matter that he'd just taken the case; Cloutier decided to take action immediately. The law was the law. Buzz and Kim, despite what they *thought* they knew, would have to follow the law or be subject to a contempt order. He also thought it was important that both of Kim's attorneys knew "what Kim had been saying." After all, the probate court order "was clearly [being] violated." He wanted to establish a new visitation schedule, and by doing so, he had hoped the "level of hostility would decrease. . . ."

By the end of the letter, Cloutier urged both attorneys to consult with Kim on the matter right away. Then he made an idle threat: if something wasn't done immediately, he would have "no hesitation whatsoever in bringing the matter to the Superior Court."

Along with sending a copy of the letter to the Carpenters, Cloutier indicated that he had copied "Attorney Beth Carpenter" on the letter, too. Why? Well, it was anybody's guess.

The superior court might have been the Carpenters' best bet at this point. For one, Buzz and Kim didn't have the money to pay for costs incurred if the case went to the superior court; they would have to rely on public defenders, who were generally inundated with cases. Two, it would send a message to everyone involved that the Carpenters weren't going anywhere. They were taking this custody issue as far as they could.

Although they weren't wealthy by any means, the Carpenters could acquire funding for such a battle if they needed to. They owned a home. They had pensions. They had a savings account. Maybe this was the only way they could really get through to Kim that they were serious. Once the supreme court had heard their case, there was no way they would be denied—at the least—scheduled visitations.

From the time Haiman Clein and Beth Ann began working together after Clein's memo, it was obvious to Clein the memo had had little impact on Beth Ann. Rebecca was still a steady topic of conversation whenever she and Clein were together.

"The Rebecca discussions," Clein recalled later, "borderlined on hourly. I would say daily—but more than daily! And it wasn't just with me."

In fact, things got worse, not better. Once Cloutier became involved, Beth Ann became even more obsessed with knowing what was going on. She would phone home and ask questions. She would call Joseph Jebran and tell him about what she learned. When she would sit down with Clein to go over work-related issues, she was either off somewhere else in thought, or just not interested in anything besides Rebecca.

Instead of disciplining her, however, Clein decided to begin working with her on a supervisory level. For the most part, Beth Ann handled real estate closings, divorce proceedings and personal injury claims, and she met with clients. Clein figured he could help her out and keep an eye on her at the same time.

Looking at Beth Ann, an attractive twenty-nine-year-old law school grad with a sexy smile and shoulder-length red hair, it wasn't a hard decision for Clein to make. He had already had numerous affairs on Bonnie by this point. Who was to say Beth Ann wouldn't be interested?

So he decided to begin listening to her problems.

Within just a few weeks of listening to countless stories of abuse and mistreatment, Clein made a suggestion one day. They were sitting around the office, going through some work, and Clein told Beth Ann that he would talk to Bonnie and, with her blessing, take temporary custody of Rebecca. He had four kids at home himself. Why not take Rebecca and, in turn, help move the matter along? The sooner he cleared things up with Rebecca, the sooner he had his employee back, working at peak efficiency.

It was a noble gesture—but one that many agreed later was more likely based on malevolence than dignity.

Based on the conversations Clein and Beth Ann began

to have, the picture he began developing of Buzz was of a man who was not capable of taking care of a cat, much less a small child with health problems. As Beth Ann had been saying to just about everyone right along, she also told Clein that Buzz was abusing Rebecca. He and Kim were living in deplorable conditions. Buzz was hotheaded and incapable of providing for a family; he was a very dangerous person for Rebecca to be around. Although he had never met Buzz, Clein had no reason to believe that anything Beth Ann was saying wasn't true.

One day, shortly before an upcoming court date to discuss visitations, Buzz walked into Clein's New London office. Suddenly the infamous "abuser" he had been hearing so much about for the past two months was standing in front of Clein.

"He came in demanding a file," Clein recalled later. "A file that she had from the probate proceeding. . . . Beth Ann either didn't have it at the moment or didn't want to give it to him."

Buzz was "animated," Clein remembered. Very demanding. He wanted that file and wasn't going to take no for an answer.

"Where is it?" Buzz barked at Beth Ann.

"It's not here at the moment. It's not available!"

Clein, standing there looking at the two of them, said, "We'll see that it gets to your attorney."

With that, Buzz left without saying anything more.

Be it the pressure that Thomas Cloutier was beginning to put on them, or the fact that Buzz and Kim wanted to work things out, they began letting Rebecca see the Carpenters on occasion—but only in public places. Since Buzz and Kim had stopped visitations, Beth Ann and the Carpenters had been calling every day, sometimes three and four times a day to speak with Rebecca. They would even go to Kim's work, Kim later claimed, and harass her there.

One afternoon, in front of Rebecca, Dick exploded. "You whore!" he screamed.

Other times, they'd meet at a local McDonald's. But it always seemed to turn into a fiasco, with Kim and Buzz leaving in a rush. There was one instance, Kim later said, when Cynthia pulled Rebecca in close and said, "You'll be coming home soon."

It was the wrong thing to say to an already confused and conflicted child. Any adult could have surmised that. What was odd was that Cynthia held two master's degrees, one of which was in psychology. Why would she do such a thing?

At best, the entire ordeal was disconcerting and was likely to blow up in somebody's face somewhere down the road. No one, it seemed, was interested in compromising for the sake of Rebecca. At worse, things had already escalated to a point from which there was perhaps no return. Sooner or later, something—or someone—was going to snap. No matter where Buzz and the Carpenters met, they couldn't get together without some sort of argument or confrontation.

Chapter 20

With Kim three months pregnant and the custody battle for Rebecca at the forefront of daily life for both families, on January 17, 1993, a rather brisk and dry winter day, Buzz and Kim, joined by family and friends, got married.

The ceremony was held at the Clinton house in Old Lyme. Buzz and Kim had enough class to invite Beth Ann, Richard, Dick and Cynthia, all the while thinking they would probably skip the event.

Shockingly, though, Beth Ann and Cynthia showed up, but Dick and Richard refused.

Later, many said the only reason Cynthia and Beth Ann attended was to see Rebecca—and, with all that was going on at the time, it wasn't such a stretch to believe that there might have been some truth to that assumption. They hadn't spent any real quality time with Rebecca since fall 1992. And ever since the alleged Joseph Jebran sexual abuse incident a month ago, they really hadn't seen her at all.

Buzz had a smile, Dee later said, "that could light up a room" the moment he entered. He didn't need snazzy clothes, expensive jewelry, or slick shoes to accentuate his striking presence. Buzz could turn heads just by wearing a T-shirt and a pair of whitewashed jeans. Yet, on his wedding day, Buzz went all out. He donned a silky white tuxedo with a ruby red cummerbund and bow tie to match and had gotten his hair cut short. He smiled with confidence at every opportunity as he made his way through the house, greeting guests after he and Kim had taken their vows.

"It was hard not to like Buzz Clinton," an old friend said later. "There was just something about him."

Kim, noticeably pregnant, her stomach protruding out from a full, body-length knitted white gown Dee's mother had made for Dee many years before, was beaming with happiness as if she hadn't a care in the world. She seemed to be able to put aside any animosity she harbored and let the day, with all its happiness and grace, unfold at will. After all, no matter what anybody had said about Kim or Buzz, today was their day.

Kim wore her hair pulled back and tied up in a pink bow and a white carnation with red and white baby's breath pinned to her right side that only accentuated her hair's glowing beauty. In one photo, Kim was smiling openmouthed, holding a camera-shy Rebecca up to her chest, while the child, in one of her signature moments, chewed on her fingers. Mother and daughter were happy.

Rebecca had been dressed like a princess: a Valentine's Day–red blouse with a white bow pinned to the front, cotton white undergarments and Shirley Temple–like black shoes. Her reddish blond hair—like her mother's—sparkled like gold dust as Buzz's relatives bugged her to pose for photos.

The Clinton family adored Rebecca. They agreed the child made Buzz a better person—or, rather, a person who wanted to do better.

As Beth Ann and Cynthia made their way through the reception, they failed to socialize with other guests. Instead, they followed Rebecca around the house as if it were the last time they were ever going to see her. They brought no gift or card, and they refused to eat.

While Kim and Buzz celebrated the first days of their marriage and prepared for the birth of their first child, attorney Thomas Cloutier worked doggedly on the Carpenters' case.

On January 19, only two days after the wedding, Thomas Cloutier filed several complaints with the New London Superior Court backing up Cynthia's claim that Buzz and Kim had reneged on their earlier court-ordered agreement for visitations. In one complaint, Cloutier argued that Kim had "both, by acts of omission and commission, demonstrated that continued custody of her minor child is not in the best interests of said minor child."

The second complaint introduced a new dynamic: money.

"The plaintiffs," Cloutier wrote, "claim money damages. . . . The amount, legal interest or property in demand are less than $15,000, exclusive of interest and costs."

On all the documents, Dick and Cynthia were listed as plaintiffs. Beth Ann, probably at the behest of Haiman Clein, was out of the picture—at least legally.

In his application for "temporary custody and temporary restraining order," Cloutier motioned that "Cynthia is entitled to visitation rights . . . by virtue of an order for the Probate Court . . . entered on December 15, 1992. . . ."

But there were inconsistencies in the complaints insofar as Buzz and Kim were concerned. Cloutier wrote that Rebecca had been returned to Kim back on December 20, 1992, at 5:50 P.M. (the Joseph Jebran sexual abuse incident), and "the said minor child had no bruises of any kind or nature on her body, nor was she harmed in any manner."

This simply wasn't true, according to Kim and Buzz, and later was verified by hospital records. Cynthia's own statements to Kim even disputed it. One of the last times she had seen Kim, Cynthia had acknowledged the bruises on Rebecca's face, telling Kim that she would never do anything to hurt the child.

"It had come to the plantiffs' attention that the minor child . . . was brought to the emergency room . . . during the evening of December 20, 1992, and, upon information and belief, she apparently had a black eye or eyes," Cloutier wrote. Then, for the first time, Clein's name came up. "The plaintiffs request an emergency temporary custody . . . in favor of either the plaintiffs or attorney and Mrs. Haiman Clein, who have agreed to assume temporary custody of the minor child until further order of the court."

The Carpenters, it seemed, would rather see Rebecca live with a total stranger—Beth Ann had just met Clein, and the Carpenters themselves had only met him once or twice—rather than her own mother.

Most families give money to their children as a wedding gift; the Carpenters, merely two days after Buzz and Kim had tied the knot, unloaded a barrage of motions and court orders on them, which put them in a position to have to explain themselves all over again.

On January 30, a deputy sheriff showed up at Buzz and Kim's home in Old Lyme and served them with a summons. A judge would once again decide on where Rebecca would spend her days and how they were adhering to an earlier order by the court to allow the Carpenters visits with the child.

It disgusted Buzz to think that the Carpenters could be so heartless as to want their own daughter and granddaughter to be broken apart. He vowed not to let it happen, regardless of what the courts decided. He and Kim had custody of Rebecca. How could the Carpenters continually drag them into court to try to win custody after a judge had agreed that the best place for Rebecca was with her mother?

It seemed coldhearted, as if there were more to it than just custody. Perhaps it *was* more personal, Buzz often wondered. After all, did the Carpenters, nearing retirement age, actually want to raise a toddler?

One of the things that upset Kim was the way Rebecca referred to her grandparents. She called Cynthia "Mom," Dick "Poppy." How could Cynthia, Kim felt, let that go on?

But Cynthia, like the rest of the Carpenters, seemed to care about only one thing: getting custody away from Buzz and Kim.

In all due respect to Cynthia, she had a bond with Rebecca that not too many grandparents can boast about. She had been involved in Rebecca's life since the very moment she had been born. Cynthia was Kim's Lamaze coach and present during the birth, coaching Kim along. Between August 1990, when Rebecca was born, and December 1990, Cynthia was with Kim and Rebecca every day, nearly all day long.

But Kim's life wasn't centered around her mother any longer. Things had changed since then. Between December 20, 1992, and late January 1993, the Carpenters had spent all of about five hours with Rebecca. And according to Kim, she and Buzz had good reason not to let the Carpenters be involved in Rebecca's life. Kim claimed her parents had been making things up all along, and they had no trouble lying to get what they wanted—something that started back when Kim had first met Buzz and she was locked out of her own home.

"I asked for a key," Kim later said, referring to the day after she had gotten locked out of her house. "I didn't get a key."

The Carpenters made her feel, from that moment on, as if she weren't capable of taking care of Rebecca—that she was an incompetent parent and mother. They began questioning everything she did and began taking control of Rebecca's life. There was even one time when the Carpenters had taken Rebecca on vacation without letting Kim know.

Kim had been at work. When she walked into the house after her shift to pick up Rebecca, she asked Beth Ann where everyone was.

"They went on vacation!" Beth Ann snapped.

"You mean they took Rebecca with them?"

"Yeah!"

Kim had no idea where Rebecca was for about a week.

As January gave way to February, Buzz began doing some serious research on child-parent guardianship laws in Arizona. He had mentioned last year that he was thinking of moving Kim and Rebecca out to Arizona after he got his CNA license, but now he was ready to go forward with it. Things were spiraling out of control. The Carpenters were going to stop at nothing to get custody of Rebecca.

Buzz's father, Buck, had grown up in the Tucson area and had plenty of connections, many of whom vowed to help Buzz if he ever decided to make the move. One of Buck's closest friends owned a heating and air conditioner business. If, for some reason, Buzz couldn't find work as a CNA, Buck's friend said he would guarantee Buzz a job working for him. Buzz had also found out that a CNA job paid more in Arizona than it did in Connecticut. Also, the cost of living was cheaper. Besides his family, Buzz had nothing holding him back. He often said he was just going to sell his tow truck one day, wake up in the middle of the night and leave. No notice. No warning. Just pack up and go.

"Buzz had always been the type of guy who would continually throw shit against the wall," Charlie Snyder later said, "yet none of it would stick. When he came to me around this same time and told me he was thinking about moving to Arizona, he was at a point in his life where some of that shit was finally beginning to stick. He was going to school. Had just gotten married. They had custody of Rebecca. Kim was pregnant. He'd stopped hanging around with all those troublemakers he'd ran with and just wanted to provide a life for his family. The Carpenters were making that very difficult for him."

DCYS social worker Teresa Jenkins had looked at the Carpenter-Clinton case once again to find out how things were going. By February 4, Jenkins filed a report that went through most of the problems the families had had during the past six months. At the end of the report, Jenkins gave her opinion of how the case had progressed.

Contrary to what Beth Ann had told Joseph Jebran, Jenkins reported that Kim had identified the perpetrator of the alleged sexual abuse as "unknown." There was no mention of Jebran's name anywhere in Jenkins's report. It was just more spin on Beth Ann's part. She had called Jebran and worried him for nothing.

Furthermore, Kim had explained to Jenkins why she wasn't allowing her parents to see Rebecca overnight: because there was an investigation of sexual abuse going on. Kim thought it was in Rebecca's best interest to keep her home and only see the Carpenters at a "centralized location."

Jenkins agreed it was a logical thing for a mother to do. Kim was, after all, acting as any concerned guardian might.

"Since Rebecca's placement back with her mother on December 15, 1992, she has adjusted very well and has not exhibited any negative behaviors since that time," Jenkins wrote.

Guardianship, the main thrust of the fighting and bickering, should remain with Kim and Buzz, Jenkins suggested, "as [Kim] has not put her daughter in any danger or put her at risk in any way."

The report, written by a professional who had been

trained to sniff out abuse of any kind, was in total contrast to what Beth Ann and Cynthia had been saying.

Ending the report was perhaps the most infuriating statement that any professional could have said to the Carpenters at the time: "As for visitation with maternal grandparents, it should be solely up to Kim Carpenter-Clinton."

Any lawyer knew that probate judges relied heavily on these types of reports for basing their decisions. What would happen now?

Finally, Teresa Jenkins made the recommendation that Rebecca should remain with Kim and Buzz Clinton.

A month went by, and things remained heated. Kim and Buzz refused to allow the Carpenters to see Rebecca and, at times, even speak to her on the telephone. Then, on March 2, Thomas Cloutier filed another complaint with the court which specifically asked for "the grandparents" to receive visitation and "specific access by telephone . . . pending a full hearing. . . ."

Three weeks later, Beth Ann sent Cloutier a fax, detailing how Buzz was beginning to cause the family more trouble.

According to Beth Ann's fax, Cynthia said that Buzz had called the Carpenters to talk about things, but Cynthia insisted that she speak with Kim. Cynthia didn't want to deal with Buzz. She saw him as someone with whom she couldn't negotiate. Kim was her daughter and Rebecca her granddaughter. Anything having to do with either of them would have to be talked about with Kim, not Buzz.

"You're not allowed to speak with her," Buzz told Cynthia.

"Why not?"

"Because you upset her."

"She's never indicated to me that I upset her by anything I said."

"Well, that's tough. . . ."

"What happened the other night at McDonald's?" Cynthia wanted to know.

A few days before the phone call, Buzz and Kim had agreed to meet the Carpenters at a local McDonald's. It turned into, Cynthia suggested, a shouting match that Buzz had control over from the start. Cynthia said Buzz had become "insulting." He had said he'd wanted to sit down and speak with Dick and Cynthia about things, but he insisted on tape-recording the conversation. That's when Dick refused to talk. Cynthia then said she didn't like the idea of Buzz's bringing along a tape recorder. All of a sudden, Cynthia said, Buzz became hostile and insulting.

"You can't be a grandmother if you don't know how to be a mother," Buzz said in a rage. He then said he was in the process of obtaining a restraining order to bar the Carpenters from talking to Kim and bothering her at work.

"You're harassing her!" Buzz yelled. Then, sometime later, "If I ever see you on Old Stagecoach Road, I will run you off the road with my tow truck. I'm Rebecca's father! I will tell *you* what the rules are. If you continue to give me problems, so help me God, I will disappear with Kim and Rebecca. I'm adopting Rebecca shortly, anyway."

At that point, Buzz said, "The psychologist says that you are the ones causing Rebecca problems!"

It didn't take long after Buzz spoke his peace to pack Kim and Rebecca up and leave McDonald's. The Carpenters were left with yet one more reason to continue with their fight. In their view, Buzz had snapped. He was living up to everything they had said he was.

Cynthia's testimony of the events leading up to that showdown at McDonald's ended by stating that every time Buzz called the Carpenters and said he would like to "put a resolution to the problems" he "immediately began by denying" Cynthia access to Kim.

The last time they had spoken, Buzz said, "I am

Rebecca's father. I control the situation. If you *ever* want to see Kim or Rebecca again, you will cooperate with me; or I will disappear with them."

It was clear that Buzz was finished with any type of negotiation. He had put up with the Carpenters' rules long enough. He and Kim were married now. Kim was expecting their first child. He was finished playing their games.

With that, Kim's court-appointed lawyers filed a restraining order, urging the court to stop the Carpenters from "harassing, assaulting, or molesting the defendant until further order of the court."

A hearing had been scheduled for April 6, 1993. Several new state counselors and attorneys had since become involved in what now appeared to be a situation that was turning uglier with each passing day. Buzz, Kim and the Carpenters just couldn't come to any sort of agreement on their own. There needed to be mediation.

Linda Yuhas, a family relations counselor, had recently become involved and began looking into the case more closely. She referred the matter of visitation to the court, stipulating the need for a hearing to resolve it.

During court proceedings, Rebecca sat with Buzz and Kim while the Carpenters sat on the other side of the room. Whenever Kim would look at Beth Ann or her parents, she would "shake," Dee later recalled.

By the end of the day, the judge made a decision. The Carpenters would be allowed unsupervised visitation with Rebecca, but they were ordered not to engage in any discussion with the child about Kim or Buzz. The court, the judge warned, would take action if they did.

Rebecca would get to see the Carpenters once a week, at the discretion of Kim, and one weekend per month. In a sense, they were right back to where they had started in October 1992.

Chapter 21

Beth Ann called Tricia Baker on April 5, 1993, and asked her if she and her fiancé, John Gaul, would like to join her and Joseph Jebran at the Treehouse Comedy Club the following weekend for dinner and drinks. "It's my birthday," Baker answered, beaming. "We'd love to."

Tricia and Beth Ann had been communicating by telephone for months now, but this was the first time they had actually made plans to go out socially. Whenever there was breaking news with Rebecca or the court, Beth Ann would phone Tricia so the two could chat.

On Saturday, April 10, John and Tricia drove to Ledyard and met Beth Ann and Joseph Jebran at the Carpenters' home.

When they walked in, they sat down in the living room and began telling Dick, Cynthia, Beth Ann and Joseph how excited they were to be going out "on the town." But, like every other time the two families had gotten together and talked, the conversation quickly turned to Rebecca.

"It's so horrible," Beth Ann said at one point, "that Rebecca is in this situation."

"Sounds terrible," Tricia said.

"He's violent," Beth Ann said. "He's a stripper! He's on lithium!"

"My tires were popped on my truck," Dick Carpenter added at one point. "I know Buzz did it."

When the conversation shifted to Buzz's desire to adopt Rebecca, Beth Ann became angry and loud.

"It's *not* going to happen," she insisted.

It was obvious to John and Tricia that the source of the Carpenters' problems was Buzz. Kim's name barely came up in conversation.

As Beth Ann and Cynthia continued to talk about Rebecca and the abuse they thought Buzz was responsible for, John and Tricia sat and listened, shaking their heads in disbelief.

How could someone do those things to a child?

During the days and weeks following the dinner, Beth Ann and Tricia became as close as two friends could possibly become. They began talking on the phone, Tricia later said, every day, and hung out together at night. They went shopping. Tricia's mother and father owned a beachfront home in Waterford. When the weather turned warmer, Beth Ann would stop by and lie out on the beach with Tricia. There were times when Tricia would go down to Beth Ann's office in New London and just sit and talk.

"Sometimes once, twice a week—sometimes it seemed like I was there almost every day," Tricia recalled.

When it came time for Beth Ann to go in front of the Washington, DC, bar to get sworn in as an attorney, Beth Ann invited Tricia.

The scope of their conversations was always geared toward Rebecca, the custody fight and how Buzz was this vicious abuser who needed to be stopped.

It was a campaign: a well-thought-out dialogue scripted around how awful a person Buzz was.

Tricia, a good person at heart, fell for it all. She felt sorry for Rebecca, Beth Ann and the family. If there was anything she and John could do to help, Tricia would say, she would discuss it with John and do what she could.

It wasn't obvious to Tricia right away, but the friendship was based on only what Beth Ann could get out of her and John, nothing more. It had little to do with Beth Ann's liking Tricia as a person. In fact, they were two totally different people, with very little in common. Beth Ann was a professional, a lawyer who was just beginning her career; Tricia worked at a hospital, her fiancé a blue-collar guy. Many people said later the only reason Beth Ann had befriended Tricia to begin with was to further the Carpenters' goal of gaining custody of Rebecca.

With the blessing of her fiancé, Tricia Baker took control of the situation almost immediately after Beth Ann had baited her. After discussing things with John, the couple decided first to fight for visitation and, later, custody. Based on what Cynthia and Beth Ann had hammered into Tricia and John over a two-month period, beginning on Tricia's birthday in April, Tricia and John concluded they couldn't sit by and let Buzz abuse Rebecca without doing anything about it.

So she and John began meeting with the Carpenters at their Ledyard home so they could begin the process of getting to know Rebecca and begin devising a plan to gain custody.

Regarding the visits at the Carpenter house with Rebecca, Cynthia and Beth Ann told Tricia they didn't want her or John at the house if Kim was dropping off Rebecca.

"Why?" Tricia asked.

"Because it wouldn't look good," Beth Ann said.

Cynthia and Beth Ann wanted to keep John and Tricia—and what they were about to do—a secret for as long as they could.

The first thing Beth Ann did, once she knew John and Tricia were on board, was find them a good family lawyer. Miriam Gardner-Frum, who had a reputation around town as a tough probate-type lawyer, had an office just down the block from Clein's.

"She's perfect," Beth Ann told Tricia one morning. "You guys will like her."

Then, when Tricia and John indicated that they were financially strapped and couldn't really afford a lawyer, Beth Ann told them not to worry about it. She and her parents would come up with whatever funds they needed to retain Gardner-Frum.

Soon after that, the four of them—John, Tricia, Beth Ann and Cynthia—began meeting regularly to discuss a plan of attack.

During one visit, the entire Carpenter family, including son Richard, told John and Tricia repeatedly that it would be in the "best interest" of Rebecca if they were "in her life." They made it clear that because John was the biological father, he had rights that no one else had. He needed to exercise those rights, if not for himself, then for Rebecca.

Tricia and John didn't need a sales pitch at this point. They were convinced. The Carpenters, however, continued accusing Buzz of abusing Rebecca.

That same night, Beth Ann and Cynthia told Tricia and John they would "help with child support [payments] and everything if they would just get her," meaning, of course, Rebecca.

A short time later, Beth Ann called Tricia and told her that everything was all set.

"What do you mean?" Tricia asked.

"You can come to my office and pick up a check to give to Miriam Gardner-Frum."

A day later, Tricia showed up and picked up two checks for $750 to give to Gardner-Frum. What was odd, however, was that they were cashier's checks, drawn from a local bank, not from Beth Ann's personal account.

"What's with the bank checks?" Tricia asked.

"The money," Beth Ann explained, "has to come from you, not me. I'm a lawyer. It would be a 'conflict of interest' because we already have a case pending."

When Tricia heard Beth Ann mention conflict of interest, she thought, *Oh, what the hell . . . she's an attorney. She should know better than me what to do.*

With a bank check, Beth Ann further explained, Tricia could go to the bank it was drawn on, cash it, then either give Gardner-Frum the cash or deposit it into her own account and write a check herself.

At a second meeting, Beth Ann handed Tricia a file as thick as a paperback novel.

"What's this?"

"Everything you'll need!"

It was all there: DCYS reports, hospital records, court records, reports, personal correspondence between the Carpenters and Clintons and, oddly enough, private investigation reports written by a local private investigator the Carpenters had hired some time ago.

Indeed, a local Thomas Magnum–type detective had been looking into Buzz's life now for a few months, trying to get the dish on "old Buzzy Boy."

To makes things even easier for Tricia and John, Dick offered John a job in his landscaping company, and John gladly accepted.

When Trish and John sat down and began to hash out what to do first, it took them all of about five minutes to come to the conclusion that Rebecca needed to be taken away from Buzz and Kim—at any cost. Based on what the Carpenters had been saying, Buzz and Kim were the worst parents a child could have.

"The Carpenters would take photos of Rebecca when she would come over for a visit," Tricia recalled. They weren't "Kodak moment" photos. Rebecca wasn't sitting on the couch, or playing with her Barbies, or running around the yard pretending to be Wonder Woman. Instead, she was posing, exposing certain sections of her anatomy, which made the photos look more like mug shots than anything else.

The photos were to prove abuse, Beth Ann told Tricia when Tricia asked about them. Whenever Kim and Buzz would drop Rebecca off, Beth Ann said she was dirty. The Carpenters, she explained, just wanted to document it so they had hard evidence when the time came.

But every time Tricia had seen the child, sometimes only minutes after Kim had dropped her off, she always looked "beautiful." There wasn't one time where Tricia could remember that Rebecca looked anything like Beth Ann and Cynthia had described.

Later, Dee Clinton would say the same thing: whenever Rebecca left the house, she was always bathed and dressed well.

Yet it wasn't only dirty clothing, Tricia soon realized, that Beth Ann was exaggerating. One time, Beth Ann called Tricia and told her that Rebecca had shown up at the house with rope burns around her neck.

"*What?*" Tricia asked. She was horrified.

"Yup. Rope burns . . ."

"My God, Beth. What are we going to do?"

"We took a photo. I'll show it to you the next time you come over."

Terrified for Rebecca, Tricia drove to the Carpenter house the next day and asked to see the photos.

"Take a look at that!" Beth Ann said, handing her the photos.

"I didn't see any rope burns," Tricia said later. They just weren't there.

As time passed, and Buzz and Kim tried to live up to their end of the visitation schedule set by the court, unforeseen problems always seemed to get in their way. Kim and Buzz had always had problems with their vehi-

cles. On state assistance, with Buzz not holding down a
regular nine-to-five job, transportation became more of
an issue now only because the court had made it a stipulation that Buzz and Kim drop Rebecca off with the
Carpenters.

As spring turned into summer, Buzz and Kim continually fell short on their court-ordered duties. There were
several times where they didn't drop Rebecca off or even
call the Carpenters to inform them of their car troubles.
The Carpenters, of course, were livid. It was all lies, they
insisted. Buzz was up to his old tricks again.

The court had scheduled visitations one day per week,
"to conform with [Kim's] work schedule," and one
weekend per month, from Saturday noon to Sunday
noon. There wasn't anything Buzz or Kim could do
about it. Further, Kim was ordered to deliver Rebecca
and pick her up. For a few weeks, it worked out well. But
as Buzz and Kim began to have car troubles—or so they
claimed—the visits began to slack off.

In turn, the Carpenters exercised their legal rights
and did what they had done every other time things
didn't go their way: they filed a complaint with the court.

If Buzz and Kim had, indeed, been missing visitations
because of car troubles, they would have to set up some
other type of arrangements. As Thomas Cloutier made
clear in his latest complaint, it wasn't the Carpenters'
problem that Buzz and Kim couldn't afford a car in
working order. It was their responsibility to have Rebecca
in Ledyard at the times the court had set. End of story.

This latest complaint sent the matter back into the
courtroom, which got the Family Services Unit of the superior court involved again. Linda Yuhas, a family
counselor who had worked on the case once already, was
back on it again.

The Carpenters had a solid argument. As Yuhas
investigated the matter, she began to understand that

maybe the Clintons had had some car troubles, but it was more about Buzz's wielding his power as Rebecca's stepfather.

Back on May 6, the court had set up a meeting for all the parties to discuss what had been going on. Kim "refused to engage in the mediation process without her husband. . . . ," Yuhas later reported.

Because he wasn't Rebecca's natural father, Buzz was not a party to the action, and in the eyes of the court, he couldn't participate in any of the proceedings during hearings and meetings—that is, unless he and Kim had written consent from Dick and Cynthia.

"It would be a violation of this agency's policies, Mrs. Clinton," the court told Kim, if it let Buzz participate.

When Buzz and Kim heard that, they left the meeting.

Kim was seven months pregnant at the time of the meeting. Did she need any more stress in her life? She was married to Buzz and couldn't understand why he couldn't be a part of the proceedings. He was a major part of Rebecca's life and the closest thing Rebecca had *ever* had to a traditional father figure.

In a surprising move, the Carpenters, perhaps fearing that the more friction they caused the more problems Buzz would bring to the table, decided a few days later to allow Buzz to be involved in the process.

So the Family Services Unit scheduled another date: July 1, 1993.

On June 28, Kim called family services to say she had "other obligations" that day. She and Buzz wouldn't be able to make the meeting.

"You need to reschedule your obligations, Mrs. Clinton, and attend this meeting," Kim was told.

Buzz and Kim never showed up.

It was clear to Linda Yuhas that Buzz was the cause of the most recent problems. Kim was undoubtedly yielding to Buzz's orders. The Carpenters even went so far as to agree to provide transportation for all the visits. In turn, however, they wanted extra time with Rebecca, along with a full week at some point during the summer and extra hours during the holiday season.

"Mrs. Clinton has not cooperated with this office," Yuhas wrote. "It appears that Mr. Clinton may be an influence in that regard."

She then explained that the Carpenters' expectations were neither "unreasonable or unrealistic," and she recommended the matter back to the court.

For the Sake of a Child

Chapter 22

July 12, 1993, was a Monday. The weather during the past weekend had been typical for southern New England: hot, hazy, humid. From just a casual walk to the car, sweat would roll off the body like melting candle wax. It was the peak summer vacation period. Tourists were everywhere. Beaches were packed. Boaters were out cruising the Sound, lapping up the sunshine and marvelous view of Plum Island. Fishermen were bringing in fluke and porgy by the buckets. Kids were catching crabs and clams. Young couples were running along the beach, flying kites, holding hands. Moms were reading cheesy romance novels while their toddlers made sand castles and dads drank beers.

For Buzz and Kim, the day was filled with worry and trepidation. Kim was having labor pains; Buzz was timing them.

"They might be contractions."

The next day, Kim woke Buzz up early in the morning. *"Let's go."*

By the end of the day, Buzz and Kim welcomed a new baby, Briana Clinton, into their chaotic lives. They were ecstatic. Briana looked just like Buzz: dark hair, blue eyes, dark skin. She was a beautiful, healthy girl.

To celebrate the birth, the Carpenters sent Kim a present that same night while she lay tired from giving birth.

But it wasn't a box of candy or a bouquet of fresh cut flowers.

Instead, it was a subpoena.

Buzz and Kim had been scheduled to drop Rebecca off for a visit, but because Kim had been experiencing labor pains, they thought it wouldn't be a big deal to skip the visit. On top of that, Buzz knew Kim would want Rebecca with him so the three of them could bond as a family as soon as Briana was born.

The Carpenters decided to hold Kim in contempt of the court-ordered visits.

On March 25, Haiman Clein celebrated his fifty-second birthday. Still sporting his signature Grizzly Adams beard, he was losing his hair now by the handful. He wore glasses. He was indulging in cocaine more frequently, drinking excessively and popping Prozac like Flintstone vitamins.

Walking around his office lately, however, Clein had his eyes glued on Beth Ann as though he had never seen a woman like her. By midsummer 1993, he and Beth Ann were taking lunches together and dining at some of the more elegant and expensive restaurants in town. They were even working out together at the local health spa.

Clein was totally smitten by Beth Ann's charm and grace. She was looking good and hadn't cut her red hair for several years now; it was beginning to trail down her back. She wasn't an ounce over 110 pounds. She always wore trendy clothes and expensive jewelry—and had a glow to her personality that Clein had encountered seldomly.

Still, Beth Ann's hatred for Buzz was never more fervent, while her emotional state, Clein later said, differed from day to day.

"She was happy when things were going well," Clein

recalled later. But when they weren't, she became "angrier" as time went on.

Lately, it was Buzz and Kim's thwarting of the visitations that bothered Beth Ann most. They were never home when they were supposed to be and always made it difficult for the Carpenters and Beth Ann to see Rebecca.

"Rebecca has an eye problem," she told Clein one day. "Kim and Buzz aren't taking care of it."

"That's horrible," Clein offered. By this time, he and Bonnie had dropped their pledge to adopt Rebecca, and the subject was hardly ever brought up.

Beth Ann made no direct allegations of sexual abuse on Buzz's part, but it was certainly implicit, Clein later remembered. In a rage, she would say things such as: "Buzz is forcing Rebecca to sleep in his bed!" From that, Clein assumed the worst.

Tricia Baker had been showing up at the office every other day. Beth Ann and Tricia, Clein began to notice, would go out to lunch or just sit and talk about the custody fight. It occurred to Clein that other than Rebecca, the two women had little in common. Clein had met several of Beth Ann's friends by this point, but "Tricia didn't look to me," Clein later offered, "like the type of girl Beth would normally associate with."

Like many other people, he thought the relationship was odd. So he asked Beth Ann what Tricia's role was. There had to be, Clein surmised, a logical explanation as to why Beth Ann was hanging out with her so much.

"John Gaul is Rebecca's natural father and is pursuing custody," Beth Ann explained.

She then told Clein that Tricia was John's fiancée. They were getting married in a few weeks.

"How do you feel about John getting custody?"

Because it would ultimately help the Carpenters achieve their goal one way or the other, Beth Ann said she "favored" it. Even encouraged it. After all, it had been Beth Ann who had sought out John Gaul initially.

Little did Beth Ann know, however, that John was beginning to have second thoughts about pursuing custody. He knew it was going to be a battle. He knew it would cost him a ton of money, regardless of how much the Carpenters had offered to pay. Not to mention that Rebecca wasn't really bonding with John they way he'd hoped.

In contrast, Tricia had become emotionally attached to the child by this point. Beth Ann had really been playing up the notion that Rebecca could replace the child that Tricia and John could never have, and Tricia was lapping it up.

John was more grounded. He realized they were starting a life together. Suddenly it all seemed too much to bear. Less than a year ago, they had not known Rebecca existed. Now they were contemplating getting custody of her?

Tricia's parents, Judy and Harry Baker, were smart, successful people. They owned a spacious stucco home on the ocean in Waterford, were respected members of the community, had been happily married for decades and were perfect role models for Tricia.

By late summer, the Bakers had told Tricia they honestly thought Beth Ann's friendship was transparent. They said Beth Ann was using Tricia to further her own agenda. Tricia, though, was perhaps blinded by emotion. She accepted people at face value. She never believed Beth Ann was anything less than a friend. In fact, Tricia had informed her parents recently that she had even invited Beth Ann to her wedding.

Perhaps against their better judgment, the Bakers didn't argue their point. Tricia was old enough to make her own mistakes.

When Beth Ann heard that she had been invited to

the wedding, she asked Tricia about Richard, Dick and Cynthia.

"They can come, too, right?"

"Of course," Tricia said.

With a court date set for mid-August to resolve the issue of visitations, Carolyn Brotherton, Kim's attorney, filed a motion on July 29, 1993, to withdraw herself from the case.

Why?

"There has been a complete breakdown of the attorney-client relationship."

Buzz was rubbing his nose into the entire matter, trying to take control of every facet of it. According to some, Brotherton wanted more money. It had required more work than she had anticipated. Buzz and Kim were broke, and they told her they couldn't afford it. Buzz had scraped to come up with the $700 retainer, but now, some later claimed, Brotherton wanted $900 more.

Buzz told Brotherton he wanted all the files from the case. She said as long as he gave her more money, he could have whatever he wanted.

Nevertheless, here they were, a month before an important court date, and Buzz and Kim were without counsel.

Being the resilient person he was, with the court's permission, Buzz decided to represent Kim himself. Dee and Buck had always taught their son to fight. No matter what, keep going forward. Buzz knew the case better than any attorney they could bring in at this late period, anyway. Why not give it a shot? They didn't stand much to lose. The court date wasn't about custody; it was about visitations.

Convincing a court of law to agree to let a layman act as counsel for his wife in a custody matter wasn't the easiest thing to do, however. But after Buzz filed all the appro-

priate paperwork, the court agreed, to everyone's amazement, to let him represent Kim—if only for the August 16,
1993, hearing date.

Weeks prior to the court date, Buzz had gone down to
the court to file a restraining order against Dick and Cynthia. Perhaps it was part of his legal strategy, or maybe the
Carpenters were just getting on his nerves again? Either
way, the court rejected the order and advised Buzz that he
was "not eligible because he did not fill the statutory re-
quirement to get" the order.

On August 16, 1993, in the New London Superior
Court building directly across the street from Haiman
Clein's law office, the Carpenters and Clintons showed up
to square off.

Everyone was there. Buzz and Kim sat on one side of
the room, while Beth Ann sat on the opposite side, yet
only yards away. Haiman Clein and Dick Carpenter sat
next to her. Cynthia would be asked to testify, as would
Kim.

At the end of the day, what the hearing came down to—
and the judge interrupted proceedings about two-thirds
of the way through to point it out—was, "Why has [Kim]
not complied with the court order regarding visitation?
Has she any explanation for that?"

In the eyes of the court, Kim had not lived up to her
end of the court's previous order. The judge wanted to
know why.

It was a simple request.

Ultimately the judge ordered visitations one weekend
a month and one day a week. "The parties are going to
have to agree on that," he said. "I must caution the defendant, Kim Louise Clinton, that she must follow this
order or she will be found in contempt and she could *go
to jail.*" Now turning his attention toward Buzz, "So you
best make sure that she does obey the court's order . . . ,"
the judge said.

Essentially, the Carpenters had won.

As Buzz, Kim and the Carpenters began to file out of the courtroom, Buzz leaned over and said something to Dick Carpenter in passing. Just then, Beth Ann, Cynthia and Dick, who had sat and listened to the proceedings without saying much of anything, jumped up and hurriedly followed Buzz as he made his way out through the double doors. With all four of them standing by the doors, the Carpenters began to speak in "harsh, muffled tones," Deputy Chief Clerk David Gage later said.

"You could see that they were very angry at each other," Gage added. "There were lots of hand gestures, and all parties became very animated."

"Why in the hell don't you leave us alone?" Beth Ann screamed at Buzz.

"The custody battle of Rebecca is none of your business," Buzz shouted back.

Then they began yelling at each other "very loudly," Liz Hall, the judicial marshal who was standing next to them, recalled later.

After that, the pushing and shoving started.

While Buzz and Beth Ann pushed each other back and forth, Cynthia and Dick began yelling at Buzz. Making their way to the next set of double doors, they all became "logjammed," Hall remembered, and couldn't get out without rubbing up against one another.

So Hall stepped in between to make sure no one got hurt. "Calm down," she said.

As Hall escorted them out of the courtroom, sending Buzz one way and the Carpenters the other, Beth Ann began to say something.

Buzz, who had begun to walk away, turned and stopped.

"I will kill your ass!" Beth Ann shouted, staring at Buzz.

Hearing that, Buzz just walked away.

Liz Hall asked Beth Ann, who was crying now, if Buzz

was her husband. Hall was confused. She didn't know much about the case.

"No! He's my brother-in-law," Beth Ann said through clenched teeth. "I don't know why he is doing this to our family. He wants to take Rebecca. He's no good."

Chapter 23

A few days after Beth Ann had told Buzz she'd "kill" his "ass," family services referred the case to Ingrid Comeir, a seasoned gray-haired veteran of the agency who was brought in as a negotiator. Comeir's first order of business was to set up visitations between Rebecca and her natural father, John Gaul. Comeir, of course, had no idea that John and Tricia had been visiting Rebecca for nearly a year already.

Toward the end of August, John and Tricia, days away from their wedding, had accepted an invitation to a Labor Day picnic the Carpenters were hosting at their Ledyard home. It was to be a family gathering. Tricia and John had been spending a lot of time with Rebecca lately, trying to get closer to her. But Rebecca, for whatever reason, didn't want any part of them. Perhaps the picnic would help change that.

During the past six months, Tricia and John spent weekends at the Carpenters' when Rebecca was there. John noticed that "even though Rebecca had her own room and bed in the home," Beth Ann would sleep with the child.

Also, at this time, Dick and Beth Ann repeatedly expressed to John and Tricia their hatred for Buzz. They made little mention of Kim. It was always about Buzz: the abuse, the dancing (which he had been through with for some time now), the fact that he was thinking of moving Rebecca and Kim out to Arizona and that he was going to adopt her.

It was all too much for them.

But by the end of August, John had decided that fighting Buzz and Kim for custody wasn't such a good idea anymore. Tricia, undoubtedly still seduced by Beth Ann's counterfeit friendship, believed Beth Ann and Cynthia were doing the right thing for Rebecca and that Buzz was abusing the child. It was her and John's responsibility to protect Rebecca any way they could. They had to forget about themselves and concentrate on the child.

Tricia, though, began to have second thoughts, too, on August 28, the day of her wedding.

The Carpenters sat together at a table near the bride and groom's. Although it was Tricia and John's day, to anyone who would listen, the Carpenters carried on about Buzz and how much they disliked him. It was all Buzz's fault. Without him, there would be no trouble. What were they supposed to do, just roll over and forget everything?

"The entire Carpenter family hated Buzz," Tricia said later. "Dick said to me that 'ten thousand dollars could take care of the problem'—and I knew he was referring to Buzz and hiring someone to kill him."

There were others, too, who had heard Dick say the same thing during the wedding.

Beth Ann called Tricia a day or so before the Labor Day picnic with some bad news. "We don't want you and John to come to the picnic," she said.

"Why not?"

"Well, Kim and Buzz are going to be there."

Tricia was hurt and, at the same time, shocked. "Okay," she told Beth Ann. "No problem."

She wondered why the Carpenters would invite Buzz. There had to be some kind of motive behind it.

Buzz thought the gesture was a bit strange, too. If the Carpenters had just wanted to see Rebecca, they could have either said so, or invited Kim and Rebecca and not him.

Dee Clinton later said that to Buzz, any situation was salvageable. Any problem could be worked out. Maybe the Carpenters were finally giving up? By this time, there was no chance of their getting custody of Rebecca. And with Buzz now determined to move to Arizona, what other option did they have? If they wanted to see Rebecca, they would have to involve Buzz.

Whenever Buzz was torn about a decision, he usually turned to his mother for guidance.

"What's up with this picnic, Ma?" Buzz asked Dee one day. "Do you think we should go?"

"Maybe you and Kim *should* go," Dee said. "Perhaps they want to work things out."

The picnic didn't turn out to be all that bad. There was no trouble for Buzz or Kim. The Carpenters even acted as if they were perhaps accepting Buzz into the family for the first time. At one point, Kim later remembered, they even asked Buzz to stand next to the fireplace in their living room, an old relic of a thing with a worn mantelpiece above it, so they could snap a family photo of him, Kim and Rebecca.

Buzz obliged.

Sometime later, however, that seemingly innocent photo would, in many ways, contribute to his death.

Days after the Labor Day picnic, John Gaul made it clear not only to Ingrid Comeir, but to the Carpenters, that he wasn't interested in pursuing custody of Rebecca—that he and Tricia had talked it over and thought it was in the best interest of their marriage not to take the issue any further. They still wanted to maintain a relationship with

Rebecca, of course. But fighting for custody was not something they wanted to pursue any longer.

Interestingly enough, once Tricia and John told everyone how they felt, it was the last time they ever heard from the Carpenters. Beth Ann, who had been calling Tricia almost daily for the past eight months to a year, taking her out to expensive dinners and on trips, never called her again.

Anyone in the New London law office of Haiman Clein who had witnessed his relationship with Beth Ann blossom throughout the summer couldn't ignore the fact that by October 1993, Clein and Beth Ann were an item. They no longer were trying to hide it. In September, Beth Ann had rented a luxurious, $1,032-a-month condo at the upscale Norwich Inn and Spa, about ten minutes from her parents' home in Ledyard. Most of the condos had come furnished with the best furniture money could buy, but Beth Ann insisted it be removed, Clein later said, so she could replace it with her own. On top of that, she now drove a brand-new BMW. And many began wondering where all her money was coming from.

Beth Ann's income had risen remarkably within the same time period. She went from making about $27,000 a year to $50,000, without any notice, Joseph Jebran later remembered. She was still seeing Joseph Jebran and, from his standpoint, their relationship was still going strong. He was still sending his checks home, and she was still sending him back a stipend to live on and allocating the remainder to his bills.

Clein was the first to admit that he had become obsessed with Beth Ann by this point. Melissa Jolley, a twenty-eight-year-old local woman who worked as Clein's office manager and bookkeeper, recalled later how Clein had one day described his relationship with Beth

Ann. Holding up a copy of the novel *Damage,* Clein said to Jolley, "You should buy a copy. It's about Beth Ann and me!"

Damage is about a successful doctor who becomes obsessed with his son's fiancée, who is half his age. The book has been described by critics as a "ruthless story . . . an implacable work of the erotic imagination."

For Clein, however, Josephine Hart's highly praised novel was based on a reality he was now living.

By the beginning of November, Clein was calling Beth Ann several times a day whenever he was out of the office and seeing her at night whenever he could. They began to go out for drinks after work and on weekends. They talked about Buzz, Rebecca, Kim, work—and anything else Beth Ann wanted.

One night, Beth Ann looked at Clein and asked, "Do business trips ever come up?"

Clein felt a strong impression that she wanted to go. She seemed interested in the prospect of being alone with him.

"I have a trip coming up in November to Florida to see a client," Clein said. "Would you like to go?"

Beth Ann smiled. "Yes," she said. "Yes. Yes. And yes!"

After that conversation, Beth Ann began calling Clein almost daily, and she began spending all of her free time, besides the weekends Joseph Jebran was around, with Clein. "Flirting," Clein later recalled. It seemed to him that she was flirting with him now in a more sexual way. There was chemistry. The atmosphere was more charged. Clein, of course, was flattered. Here was a woman nearly half his age, a beautiful redhead with skin like porcelain who could have had any number of men, interested in *him.*

"All the signals I was getting I perceived as positive," Clein later said.

As luck would have it, the trip to Florida was scheduled

for November 22—a day before Beth Ann's thirtieth birthday. Celebrating it together, in the sunshine and warmth of Naples, Florida, one of the wealthiest areas on the Gulf Coast, would be like something out of a fairy tale.

As Beth Ann and Clein made their way to Florida, as usual, she began talking about the custody fight. As Clein would find out, the entire trip soon became a lobbying campaign for Rebecca.

"It is hopeless," Beth Ann said. Then she explained how bleak the future for Rebecca looked. There was no way a court was going to award the Carpenters custody, especially now that Buzz and Kim were married and had been bringing Rebecca up for almost a year. In fact, just a few weeks before the Florida trip, Buzz, Kim and Rebecca had moved into a two-bedroom apartment in East Lyme. They were finally out of the Clintons' house and on their own. Buzz had qualified for a position at Vinal Tech to begin his course for becoming a CNA, slated to start school within the next few months. In the eyes of family services, Buzz and Kim were doing everything by the book.

"Beth Ann was in constant agitation over it," Clein recalled later.

In Florida, they dined at the finest restaurants and stayed at a resort hotel—and by the second night, when the maelstrom of lust was too much, they had sex.

When they returned, Clein began sleeping with Beth Ann just about every day. As they grew closer sexually, Beth Ann began to pour it on about her concerns for Rebecca's welfare.

"My family is continually upset and frustrated," she told Clein one morning as they lay in bed. "We're continually worried that Rebecca is being abused."

A week or so later, Clein was talking to Beth Ann's brother, Richard, on the phone. Richard was crying, Clein remembered later.

"What's wrong? Why are you crying?"

"Something terrible has happened to Rebecca. She's being abused."

By the first week of December, Beth Ann became even more concerned that things were only getting worse for Rebecca.

"The whole family is upset," she told Clein. She was crying. "I fear that my father or brother might kill Buzz."

Ingrid Comeir, the counselor appointed by the court to keep an eye on the situation, began to receive calls from Cynthia and Buzz by the end of December. They were making accusations against each other. Most of the time, they were calling to say that the other had done something horrendous to Rebecca.

As the frustration mounted, Beth Ann continued her daily testaments to Clein, implying that the only alternative left was to get rid of Buzz.

"As long as he's alive," Beth Ann said one morning, "Rebecca is never going to be safe, and we'll never get her!"

Then a few days later, Beth Ann called Clein in a rage. "What happened, Beth?" Clein asked. "She was in high anxiety, weeping, bordering on being hysterical about it," he remembered.

But she wouldn't say exactly what had happened. Only: "As long as he's alive, Rebecca will never be safe. We will never get her!"

"Jesus, *what* happened?"

Beth Ann then had a request. "Will you help me?" she asked matter-of-factly.

"What?"

"Will you kill him for me?"

Clein was taken aback. He hadn't expected to hear such a thing from someone he felt so close to, someone with whom he was now in love.

"No!" he said.

Beth Ann then began weeping more profoundly.

"Listen," he offered. "I won't, but I know someone who would. But I'm unsure at this point."

Clein wanted to check it out before making any promises.

The following day, he told Beth Ann that he had spoken to an old client of his about it.

"What's his name?" she asked.

"Mark Despres."

Over the next few days, Beth Ann was "pretty intent" on hiring Despres, Clein later said. But Clein wanted to be sure she was serious. So he asked her again.

"Go ahead," she said.

"With what?" Clein wanted to hear once again.

"The killing."

Chapter 24

In the months since Haiman Clein and Beth Ann began sleeping together, Clein, now a love-struck Romeo, had said numerous times he'd do anything Beth Ann asked of him. Nary had a day gone by where the two lovebirds didn't see each other, have sex or talk about what was now the main thrust and focus of their relationship: the decision between them to have Buzz Clinton killed. For Clein, he believed wholeheartedly that Buzz was the worst kind of human being imaginable—a sexual predator of children—and deserved a death sentence for his actions.

Yet, even if it were true, for two lawyers to put themselves in a position of judge, jury and executioner, many would later argue, made people like Beth Ann and Clein no better.

Clein had represented Mark Despres in the past on several occasions: notably, a gun possession charge, his divorce from Diana Trevethan and a real estate matter that had earned Despres a rather large payday for a piece of property he had owned. They had become good friends throughout the years. By the end of 1993, though, Despres was more to Clein than just a friend. Clein had been buying cocaine from Despres in large quantities for quite some time. It was that drug dealer–customer relationship that got Clein thinking, after Beth Ann had confronted him with the notion of having Buzz killed, that Despres just might be the man for the job.

Despres had told Clein he distributed cocaine mainly in the New York area. Others claimed Despres had been dealing cocaine out of a local bar in Ivoryton.

Nevertheless, one day, while Despres and Clein were discussing how Despres sold his drugs, Despres mentioned that he had to "off" people once in a while because of the dangerous situations he found himself in while in New York. Clein wasn't all that surprised, he later said, that Despres had been involved in that type of behavior. He had almost expected it of him.

When Beth Ann asked Clein to kill Buzz, Clein remembered that previous conversation and thought, *Mark's done it before. Why not ask him?*

"I can trust him," Clein said he told Beth Ann in late December when they were discussing hiring Despres. "I know Mark."

From there, it was only a matter of asking.

With that, Clein called Mark one morning and told him he had a job for him—and it wasn't making another dollhouse for his wife, or picking up a bag of dope.

"Come into the New London office," Clein said. "I need to talk to you."

A day later, Despres showed up.

Clein took him into a side office—according to Despres and Clein—and asked Beth Ann to join them.

"I have some personal things for you to do," Clein said as Beth Ann looked on in quiet desperation. "I want you to take care of—*murder*—this real bad guy who is molesting a young girl. Can you make this person disappear?"

"All right," Despres said, shrugging his shoulders as if Clein had ordered another bag of dope.

"We can talk about it further later on," Clein said.

A few days after that first meeting, Clein had Despres come back to his office. This time, however, Beth Ann wasn't around.

"I'm involved with a woman whose niece is being abused—and the only way to stop the abuse is to have him killed. Would you do it for us?"

"Yes," Despres said.

Despres then explained how he wasn't interested in who the woman was, and didn't ask about her. Later, though, Despres admitted that he knew immediately it was Beth Ann.

Clein, however, had sent Beth Ann out of the office before Despres had arrived because he didn't want Despres to see her again.

Being around Mark Despres, former friends recalled later, could be kind of intimidating. He was a very large man, about six feet one inches, three hundred pounds. Clein, a big man himself at six feet two inches, two hundred pounds, knew that underneath the baggy clothes Despres usually wore was a rock-solid machine of a man. Despres was brawny, like an NFL lineman, and his square shoulders seemingly ran all the way down to the ground. He had a biker appearance to him that was creepy and brassy.

As the two men continued to talk of the killing during that second meeting, at one point, Clein told Mark that the person he would be looking for was a local man named Anson Clinton.

"Is his nickname Buzz?" Despres asked.

Clein was surprised. "You know him?"

"Yup."

"How?"

"I know some people who have had some bad drug deals with him, and he isn't very well-liked."

Clein shrugged. Okay, he said. Perhaps it made him

feel a bit more certain about what he and Beth Ann were doing.

Next they began discussing the details. "I need a gun and a car," Despres said. "An *old* car."

"Okay—"

"When I did this before," Despres added, interrupting Clein, "I used an old car to dispose of the body. I'll do the same thing."

"All right," Clein agreed.

"I want eight thousand dollars."

"I can do that."

"I'll need to know where he lives and works. I want marker plate numbers. I'll figure out how to hook up with him or something like that."

Clein really didn't know much about Buzz besides what Beth Ann had told him. And she hadn't yet said where Buzz lived or worked.

"I'll get that information," Clein said as the meeting drew to a close. "Don't worry about it."

Near Christmastime, Clein called Despres and told him he had all the information he had previously requested, and that he needed to come into the office. Giving it to him over the telephone wasn't a good idea. In between the time they had last met, Clein had given Despres an envelope containing $3,500. It was a down payment for the murder, Clein later said, enough money to buy a car and gun.

Later that day, with Despres sitting in Clein's office, Clein got up and said, "I'll be right back. . . . Give me a few minutes."

Clein then walked across the small hallway into Beth Ann's office. She was waiting for him.

"I need that info," he said.

"Hold on," Beth Ann replied.

As Clein stood there and waited, he later recalled, Beth Ann called her mother, Cynthia, and asked for

Buzz's address. Then she inquired, "Where does he work? What's the name on the side of his tow truck?"

Beth Ann, Clein later added, never told her mother why she needed the information—at least not while Clein was standing there.

After she was finished writing everything down, Beth Ann handed the piece of paper to Clein.

"I'll rewrite it in my own handwriting and throw this piece of paper away," Clein reassured her.

While Clein passed through the hallway, he stopped in the rest room and tore off a piece of paper towel.

Despres was waiting patiently when Clein came back into the office a few minutes later. Beth Ann stayed in her office.

"What's up?" Despres asked.

"Here," Clein offered, after copying the information down on the piece of paper towel.

"All right, then. We're all set?"

"Yeah," Clein said. "But throw that piece of paper away after you've memorized the info."

Clein then reached into his pocket and took out another $500 in cash and gave it to Despres. "In a few days, I'll have another fifteen hundred for you," he promised.

Despres seemed satisfied with that.

Clein's New London office usually held its annual Christmas party for clients a few days before the holidays began. Beth Ann and Clein had gone out the day of the party to lunch and showed up later that evening as it was already in full swing.

When she and Clein walked up to the door, Mark Despres was sitting in the lobby area waiting for them.

Dressed from head to toe in camouflage army fatigues, Despres had taken on the role of a hired killer to a rather perplexing extreme. Here was this massive human being, dressed like a marine ready to do battle in the jungles of Vietnam, sitting in the lobby of Clein's law office with scores of festive professional people mingling around in the background. He had even dyed his hair. It was a surreal sight—quite opposite from the Hollywood stereotype: good-looking male, usually of Italian heritage, dressed in all black, packing a silencer.

When Clein first looked at Despres sitting there, he felt uneasy. It was as if Despres were getting a thrill out of the whole thing. He seemed enthusiastic about what was ahead. Beth Ann was nervous, no doubt scared someone was going to see them together and begin thinking something was up.

When Clein and Despres entered Clein's office after getting some food and drink and talking with guests for a moment, Despres opened his jacket.

"Check it out, Haiman!" he said, smiling.

"You're risking a lot by going around like this," Clein said, shaking his head.

Despres had a huge handgun tucked inside a shoulder holster he was wearing.

Beth Ann then walked in. They all sat down and spoke very briefly. In Clein's mind, the meeting was a way for the three of them to get acquainted. They had entered into this agreement together. At least they should know one another before Despres went through with the hit. Hiding Beth Ann from Despres wasn't possible anymore, nor was it feasible, Clein had surmised. There was just no way to keep her out of it.

"This is the guy who is helping us with *that*," Clein said to Beth Ann, looking over at Despres. It was an "oblique reference," Clein later admitted. Even though he had made it in front of Despres, Clein was confident he still hadn't confirmed to Despres that Beth Ann was the same person behind it all. Clein wasn't stupid. He hadn't gone to law school for nothing. He may not have been a criminal lawyer, but he knew the law. If Beth Ann's name was never used specifically, there might be problems for anyone who might accuse her later on.

"Mark made the connection [that it was Beth Ann] very quickly, though," Clein recalled.

Later that week, when Clein was talking to Despres on the phone one night, Despres said, "I knew that's who you were talking about when I had seen her the first time."

"Yup," Clein finally confirmed. "That's her, all right."

Mark Despres met with Clein again in the early part of January 1994, and they further discussed how and where Buzz would be killed. Clein, perhaps wanting Despres to know why a lawyer with such a standing in the community would call a hit on a man he hardly knew, explained one time that he'd tried to take care of the matter in court, but he had failed. Murder, Clein insisted, was the only option they had left. Buzz, after all, was molesting the young girl. What else could they do?

Despres agreed. To him, Buzz was nothing more than a "scumbag" who deserved death. Molesting little girls, even to a criminal, was one of the worst offenses imaginable. In prison, "diddlers," as they are commonly known, receive the most violent treatment from other inmates. One could butcher his own mother and father or rob a local church, but touch a kid and you're doomed.

No one, however, discussed evidence. Where was all the evidence that Buzz had molested the girl?

There was none.

Around this same time, Chris Despres, Mark's son, had not been getting along well with his mother, Diana Trevethan. So it was agreed that the best thing for Chris would be to move in with Mark.

Diana Trevethan, perhaps against her better judgment, agreed that Chris should go live with Mark.

At fifteen, Chris began going to Valley Regional Tech High School when he moved in with Mark. He was thrilled by his father's unique talent of ripping apart car engines and putting them back together again, doing bodywork, along with how Mark had worked with his hands. In that respect, Chris wanted to follow in Mark's footsteps. Living with dad, Chris later said, was a way not only to get closer to him, but to learn mechanics.

Soon after moving in, Chris began to skip school. To his surprise, Mark would even pick him up at school and encourage his truancy. Mark himself was never interested in school. He'd left in the eighth grade and never returned. Some later said Mark's father, who had left the home when Mark was five, had beaten him and emotionally abused him for the short time he was around. Because of that, Mark hadn't really known how to be a father. Even though Mark's mother, Esther Lockwood, had remarried a man who treated Mark decently, Mark never really had a parental example to follow, Lockwood later said.

When he would pick Chris up from school, or on the days when Chris decided not to even bother going, they would go out and ride ATVs or just hang out at Fremut Texaco, the local garage in Essex where Mark had been working as a used-car salesman along with Joe Fremut. Sometimes, when Mark and Chris were bored, they would go out in the back of Despres's Winthrop Road home in Essex or Fremut Texaco and fire one of Mark's twenty weapons, setting up bottles and cans and taking target practice.

Fremut Texaco, which was on the other side of Essex, became a place for Mark and Chris to kill some time while Joe Fremut worked in the garage and sold cars. Despres had always considered Fremut one of his closest friends.

But Fremut viewed the relationship differently, he later admitted. He would call Mark "Fatboy" behind his

Twenty-six-year-old Anson "Buzz" Clinton, in 1992, two years before he was gunned down.

Buzz Clinton and his younger brother, Billy.

Easter Sunday, 1986. From left: Buzz Clinton; his sister, Suzanne; his father, Buck; and his brother, Billy.

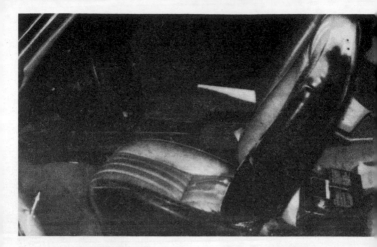

The inside of Buzz Clinton's 1981 Pontiac Firebird as the
Connecticut State Police Major Crime Squad
found it on March 10, 1994.
(Courtesy of Clerk's Office, New London Superior Court)

An aerial view of Exit 72 off Interstate
95 in East Lyme, Connecticut, where
Buzz Clinton was found shot to death
on March 10, 1994. *(Courtesy of
Clerk's Office, New London Superior Court)*

This copper-covered .38 caliber
bullet was taken from Buzz Clinton's
chest cavity. *(Courtesy of John Brand)*

The Eastern District Major Crime Squad of the Connecticut State Police in Norwich, Connecticut, was the hub of the Buzz Clinton murder investigation. *(Author's photo)*

John Turner, a 20-year veteran of the Connecticut State Police, was one of the detectives leading the investigation into Clinton's death. *(Author's photo)*

Detective Richard "Reggie" Wardell was instrumental in getting hired hitman Mark Despres to expose the conspiracy behind Buzz Clinton's murder. *(Author's photo)*

Detective Marty Graham worked for years to bring those responsible for Buzz Clinton's death to justice. *(Author's photo)*

Kim Carpenter-Clinton, Buzz's wife, in her 1984 high school yearbook photo. *(Courtesy of Ledyard High School yearbook)*

In 1992, Buzz Clinton converted this tool shed on his parents' property into a fully functional "detached bedroom." *(Author's photo)*

The Clinton residence in Old Lyme, Connecticut, where Buzz Clinton grew up. *(Author's photo)*

Kim Carpenter and Anson "Buzz" Clinton on their wedding day, January 17, 1993.

Cynthia Carpenter, Kim's mother (in middle, leaning over, talking to Rebecca), lost custody of Rebecca only weeks before this photo was taken.

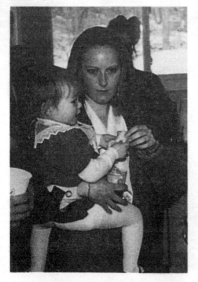

Beth Ann Carpenter with her niece, Rebecca, during her sister Kim's wedding ceremony.

Cynthia and Dick Carpenter were photographed by detectives.
(Courtesy of Connecticut State Police Crime Lab)

Beth Ann Carpenter's senior class photo, 1981. *(Courtesy of Ledyard High School yearbook)*

Beth Ann Carpenter lived in this lavish condominium at the Norwich Inn & Spa resort, in Norwich, Connecticut. *(Author's photo)*

In the late eighties, attorney Haiman Long Clein built a lucrative practice catering to Connecticut's powerful and rich.
(Courtesy of Connecticut State Police Crime Lab)

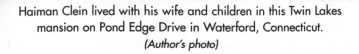

Haiman Clein lived with his wife and children in this Twin Lakes mansion on Pond Edge Drive in Waterford, Connecticut.
(Author's photo)

Acting on a tip, investigators of Buzz Clinton's death first searched for evidence at the Fremut Texaco in Essex, Connecticut.
(Author's photo)

Buzz Clinton thought he was going to sell this tow truck on the night he was murdered.

The area in back of the Fremut Texaco, where Mark Despres and Joe Fremut rehearsed how they were going to kill Buzz Clinton. *(Courtesy of Clerk's Office, New London Superior Court)*

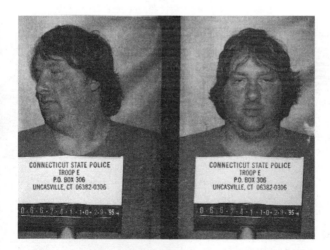

Mark Despres was arrested on October 29, 1995, after arming himself with an AK-47 and leading Connecticut State Police on a 12-hour manhunt. *(Courtesy of Connecticut State Police Crime Lab)*

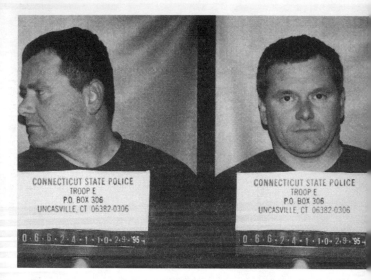

Joe Fremut exposed Mark Despres's involvement in the murder
shortly after detectives arrested him.
(Courtesy of Connecticut State Police Crime Lab)

After spending months on
the run, Haiman Clein
was arrested by the FBI in
Long Beach, California,
in early 1996.
*(Courtesy of Connecticut
State Police Crime Lab)*

Dee and Buck Clinton had this house built on their property for Kim and her kids shortly after Buzz was murdered.
(Author's photo)

Eight weeks after Buzz was murdered, Kim Clinton gave birth to his son, Anson Clinton IV.

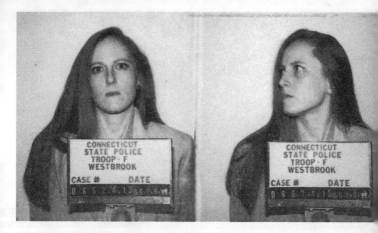

After authorities in Ireland tracked her down and extradited her
back to the United States, Beth Ann Carpenter posed
for a mug shot on June 19, 1999.
(Courtesy of Connecticut State Police Crime Lab)

Beth Ann Carpenter at her parents' Ledyard home in November
2000, after her bond was reduced from $1 million to $150,000.
(Courtesy of Connecticut State Police Crime Lab)

Chris Despres (20 years old here) was only 15 when he watched in horror as his father murdered Buzz Clinton.

In June 2002, convicted murderer Mark Despres was photographed at MacDougall-Walker Correctional Institution, in Suffield, Connecticut. *(Courtesy of Connecticut Bureau of Prisons)*

Haiman Long Clein, at 56, on September 23, 1997, two years before he took a plea bargain for his role in Buzz Clinton's murder. *(Courtesy of Connecticut Bureau of Prisons)*

After she was found guilty of capital felony, murder and conspiracy to commit murder, Beth Ann Carpenter was photographed at the York Correctional Facility for Women in Niantic, Connecticut, on April 24, 2002. *(Courtesy of Connecticut Bureau of Prisons)*

back and make fun of him. Even to his face, Fremut would say insulting things such as, "Hi, fat fuck!"

Fremut and Catherine White, his drug-addict, prostitute girlfriend, were known as "Bonnie and Clyde." Despres, Fremut and White were often collectively called the "Three Stooges." They all carried guns.

But Mark and Chris not only had shooting guns, skipping school and riding ATVs in common; Mark had recently started turning his son onto something altogether more sinister. According to an old friend and, later, investigators, Mark and Chris would spray-paint pentagrams on the floor of Despres's apartment, fill the room with lit candles and hold satanic rituals and séances, reciting verses from satanic literature.

"Chris said that he was really scared one night—that he had seen something during one of the séances," a friend later recalled. "Because of that, Chris didn't like doing it. But Mark was *really* into it." Recalling how Mark treated Chris during this time, that same friend added, "Just the fact that he always treated Chris like a buddy and not a son. And that he encouraged him to do bad things, like go ahead and skip school or work so they could ride three-wheelers . . . drink and smoke pot. Mark was boisterous and loud. Kind of obnoxious. He thought he was—and I guess he really was—a tough guy."

Others claimed Chris and Mark would have rituals out in back of Despres's property in the woods involving fire and orgies with young girls—all in the name of Mark's master, Satan.

To Chris, skipping school and smoking pot with his father was a dream come true. He was living as an adult, basically doing whatever he wanted, and Mark could have cared less. Mark would even buy Chris alcohol and pot. On some days, while most other kids were in school learning about the Civil War or economics, Chris and his dad were out partying with Chris's friends, many of whom were young girls.

Unbeknownst to Chris, Mark had ulterior motives for the parties, a former friend claimed. For when Chris was not around, Mark would put the moves on Chris's girl-friends. Apparently, Mark liked little girls and had begun dating a fifteen-year-old recently.

It was odd that Buzz's alleged behavior was so appalling to Mark Despres—because, when it came down to it, Mark Despres, at thirty-four, was himself doing the exact same thing the Carpenters and Haiman Clein were accusing Buzz of doing.

Chapter 25

If Beth Ann had any doubts about Haiman Clein's devotion, they disappeared when she began receiving love letters from Clein during the latter part of 1993 and the beginning of 1994.

The first letter, dated December 30, 1993, was gentle and caring, mirroring a note a love-crazed adolescent might slip to his girlfriend during class. In the opening paragraph, Clein wrote of his loyalty to the relationship. He said he was "sincere in [his] desire and belief that somehow [they would] end up together. . . ." He spoke of how awful it would be not to see her again—"And I don't mean around the office!" Ending the brief letter, he said he felt an "intense" love for Beth Ann every "moment" he was "awake."

It was clear that Clein, who would turn fifty-three on March 25, had become obsessed with Beth Ann.

On the one hand, the letter was an innocent sign of love. Clein's heart was aching. But on the other, that terse letter, so seemingly harmless and sincere, would be the last time Clein would hold back his innermost feelings. Perhaps he couldn't help himself? Or maybe he had become so increasingly fixated with a woman nearly half his age, was so strung out on cocaine, alcohol and Prozac that he'd lost total control of the little bit of sanity he had left.

Either way, Beth Ann was about to get to know the *real* Haiman Clein.

In a letter dated January 3, Clein began to describe how he had become turned on by just about anything Beth Ann did. "I am sitting here thinking about you and, of course, your beautiful body." Then he said he loved her "skin" and "smells."

"When I start being turned on by someone's 'armpits,'" Clein wrote, "I know I'm in trouble. . . ."

The letter ended with a long admission of how Clein yearned to be with Beth Ann forever. It was a dream come true, he suggested. He was abandoning his better judgment and allowing his lust to make decisions for him. He also admitted that he wasn't so sure it was a good thing.

A few weeks went by without another letter. Then, on January 24, Clein penned one of his most troubling literary achievements to date. Indeed, the crowning jewel of love-letter writing—a document that would leave absolutely nothing to the imagination.

The letter was rife with sexual fantasies of the most bizarre type. Clein was in the midst, it was easy to tell, of losing the little bit of self-control he had left. By the time Beth Ann was finished reading the letter, she must have known that she could have ordered Clein to kill the pope and he would have agreed.

Clein opened the letter by saying he could not "survive" or "live" without her. "Every second of my day is filled with you." He then admitted that the minute she showed any type of "affection" for him, or paid attention to him in the slightest way, he became a "basket case." For whatever reason, Clein felt the need to say next that he "appreciated good-looking women, breasts in all condition, and responded to a heavy pass every now and then—but I have not had a relationship with anyone while living or going with another."

It was nonsense. He was cheating on his wife, Bonnie, with Beth Ann. He may not have had a "relationship" with anyone else, but, as many of his friends would later claim, he'd slept with just about any woman who'd have him.

He wrote next that, in his mind, the relationship between the two of them "was not an affair." It was his "heart as it had never been tugged or tested." Perhaps referring to the recent plot to murder Buzz, Clein said he would do "anything" for Beth Ann and "to protect me." He admitted that the "thought" of someone's threatening her "in any way," or making her feel "bad or hurt," made him "crazy."

After saying he had tried to "strangle" someone because he thought this unnamed person was being "offensive" to her, Clein said he hoped that the person did not take "it" any further. He was talking about an incident that happened in court one day, when Beth Ann had had some problems with someone in the courtroom.

Then, ironically, after saying how much he "respected" her, Clein began to show his true colors. "I love your ass," he wrote, "and want to taste it."

If he had stopped there, it would have been seen as nothing more than a humorous gesture or personal compliment between two adults.

But he continued.

"I want you to give me everything from inside of you." Then he said he "realized" he was probably sounding pretty disturbed by admitting to it, but "I want to taste your ass," he continued, "after you have gone to the bathroom."

He then asked Beth Ann to burn the letter after reading it, and to forgive him for what he was saying. Still he felt the need to continue.

He wrote next that he wanted Beth Ann to defecate on top of him. Afterward, he suggested, he would "spread it over [his] chest." When he was done with this so-called human mud bath, he saw Beth Ann, in a dominating role, ordering him to take a shower.

He admitted that their relationship had become "more than it should be."

Then he asked her not to be "grossed out" by what he was suggesting. It was obvious that they hadn't done anything like this in the bedroom before, but maybe this was Clein's way of suggesting they start. Regardless, he then said he "loved the thought of being inside" her, "especially [her] ass." Hinting at perhaps his own sexual dysfunction, Clein expressed next how worried he was at the thought of not being able to satisfy her fully. Then he said that, to him, she was this "powerful and strong figure who could command the earth."

Beth Ann had Clein right where she wanted him. Clein had hired a man to kill her brother-in-law, and now he was having anxiety over not being able to perform sexually in bed. It was all about Beth Ann. Whatever she wanted, she would get.

Ending the letter, Clein said that he wished "he could give [her] everything in the world"—which, in Beth Ann's mind, he was about to do.

During the early part of January, Joe Fremut and Mark Despres had gone to a car auction to purchase a few vehicles for Fremut Texaco. While they were walking around, Mark said, "Joey, guess what?"

"Yeah?"

"I joined this Devil worship cult."

Despres then stuck out his hand. Fremut looked down. There were three numeral 6s burned into Mark's hand. This was odd to Fremut, he later said, because Mark had always been a devout Christian.

"Come on, Mark. What's going on?"

"I denounce God now and worship Satan."

"What are you going to get out of that?"

"These people in the cult have connections to do hits, to kill people."

A few days later, they went to another auction.

"Listen," Despres explained as they walked around, "I have my first contract. It's a guy on the other side of the river."

The next day, Despres met Fremut at Despres's apartment. Fremut later recalled the conversation.

"His name is Buzz," Despres confessed. "He's a child molester. His own father-in-law is paying the money to have it done. I want you to help me. The money—about ten thousand dollars—will go to me through my attorney from the victim's father-in-law."

Dick Carpenter?

Despres met with Fremut again later and, according to Despres, they began discussing Fremut's role in the murder for hire.

"We would get paid eight thousand," Despres told Fremut.

"I also have a murder to do, Mark," Fremut said, not taking Despres seriously. "Will you help *me*?"

Fremut explained he wanted to go out to California and kill Catherine White's pimp. Despres knew White well. She would hang around with Despres's longtime girlfriend, Jocelyn Johnson, when the two men got together.

Investigators later said that the main reason why Fremut wanted White's pimp dead was because Fremut wanted her exclusively. There were reports that White would take a john up to a hotel room and, once there, Fremut would roll the guy for everything he had. Perhaps White's pimp was pissed off that Fremut was cutting in on his action.

"So you'll help me?" Despres asked.

"If you'll help me," Fremut said.

A day or so later, Despres went back to Haiman Clein's

office in New London to discuss further the payment plan they had originally set up. Despres wanted to be paid in full, he said. He had already gotten some money from Clein, which he never told Fremut about, and wanted to know when the rest of it was coming.

"Listen, Mark, there's a little problem. I only have five thousand dollars," Clein said.

"I could get it done for that," Despres offered.

When Clein realized that Despres wasn't going to haggle over the price, he told him to hold on for a moment, then walked out of the room.

Minutes later, Clein returned with Beth Ann.

As she sat and wept quietly, Clein later recalled, he explained to Despres that she was "financially strapped." He wanted Despres to be well aware of the fact that *he* was the one who was responsible for paying him, *not* Beth Ann.

Despres said he understood.

Paying Mark Despres to murder Buzz Clinton wasn't apparently at the top of Haiman Clein's growing list of debts. On February 14, Valentine's Day, Clein—in near financial ruin, on the verge of losing his Watertown home to the bank, his investment properties crumbling like Lincoln Logs, his law practice nearly out of business—gave Beth Ann a $5,000 necklace.

A few weeks after that, he gave her a $2,530 ring.

Investigators would track down later where Clein bought the jewelry. The $2,530 ring was purchased in Winter Park, Florida. Oddly enough, Clein, at this point in his life, was broke.

So where was he getting all this money to buy Beth Ann nearly $8,000 worth of jewelry in the span of two weeks?

Walter Cox had been a wealthy client of Clein's for years. Clein had handled fiduciary matters for Cox: estate planning, business matters, etc. Examining Cox's

American Express records, investigators found that Clein had not only paid for a trip to Florida for his entire family (Bonnie and the four kids), but bought the jewelry for Beth Ann with Cox's American Express card while they were there.

Clein would admit later to embezzling nearly $500,000 from Cox.

With the end of February quickly approaching, Mark Despres began telling people he was going to begin following Buzz around town, looking for a suitable time to, as he explained it to Joe Fremut, "do him."

But there was only one problem: Despres was having trouble locating him. Despres would sit out in the parking lot of Pettipaug Manor, the convalescent home where Buzz had been working now for the past few weeks, and wait for him to emerge. Or maybe he would drive over to Buzz's apartment in East Lyme and just sit in the parking lot.

But after a week or so, the opportunity never presented itself, Despres later said. Plus, he still wasn't sure what Buzz actually looked like.

There was one time when Despres and Fremut had driven to Pettipaug Manor to stake out Buzz's tow truck. Since the time Despres had told Fremut about the murder-for-hire plot, Fremut had suggested they capture Buzz, torture him, wrap him in a blanket and throw him into the nearby Niantic River. Clein had explained to Despres that Buzz drove a tow truck. So Despres and Fremut drove into the rear parking lot of Pettipaug Manor and began looking for it one day. When they didn't spot what Clein had described as a "red wrecker," Despres drove Fremut back to his house and went home.

As the days passed, and Despres began to track Buzz's movements more thoroughly, he opted not to bring Fremut. Instead, Despres began bringing along Chris, his fifteen-year-old son.

One of the first times Chris had gotten an inkling that there was something going on was at the local IGA supermarket in downtown Essex. Mark and Chris were walking around the store when they happened to come upon Clein as he was shopping.

Mark sent Chris away. He said he had some private business with Clein. A few minutes later, when Mark returned and met Chris in the car, Chris asked him about his conversation with Clein.

"Nothing," Mark said. "Don't worry about it."

Days later, however, when pressed again, Mark explained the entire murder-for-hire plot to Chris.

"I've been paid ten thousand dollars to kill a man from Old Lyme," Mark told his son, as if they were discussing a contract Mark had received to paint a house.

When Chris thought about it, he later said, he considered it to be a joke. He really didn't think his father and Fremut were serious about going through with it.

When Mark couldn't locate Buzz, he went over to Fremut Texaco to talk it over with Fremut. He needed some advice. He knew Fremut would set him straight.

Catherine White was there when Despres showed up. She was inside the lobby area of the garage, just hanging around, while Mark and Joe were around the corner in the garage. They couldn't see White, but she could clearly hear what they were talking about.

"I'm having trouble locating this guy," Despres said in frustration. "I've been watching him for several days, but I can't get him alone."

"Well, Mark, don't worry about it—"

"Don't worry about it? Everywhere he goes is not a good place to get this done."

"Listen," Fremut said, "where there's a will, there's a way."

Convinced there must be another way, days later,

Despres went back to Fremut Texaco to discuss other options. Again White was there.

White watched as the two men went out in the back of the garage and began test-firing several different weapons. Several skeletons of junk cars lay around the property. It was a Sunday. Business was slow. With no one around, Despres and Fremut took turns. Fremut sat in a car with the windows rolled up and fired a weapon while Despres stood outside and listened.

Fremut stepped out of the car, and he and Despres talked about how loud the gun sounded from outside the vehicle. They wanted to be sure that if they shot Buzz inside a car, the noise wouldn't attract any attention.

As the day progressed, White looked on as Despres and Fremut test-fired several different guns under different conditions. Sometimes Fremut would turn the radio on in the car and fire off a few rounds, increasing the volume in increments.

"How was that?" he'd yell afterward.

At one point, Fremut broke out a crossbow, and they started taking target practice. Despres admitted later that they were checking the various weapons for "accuracy, distance and power." Despres thought perhaps he was going to have to kill Buzz from afar, and he wanted to be sure he had the right weapon for the job.

Days later, Fremut and White went over to Despres's apartment. Despres wanted to show Fremut a .25-caliber automatic pistol he owned. For the past week or so, Fremut and Despres had been discussing making a silencer and even purchased a handbook on how to do it. Despres had called Fremut up to say he'd made a silencer for a 9mm Fremut owned. He wanted to show it to him.

After showing Fremut how the silencer fit perfectly on the weapon, Despres said, "Let's go out back and try it out."

Despres also brought a .38-caliber Saturday night

special he'd owned and a .22-caliber rifle. The .38 had a brown handle, White later recalled, and a black frame. The serial numbers, she noticed, had been filed off. In their place, Despres had engraved FUCK YOU PIG.

"Where'd you get that?" Fremut asked Despres.

"A biker friend of mine I buy my cocaine from."

As they took turns firing the various weapons, White listened as Despres explained to Fremut how he had been stalking Buzz lately.

"I've been standing behind his house, watching him at night. But the person who wants it done doesn't want any of his kids around when I do it."

Sometime later, Despres finally confessed to Fremut that he was getting paid between $5,000 and $10,000. This time, Fremut believed him.

When Fremut heard the amount, he laughed. "It doesn't seem like a lot of money to shoot someone, Mark," he said.

Mark Despres called Haiman Clein a few days after he and Joe Fremut had practiced firing weapons and told Clein he was having trouble finding Buzz. He thought he had seen him a few times, but he just wasn't sure it was Buzz. He didn't need to tell Clein that it would be a disaster if he killed the wrong guy.

"Come in today! We need to talk," Clein said.

As Despres sat down in Clein's office later that afternoon, Clein began pacing. Then he started yelling at Mark. It was obvious from what Clein had to say that Beth Ann was putting the squeeze on him to get the job done.

"Why the fuck is this not done yet?" Clein asked in a rage. "Huh? It's taking too fucking long. Just get it done!"

"I'll give you back the money if you want," Despres offered.

Turning red, Clein began walking out of the room.

But before opening the door, he said, "You stay right here, Mark. Don't move."

When Clein returned, Beth Ann was behind him.

"He drives a black Firebird," Beth Ann mumbled in a whisper, looking at Despres. Then, without saying anything else, she handed Clein a photograph of Buzz, Kim, and Rebecca. They were standing, Clein later recalled, in "front of a hearth." Clein recognized it immediately as being the one in the living room of the Carpenters' Ledyard home.

"It was a wooden hearth, not a big fireplace or anything like that," Clein said later. "If you walk into the house, it's to the left."

Clein had been over to the Carpenters' house several times. Beth Ann had told him previously that she had gotten the photograph from her parents. Many later speculated that the photo must have been taken when Buzz and Kim went over to the Carpenters for the 1993 Labor Day picnic. In all likelihood, it was the only time the Carpenters would've had a chance to photograph Buzz at their house. They had been fighting with the man for nearly a year by that point. Taking family photographs didn't seem to be at the top of their priority list.

With Despres sitting patiently, not saying much, Clein pulled a pair of scissors out of his desk drawer and cut Buzz's face, from the neck up, out of the photograph. The new photo was about the size of a nickel.

"Here," Clein said, handing Despres the cutout. "Now you go find that motherfucker!"

Chapter 26

During the afternoon of February 20, 1994, Catherine White and Joe Fremut were hanging around Fremut Texaco when Mark Despres pulled into the parking lot, parked his car by one of the garage bays, got out and walked casually over to where they were standing. As was generally the case lately, Chris Despres was right behind his dad.

"Catherine, go do something," Fremut said, wiping his hands off with a rag.

"I can't find the opportune time to do him, Joe," Despres said in frustration. "I've been following him around but just can't seem to get him alone."

"Continue to follow him around," Fremut urged. "The moment will present itself."

Later that night, White finally confronted Fremut about what she suspected.

"Mark picked up this contract for eight thousand dollars to do this guy from Old Lyme," Fremut said without hesitation.

This was the first time White had heard directly from Fremut that he and Despres were going to kill someone.

Things abruptly changed one day near the end of February. Clein and Beth Ann had gotten into, Clein later said, a "petty argument," and Clein got so upset at her that he called the murder off.

"Forget about it," Clein told Despres over the phone the following day.

At first, Despres didn't say anything.

"You hear me?" Clein said again.

"Okay," Despres said. Then, thinking about it for a moment, he asked, "Do you want me to lower the price?"

"*No!* It's off."

Later, Clein explained that it was possibly his moral compass on that day beckoning him to look for a reason to call it off. He said the argument had been so trivial it shouldn't have been enough to make him mad enough to cancel the contract. "I reasoned with myself that I shouldn't be doing this for her—that why should I do this for her? I might have just been looking for a reason to call it off."

Somewhat amazed by the recent turn of events, after realizing how serious Clein was, Despres said, "Fine, no problem."

Later that night, Clein showed up at Beth Ann's condo and explained how he'd called it off.

Beth Ann didn't say much of anything one way or the other, Clein later said, and just let it go.

At least for the time being.

Haiman Clein and Beth Ann's life together stayed pretty much plain and simple for the next week or so. They continued sleeping together, dining out and working together, but the subject of Buzz's murder, according to Clein, hadn't been as much a part of their conversation as it had been in recent months. Throughout the past few weeks, Beth Ann had noticed an increase in Clein's anxiety, though. He would sweat profusely, she later said. He would shake. His skin was pasty and clammy. There were times when he would become enraged for no apparent reason. They might be driving down the road and Clein would snap and begin banging his head against the windshield. She suspected he was abusing drugs, but she never called him on it.

A short time after they had first slept together back in November 1993, Beth Ann went to Clein and explained how ashamed she felt about the relationship. He was married, for heaven's sake. He had children. He was her boss.

"Bonnie and I," Clein admitted, "haven't had sex in three years. She criticizes me for all of my business failures. Anyway, she's having an affair with a Connecticut college professor!"

By then, Beth Ann later admitted, she was in love with Clein.

"I was impressed by his stature." He was an older man, a professional. "He was the board director at a local bank. I looked up to him."

She said she could learn things from Clein that she couldn't from anyone else. Since the affair had begun, Clein had made a key to Beth Ann's condo. He would leave work early and go cook for her. While she shopped or worked out, he would prepare gourmet dinners. He would show up the next morning with doughnuts and coffee.

But now, three months later, they were planning a murder together. Gourmet dinners, trips to Florida, working out at the local spa and shopping excursions seemed like some domestic fantasy. They were in this thing together now. Unless Beth Ann wanted to call it off completely, as she had said, there was no turning back.

Beth Ann was on the phone one afternoon near the end of February talking to someone in her family, when suddenly she broke into tears, crying as if there had been a death in the family. Hysterical, Clein later remembered, she began shaking, mumbling things he couldn't understand.

Something had happened to Rebecca, Beth Ann said after hanging up—something really, *really* bad.

"What is it?" Clein asked. "Tell me."

"Buzz locked Rebecca in the basement. . . . She had a burn mark on her back. The whole family is upset."

Indeed, the entire Carpenter family, Clein soon learned, had been in a frenzy over the incident ever since they'd picked Rebecca up for the weekend.

Moments later, Clein and Beth Ann took off to her Norwich condo. As they drove, Clein picked up his cell phone and called Cynthia Carpenter. Beth Ann, sitting beside him, was panic-stricken and crying; she was carrying on about how bad the situation still was for Rebecca.

"It won't go on much longer," Clein promised Cynthia over the phone. "It" wasn't stated, but it was certainly implicit: "it" meant the alleged abuse Buzz was perpetrating against Rebecca.

Locked in the cellar? A burn mark on her back?

When they got to Beth Ann's condo, she asked Clein if he could "call Mark and tell him to go ahead with it?" Looking into his eyes, as serious as she had ever been, she said, "I'll pay for it if I have to."

"I will," Clein reassured her. "Don't worry about it."

At the office the next day, Beth Ann repeated her previous offer. "I'll pay the remaining three thousand. You *have* to get Mark to go through with it."

Buzz was never charged with any type of abuse against Rebecca. Neither DCYS, the Family Services Unit, which had investigated every allegation made against Buzz, nor the state's attorney's office ever brought charges against him for abuse of any kind. It was all lies, many later said, made up to convince those involved to kill Buzz. This most recent event arose from an incident that took place at Buzz and Kim's new apartment. Rebecca, Dee Clinton later said, had fallen against a space heater and burned her back. The entire Clinton family had heard about it. Buzz had never locked her in the basement or burned her with a cigarette. The story had been fabricated, many later claimed, to get Clein back into the mind-set of rehiring Despres to kill Buzz.

"What did Haiman say about that incident that led him to reinstate this murder?" Kevin Kane , Connecticut State's attorney, later asked. "It was those phone calls in which [Beth Ann] was so upset from talking about Rebecca having been burned."

The issue of Rebecca's being burned quickly worked its way to the murder team. Within days, Clein told Despres, which only solidified Despres's personal theory that Buzz was a "scumbag" who deserved to die; then Despres told Fremut, who told White, and finally Chris found out.

After explaining to Chris that Buzz had to die because he was abusing a child, Despres said, "He's putting cigarettes out on [her] back, for Christ's sake."

What more proof was needed? Despres reasoned. The courts weren't doing anything. The Carpenters weren't doing anything. It was time Buzz Clinton paid for his repulsive acts against children.

Despres had been game since day one; he needed very little convincing. To him, Buzz was a child molester. So when Clein called him back and told him to go through with it, Despres said, "No problem."

Still, Mark had to convince Chris that they were doing the right thing.

A former friend of Mark Despres's recalled later how Mark had justified the murder to Chris; told him how he had proof that Buzz was sexually abusing Rebecca.

"Chris told me that Mark played some tape for him that had the child being abused. Whoever had approached them to do this said it was awful that there was a screaming child on the tape. . . . The reason they were going to do the hit was that there was this child screaming on the tape."

According to that same friend, Mark believed the tape

was of Buzz raping Rebecca. He said Clein had played the tape for him one day when he was in his office. Clein insisted that the man on the tape was Buzz and the screaming child was Rebecca.

This seems almost impossible, however.

If Mark believed that a person would record himself raping a child, or that a third party would record it but not do anything to stop it, then Clein could have probably talked Mark Despres into anything. He was as gullible as a child.

Nonetheless, regardless of the truth, this tape was positive proof to Mark that Buzz "needed to be taken off the face of the earth"—and murder, in Mark Despres's twisted mind, was the only justifiable way to accomplish that task.

By the beginning of March, seven different people— Mark Despres, Haiman Clein, Beth Ann Carpenter, Chris Despres, Catherine White, Jocelyn Johnson, and Joe Fremut—knew of the plot to murder Buzz. Yet no one went to the police and, subsequently, saved Buzz's life.

Chapter 27

If he had his way, inside of the next few weeks, Mark Despres would be basking in the sunshine of Florida, living off the blood money he was being paid to kill Buzz—that is, providing he could get Buzz alone somewhere.

During the first week of March, Despres had even called Pettipaug a few times from a pay phone across the street from Fremut Texaco to see if Buzz had been working. But he never seemed to be there when Despres phoned.

With that, Despres's frustration began to mount.

On March 6, 1994, Despres picked up Fremut, and they drove to Pettipaug for the second time that week. This was it. No more screwing around. They were going to find Buzz Clinton, stuff him into the car and, on some remote stretch of road, blow his brains out—the same way they had rehearsed.

Before they got to the parking lot, Fremut took the wheel. Then he pulled around into the rear parking lot of the building, dropped off Despres and drove around to the front of the building, where he waited for Despres to give him the signal that Buzz's tow truck was parked out back.

"We were just looking to follow [Buzz] . . . so we could get an idea where [he] goes . . . so we could shoot him," Despres later recalled.

But Buzz wasn't anywhere to be found.

The following day, Clein called.

"Have you found him?"

"Nope."

"Come into the office!"

Later that day, Despres drove to New London.

"What the fuck is going on?" Clein demanded. He and Despres hadn't spoken for some time. Clein assumed Despres was close to finishing the job. He expected to pick up the newspaper any day now and see that it had been done.

"He must be driving something else. I can't locate him," Despres said.

Despres's instincts were spot on. Buzz had been driving a Pontiac Firebird he and Kim had recently purchased. The tow truck hadn't been running well.

Clein had always been unsparing and strict, like a scolding parent, when conveying his demands to Despres. Despres, whose own father had hit him repeatedly and left him, perhaps looked to Clein as the father figure he never had. In one way, Despres, a man certainly capable of snapping Clein's neck as if it were a twig, was frightened of Clein. If Clein was capable of commissioning one murder, why not two? Despres even went to his on-again, off-again girlfriend, Jocelyn Johnson, one night and admitted how scared he was. He told Johnson Clein had given him a photograph of Buzz, but he was still having trouble identifying him from the photograph alone. He told her that Clein was "aggravated" that the murder hadn't yet been carried out, and Clein had even threatened his life, saying at one point, "You'll be next if you don't carry out the murder." Despres gave Johnson the "impression," she later said, that he "didn't want to go through with" it. But he was terrified and felt he had to because he'd already spent the down payment Clein had given him to buy a gun and car.

As Despres shuffled a bit in his chair, watching Clein

grow angrier because Buzz was still alive, Despres said, "I called him a couple of times, Haiman—"

"What the hell for?" Clein asked, interrupting.

"I was thinking of asking him to tow a car for me."

"You're making me look like an *asshole!*" Clein screamed.

"This isn't something you can just do anywhere, Haiman."

During one of their first meetings, Clein had been very specific regarding how he wanted Buzz killed, making a point to tell Despres *not* to kill Buzz in front of his children or near his home. He wanted it done privately, he said, with no one around. But things were clearly different now. Something had dramatically changed the stakes.

"Do it on the fucking sidewalk," Clein said. "On the road. *Anywhere!* Just fucking do it!"

Out of the corner of his eye, Despres could see Beth Ann through the door window in Clein's office. She was peering in from her office, undoubtedly curious about what was being said.

Despres then asked Clein if he wanted his money back.

"No. Just get it done."

"How?"

"His wrecker is for sale. Just call him up and tell him you want to look at the wrecker—and then . . . get rid of him!"

Since being hired by Clein, Despres had made it a habit to stop and let Fremut in on the latest details about the murder plan. So after leaving Clein's office, Despres drove to Fremut's to talk.

"His wrecker is for sale," Despres told Fremut as they stood outside in the parking lot. "The best way for us to get rid of him is to make believe we're going to buy the wrecker."

"Sounds like a good enough idea to me," Fremut said.

Despres then walked across the street, called Buzz and explained that he wanted to look at the wrecker.

"I'm too tired to come out," Buzz said. "Call me tomorrow night."

Despres hung up and walked back to the garage.

"So?" Fremut asked.

"He said he's too tired."

Despres was clearly disappointed. Things had gone on too long. It seemed the longer they waited, the harder it was becoming.

"Keep trying," Fremut urged.

The same scenario played out twenty-four hours later when Despres called Buzz again from the same pay phone.

"I'm too tired," Buzz repeated. "Try me again tomorrow night."

Dee Clinton had recently turned forty-seven. She owned a successful kennel and had raised three beautiful children. She never wanted anything more. Buck Clinton was the wrestling coach at Wethersfield High School. He had been involved with the sport his entire life. His kids respected him. The Clintons had had their share of troubles, but they always came together as a family to overcome whatever obstacle was put in their way. Since Dee had gotten to know Kim over the past year and a half, she began to understand that Kim was one of the main reasons why her son had changed so much lately. Buzz seemed ready to settle down. Now, with this issue of custody almost behind them, Dee surmised that Buzz, Kim, Rebecca and Briana could begin their lives together as a family—but, more important, without any meddling from the Carpenters.

On March 9, 1994, Dee had been over at Buzz and Kim's apartment because Briana had been ill, which was likely the reason why Buzz had told Despres for two consecutive days that he couldn't meet him. Buzz wanted to be home with his daughter. She was sick. Everything else could wait.

Dee brought a pair of shoes for Rebecca and some medicine for Briana when she showed up that night. Buzz was on the couch. Kim was sitting on the floor holding Briana. Rebecca was her old self, "buzzing around the living room," having a grand old time, Dee later recalled.

While she was there, Buzz had taken a call. When he got off the phone, he told Dee it was "the guy I'm going to meet. He wants to look at my wrecker. When you get home tonight, Ma, put my battery on the charger. I need to charge it before I meet him."

Dee said she would.

"I'll bring the battery back here tomorrow," Dee said, and explained that she was coming back over anyway to pick up Kim so they could go shopping. Dee said she'd be there around 6:00 P.M.. By her bringing the battery, she added, it would save Buzz a trip.

"Sounds good to me, Ma."

Around 5:30 P.M., on March 10, Mark Despres drove over to Fremut Texaco with Chris. Catherine White, along with a friend of hers, was at the garage hanging around.

"I'm going to call Clinton about the wrecker," Despres said after pulling Fremut aside for a moment.

"I'll come with you," Fremut said.

Mark and Chris, after talking with Fremut for a few moments, got into Despres's car and hightailed it out of the parking lot. Fremut and White followed.

About fifteen minutes later, near 6:00 P.M., with Fremut behind him, Despres pulled off Exit 64, on Interstate 95 in Westbrook. One of Connecticut's many state police barracks was up ahead, not more than half a mile away. At the end of the exit, Despres pulled into a commuter parking lot where there was a pay phone.

As White watched, Fremut and Despres got out of

their cars and walked toward the pay phone. But before they approached the phone, Fremut grabbed Despres by the arm.

"I can't come with you," he said. "I have something else I need to do tonight."

"So I'm supposed to go by *myself?*" Despres had planned the murder with Fremut from the start. Here it was, *show time,* and Fremut was bailing out?

"Just go do it! It's no big deal."

"What the fuck, Joe?"

Just then, Chris came walking up.

"Bring Chris with you," Fremut suggested, pointing at him. "Have him do it for you."

"Yeah, right."

What at first seemed like an idiotic suggestion became one of the only options Mark had left.

So he asked Chris if he wanted to go along.

"I want three hundred dollars and a gun," Chris said.

"I'll throw in a bag of weed, too," Mark said.

Mark later said he would have given Chris the money and weed anyway. It didn't matter that Chris had agreed to go along.

Fremut then got into his car and took off. A disgusted Despres watched Fremut barrel out of the parking lot. Then he picked up the telephone and called Buzz.

"So, can I take a look at the wrecker tonight, or what?" Despres asked when Buzz answered.

"Sure. I can show it to you anytime tonight," Buzz said.

"How is it? In good shape?"

Buzz had painted it recently. It was old, but it looked as if it had been well taken care of.

Despres later said he then made small talk with Buzz so as to make the call seem legit.

"It's bad on gas," Buzz offered.

They then agreed to meet at the Howard Johnson restaurant parking lot, in Old Saybrook. HoJo's, as it was called, was at the intersection of Route 9 and Interstate 95. The Connecticut River, which runs parallel to Route 9, dumps into the Atlantic Ocean at the same intersection. The Baldwin Bridge acts as somewhat of a town line between Old Lyme and Old Saybrook.

"How's seven o'clock?" Buzz asked Despres.

"I'll see you then."

Shortly after Buzz hung up with Despres, Dee phoned to tell him that she was running late and wouldn't have a chance to drop off the battery until later on that night when she picked Kim up to go shopping.

"I'm not going to make it by six, Buzz," Dee said. "There's no way I can finish all of my work. Sorry."

"I need that battery. I'm meeting this guy."

"The earliest I can do is seven."

"Just leave the battery out. I'll pick it up on my way out."

When Mark and Chris arrived at Despres's Deep River home after talking to Buzz, Mark pulled his .38-caliber Saturday night special out of the drawer where he stored it, loaded six rounds and put it in his shoulder holster.

The gun, bought sometime in early 1994, had been purchased by Jocelyn Johnson, Despres's girlfriend, at Ron's Gun Shop, in Niantic. Despres was with Johnson when she purchased it, and had even picked it out.

After loading his gun, Mark sat down next to Chris to watch television. It was about 6:45 P.M. They didn't have to meet Buzz until somewhere around 7:00 P.M. With HoJo's about a ten-minute drive south on Route 9, there wasn't much left to do except wait.

Despres had traded in his white Buick Skylark and purchased a blue Buick Regal for the specific reason of killing Buzz. The plan was to meet with Buzz and tell him he wanted to take the wrecker for a drive to check it out. Despres would then tell Buzz that Chris would follow them in the Regal. Once they got going, Despres would pull off somewhere in the woods and blow Buzz's brains out in the truck.

As Chris and Mark were getting ready to take off for Old Saybrook, Chris asked what they were going to do. The boy still seemed to think it was, perhaps, all a joke.

"We're going to kill that guy," Despres said matter-of-factly.

If Chris had thought his dad would never go through with the actual murder, now it was clear that he was serious. Chris watched as his dad loaded a weapon, shouldered it and made several calls over a two-day period to hook up a meeting with Buzz. There was even one time a few days back when Despres and Fremut were fanning through the *Bargain News,* a local newspaper that sold cars and trucks, and came upon a For-Sale ad Buzz had placed for the wrecker. Mark recognized the phone number in the ad as being the same as the number on Buzz's tow truck. When Mark and Joe began discussing the notion of calling Buzz and luring him away under the guise of buying the tow truck, Chris's name came up as being the possible triggerman.

Then, as Mark walked away for a minute as the three of them were sitting around and joking about things, Fremut put his arm around Chris and, slapping him on the back as though he'd just whacked a two-run homer for his Little League team, said, "I'm going to make you a hit man, Chris!"

They all laughed.

Chris could do nothing else except look at Fremut and wonder what he was getting himself mixed up in. What seemed at first like a plot for some sort of twisted game of Dungeons & Dragons was now materializing into reality.

When Buzz showed up at his parents' house in Old Lyme to pick up the battery, Buck was cooking dinner. In the foyer, to the right, on the wall, were photos of

Buzz and all the kids. The Clinton home wasn't by any means one of the larger homes in Old Lyme, but it was a warm place of solitude and strength for Buzz Clinton. He knew his family loved him. Buck and Dee, although they were tough on their son when he needed it, would have done anything for Buzz—and usually did.

"You stayin' for supper, Buzz?" Buck asked.

"No. I'm in a rush, Dad. I've got to get out of here as soon as possible."

As they were talking, Suzanne, Buzz's sister, came running into the kitchen. There was a play area off to the side of the kitchen where Suzanne had been playing when Buzz arrived. Suzanne looked up to her much older brother as though he were a movie star. She adored and idolized him.

"Buzz was her everything," Dee recalled later.

Buzz had always found the time to stop whatever he was doing and give his sister a hug and kiss on the cheek, or maybe even play with her if he had enough time. Tonight was no different.

After Suzanne hugged Buzz and kissed him on the cheek, she said in her comforting and well-mannered voice, "I love you, Buzz Clinton."

"I love you, too, honey. But I have to get going now."

With that, Buzz walked out the door of his childhood home en route toward a death sentence for which he had no idea he had already been tried, convicted and sentenced.

Chris and Mark showed up at HoJo's early, about 7:05 P.M. As soon as Mark pulled into the parking lot and spied who he thought was Buzz waiting for him, he knew he would have to scrap his previous plan of killing him in the wrecker—because Buzz was driving the old beatup Firebird he and Kim had just bought.

Curious as to why Buzz wasn't driving the wrecker,

Despres pulled up alongside, rolled down his window and asked, "Are you the guy with the wrecker?"

"Yes," Buzz said. "I want you to follow me to Niantic, where my house is. I'll show you the wrecker there."

Despres looked at his son for a moment without saying anything. Then, turning to Buzz, he said, "That'll work."

Buzz pulled out of the HoJo's parking lot and began heading north on Interstate 95. Despres, his mind racing, stayed right behind him.

Despres was stuck. How the hell was he going to do it? He hadn't made a contingency plan.

After Buzz drove over the Baldwin Bridge and continued on I-95 for about three minutes, he put his blinker on to get off on Exit 72, the Rocky Neck State Park Beach connector.

For Mark Despres, it was the perfect spot to commit murder.

"It was a spur-of-the-moment thing," Despres later said. "No cars were coming."

As the two men drifted off the exit and began merging onto the connector, Chris, as Mark began flashing his lights at Buzz, asked what was going on. Buzz's apartment was only miles down the road; they were going to be there in a few minutes.

"I'm going to kill him right here," Mark said.

About midway down the connector, Buzz noticed that Despres was flashing his lights, so he pulled over.

With his car still running, the driver's-side door wide open, Buzz got out and began walking toward Despres's vehicle. Chris, looking down at the floorboards, knowing what was about to happen, froze. Reality and fantasy had now merged into a seamless blur of what Chris had thought all along was some sort of joke.

"What's going on?" Buzz asked as he moved toward Despres.

"I need to get some gas," Despres said as he got out of his car.

Without even thinking about what he was doing, Despres used his driver's-side door as a rest to steady his .38, pointed it at Buzz and fired.

It took only seconds. Chris never looked up. He only heard the shots and saw flashes of light, like lightning, out of the corner of his eye.

Despres, quickly getting back into his car, watched as Buzz fell to the ground like a rag doll. Stunned, Chris turned and saw headlights coming over the crest of the hill in back of them.

A witness?

As the car came closer, Mark put the car in reverse—he had to back up a bit to get around Buzz's body—hit the gas pedal and sped away.

"He backed up a little first," Chris remembered later. "Turned left and drove off. I believe he ran over [Buzz]."

"I heard a thump under the car," Despres added later, "and realized I ran [him] over."

Chapter 28

In what seemed like only seconds to Chris Despres, he and his father had driven from the Rocky Neck connector back to the Baldwin Bridge. When they had left the scene, Mark said later, he thought he was "going about eighty or ninety miles per hour." Making a hard right at the end of the connector, Despres's car went into a four-wheel slide as he twisted and turned the steering wheel to keep the vehicle on the road.

"Dad," Chris screamed, "don't crash it now!"

When they arrived at Despres's apartment, Mark pulled up alongside the garage. Scared, Chris took off inside while Mark went into the garage.

Once inside the garage, Mark took out a ball-peen hammer and, with violent strikes, began thrashing at the gun as small portions of it broke off and scattered. Then he got out a die grinder. The gun had no serial number, but he still needed to, as Clein had suggested, dismantle it.

By 9:00 P.M., Mark had the gun broken down into several pieces, some of which he placed in his coat pocket. After sweeping what he could off the floor, he grabbed Chris and took off to Fremut's apartment. Catherine White was there when they showed up. She remembered later that Mark was "frantic" and manic when they arrived.

"I did it, Joe," Despres said in front of White.

Fremut didn't say anything. Instead, he grabbed Mark by the arm and pulled him into the hallway.

"I didn't know when to stop, Joe. I didn't . . . I . . . ," Mark said, talking fast.

"What?"

"It was a rush, Joe."

At that point, Mark and Joe took off, most likely to get rid of whatever was left of the gun. Fremut had tools in the garage, and investigators later found pieces of the weapon in the Dumpster out back of Fremut Texaco. Although White didn't see them do it, it was possible they had gone into Fremut's garage and cut the gun into smaller pieces.

With Joe and Mark gone, Chris sat with White inside Fremut's apartment and talked.

"Have you been with your dad all night?" White asked.

"My dad's cool," Chris said. He was smiling and seemed unmoved by the night's events. "He said he's going to buy me a motorbike and take me camping." Then he added, "I feel like smoking some drugs about now."

Forty-five minutes after Mark and Joe had taken off, they returned. Without saying much, Mark motioned to Chris that it was time to go.

While driving south along Route 9, Mark pulled off Exit 3. Down at the end of the exit, to the right, was a Sunoco station.

Just off the exit ramp, Mark stopped the car, had Chris roll down his window, and told him to throw a few pieces of the .38 into the woods behind the Sunoco station.

After that, Mark hopped back onto Route 9 south and eventually ended up back on Interstate 95, heading north, in the direction of the Rocky Neck connector. Mark had decided to drive over to Jocelyn Johnson's house in Old Lyme and hang out for a while. He was confused. He had just killed a man. As with most inexperienced murderers,

Mark had planned everything up until the time of the actual murder. Now he was scrambling around, trying to get rid of evidence, wondering what to do next.

While crossing the Baldwin Bridge for the second time that night, Mark stopped midway over the bridge and threw the remaining pieces of the weapon into the Connecticut River below him. Less than a mile away, state police, local police and several bystanders were standing over the dead body of Anson "Buzz" Clinton. Dee Clinton was sitting in traffic only yards from where her son lay dead in the road—and she didn't even know what was going on. Kim, seven months pregnant, unknowingly now a widow, was at home waiting for Dee to pick her up so they could go shopping.

When Chris and Mark arrived at Jocelyn Johnson's house, Mark spied Johnson's brother working on his car in the garage. Chris stayed in the car. Mark walked past Johnson's brother without saying a word.

After only about five minutes, Mark emerged from Johnson's house, having only made "small talk" with her, he later said, and he and Chris drove back home.

When they arrived, Mark turned on the television. And after watching the nightly news, he and Chris went to sleep.

Early the next morning, March 11, at about 6:30, Beth Ann called Haiman Clein at his home. Clein was in bed with his wife. They had been sleeping when the phone rang.

"Buzz has been killed," Beth Ann said in a nervous slather of words. "Come over right away. I'm afraid. Scared. Come now!"

"I'll be right over."

While Clein was pulling up his trousers, Bonnie Clein woke up.

"What's going on?"

"Buzz Clinton," Haiman said, "has been killed. I'm going over to Beth's to see if anybody needs me."

Clein had been urging Despres for about the past two weeks to get the job done. Driving over to Beth Ann's, Clein now knew he had but only a few things left to do—the first, of course, was to pay Despres the remainder of the money he owed him. If Clein had had the upper hand on March 10 and the days preceding it, Despres now controlled the situation. Clein wasn't stupid. He knew Despres would be calling him shortly for the money.

As if it were just another day, Clein stopped first at a doughnut shop down the street from Beth Ann's condo to pick up coffee and doughnuts. But as soon as he opened the door to her condo, he could tell Beth Ann had been devastated by what had happened.

"She was scared out of her mind," Clein later said.

Setting the doughnuts and coffee on the counter, Clein tried reassuring her that everything was going to be all right. "You don't have to be scared," he said. "No one can know about anything."

As far as Clein understood it, he, Despres and Beth Ann were the only ones who had known about the murder. In truth, though, seven different people were involved—one of whom was a teenager. The chances of one of them not coming forward once the pressure was put on were unrealistic. Mark Despres had broken the one golden rule any professional hit man adhered to: tell no one.

While Clein comforted Beth Ann, telling her repeatedly that everything was going to be okay, she began pointing at the ceiling. Then, pulling Clein down toward her, she whispered into his ear, "Bugs."

"It couldn't be," Clein said.

Indeed, there was no chance that law enforcement, even if it had known that Clein and Beth Ann had been involved, could have placed a bug in her condo that quickly. It was impossible.

But for Beth Ann, fear had now replaced any hate she had for Buzz. She was petrified that someone was going to find out. It was another sign, some later concluded, of her guilt.

During the two hours Clein spent at Beth Ann's condo that morning, he later said, she had "several conversations" with her parents by telephone. But every time Clein tried to bring up the murder and discuss their next move, she would put her hand over his mouth and tell him, in a whisper, to keep quiet. Then she'd point to the ceiling . . .

Bugs.

After speaking to her parents one final time that morning, Beth Ann hung up the phone and told Clein the cops were in Ledyard asking her parents questions. "We need to get over there right now."

"Okay," Clein said. Then he said, "Relax, would you?"

Bugs.

During the car ride, Beth Ann refused to discuss anything having to do with the murder. The car was bugged, she repeated over and over and over. Clein later said she was "frantic," worried sick that someone was listening to their every word.

Mark Despres had finally gotten hold of Clein on Friday, March 11, the day after the killing. Clein said he couldn't meet with Despres on that particular day, but they would hook up soon. During the conversation, Despres told Clein everything he could remember about the details of the murder—including the fact he had brought along Chris.

"But I need the rest of that money, Haiman," Despres begged.

Clein fell silent, then said, "Meet me at the office on Monday."

Over the past few days, Beth Ann had become so obsessed with the notion of the cops tracking her and

Clein's every move and listening in on their conversations that she refused to speak to him at all. When Clein finally told her what Despres had said about bringing along Chris, it only added to her paranoia. Every time she saw Clein, she wouldn't utter a word without first patting him down to see if he was wired like an informant. To Clein, it wasn't a big deal. He felt closer to her now than he ever had.

The only thing that bothered Clein was that they weren't discussing things enough. They needed to talk about times, dates and where they were on the day of the murder.

One day, as Beth Ann was patting Clein down, she whispered, "I'm in denial, Haiman."

Clein didn't know what to think, so he continued trying to get her to talk. But she repeatedly refused.

Then they took off with two other couples to Madison Square Garden in New York City for a college basketball tournament. Clein had insisted they go. They had to do normal things.

While in their New York hotel room, Clein thought it was the perfect place to discuss the murder and how they were going to handle the next few weeks and months. But Beth Ann "freaked out" and kept "shushing" him, not letting him finish a thought. Then she would walk around the room and point behind the radiators and up at the ceiling.

Bugs.

When they got inside a cab to go downtown, Clein tried once again to talk about things, but she shook her head, held her fingers to her lips and pointed at the cabdriver.

"We can't talk. *Shhh* . . ."

Chapter 29

By Saturday, March 12, 1994, the impact of her eldest son's death had finally hit Dee Clinton. Like any mother, Dee was consumed by grief and sorrow. She had sat in traffic on the night her son was murdered, merely yards away from his dead body, and didn't know it until later that night when state police gave her the heartbreaking news. Now, days later, with the cruelty and horror of Buzz's death unearthed, Dee somehow had to find the strength to manage a business and plan a funeral.

How life could change in an instant.

Suzanne Clinton was old enough to understand what had happened to her brother, and his death hit her, perhaps, the hardest.

During the morning hours of March 11, Dee was fiddling around in the kitchen when Suzanne came running out of her bedroom after talking to Billy, her younger brother. Dee had to take only one look at Suzanne's face to know what little Billy had said.

"Billy said," Suzanne began saying . . . and then dropped to her knees and began crying.

"Buzz," Dee later said, "was Suzanne's 'everything.' He was gone this time for good. He wasn't coming back. And she knew it."

After Dee consoled Suzanne, she walked out to the kennel and turned to a poster she'd put up some years before and just stared at it. A devout woman who believed wholeheartedly in God and His role in everyday life, it was one of Dee's favorite pieces of literature to meditate on. Now, she thought, was as good a time as any to take the words in:

> One night I dreamed I was walking along the beach with the Lord.
> Many scenes from my life flashed across the sky.
> In each scene I noticed footprints in the sand. . . .

In the poem, the man asked why there had been only one set of footprints in the sand at times in his life when he needed the Lord the most. The Lord said it was at that moment when He was carrying the man.

"Footprints in the Sand," written by Margaret Fishback Powers, was a popular, inspirational poem based on faith, hope and belief in Jesus Christ that one can get through anything with enough faith. Dee relied on the poem's resonance to get her through what was amounting to be the toughest thing she ever had to deal with.

After reading the poem, Dee sat down and said out loud, "Dear Lord, You'd better be carrying my ass, because there's no way in hell I am going to be able to get through this without You."

On Saturday, March 12, Dee woke early and, to her surprise, felt an "unbelievable amount of peace rush over" her. She was able to accept the fact that someone had taken her son's life and there was nothing she could do about it. Buzz was dead. He wasn't coming home.

Still, she had a sense that it was going to be okay.

As sure as her feeling of peace was, it also bothered Dee. *Why?* she thought. *Is there something wrong with me?* Maybe it was the beginning of a nervous breakdown? There was no way she should feel this calm and this tolerant over having to bury her son in a few days.

When Dee got out of bed, the eulogy for her son's funeral she had been putting off writing, out of nowhere, began to come to her as if someone was dictating it.

Get a paper and pen and write it down, she said to herself. *Don't wait. Do it now.*

While writing, Dee recalled later, she was in a state of subconsciousness, as if she had no idea what she was writing or where it was coming from.

"It just came out."

In the middle of composing the eulogy, however, something else happened. Without warning, Dee stopped writing and went back to bed, lay down and began to cry. At first, it was just mild sobbing that went along with grief. But then, after a few moments, she began to go into a "guttural cry so deep and physically painful that it was worse than any labor pain" she had ever experienced—as if every pleasant moment she had ever spent with her son was somehow coming back to her in the form of tears and pain.

But as Dee held on to her stomach, rocking back and forth like a junkie, shaking and crying, she began to think about the eulogy.

If I continue in this dark, desolate and hurtful place, I will lose the eulogy.

She couldn't let that happen.

"I can't explain it. But in the blink of an eye, I was back in that peace I had left a moment earlier."

Dee later explained that ever since that morning, she had come to terms with her son's death, accepted it and decided not to waste time on tears and anguish. "How my son got that way, however," she added, "is not okay. But I have come to accept that he is gone."

As the ED-MCS began to investigate Buzz's death during the middle part of March 1994, questioning the Carpenters, Buzz's former friends and relatives, trying to piece together what had happened during his final days,

Beth Ann had some rather remarkable news for Haiman Clein—a bit of information that would surely throw a wrench in their wheel of deception and secrecy.

"I'm pregnant," Beth Ann told Clein one night in late March.

"What?"

But that wasn't the end of it. "Twins!" she added. "I'm going to have twins, Haiman."

On Monday, March 14, Mark Despres arrived at Haiman Clein's office at about 2:30 P.M. Clein's legal secretary, Marilyn Rubitski, and Beth Ann were there when Despres walked in. As soon as Clein saw Despres, he grabbed him by the arm, retreated into his office and closed the door behind them.

"It's done, huh?" Clein said first, in almost a celebratory fashion.

"Yes."

After a moment of small talk, for a second time, Despres laid out exactly what had happened, leaving no detail out.

"So, you took your son with you?" Clein asked.

"Yeah," Despres said.

Despite his thinking that bringing along a fifteen-year-old kid to commit a murder for hire wasn't the smartest thing in the world to do, Clein didn't say much more about it. Instead, he walked over to Despres and hugged him as if he were indoctrinating him into the Mafia.

"We're married now, Mark," Clein said. "You know that, don't you?"

After Clein sat down at his desk, Despres asked, "What have you heard?"

"The cops are investigating everyone in the family. I'm staying away because I'm a friend of the family."

"What else?"

"I hope the fuck you got rid of that gun and car, Mark."

"I took care of it."

Despres was desperate now to get the rest of his money so he could plot his next move. To complicate matters further, he had been running around town with a young girl, *Jackie Powers*, he had met in December 1993, and she was now living with him and Chris. In fact, at one time, Chris had been dating the same girl, an old family friend later claimed. She was only fifteen. Mark had been telling people he planned to go to Florida with her as soon as Clein paid him off. He was going to open a body shop in Daytona and just lay low. He was also saying that he hadn't slept much since the murder, but Chris had been sleeping just fine.

The car Despres had used in the murder had been sold to a dealer in Lyme, Despres then explained to Clein. The gun was gone, too.

"Follow me to the bank," Clein said. "I'll get you some more money."

Within minutes, Mark and Chris were sitting in the parking lot of the Bank of Southeastern Connecticut in Waterford, just a few miles up the road from Clein's law office, waiting for Clein, who had since gone into the bank.

A few moments later, Clein emerged from the bank carrying an envelope.

"Don't come and see me for a while," Clein said, handing Despres the envelope. Mark took a quick peek inside while Clein continued to talk. There were thirty-five $100 bills inside.

"Okay," Despres said.

"Lay very low, Mark."

Despres said he understood.

Leaving the bank, Despres drove to Fremut Texaco.

When he and Chris arrived at what had become their home away from home for the past few weeks, Joe Fremut walked over and, as though he were proud of what they had done, smiled.

"He paid you, didn't he?" Fremut asked when Despres approached him.

"Yeah," Despres said. "He paid me."

By this time, Catherine White had joined Fremut and Despres. Despres had mentioned that they should go around to the back of the garage and talk. It was more secluded.

"You did a good job," Fremut said. "What are you going to do with the money?"

Despres said he wanted to open up a body shop in Florida.

By this point, Despres felt Fremut was itching to get his hands on some of the money. He kept referring to "the money, the money." How much? When was the rest of it coming? He kept prying. Despres was getting frustrated. He wasn't going to give Fremut a dime. After all, Fremut hadn't done anything but plan the murder. He hadn't carried out on his earlier promise to go along with Despres. Why should he get anything?

"You should go to the casino and spend that money," Fremut suggested, explaining how the casino was the perfect place to launder it.

With her shoulder-length brown hair, Old Lyme resident Jocelyn Johnson was a slim, fit, relatively tall and plain-looking woman in her late thirties. She had known Mark Despres, and had dated him, over the past twelve years. An avid rider of horses, Johnson was, some later said, one of the only good things Mark Despres had going in his life at the time he killed Buzz Clinton.

"I always thought she was nice . . . good for Mark," a person who knew Johnson later said. "She seemed to have had her head on straight. She was always pleasant."

On one or two occasions, Despres had told Johnson about his plans to murder Buzz long before he had carried them out. He would also, Johnson later said, make comments regarding the progress he was making. One time, he'd even admitted that Haiman Clein had hired him.

But Johnson always wrote it off as another one of Despres's harebrained schemes and never took him seriously.

In just about everyone's estimation, Mark Despres was good with his hands, had little problem fixing anything wrong with a car and had made sculptures out of metal and wood he used to give people as gifts. His mother later said he had even nursed animals back to life when he was younger. He helped people. He cared about people. He could fix anything.

But the one thing Mark Despres couldn't do was fix the fact that he was now, among all those other things, a cold-blooded murderer who was scurrying around like a hunted rabbit wondering what to do next.

With the thought of what Joe Fremut had said regarding laundering the money, Despres picked Johnson up at her home around March 16 and drove to the Foxwoods casino in Ledyard. Fremut had made a valid point when he suggested Despres launder the cash.

After exchanging the cash for chips, Despres hit the blackjack tables and, he later said, "lost."

As Johnson stood by and watched, at one point, she mentioned how she'd seen on the news that someone had been killed in East Lyme. Apparently, she still hadn't convinced herself that Despres had been serious about the murder. Up until that point, she and Despres hadn't discussed it much. But having seen the news report, putting two and two together, Johnson wanted to know if Despres had had anything to do with it.

"I told her I did," Despres later said.

Later that night, Despres let Johnson in on all the details.

"I told [her] that Haiman Clein was the one who paid me to get rid of a guy who was molesting a little girl."

Johnson now had no choice but to believe what she was hearing. Yet regardless of whether she believed him, Jocelyn Johnson sat on the information and ultimately decided, for whatever reason, not to go to the police. Instead she continued her relationship with Despres.

Joseph Jebran had drifted apart from Beth Ann during the past six months or so; in many ways, though, he still continued to view the relationship as salvageable. Beth Ann still took care of Jebran's money and picked him up at the train depot when he came home on weekends. None of that had changed. The only difference now? Beth Ann was sleeping with Clein behind Jebran's back.

In early April, when Beth Ann showed up at the New London train station to pick Joseph up for the weekend, she seemed a bit nervous. Something was obviously wrong, Jebran thought.

"What's going on, Beth?" he asked.

Beth Ann began crying. "Nothing."

"*Nothing?* What is it? Tell me."

"I've been seeing Haiman," she finally admitted.

Joseph had had his suspicions, he later said. He may have been a bit naive, but he wasn't stupid. He knew something had been going on.

"Okay," he replied.

"There's more, though," Beth Ann continued. "I got pregnant."

It was the last thing Jebran had expected to hear. He still loved her. It was clear in the letters and cards he had sent her. They had known each other for about six years. With this latest news, however, he now knew there was no chance for them. It was over, whether he wanted to admit it or not.

"I had a miscarriage," Beth Ann further explained. She didn't mention, according to what Joseph later said, that she had been carrying twins and had lost only one child. Or that the other child she was carrying was still alive. Joseph Jebran, on that day, was left with the impression that she wasn't pregnant anymore.

"Would you have kept the baby if you hadn't had a miscarriage?" he then asked.

"Yes! Of course. It's been rough on me, Joseph. I've had a tough time. With Haiman still being married, I'm jealous."

Jebran was appalled. Here she was wanting sympathy from a man she had two-timed, a man who had given her whatever she wanted.

By this point in the conversation, Jebran had heard enough. To get her off a subject that was, undoubtedly, ripping his heart out with each word spoken, Jebran began asking about Buzz and the murder investigation.

"Who do you think killed Buzz?" he asked.

"It was probably drug-related," Beth Ann said.

It was better, Joseph suggested, that Beth Ann drop him off at his cousin's house in New London. He couldn't stay at the Carpenters' house in Ledyard anymore. Murder? Miscarriage? Haiman Clein? Joseph Jebran wanted no part of it.

"I said," Jebran recalled later, "'I'm not going to give her any more of my time. I'm not going to give her the opportunity to get any more help or anything from me. I'm out the door. . . .'"

Beth Ann called Joseph's cousin the following night, looking for him, but Jebran's cousin told her he was gone.

"Don't call here again, either!"

With her husband dead now for about eight weeks, Kim Clinton, on the morning of May 12, 1994, went into labor. Fifteen hours later, Buzz's son, Anson Clinton IV, a healthy and vivacious child with a thick shock of black hair like his dad's, came into a world that, for him, would never include his natural father. What should have been a day of joyous celebration was marred by the sad fact that Buzz would never get a chance to lay eyes on a son he had been so much looking forward to raising. Buzz had made mistakes with his first son, Michael. He was the first to admit that. But the birth of Anson was going to give Buzz the chance to fix those mistakes. He had dreamed of watching his son wrestle, like he had, play baseball and football.

Since Buzz's murder, Kim had given her immediate family full access to Rebecca, surprising to the Clinton family. The Carpenters, including Beth Ann, were spending more time with Rebecca now than they ever had. In fact, Haiman Clein later said that Beth Ann was a different person after getting to see Rebecca again regularly. The entire Carpenter family was ecstatic, he added, over how they were able to rebuild the relationship Buzz had seemingly severed.

For the Carpenters, in many ways, the situation was back to the way it had been before Buzz had entered the picture.

The Job

Chapter 30

No matter how much a murderer tries, he will unknowingly leave behind clues to his crime at the scene. It is inevitable. It could be a footprint. A piece of chewing gum. One strand of hair. Or a microscopic fiber torn off a shirt during a struggle. Or some type of DNA not visible to the human eye.

For the investigator, it may not be much, but there is *always* something left behind at the crime scene.

Even the best investigators are stumped at times, however. A fiber (the male), for instance, is no good to a forensic scientist without a mate (the female) to match it against. Years—even decades—can go by without a break in a case that has produced little forensic evidence.

This is when investigators rely on witnesses.

Take the case of two El Segundo, California, cops who were shot to death in the same manner as Buzz Clinton some forty-five years before the crime was solved.

In 1957, El Segundo cops Milton G. Curtis and Richard A. Phillips, both in their twenties, were ambushed after they stopped a suspected rapist and car thief who had been driving a reported stolen vehicle. After killing both cops, the man escaped and a nationwide manhunt began. Thousands of leads poured in. But as the years passed, the case became as cold as a star-filled winter night in Alaska. It wasn't until the man, well into his sixtics (he was in his twenties when he committed the crime), had moved to the East Coast, settled down with a family and had probably forgotten about the notion of ever being caught that he was arrested.

How could a case go unsolved for four decades and suddenly be solved overnight?

An anonymous phone tip.

In the El Segundo case, someone had phoned in a tip that a man had been overheard bragging about getting away with a decades-old murder. A year before the man had ambushed the two cops, he had committed a burglary. His fingerprints had been on file since then. With the technology made available to investigators some forty years later, coupled with the phone tip, the fingerprints in both cases—the robbery and cop murders—were eventually matched up. Subsequently a cop who hadn't even been born when the murders had taken place was able to make a case against the man.

In Buzz Clinton's case, that break wouldn't take forty years—but only three months. And it would come in the form of a phone call from Joe Fremut's twenty-four-year-old live-in girlfriend, Catherine White.

When White had made what the detectives involved later referred to as her "heroic" phone call to the Connecticut State Police on May 25, implicating Mark Despres and Joe Fremut in Buzz Clinton's death, investigators had gotten that one lead they had been looking for all along: one solid piece of information that had been missing from the chain of evidence.

"This was a whodunit case from day one," Detective Marty Graham said. "We were stumped. We had our ideas, of course. But did we have it narrowed down to specifics? No. We thought we knew who did it, but we didn't have any names."

"Cathy White, a hero, gave us names," Detective John

Turner added. "Up until that phone call, there was no evidence. We were running out of leads."

All agreed, without White, Buzz Clinton's murder would have likely never been solved.

In one way, White had broken the case wide open with her courageous phone call. But in another way, the investigation had broadened, as detectives suspected it would all along. As Turner, who had somewhat taken control of the investigation along with Marty Graham and Reggie Wardell, began to interview White, it became absolutely clear that there was more to Clinton's death than just a murder-for-hire contract by two thugs who would likely have trouble pulling off a convenience store holdup without getting caught.

For one, White had mentioned to Turner that she had overheard Despres one day telling Fremut that it "was the father-in-law of [Buzz] who set the murder up through an attorney because he was tired of his grandchildren being molested by his son-in-law and of his pregnant daughter being abused."

This fell more in line with what investigators had already suspected: Dick Carpenter and Buzz Clinton had a common hatred for each other that ran far deeper than most father- and son-in-laws who didn't get along. They had suspected that Dick Carpenter had had something to do with Buzz's death from the get-go. They had asked him to take a polygraph test on several occasions, but he always refused. Then there was Old Lyme police officer Joe Dunn's contention that merely weeks before Buzz's death, Buzz had said that if he ever turned up dead, Dick Carpenter should be the first person cops go to.

Considering what White was now saying, it was a viable proposition to think that Dick Carpenter had been the one to set this entire murder-for-hire plot in motion, or at least plant the seed in someone else's mind.

As Turner and Graham began talking to White, she

explained why she had chosen to come forward months later.

On or about May 22, White explained, she had asked Fremut about what she had been suspecting for quite some time: he and Despres had planned and carried out the East Lyme murder that had been all over the news. To her chagrin, Fremut told her everything. The next day, May 23, White called Despres and asked him for a ride to JFK Airport. White told Despres she wanted to leave Fremut. She was scared of him. As they talked, White told Despres that Fremut had given her details of Buzz's murder.

"Joe was not supposed to tell *anyone* about that. That information is supposed to be confidential," an angry Despres warned White.

With that, White said she was terrified. She took Despres's words as a threat to back off. After all, he had already killed once.

So she phoned the Montville State Police barracks and reported what she knew.

"I asked Joe," White continued to explain to John Turner, "and he told me that Mark had picked up a contract for eight thousand dollars 'to do this guy.'"

"Where did he get the contract?" Turner asked.

"He told me that Mark picked it up through this Devil worship group that he belongs to in Deep River."

Another reason White said she didn't come forward sooner was that she didn't believe Despres would ever "do it." She thought he would, like Fremut, "back down."

To back up further what she was saying, White suggested Turner speak with John Filippi, one of Fremut's friends. White said Filippi knew some things that might help—including who it was who paid Mark Despres for "the job," as Filippi later called it

Early in the morning of May 26, Detective Chet Harris, a member of the narcotics task force who had already developed a "working relationship" with Mark Despres over the years, made a phone call to Despres. Harris said he could pay him for some information he needed if they met at Eagle Rock, an undeveloped cul-de-sac in Essex.

Despres, who had just turned thirty-five, appeared dirty and unkempt when he arrived at Eagle Rock. Harris had set up the meeting after Catherine White had given Detective John Turner Despres's name.

Despres showed up at about 10:00 A.M. Harris, Turner and Detective John Szamocki were waiting for him. As soon as Despres got out of his car and walked over to Harris, Harris said, "The phone call was a ruse, Mark. My real purpose was to have you talk to Turner and Szamocki. They need to ask you some questions."

"All right," Despres said.

Despres then got into Turner's vehicle. As Harris waited outside, Szamocki got in the backseat, while Despres sat down in the passenger side.

"We want to ask you some questions about an incident that happened in East Lyme," Turner said. "The murder of Buzz Clinton."

Despres paused and didn't say anything at first. But through his facial expressions, it was clear to Turner that something was wrong. He looked worried, nervous, pale and sweaty.

After a moment, Despres nodded. "I know," he said. "I know."

"Do you understand what I'm saying, Mark?" Turner asked.

"Yeah, but I . . . I . . . I think I should contact my attorney."

"That's easy enough," Turner said, handing Despres his cell phone. "Who is your attorney, anyway?"

"Haiman Clein."

It was the first time Haiman Clein's name had entered into the investigation.

* * *

Chet Harris had already met with Despres at Despres's apartment in Deep River earlier that same morning and asked him if he was involved in the murder of a "man on the connector in East Lyme" back in March.

To Harris's amazement, Despres acknowledged that he was "deeply involved in the murder of Anson 'Buzz' Clinton," Harris later noted in his report of that meeting.

"Despres admitted being present when Clinton was killed."

"There was someone else there, too," Despres mentioned when Harris pressed him for more details.

"Who was that?"

"I don't want to say."

As the interview with Turner and Szamocki continued, Despres began to change his demeanor somewhat and became more innacurate with his statements and secretive, shifting and stirring in his seat. Turner, of course, wanted to know who else had been behind the murder. Not just Fremut—they knew that already—but the actual mastermind of it all. In other words, who had paid Despres for the job?

Despres then got out of Turner's car and walked over to Chet Harris, someone with whom he felt more comfortable.

"Could you help them out at all, Mark?" Harris asked.

Despres shrugged.

"Do you know anything about that murder?"

"I know the whole deal," Despres admitted.

"Did you tell them that?"

"No, I'm telling *you*."

"Why didn't you tell them?"

"I cannot go to jail! I would rather kill myself than go to jail."

"Tell *me*, then," Harris encouraged.

"I'll tell you everything, Chet . . . but only after I speak with my attorney."

Harris and Despres, along with another detective who had been there, then walked over to where Turner and Szamocki were standing.

After a long discussion about Despres's desire to get a lawyer before he said anything more, Turner said, "We're going to issue a search warrant for your apartment today, Mark."

"You won't find anything."

Turner ignored it, then he asked, "What's up with Chris, your son?"

"Ah, Chris has been living with me, but I kicked him out. He was out of control. He wouldn't do anything he was told."

Before getting into his car and leaving, Despres said he was going directly to see Haiman Clein.

Hours later, as Chet Harris sat outside Despres's apartment, waiting for him to return, Despres pulled into the driveway, and walked up to Harris's car.

"Did you get a chance to speak with your lawyer?" Harris asked.

"Yes. But he referred me to another lawyer." Despres then took a piece of paper out of his pocket with the lawyer's name on it and showed it to Harris. "They both advised me not to say anything more."

"You looked stress out, Mark. You all right?"

"Look, there's no good way out of this situation. I cannot tolerate jail—even for one day! If I do talk, though, it'll be to you, Chet."

Harris shook his head. He understood.

"I'm not going to jail," Despres said again. "I'd rather be dead than go to jail for twenty or thirty years."

Harris didn't know what to say.

"Is Joe in trouble, too?" Despres asked, then explained how he had seen Fremut sitting in a cruiser earlier, talking to a trooper.

"I'm unaware of Joe Fremut's involvement in this case, Mark."

"You won't find anything in my apartment," Despres said before walking away. "I'm going to drive around for a while and think this through."

Harris soon left.

About an hour later, Harris ended up at Fremut Texaco, where other detectives were questioning Joe Fremut. Pulling in, Harris spied Despres sitting in his car near the south side of the garage, so he approached him.

"You okay, Mark? How you feeling?"

Despres waved his hand in the air. "So-so," he said softly. "Joe isn't involved," he added.

"By the look on your face, Mark, I can tell you want to talk."

"I don't want to go to jail, Chet."

For the next fifteen minutes, Despres and Harris discussed the guns Despres said they were going to find in his apartment when they searched it. Despres was concerned about the silencer. He was worried he'd "get in trouble" for having it.

"You may be arrested, Mark," Harris warned.

Chet Harris had been going back and forth between the Fremut interrogation going on inside the garage and where Despres was sitting in his car. At one point, Harris asked, "You want to talk to me about Buzz Clinton, Mark?"

Despres didn't say anything.

"Are you deeply involved?"

"Yes."

"Was there someone else present at the murder?"

"Yes."

"Who's that?"

"Listen, I can't say anything more. I have to go."

"You're free to go, Mark."

During the course of the day, Despres had been on an emotional roller coaster, sure that the ED-MCS was going to bust him at any moment. In one sense, he was coming to grips with the fact that he might end up in jail within the next few days—which was something, he had made clear, he could not accept. Chet Harris, an experienced investigator, knew it was only a matter of time before Despres rolled over. So when Despres left Fremut Texaco, Harris waited awhile and drove back over to Despres's apartment to see if he could talk to him some more. Turner and his crew were preparing to serve a search warrant at Despres's apartment. Harris figured he could help out on both fronts.

When he got there, Despres was sitting in his car in the driveway. Jackie Powers, his fifteen-year-old live-in girlfriend, sat next to him.

"I want to drive around with Jackie," Despres told Harris, "while you guys conduct the search."

"Could you step out of the car, Mark?" Harris said in a nonthreatening tone. "Let's talk in private."

Despres turned to Jackie. "I'll be right back."

"I'm concerned for the girl, Mark," Harris said as they walked away.

"Don't be. I just want to spend some time with her."

"I will not allow a *juvenile*, under these circumstances, to leave with you."

Harris was a bit more firm now in his inflection, letting Despres know who was in control.

"Nothing is going to happen to her, Chet."

"You admitted to me that you were involved with Buzz Clinton's murder, Mark. You're free to go, but she's staying here!"

Detective Reggie Wardell had walked over while Harris was questioning Despres. By this point, Turner and his team had arrived to serve the search warrant and were scouring the area.

"You're not leaving with her, Mr. Despres," Wardell said. "We can't let you do that."

Despres agreed—and took off without the girl, who was eventually turned over to her mother.

Chapter 31

Mark Despres's apartment was adjacent to his mother's house, a modest, raised ranch-style home with faded yellow paint and a well-kept yard. On the same property, near the edge of Winthrop Road, the apartment Despres lived in was nothing more than a two-car garage, with a large loft above it. Despres had lived there on and off since he and his wife, Diana Trevethan, had divorced back in the early 1980s.

After wading through piles of garbage inside Despres' apartment, the ED-MCS found a few interesting items right away. While sifting through phone bills, motor vehicle records, address books and other common items, John Turner found what Joe Fremut had predicted he would earlier that day: a 9mm Taurus handgun.

It was a good start. Anytime a source's information was accurate, Turner recalled later, "It means this person can somewhat be trusted."

Next to the gun was a homemade silencer. It looked as if it had been recently attached and detached, with broken shards of solder visible on both the weapon and the silencer. Owning a silencer is a crime. At the least, Despres could be arrested on that charge.

Despres had come back after driving around for a while and was waiting outside while the search continued.

"That's Joe's gun," Despres said when Turner approached him with it.

As the search progressed, what could have been seen as an arsenal of weaponry by some was merely a weak collection of hunting rifles and old, rusted guns that many a household in the area probably had on hand: .22-caliber Derringer, .22-caliber L.R. revolver, .22-caliber long rifle, a shot gun (Long Tom), an old Civil War–era rifle dating back to 1876, a service rifle, .22-caliber Winchester, .54-caliber black powder rifle, two Mossberg shotguns, a second black powder rifle (this one a .50 caliber), .30-caliber rifle made by Plainfield, .22-caliber rifle made by Chipmunk; Ithaca M49 rifle and a Crossman air gun.

Within Despres's massive inventory of handguns and collector's rifles, however, was no sign of what detectives were looking for—the .38 that had killed Buzz.

Also of interest to detectives was some satanic literature found out in the open on a table, scores of burned candles, a Ouija board, and a red pentagram spray-painted on the floor.

"We came up with a lot of little pieces of evidence," Turner said later, "that, most important, corroborated what Catherine White had told us about. That's when we knew we had a trustworthy source. Everything Cathy White described was there."

Days later, the 9mm the ED-MCS had confiscated was given to the ATF, along with a request for a trace. Within a few days, it was learned that the gun had been shipped from Westfield, Massachusetts, to Hoffman Gun Center in Newington, Connecticut, on March 13, 1989. After checking with Hoffman, Turner found out that Despres had been telling the truth when he said it was Fremut's gun because Hoffman listed the owner (or purchaser of the weapon) as Joseph Fremut.

On June 2, detectives and state troopers spent hours

rummaging through every crevice of Fremut Texaco, hoping to come up with something to tie Fremut to Buzz's death. Near the end of their search, Detective Marty Graham hit the jackpot in the bottom of the Dumpster out back. He found various papers, gun parts and live ammo buried under some garbage and old car parts.

A few days later, the Connecticut State Police Forensic Laboratory confirmed that the ammo taken from Fremut's Dumpster was the same caliber as the bullets extracted from Buzz's body. What was more important, however, was that the ammo was manufactured by the same company that had manufactured the bullets that killed Buzz Clinton.

A few days after Catherine White had made "the call," she went to Joe Fremut's apartment and took a sawed-off shotgun and a .38-caliber pistol, hid them in an overnight bag and boarded a train alone to California.

When Fremut found out what White had done, he contacted Despres and told him they were flying out to California right away to meet White and, as Fremut had suggested months earlier, kill White's pimp, who lived in the San Francisco area.

Fremut, Despres later explained, had "intentions of robbing and torturing [the] pimp." Despres decided to go along, if not to help out Fremut, but rather just to get out of Connecticut and away from the cops. However, when Despres arrived in California, he abruptly changed his mind and flew back to Connecticut without learning the fate of White's pimp. Despres's heart was in Florida. His Deep River apartment and mother's home had been searched already. He had told detectives he was there on the night Buzz had been killed. He knew an arrest was imminent.

Arriving back in Connecticut from California in early

June, Despres contacted Haiman Clein right away; he desperately needed the rest of his money.

The next day, Despres asked his mother, Esther Lockwood, if she would go to Clein's office and pick up an envelope for him.

As she drove back from Clein's office, Despres's mother peeked inside the envelope, she later said, and saw about $1,500 in cash.

As soon as Despres got his hands on the money, he ran scared and picked up his fifteen-year-old girlfriend, Jackie Powers, and went to Florida.

As soon as he arrived, Despres began calling Clein, using the code name Edward Schwartz, demanding the rest of his money. Clein had given Despres about $5,000 by this point, but the deal had been for $8,000. Despres held the cards now. He could turn Clein in at any time.

"Where's my money?"

To be safe, Clein told Despres not to call the office anymore—using the Edward Schwartz name or not.

When Despres pushed Clein for an exact delivery date for his cash, Clein said, "You'll get your money, Mark. Hold tight."

Over the next few weeks, at increments of between $200 to $800, using a fictional name and return address, Clein began overnighting Despres more money.

During the first phone call Despres had made to Clein, he explained that his apartment had been searched. He said he was worried. He said he needed a lawyer. He said Clein had promised him a lawyer if it ever got to this point, and he reminded Clein that he had also promised bail money, a passport and a ticket out of the country if the cops started asking questions.

"What the fuck am I supposed to do now, Haiman?" Despres wanted to know.

For Clein, it was the first time he'd heard that Despres's apartment had been searched.

"I don't know, Mark. I'm not a criminal attorney. But I'll figure something out. Hang in there."

Clein was scared, he later said, when he heard news of the search. He knew that once the cops got their hands on Despres, he was going to cave in like the paid informant he was. From there, Beth Ann's name would come up. With Chris Despres involved, Clein knew, the cops would, undoubtedly, use him as a negotiating tactic.

Fear and worry drove Clein to call Bob Axelrod— an old friend and noted criminal attorney from Meriden, Connecticut, who had opened a second office and an antiques store in Florida—a day or so after he spoke to Despres. Axelrod had been an attorney for about twenty-five years. He and Clein had known each other for about fifteen years. Lawyers like Axelrod, however, commanded large retainers—something in the neighborhood of what neither Mark Despres nor Haiman Clein could afford.

Nonetheless, Clein was a friend of Axelrod's. He needed advice.

After Clein finished talking with Despres and went to see Axelrod, he told Beth Ann what was going on.

"Let's step outside," Beth Ann whispered. "Bugs," she added, pointing around the New London law office. "Bugs, Haiman."

Clein followed her outside.

"Bob Axelrod is flying in from Florida," Clein explained when they got outside. "He's going to handle this. I don't want you to worry."

Then Clein told her why he had called Axelrod. So far, they were clear. There was no reason to begin panicking. Their names hadn't even come up.

"I want to go to Bob's office," Beth Ann demanded. "I want him to represent *us*, too."

This made sense to Clein, but frightened him at the same time. Having recently upped his Prozac and alcohol intake, most likely to supplement the cocaine he wasn't getting from Despres anymore, Clein was climbing the walls with concern. The cops were scurrying around, gathering evidence, writing up search and seizure warrants, interviewing people. It was only a matter of time before they came knocking on his door.

About three days later, as Clein and Beth Ann drove to Axelrod's Meriden office, about a forty-five minute drive from New London, Clein told Beth Ann he was going to tell Axelrod "everything" when they got there.

This didn't bode well with Beth Ann. She became "agitated," Clein later said, and began groping him, checking to see if he was wired.

Bugs.

After not finding anything, she began to shout, "Pull over! Pull over!"

"What are you—"

"I said pull over, damnitall!"

Bugs.

Route 9, near Middletown, Connecticut, is a two-lane highway, with the Connecticut River racing swiftly toward the Atlantic Ocean on one side and a thick, dense wooded area on the other. Clein, afraid he was going to get in an accident, pulled off to the shoulder of the road.

The car hadn't even come to a complete stop when Beth Ann began to rummage through it as though she had dropped a burning cigarette.

Bugs.

She looked under the seats. In between the seats. In the glove compartment. Under the sun visors. Anywhere she felt Clein could be hiding a wire.

Bugs.

"We should tell him the truth," Clein said after he calmed Beth Ann down and they got back on the road.

Silence.

"Beth?"

She then made it clear that she was finished talking. She was terrified that Clein, a man whose baby she was carrying, a man she was in love with, was setting her up.

Ultimately Beth Ann's intuition was correct. Because only days after he and Beth Ann had met with Bob Axelrod regarding Mark Despres, Clein called Axelrod back and retained him for himself.

When Axelrod asked why, Clein told him everything.

After that conversation, Axelrod told Beth Ann that he could not represent her, too. Then he called Hugh Keefe, a noted criminal defense attorney from New Haven whom Axelrod had known for several years.

"I was sarcastic and hinted around enough," Axelrod told investigators later, "to let him know what she was involved in. . . . I did tell Keefe that both Beth and Haiman would probably be arrested as someone who hired a hit man."

Chapter 32

At the behest of Bob Axelrod, on June 2, Haiman Clein drove Beth Ann to New Haven to meet with Hugh Keefe. According to Axelrod, Beth Ann wouldn't let Clein speak to him without her being present. Even if Axelrod called Clein's office, Beth Ann demanded to listen in on another line. She would harass Clein in front of Axelrod. She would demand to be present at *any* and *all* meetings and conversations. Axelrod was having a difficult time getting anything out of Clein.

Beth Ann met with Keefe on June 2 while Clein waited in the reception area of Keefe's office. In private, she told Keefe that she was pregnant with Clein's child, had carried on a romantic relationship with him since November 1993 and he was involved in her brother-in-law's murder. She also said her family had been involved with litigation against her sister, who had been married to Buzz at the time of his death.

When Keefe asked Beth Ann if she was involved in the murder, she "denied any involvement," Keefe later said, ". . . but was afraid she would get tainted with part of the blame because of her close relationship with Clein. . . ."

After asking Keefe for "advice and representation concerning her father," Beth Ann asked, "How can I best protect myself . . . ? I want advice on severing my relationship from Haiman's law firm. . . ."

Before ending the brief meeting, Keefe told her she should speak to his partner, Robert Lynch, who had some expertise in that area.

Still, there was the matter of a large retainer fee Beth Ann needed so she could formally hire Keefe as counsel. Where was she going to get the money?

A few days later, Clein drafted a check from his trust fund for $5,000 and gave it to Beth Ann so she could pass it along to Keefe. Just like that, the same woman who had finished telling Keefe she wanted to sever her relationship with Haiman Clein for fear of being branded a murderer by association accepted a check from Clein for $5,000 to hire one of the most prominent criminal defense attorneys in Connecticut.

At the young age of fifteen, Chris Despres had already seen more than most people saw in a lifetime. He had sat by and watched as his father committed a savage murder. He had participated with his father in satanic worshiping ceremonies and séances. He had been smoking pot and drinking.

It wasn't a surprise to anyone who knew Chris to learn that in the early part of June, depression infected him like a flu virus. His father was gone, no less with a girl Chris had dated at one time. He had information that could put his father on death row, even if he didn't realize it. The weight of everything was just too much.

After Mark left for Florida, Chris had no reason to stick around town. So he moved back to Newington into his mother's house and began to attend school regularly.

Chris had been friends with a shy, older woman, *Margaret Long,* for years. She had dated a guy whose younger brother had been a friend of Chris's. She would see Chris from time to time through that friendship. Unassuming and a bit reticent, Margaret was a good listener and a friend to Chris.

After spending only a few weeks in Newington, Chris and his mom decided it might be best if he went to live with her father and sister in Old Saybrook. This way, Chris wouldn't have to change schools. He could go back to school in Essex and try to lead a somewhat normal life.

At the same time Chris moved in with his aunt and grandfather, Margaret had broken up with her longtime boyfriend. One thing led to another, and Chris and Margaret began dating. They had already known each other, so dating only seemed natural. Something had been bothering Chris, though, Margaret quickly realized. But he refused to talk about it when she asked.

"I knew there was something wrong," she said, "but I never knew what it was—at least not at that time. Chris would never talk about anything. As I got closer to him, I learned that he liked to keep things bottled up."

One thing was utterly clear to Margaret during the first few weeks of their relationship, however: Chris wanted nothing to do with his father. For one, he was angry that Mark had run off with "his girlfriend" and left him to fend for himself. Two, there was something else that had happened between Chris and Mark that Chris didn't want to talk about.

Regarding a fifteen-year-old girl's taking off to Florida with a man old enough to be her father, Margaret later said that the girl's parents knew she had run off with Mark, but did nothing to stop it. Others even claimed that the girl's parents had given Mark permission to take her.

By Thursday, June 30, 1994, John Turner and Marty Graham tracked down John Filippi, a friend of Joe Fremut's with whom Catherine White had suggested they talk. Filippi appeared anxious when they showed up. He was obviously worried about something.

"I heard about the murder from Cathy White," Filippi explained. "But anything I say will put me in danger. Joe Fremut might do something to me if he finds out I'm talking to you."

"When did you hear about the murder?" Turner asked in his trademark Joe Friday–like delivery.

"I don't know. Must have been about two weeks after it happened."

Filippi, who had just gotten out of jail on March 8 and, admittedly, started dealing drugs for Joe Fremut immediately afterward, went on to explain how he had driven White, a guy named Jed, and Filippi's girlfriend, Elizabeth Stranland, to Hartford one afternoon to buy some heroin. During the car ride, White began talking to Jed about how Despres and Fremut had "killed someone on the highway in East Lyme." She said she was afraid Fremut was going to kill her next.

"Don't say that, Cathy," Filippi said when he heard White mention it. "Don't make things up like that. Joe will kick your ass if he finds out."

"I'm not going down alone," White said. "I'll take that motherfucker with me!"

When Filippi saw Fremut the next day, he rolled over on White without a second thought.

"Be quiet about that!" Fremut warned. Then he asked Filippi if he would take two "dummy bags" of heroin containing rat poison and give them to Stranland and White.

"What?"

"They know too much," Fremut said. "They're talking too much shit."

Filippi refused. He later told White and Stranland to watch their backs because Fremut was out to kill them.

As Graham and Turner interviewed Filippi, they confirmed he had set Fremut up with a silencer.

Next they wanted to know if Filippi had heard who had paid Fremut and Despres to murder Buzz.

"They were being paid," Filippi said, "to do the hit by the victim's family, who I understood was either the wife of the victim or the father-in-law."

By June 16, Beth Ann and Haiman Clein's relationship was breaking down. Clein was beginning to tell her that he wanted out of the relationship, saying he couldn't leave Bonnie, the mother of his four kids, as he had originally promised. It was an abrupt change of heart from a man who, just a few months ago, had written to Beth Ann that—besides him wanting her to defecate on him—he would rather die than be without her. This made some later wonder if Clein's lawyer, Bob Axelrod, had put him up to terminating the relationship.

In 1992, before Beth Ann had even known Clein, she met thirty-six-year-old Diana Hendelman at the local Gold's Gym in Waterford. They became fast friends and started hanging out together. Beth Ann, Hendelman recalled years later, was "quiet" at first, but she opened up later when their relationship became more personal. Within a short time, Beth Ann told Diana about Joseph Jebran. She said Joseph viewed the relationship differently than she—that although they were intimate, it was more or less a "friends with benefits" thing.

When Beth Ann met Clein and later began talking to Diana about him, she admitted that the relationship was more intimate and sexual. She told how she was infatuated by Clein's status, presumed wealth and stature in the community. But in Diana Hendelman's view, she believed it was more about obsession than anything else.

Throughout the course of their friendship, Diana had met Clein on about three separate occasions.

"I was shocked," she recalled later, "when I saw Clein and realized how much older he was than Beth Ann."

It *was* an odd match. On one hand, there was Joseph Jebran: young, single, successful, good-looking, suave and charming; on the other, there was Haiman Clein: old enough to be her father, a chronic abuser of alcohol and cocaine, on Prozac, financially sinking and sharing his wife sexually with clients and friends.

Beth Ann, however, never told Diana about the problems her family was having with Buzz, Kim and the custody matter. It never came up. Nevertheless, Diana and Beth Ann remained friends throughout the entire time Beth Ann and Clein had hired Despres to murder Buzz. As Beth Ann and Clein's relationship began to deteriorate, Beth Ann began to lean on Diana for support.

June 17, 1994, was a night Diana Hendelman remembered with vivid accuracy years later because Beth Ann had called her while she and her husband, Martin, were watching the minute-by-minute coverage of O.J. Simpson's infamous flight in his white Bronco on a California freeway. They were supposed to meet Beth Ann for dinner. But shortly before they were going to drag themselves away from the television set to leave, Beth Ann phoned.

"I'm on my cell phone," Beth Ann said.

"Are we going to dinner?"

"No!"

Beth Ann, Diana recalled, was "hysterical" and manic.

"Where are you?" Diana asked.

"I'm outside Haiman's house. . . ."

Hendelman heard loud noises, banging and clanking. Beth Ann, she then learned, was trying to break in.

"What are you doing, Beth?"

"I'm going in to confront that bitch Bonnie about our relationship."

"What?"

Hendelman knew there was some friction between

Bonnie and Beth Ann. Bonnie had known that Clein
had been unfaithful for most of their marriage—she had
even participated sexually in some of the relationships
herself. But Beth Ann was staking her claim. She wanted
Bonnie out of the picture. Clein, however, wanted nothing to do with Beth Ann anymore. He was trying to
distance himself from her as much as possible.

Beth Ann wasn't going to hear of it. She was under the
impression that since she was still carrying one of his ba-
bies, Clein was going to drop Bonnie and marry her.

Sometime later, she even tracked Clein, Bonnie and
the kids down at a local restaurant. While they were eating, Beth Ann stormed in and began fighting with Clein.
A week or so later, while Clein, Bonnie and the kids were
en route to upstate New York for a long weekend, she
phoned Clein on his cell phone and demanded he meet
her on the side of the highway. With Bonnie and kids in
the car looking on, Beth Ann tore into Clein, asking why
he was going away for the weekend with everything that
was happening.

When Clein said he had to go, Beth Ann shouted,
"Cops like to arrest people on weekends, too, you know."

Clein's kids even got into the act. One time, when
Beth Ann, acting insane and obsessive, showed up at
Clein's house, one of Clein's kids used a slingshot and
rocks to chase her away. There was another time when
Beth Ann, despite Clein and Bonnie's insistence that the
relationship was over, waved a pair of his underwear in
front of Bonnie's face, implying that she was still sleeping with him.

Oddly enough, however, when it came time for Beth
Ann to abort the second child she was carrying, detectives from the ED-MCS were shocked to learn that it
hadn't been Diana Hendelman who had driven Beth
Ann to the doctor to get the abortion.

Detectives later claimed it was Bonnie.

Chapter 33

John Turner and Marty Graham had a feeling that Catherine White knew much more than she was admitting to. However, they also knew the rules where sources were concerned: don't intimidate or push; instead, let them give information at their own pace. Catherine White would open up. It was only a matter of when.

On August 26, Turner received a call from Reggie Wardell that he had been hoping to receive ever since first talking to White back in May.

"Listen, John, Cathy White was arrested by the Madison Police Department on a failure-to-appear DWI warrant. They have her in custody."

"I'll be right there," Turner said.

White had been moving around so much after she made that initial call to police that Turner and his crew had a hard time keeping track of her. She was never in one place more than a day, but now they had her locked up.

"Everyone found out about what I did," White said when Turner and Wardell walked in. "Thanks a lot! I'm scared as hell now."

"Relax, Cathy. We'll take care of it."

"I'll give you more info, but I am *not* putting it in writing."

"Talk to us, Cathy."

Over the next hour, White began to open up a bit

more. She said "the whole thing" was "set up" by an "attorney" for "the father-in-law." This attorney, White insisted, had "hired Mark Despres."

"Okay . . ."

"Mark received a phone call one day when we were all driving to New York to buy drugs for this same attorney."

"Wait a minute. So, Mark is selling 'this attorney' drugs, too?"

"Yeah. That's why the attorney felt comfortable hiring Mark; he knew him."

"Is there anyone else who can back this up?"

"Mark's fifteen-year-old girlfriend and Mark's brother."

White then gave Turner and Wardell their names. Then she said that Joe Fremut knew about the murder, but he was not "directly involved."

"What else?"

"Well, I know you've been speaking to John Filippi and his girlfriend, Liz Stranland."

"We do what we have to do, Cathy."

"You're wasting your time. They don't know anything. All they know they got from me."

By the end of the conversation, White said she didn't know where she'd be in the coming months. If they wanted to get hold of her, they would have to contact her friend in California, and she would get her the message.

As Turner, Wardell and Graham began checking White's latest information, it turned out to be so accurate they ended up using it as a litmus test to find out if some of their other sources were telling the truth.

"Call Cathy White what you want," Marty Graham said later, "but she was very much a hero in this thing. We didn't know who these people were before she came forward. So, it really didn't matter what kind of background she had. She brought new names into this thing every time we spoke to her."

* * *

With the insurance money from Buzz's death, Dee and Buck Clinton began building Kim and the kids a rather spacious house with a three-car garage underneath it on their property shortly after Buzz was buried; in fact, the house was a lot nicer than the one Dee and Buck lived in themselves. But Dee didn't mind. She wanted to take care of her daughter-in-law and grandchildren the same way Buzz would have.

Around the middle of summer, with the house still under construction and Kim and the kids sleeping on the floor in Dee's living room, Kim moved out.

Where did she go? To one of Buzz's old friends, the ED-MCS's first suspect, Rob Ferguson.

"Kim had undergone a complete change in character," Buck Clinton told detectives around this same time. "[She] had moved into Rob's house . . . much to the chagrin of Rob's girlfriend."

"How do you know that?"

"I've been keeping in touch with Rob. He was a business partner of my son. Through Rob, I can learn more about Buzz's friends and associates."

Like his wife, Buck was a bull. He couldn't just sit around and wait for the cops to figure out who killed his son. He had to get out there and do what he could.

"What makes you say that Kim has changed?"

"Well," Buck said, "the children seem to be less cared for by her."

"In what ways?"

"They are being bathed infrequently. She's only returned once in nearly the past two weeks to drop off dirty clothes and pick up new clothing."

The previous day, Buck had seen Kim at the end of the driveway, he said, talking to Kevin Myers, another one of Buzz's old friends. Buck said he knew Myers to be a drug user and wondered what Kim would want with him. Weeks before that, Buck said Suzanne had gone with Kim over to Rob's one day and came back talking about seeing another friend of Rob and Buzz's whom Buck knew to be involved heavily with drugs. That man, Suzanne reported, was also living with Rob.

"More important," Buck insisted, "this guy is an employee of Fremut Texaco. He must know Joey Fremut."

Then there was a phone call Buck received from Rob Ferguson one day. Ferguson sounded drunk. It was 12:30 A.M. He began by telling Buck about a conversation he'd had with Kevin Myers, who said he was "afraid of a man from New London . . ." who sells him drugs. When Ferguson asked why, Myers said, "Because I thought they were going to break his (meaning Buzz) fucking legs, not *kill* him!" When Ferguson pressed for more, Myers admitted that the "cops were on the right track."

Buck then said that Buzz had told him a day or so before his death that he had his wrecker sold to a "friend of Kevin's." In Buck's eyes, it was all beginning to add up.

Turner, Wardell and Graham, of course, knew differently—Kevin Myers, this "drug dealer," or Rob Ferguson had little, if anything, to do with Buzz's murder. But there was still an outside shot that Ferguson knew more than he was saying, though. And with this new information regarding Myers knowing Joe Fremut, there was also a chance Myers knew who was involved in the murder, too, which was what Turner, Wardell and Graham were after.

On August 16, Turner took one more stab at Ferguson to see if he had come up with anything else. On top of that, Turner wanted to make sure Ferguson was being straight with him. Turner had information in the bank now. He could play him a little bit to see if he was being truthful.

Turner first mentioned the name Kevin Myers.

"Kevin Myers," Ferguson immediately said, "came over here last week and told me how Buzz used to steal cars. We thought this is why he was maybe killed."

Myers was also involved with the same crowd who hung around Blonders Used Auto Parts. Was Buzz a car thief? Was he lifting cars for Snyder? Who knew? It seemed that anyone who ever had a beef with Buzz was now accusing him of committing all sorts of crimes. Turner knew Buzz hadn't been killed because he was stealing cars. It was an absurd theory.

"Tell me some more about Kevin Myers, Rob."

"Kevin also thinks that maybe a drug dealer friend of Buzz's from New London might have killed him."

Turner wrote down the dealer's name. "We'll check it out."

"You should," Rob said.

Before Turner left, he had one more question.

"Is Kim living here now?"

"She's been staying here on and off since June."

Chapter 34

When John Turner heard from Catherine White that Liz Stranland only knew what she had told her, he wondered if he could extract more of what White knew by simply talking to Stranland again.

Liz Stranland herself was no Mary Poppins. She was being held at Niantic Correctional Center for Women after being arrested, like White, for several failure-to-appear warrants. So Turner and Graham drove to Niantic, picked Stranland up, and brought her to Troop F. It was a more comfortable place to talk. Sources in prison sometimes get angry and resentful because of being locked up. Troop F wasn't the Hyatt Regency, but it wasn't prison, either.

Stranland said right away that she knew only what White had told her. No more.

"She told me that it was . . . what's his name . . . the victim—"

"Buzz Clinton," Turner interrupted.

"Right. Buzz. He was killed by someone hired by his wife."

This got a rise out of Turner and Graham. *Kim?* It was like looking for the source of a crack in the ice: every time they thought they were close to finding the mastermind behind Buzz's death, a new name came up and their investigation branched out farther.

As Stranland spoke, it was obvious she was confused. Yet, at the same time, she knew more than she thought. For example, she said it was Fremut who called Buzz under the ruse of buying his tow truck, and it was Despres who had been paid and ultimately pulled the trigger.

"Explain this a bit more, Liz, would you?" Graham suggested.

"Well, Mark Despres brought along his fifteen-year-old son and shot . . . Buzz six times," she said, adding, "Joey's aware of everyone who is helping, but he is also confident that he wouldn't be arrested because—and these are his words—he is 'too smart' for you guys."

Turner and Graham had to smile. They knew Fremut was nothing more than a wanna-be gangster who didn't have the guts to do half of what he told people he did.

"To me," Reggie Wardell later said, "Fremut was a weasel of a guy. A coward. But we also knew he was more dangerous than Mark Despres. We couldn't forget that."

It was clear to Turner and Graham that, like Cathy White, Liz Stranland was petrified of Fremut. Whether he carried out his threats or not, Fremut was an intimidator. He knew how to manhandle women and scare them with words.

"He talked a big game," Graham said. "He made himself out to be some gangster, but he wasn't even close."

When they asked Stranland where Fremut was, she said he was roaming around the country, hiding out.

Later, after Turner and Graham dropped Stranland back off at prison, they began to talk about their next move.

"Cathy White," Graham said.

"We have to get her to write out a statement," Turner suggested.

"Let's do it."

On September 12, Turner and Graham got a call from

the Atlantic County Jail in Mays Landing, New Jersey. White was now being held there on several charges. She was ready to talk.

White was a drug addict, exotic dancer and prostitute. One day she could be in California, the next in Florida. By a stroke of luck, she was only four hours away in New Jersey.

"Cathy would go up and down," Graham recalled. "When she was using, she wasn't much of a witness, informant. But when she wasn't, her conscience would begin eating at her. The nicest person in the world when she was straight. Truly a great person."

Her character or history never mattered much to investigators; it was the information she was providing. Time and again, it added up.

When Turner first arrived in New Jersey and laid eyes on White, he could see that she wasn't just scared anymore—she had been running for her life.

"Mark and Joey," White said first, "consider me a loose end. They know I've told you everything." She was certain she was going to be killed next.

"Do you have anything else you want to add, Cathy?" Turner asked.

"Although everything I said earlier was true, it wasn't complete."

"We kind of figured that out."

After Turner advised White of her rights, for two hours she sat and wrote out a rather telling statement: the conversations she'd heard between Despres and Fremut, those she'd had with Fremut alone and dates, times, places. It had been two weeks since White had done a bag of dope. With a clear head, she recalled every detail she could remember.

The first time White said she heard anything about Buzz's murder was back in January while she, Fremut and Despres were driving to New York. They were going into the city, she said, to "rob a pimp and throw him off a bridge."

After giving up the notion once they got there, during the ride home, White said she heard Despres brag to Fremut that he'd had several "contracts" in the past to kill people.

"Who gave you those contracts?" White said Fremut asked Despres.

"A Devil worship group I belong to in town," Despres said. White added that both Despres and his son, Chris, belonged to this same Devil worship group, "where they would go out in back of Mark's house in the woods with young girls and have orgies."

It was a few weeks later that White said she first heard Despres specifically targeting Buzz. After that, she heard Fremut and Despres routinely discussing how they were going to carry out the murder.

By the time White was finished, the ED-MCS had enough information to begin drafting arrest warrants for Fremut and Despres. But they still needed to know who the "lawyer" was who had come up in many of their conversations with sources lately. Fremut and Despres hadn't acted alone—not that they weren't smart enough, but they had no reason to kill Buzz. There was no connection. Besides that, there was this continuing notion that perhaps Dick Carpenter had hired Fremut and Despres. It seemed every time Turner and Graham turned around, someone else was fingering Dick.

In a majority of murder cases, incriminating information comes in at such a rapid pace that it's sometimes hard for detectives to keep up with it. Most cases are broken in the first twenty-four to forty-eight hours. Investigators then scramble around to put information together to serve arrest warrants. Arrest warrants have to be detailed and faultless; otherwise the information misrepresented—either mistakenly or deliberately—will come back to taint the case when it goes to court. Defense lawyers scour warrants and police reports for mistakes and inaccuracies. Good investigators are thorough, tenacious. They don't present an arrest warrant to a judge or a prosecutor until they know the charges they're bringing forth will stick. Mix murder for hire—one of the toughest crimes for prosecutors to prove—into the equation, and things get even more complicated.

Even though Turner and his colleagues had some solid anecdotal evidence that put Despres and Fremut under a guilty light, they still had to think about how tangible the evidence was. Turner had been writing up the arrest warrants almost daily since Fremut and Despres had been on their radar. He would add information whenever it came in. During the latter part of 1994, about nine months into the investigation, Turner still felt he didn't have enough yet to seek a judge's signature on the warrants. They needed more. Who was this mysterious attorney? Was it actually Haiman Clein? If so, why had he hired Despres? At this time, of course, Beth Ann's name played no part in the investigation. To the ED-MCS, she was just another grieving family member.

Jose Argarim, a thirty-three-year-old native of the Philippines who had been living in New London for the past twenty years, met Beth Ann in early October at the local Gold's Gym. Argarim, who worked for Electric Boat in Groton, liked what he saw when he first spied Beth Ann. A short time after seeing her talking to a mutual friend, Argarim asked his friend if he could introduce them. A few days later, Jose got Beth Ann's phone number and called her.

"The relationship took what I would say a normal course, and as time went on, we became very close," Jose later said. "After the first couple of months . . .

she told me that she was having an affair and was involved sexually with her boss, Haiman Clein."

Clein and Beth Ann's intimate relationship, Jose suggested, continued for a time while he was also seeing her. In January 1995, Beth Ann ended up leaving Clein's law firm under the agreement that Clein would continue paying her, and Jose helped her move out. After that, Jose Argarim began being intimate with her and began spending time at her condo. Because she was always on the phone with Clein, from time to time, Argarim would ask her if she was still seeing him.

"Only professionally," she'd say. "It's all work-related."

In March 1995, Beth Ann and Jose took a trip to Key West. As soon as they arrived, Beth Ann began acting edgy and nervous, as if she were looking over her shoulder waiting for something to happen. Two days later, to Joses's surprise, Clein showed up at the hotel where she and Argarim were staying. After Clein left, Jose went crazy, demanding to know what the hell Clein was doing in Florida at the same time they were.

"Haiman has a house in Key West," Beth Ann explained. "I didn't know he would be here."

Jose, of course, was livid. He didn't believe her. Beth Ann, however, brushed off Argarim's contempt and continued to say she had no idea Clein was going to be there. Later that night, they began fighting more loudly and aggressively. Argarim wanted to know straight up: *"Did you or did you not invite him down here?"*

"I didn't know he was going to be here, Jose. You have to believe me."

As the night progressed, Argarim became more angered by the "coincidence." She had dissed him, made a fool out of him. So the next day, he drove back to Connecticut while she stayed in Key West.

According to Jose, a month went by before he heard

anything from Beth Ann. Then, unexpectedly, she
called.

"Upset and crying," Argarim recalled later, "she [said]
she'd had a fight with Haiman." Argarim said he acted
as if he didn't care. He had been duped once—why
chance it again?

"But he pulled my hair," Beth Ann said through tears.
"He kicked me around and punched me."

"I'll be right over," Jose Argarim said.

When he arrived at her condo, he said he saw bruises
on her arms and legs. When he asked her why Clein had
hit her, she only said, "I'm never seeing him again."

One of the people who had, as far as Turner and his
colleagues could see, a close connection to Despres and
Fremut was John Filippi, Fremut's old friend who had
been commissioned once by Fremut to find him a silencer. Turner and Graham knew if they continued
working on Filippi, they could possibly find out either
where Fremut was or what he knew.

Filippi, on the other hand, just couldn't keep himself
out of trouble. In February, he'd burglarized a home in
Norwich and confessed to it a short time later. Then in
March, he broke into an office building in Essex, and
cops found his basement full of the stolen merchandise.
When detectives interviewed him about the burglaries,
Filippi mentioned that he might have more information
regarding Buzz's murder.

Back on March 12, a former girlfriend of Filippi's
phoned the state police with some rather shocking news.
She said Filippi had just called her and said he was on his
way to her house to "take care of her, her two kids and
then himself." He said he didn't care anymore about
anything.

When the woman pleaded with him to remain calm,

Filippi said, "Anson Clinton got exactly what he deserved. I gave him what he had coming. He deserved to die! You're a whore, a pig, a loser. You've ruined my life."

Chapter 35

While Haiman Clein spent his time trying to rebuild what little relationship he had left with his wife, Mark Despres continued hiding out in Florida.

Beth Ann, however, began making plans for her future.

Ali Bagherzadeh, at age thirty, had met Beth Ann back in 1987 when the two were classmates at Catholic University. Ali, born into a wealthy Middle Eastern family, had dreams of becoming a lawyer but had since abandoned them to work in his father's bank in London. After the family sold the bank in early 1995, Ali bought a company that made "steel pipes and tanks."

Beth Ann and Ali had barely kept in touch throughout the years. Months, even years, passed without a phone call or letter. But in the spring of 1995, Beth Ann called Ali in London and told him she was jobless.

Clein was talking about closing the Old Saybrook law office, she said. Things weren't going well for him financially. His employees were beginning to notice that clients' funds were disappearing more regularly, in bigger denominations. With all his finances drying up, at first Clein had objected to a severance agreement he and Beth Ann had agreed upon when she left the firm. But after meeting with her one night, perhaps falling victim to lust and temptation, Clein agreed to a healthy $1,000-per-week package.

"I'm having problems with my boss," Beth Ann explained to Ali during the phone call. "There's some internal problems. I need a job, Ali. Can you help me?"

"I can offer you a job in London as an independent contractor. You'll be self-employed. I think you're going to have problems getting a work permit, though."

By the time they finished talking, Ali agreed to give her a job for three weeks. After that, he would evaluate the situation. Beth Ann never mentioned when she would be coming. She said she wanted to secure a job so she had options once she made a decision.

It was odd that she had inquired about a job so far away from home, because on November 28, 1994, she had sent a letter to her landlord requesting an extension on her Norwich condo lease. Her landlord sent a letter back saying he would gladly grant the extension.

The question many would later ask was: why would she extend a lease on her condo if she was moving to London?

By July, John Turner had enlisted the help of the Florida Department of Law Enforcement to help keep tabs on Mark Despres as he hid out in Florida with his juvenile girlfriend. Turner wanted the Major Crime Squad in Florida, if it could, to get the girlfriend, Jackie Powers, alone and ask her some questions.

Back on May 26, 1994, after Catherine White called, Detective John Szamocki had interviewed Jackie at her home. She said she didn't know much about the murder. Despres had been smart enough not to include her in any of his discussions with Fremut. But she did know a lot about Mark Despres. She had been living with him and Chris for some time.

"Mark has one gun he keeps in his bedroom," she told Szamocki. "He keeps it next to the bed on the floor."

She also said Despres usually carried a gun on him because he had "a lot of enemies."

"Like who?" Szamocki asked.

"The only one I know of," she said, "is . . . my mom's boyfriend."

Szamocki could certainly understand how the boyfriend could be upset over the fact that a thirty-five-year-old used-car salesman was sleeping with a fifteen-year-old girl.

Another important fact from the interview was that Jackie said Mark had owned a used-car business in Florida that his sister ran for him when he wasn't around.

Before Szamocki finished, he asked Jackie about Mark and Chris's relationship.

"I know from being with Mark that both he and his son Chris believe in the Devil. They try to bring ghosts in the house and talk to them. I was never there when they did this because it scares me. Mark wears jewelry with the sign of the devil on it."

When Special Agent Michael Driscoll interviewed Jackie Powers in Florida on July 25, she didn't really have much to say, but she confirmed that Despres was still in Punta Gorda, where he had been all along. She also said he was receiving money via FedEx from someone in Connecticut, but she didn't know who. When SA Driscoll asked her if they had made plans to leave the state or were moving anytime soon, she said they were getting ready to return to Connecticut because they were out of money.

After Beth Ann told Jose Argarim that Clein had been hitting her, Argarim rekindled the relationship. And by the summer of 1995, they were closer than they'd ever been.

"We started doing things," Jose said, "with her niece Rebecca, who Beth was very fond of."

Argarim then began to get to know the entire Carpenter family, spending time at the house. Argarim assumed that Buzz was Rebecca's father because of the way they all talked about him. Curious, Argarim would ask what happened to Buzz, but he could tell it was a sour subject.

"It was obvious to me that this bothered [Beth], so I didn't talk about it again. She would tell me that she didn't want to talk about it."

While Jose believed that Beth Ann had little or no contact with Clein, friends were telling him different. When he pressed them for more information, they told him they'd seen Beth Ann around town with Clein on many occasions. Again, when Jose confronted Beth Ann, she wrote it off as business. She and Clein were partners once. They had matters to wrap up.

By the end of summer, Beth Ann told Jose she was thinking about moving to England. He asked why.

"I want to start over again, both professionally and personally."

When Argarim heard she was leaving, he began to suspect again she was seeing Clein intimately, so he retreated from the relationship.

In many ways, Beth Ann was conflicted by the end of summer 1995. She was going out of her mind, worrying about her relationship with Clein. She had told different people different things about her future. One minute, she was talking about leaving; the next moment, she was staying. Nevertheless, where it mattered, Beth Ann made every attempt to indicate she was staying in the country; in fact, in early October, she got hold of her landlord again and demanded a second extension on her lease, to which he agreed.

In truth, after news spread that capital felony murder warrants were going to be issued for Despres and Fremut, Beth Ann left the country without telling her landlord or any of her friends where she was going.

Word had hit the street by the end of the summer that Despres and Fremut were back in town. On October 27, 1995, a Friday, Turner got both arrest warrants signed.

The ED-MCS split twelve troopers and detectives into two teams of six. At the same hour, when word came down, both teams served both warrants simultaneously. It was about surprise. They couldn't give Fremut or Despres a chance to warn the other about what was going down. It could mean life or death for a cop.

By Sunday, October 29, Turner got word that Despres and Fremut were both home. Since Despres had returned from Florida, he'd ditched Jackie and had begun seeing Jocelyn Johnson again, his longtime girlfriend—a woman who had helped him purchase guns in the past. In fact, Turner had recently found out that Johnson had purchased not one, but two, AK-47 rifles. He had to believe that one or both were for Despres.

Early in the morning on October 29, Turner and Graham got word that Fremut was seen at his mother's house. So a last-minute decision was made to grab Fremut while they had the chance. Besides, Despres hadn't been seen for a few days, and they weren't sure where he was. If nothing else, Fremut might be able to assist in finding Despres.

Protected by full-body armor, Turner, Graham and several troopers arrived at Fremut's parents' house in Essex at about 8:00 A.M.

No one answered the door when Turner knocked. But after hearing movement inside the house, Turner signaled he was going to kick the door in.

As soon as Turner and his colleagues entered, Fremut's mother began screaming at them to get out: "There's no one here!" Turner, carefully eyeing the inside of the house, spied Fremut running across the balcony upstairs.

"Hold it, Joey!" Turner yelled as he identified himself. "Stop."

Fremut kept running and quickly disappeared.

When Turner got upstairs, he heard Fremut scrambling around inside a closet. He had no idea if he had a gun, so he slowly went up to the door. A moment later, after Turner made it clear there was no chance of an escape, Fremut opened the door with his hands raised and gave up without incident.

An hour later, thirty-four-year-old Joe Fremut was charged with capital felony, conspiracy to commit murder, and murder. His bond was set at $500,000, with an arraignment date set for October 31.

One down, one to go.

With Mark Despres being the woodsy, outdoor type, having fished, hunted, camped and worked outside his entire life, the thought of being behind bars was something he later said he would never submit to. No matter what, he would do everything in his power to escape even one day behind bars. With the arsenal of weaponry the ED-MCS had unearthed during an earlier search of Despres's apartment, it was almost certain that Despres was going to be armed. Jackie had told the ED-MCS he slept with a gun under his bed. He had been seen around town on occasion carrying a gun in a holster. He had killed someone, according to Catherine White. Why would he give up now without a fight?

After Turner and his team left Fremut's house, they went directly to Despres's apartment in Deep River. First they checked with Despres's mother to see if he was in the main house. Esther Lockwood indicated that the last time she saw her son he was in his apartment. Turner motioned to the troopers behind him that there was a good chance Despres was inside the apartment.

"He's probably armed. . . ."

Within minutes, the apartment was surrounded, and cops were barking out orders for Despres to come out with his hands up.

Little did they know, however, that Despres had grabbed an AK-47 Johnson had purchased for him and took off out the back door as they were converging on the scene. To his surprise, Despres made it to the woods in back of his mother's house and sat for a while on a hill watching as Turner and his crew surrounded his apartment.

"The reason he did that," Turner later said, "was so he could watch us. If we started to follow him, Despres told me later, scared he'd get caught, he was going to 'start shooting' us 'one by one.'"

Turner further explained that they were all vested, but a bulletproof vest was no match for an assault by an AK-47.

As it turned out, Despres watched for a few minutes and then retreated into the woods, a place where he surely felt he had the upper hand.

After troopers and detectives searched Despres's apartment, Turner put out an APB, tagging Despres as armed and dangerous.

Now the hunt was on for Deep River's most notorious and dangerous hired hit man.

Chapter 36

The news of Buzz Clinton's murder was a constant story in area newspapers and on television during the past few weeks as the ED-MCS moved closer to solving the case. Whenever there was a break in the story, it would be picked up by local media. WVIT TV-30, in West Hartford, Connecticut, was a staple in Connecticut households for decades. It had a large audience that included every town in the state.

Dave Kraus, a Jolly Green Giant of a man at six feet four inches, three hundred pounds, had worked at WVIT for the past year as a cameraman. During the morning hours of October 29, Kraus and WVIT reporter *Angela Ryder*, a well-known on-air personality, were in Derby covering a story unrelated to the Despres matter. When news broke that the state police had tried unsuccessfully to arrest Despres, someone at the station called Dave and Angela.

"This guy is on the loose in Deep River. The cops are looking for him. You need to get to Deep River now."

Angela was aware of the case; Dave had just moved into the area and hadn't heard much about it, so he didn't know what was going on.

They drove immediately to Despres's home in Deep River. As they were pulling up the driveway, they saw

WFSB TV and WTNH TV, the two competing stations, leaving.

"Great," Angela said, slapping her hand on the dashboard. "We missed it. Shit."

Since they were already there, they asked Despres's stepfather to answer a few questions.

"Yeah," he said, "the cops were here, but Mark took off. They're looking for him now."

Driving away from Despres's house, Dave and Angela began talking about their next move. Neither had done much research on the case, so they had no sources in the area from whom to obtain leads.

"Let's go to the Westbrook [State Police] barracks," Angela suggested. "See if we can't get a cop to give us some background to pad the story a bit?"

"I guess it won't hurt," Dave said.

As the ED-MCS searched for Mark Despres throughout the morning and into the afternoon of October 29, word had spread that Despres was on the loose. Since Chris Despres had moved back into town, he had taken a job at the same Sunoco station in Essex where he and Mark had discarded part of the murder weapon. On occasion, Chris's girlfriend, Margaret Long, brought him dinner and sat outside and ate with him.

On October 29, as Margaret and Chris were eating, they heard over a police scanner in the garage that there was a major problem going on in the Winthrop Road area.

"Hey, let's go down there," Chris suggested.

Route 145 runs from downtown Essex, near the Sunoco station, down to Route 80, or Winthrop Road, and connects in a T formation. As Chris and Margaret approached the intersection of Route 80 and 145, they saw a line of troopers blocking the road. Cars were being pulled over. Drivers were being asked questions and then allowed to proceed. The state police had a fugitive

on the loose who could very well be armed. They knew
how dangerous the situation appeared and how desperate Mark Despres was, and the police hadn't put it past
him to take a hostage.

When he pulled up to the roadblock, Chris had no
idea that all the commotion was about his dad.

"What's your business here?" a trooper asked.

"I want to check to make sure my grandmother's
okay," Chris said. "She lives right up the road. We heard
on the scanner that something's going on. Is there a
fire?"

"Who's your grandmother? Where does she live?"

"Esther Lockwood. [At] Winthrop Road," Chris said.
He looked over at Margaret, who now wondered if there
was a problem.

"Really," the trooper said, backing away from Chris's
car. "Could you step out of the vehicle, sir?"

Margaret began to shift in her seat as Chris got out
and walked away with the trooper.

"At first," Margaret later said, "I thought for sure it
had something to do with Mark. I didn't know anything
at that point about Chris's or Mark's involvement in the
murder, but Mark was always into something. Yet, I was
also scared that something happened to Esther. I liked
her very much."

When Detective Marty Graham heard from one of the
troopers that Chris Despres was sitting in a cruiser at the
roadblock, he walked over to the car and sat down next
to Chris.

"When was the last time you saw your father?" Marty
asked.

"On Saturday," Chris said. "What is this? We went out
and rode three-wheel ATVs from about one to seven."

"You know your father is wanted for murder?"

"Listen, I have no idea where my dad is now or where
he might go. Can I go now?" Chris began getting defen-

sive. "I don't know anything about the murder. I don't know where he is. Can I go?"

"Well, I guess—"

Before Graham could finish, Chris got out of the car and began walking away.

"I don't have to talk to you guys," he shouted. "I'm not under arrest."

When Chris returned to his car, he looked scared and confused, Margaret later remembered. "Something was obviously wrong—something he was keeping from me. I could feel it."

"My dad is in trouble," Chris said without hesitation when Margaret asked. "They're after him."

"What? Tell me what's going on, Chris."

"Well, they said they're going to shoot him if they catch him."

Chris didn't need to say anything more by that point. She knew that whatever Mark had gotten himself mixed up in this time was serious. It was written all over Chris's face.

Dave Kraus and Angela Ryder arrived at the Troop F barracks at about 6:30 P.M. They had spent the day tracking down a few false leads and filming some backstory footage, but nothing of any real importance turned up. Now they were hoping to get a trooper to say a few things on camera that would tide viewers over until a break in the story came.

As Dave began setting up his camera in a trooper's office, the phone rang.

"Excuse me," the trooper said while Dave and Angela continued prepping for the interview. As Dave looked on, eavesdropping on the conversation, he noticed that the trooper was becoming animated. *"What?"* the trooper barked into the phone. "Where is he?"

Then the trooper slammed the phone down and

began running out of the room. "I've got to go," he said. "Sorry."

For the moment, Angela and Dave stood there in the empty room in awe at what had just happened.

"Shit," Dave said, "maybe we better follow him, Angela, huh?"

When they got outside, they spied the trooper speeding around the corner of the building, heading for the exit of the parking lot. Troop F is on a little incline. If one is standing in the parking lot, once cars go over the crest of the hill, it's impossible to tell which way they went, left or right.

So Angela and Dave hopped in their van and began to chase the trooper. He was onto something. It wasn't necessarily concerning the Despres matter, Dave surmised, but there was a good chance it had something to do with it considering the chaotic nature of what went down as they were talking about Despres while setting up equipment.

When they got down to the bottom of the hill, however, the trooper was gone.

"Left or right?" Angela asked.

"Right," Dave said instantly. It was a hunch.

An avid lover of horseback riding, Jocelyn Johnson had gone to North Haven to ride on the morning of October 29. She was supposed to go over to Esther Lockwood's house for dinner later that night, but when she checked her phone messages after her morning ride, she found out her plans had been changed.

"Don't come over tonight," Lockwood said into Johnson's answering machine. "I'm at the police station. Mark is in trouble."

Johnson recalled later that after a day of running errands she went home and watched television. At around 8:00 P.M., Mark Despres showed up unannounced at her back door. This, however, doesn't agree with what detectives later surmised. When pressed, one detective said he felt that Jocelyn Johnson helped Mark Despres throughout the entire day on October 29, perhaps even picking him up on the road after he ran through the woods and escaped capture.

"She had bought him guns in the past—even an AK-47, for crying out loud," that same detective said. "Was it such a stretch to think that she might have helped him hide out all day, too?"

Despres was not welcome at Johnson's parents' house. Like many people in town, they simply didn't like him. That's why, Johnson later said, it shocked her to see Mark standing at the back door.

"I'm in trouble," Despres said when he arrived. "I need to get out of here right away."

"Why are you in trouble?"

"I need to get out of here," Despres said again.

"He was very unstable, and I was afraid to say no," Johnson recalled when detectives questioned her later. "I also did not want Mark [at my house] when my parents got home. So I agreed to drive him out of town."

As Johnson, who was holding a flashlight, and Despres approached Johnson's vehicle, a green 1966 Buick LeSabre, Despres whispered, "Open the trunk."

Despres then got in the trunk while a trooper surveying Johnson's parents' house looked on from up the road.

Watching Johnson's every move as she got into her car and pulled out of the driveway, the trooper called it in.

"I have a vehicle registered to one Irving Johnson traveling south on Route 156. There's a female operating the vehicle and a second person, I believe a male, was seen getting into the trunk of said vehicle."

That one phone call to dispatch set off a frenzy of calls to troopers in the area. Within a few minutes, as Johnson made her way onto Interstate 95, three more troopers had arrived and were following her.

When Johnson made her descent off Exit 66, troopers hit their lights and lined up on both sides of her car. By this time, as Johnson put on her signal and retreated to the end of the exit ramp, several more troopers had arrived.

Approaching the exit to the interstate where it intersects with the main road, Dave Kraus and Angela Ryder, after taking a right turn on Dave's hunch, stopped the van and saw eight to ten cruisers, lights on, sirens blazing, surrounding what they learned later was Jocelyn Johnson's car. It was pulled off to the side of the road near the exit ramp. As Angela and Dave pulled up, a cop came running up to the driver's-side window of their van. He had a shotgun in his hands.

"Get the *fuck* off this road. Get out of here . . . right now!"

To the left of where Dave and Angela were parked was the entrance to a self-storage company, so they pulled the van into the lot and shut it off. The cop, now approaching Johnson's vehicle, left Dave and Angela without saying anything more.

"What the hell is going on?" Dave asked Angela.

"I don't know. But get your camera ready."

One of the troopers walked up to the driver's side of Johnson's car and told her not to move. "Throw the keys out the window, ma'am."

When Johnson got out with her hands up, he asked, "Where's Mark?"

"He's in the trunk," Johnson said without hesitation.

The trooper motioned with the barrel of his gun for Johnson to walk toward the back of the vehicle. As soon as she started walking, another trooper came up from behind and cuffed her. There were now six or seven troopers, rifles in hand, pointing toward the trunk of the car, standing about ten yards away.

Dave Kraus, about thirty yards away, was stooped down low to the ground, camera in hand, facing the trunk of Johnson's car.

Show time.

"Every single cop out there had their guns drawn," Dave recalled. "Shotguns. Handguns. You name it." One unit even had dogs with them, and the dogs looked like they were ready to attack on command.

"They were going crazy, barking and jumping around."

With his camera rolling, Dave watched as a trooper walked over and, in a bellowing, deep voice, shouted, "You coming out—or what?"

Despres said something, but no one could understand him.

"You coming out or what?" the trooper asked again.

Nothing.

"You got a gun in there?"

"No!" Despres said loud and clear.

The trooper asked, "How do we know that?" and began backing away from the trunk. There was some noise, as if Despres were opening the trunk from the inside.

"That was intense," Dave Kraus recalled. "As the trunk opened, we didn't know what the hell was going to happen."

With the trunk opening slowly, a trooper stood right there ready to poke Despres in the head with his shotgun once he was in sight. When the trunk popped open, more troopers approached with their rifles pointed toward Despres's head. Despres was fully visible now. One of the dogs was sent in. While the dog began barking and snapping, four or five other troopers grabbed Despres by the hair and jacket, pulled him out of the trunk and pinned him to the ground as if he were a teenage kid. While this was going on, another trooper ran up and shoved the barrel of his shotgun into Despres's back.

"Don't move, motherfucker!"

When the troopers made Despres stand up, Dave Kraus finally understood what all the fuss was about.

"That's when I realized how big this guy was. I'm a big guy—and even I was scared shitless at the size of this man. He was wearing a camouflage ball cap and fatigues, and his hair was pulled back in a ponytail. Just one huge bastard."

Things weren't so festive and celebratory for Chris Despres now that his father had been arrested for a capital felony murder that he had witnessed. Dave Kraus's remarkable footage of Mark Despres's arrest was plastered all over the news, shown again and again. Chris couldn't seem to get away from it.

Margaret, however, began to worry. For the past several months, she had seen Chris withdraw from things that once interested him. Chris had always been quiet, Margaret knew, but lately he just wasn't himself. With the story breaking that Mark was being charged with murder, Margaret began pushing Chris to tell her exactly what was going on.

Finally Chris broke down one night. He began crying. He was, Margaret remembered later, a shell of the person he once had been. Clearly, something was eating away at him from inside his soul, and Mark's arrest only enhanced whatever pain he had already been experiencing.

"Tell me, Chris. What is it? I'm here for you," Margaret said. She loved him. She wanted to comfort him. Oddly enough, despite Chris's age, they had already discussed marriage.

"Remember the murder in Old Lyme a while ago?" Chris asked.

It was a small town. People talked. Margaret, of course, knew every detail about the murder. Who didn't?

"What is it, Chris?"

"Remember the guy who got murdered on the Rock Neck connector?"

"Yes, Chris. What are you saying? What *is* it?"

"That was my father. . . ."

"What?"

"I was there, too."

"You were there? What do you mean, you were *there?*"

"I was *there*. I watched my dad kill that guy!"

Margaret was devastated. "Totally shocked," she said later. "Mark had done nutty things, but I never dreamed he could have done that—and then to take Chris with him?"

For the next hour or so, they didn't speak. Yet as the night wore on, fidgety and wired, Chris began getting anxious. He couldn't sit still, wondering what was going to happen once the cops found out he was involved.

"Chris, come on, try to relax," Margaret said at one point.

"He offered me the opportunity to commit the murder," Chris admitted.

As if it couldn't get any worse for Margaret.

Throughout the night, Chris told Margaret everything he could remember, as if purging himself of all the guilt he had stowed away.

When cops searched Jocelyn Johnson's car, they found a .22-caliber handgun in the trunk. Apparently, Despres was armed, just as everyone had expected he might be.

Johnson was ultimately arrested for hindering prosecution and given a court date of November 11, 1995. After posting a $5,000 nonsecurity bond, she was released.

With Mark Despres and Joe Fremut in custody, the ED-MCS could get down to finding out who else was involved in Buzz Clinton's murder.

Circe's Path

Chapter 37

Dee Clinton and her family had been waiting for nearly a year and a half for *some* answers—and by early Monday morning, October 30, 1995, they had been informed that two suspects were in custody.

When newspaper reporters located Dee and asked her what she had been hearing regarding the recent arrests, Dee said, "The police have been more than fair to me, and I have to honor their wishes," she told the *Hartford Courant.* "I don't want to make their job more difficult."

With Mark Despres and Joe Fremut locked up, John Turner and Marty Graham began plotting their next move. Would Mark or Joe be forthcoming with what they knew? Would they give Turner and Graham the one thing they wanted more than anything at this point—more names? After all, Despres and Fremut didn't know exactly what Catherine White had already confessed.

Joe Fremut was especially evasive during his first interview. He indicated he was waiting for his attorney, the highly touted F. Mac Buckley, a noted criminal defense attorney from Hartford. Buckley, who would himself later face charges of embezzlement and take off in a well-publicized flight from justice, told Marty Graham after meeting with Fremut that Fremut was reluctant to talk. He was going to ride it out. But Buckley, after meeting with Fremut a second time and explaining that he was facing a possible death sentence if convicted, convinced Fremut to begin talking. Buckley, according to Graham, told Fremut that the only way he could cut a deal for him later on was if he began cooperating now.

At first, Fremut downplayed his role. He said it was all Mark's idea, and he never intended to help him.

"We knew damn well that Mark would never have killed Buzz if Fremut wasn't involved," one detective later noted. "Despres just wasn't smart enough to do it himself. He needed Joey."

Despres was stewing while in lockup. He was in his worst possible element. Having no contact with the outside, he began to think of ways to get out of the trouble he now found himself in.

At this point, Turner and Graham, based on a few off-the-record conversations they'd had with Despres, had a good indication that Haiman Clein and Beth Ann Carpenter were involved in the conspiracy, but there was nothing tangible yet linking them to the murder. At the same time, though, they knew Despres was that missing link.

Despres, however, indicated he wasn't interested in talking about anything more than what he had said already—although he told them Clein was involved.

While Turner and Graham discussed how they were going to approach Despres a second time, they heard that Clein had driven down to the courthouse where Despres was being held. Acting as Mark's attorney, Clein tried getting in to talk to him. Despres had already given Clein up in a preliminary interview Turner and Graham had conducted with him earlier that day. They knew Clein was trying to weasel his way in to see Despres so he could, most likely, warn him about talking.

By late afternoon on October 30, 1995, Turner and Graham got a judge's order to keep Clein away from Despres. Since that time, Despres had given them a statement to his involvement in the murder, fingering both Clein and Beth Ann, but would say nothing more about the details of the crime.

Clandestinely watching Clein pace the hallway inside the courthouse, Turner and Graham enjoyed a moment of reprieve in what had been a long year and a half. They wanted Clein to sweat a little. Think about things. Maybe crack under the anxiety of not knowing what was going on or what Despres was saying.

After twenty minutes of watching Clein rub his beard and wear a path in the floor tile, Turner and Graham emerged.

"We'd like to talk to you, Mr. Clein," Turner said.

"I guess," Clein said.

Sitting down, Turner said, "We need to talk to you about the murder of Buzz Clinton."

Clein immediately began playing stupid, Turner later recalled. "I don't know what you mean. I don't know what to say to that."

"You can start by telling us what you know about it, Mr. Clein. We know you know what's going on here. We know you have information that can help us out."

"Do you . . ." Clein began to say before stopping for a moment to rub his forehead. "Do you think . . . Are you looking at me as having had something to do with it?"

John Turner rarely smiled. His seriousness and stern facial features were, however, what made him one of the best interrogators the ED-MCS had on staff.

"Yes," Turner said. He and Graham suspected Clein had had some type of involvement in Buzz's murder. Then Turner added, "I don't understand, please help me understand this. Why is a person of your social stature, Mr. Clein, hanging around with a guy like Mark Despres?"

Clein then went into a long diatribe regarding his rise and fall in the real estate market. As he spoke, Turner and

Graham kept looking at each other, wondering what it all had to do with Buzz's murder.

"I was on top of the world one day," Clein ranted. "It all fell apart. You're up; you're down. That's when you start representing different types of people."

"We can understand that," Graham said.

"People with shady backgrounds," Clein continued.

"What are we talking about here, Mr. Clein?" Turner asked.

"Right! What the hell does this have to do with what we're talking about?" Graham added.

"Well, to be honest," Clein said, "eventually you become what you represent."

"We knew we had him at that point," Turner later recalled.

"I have known the Despres family," Clein continued, "for nearly twenty years, and have become close friends with Mark over that time. Mark's mother called me when he was arrested and asked for my help."

"So that's why you're here?"

"Yes."

Turner and Graham knew that Despres had been supplying Clein with cocaine, so Graham asked Clein if his connection to Despres was drug-related.

"I am insulted by that statement. But, on the other hand, I can understand where you're coming from."

"What's your relationship with"—Graham, at this point, stopped for a moment and looked at a pad he had in front of him—"Beth Ann . . . Carpenter?"

"She works with me at my law firm. And I'm not about to bring my personal life into this conversation."

"Again, you have no knowledge of Buzz Clinton's murder either before or after it took place?"

"I'm really insulted now," Clein said. "I'm really uncomfortable with talking about the case."

"Why?"

"Well, anything I say can come back to bite either Mark or myself."

"Tell us about your connection to Despres and the murder, Mr. Clein. We can talk about this here, right?"

"I'll be damned if I do, damned if I don't," Clein said. "I'm done talking."

Two days later, November 1, detectives set out to interview, as they now saw it, three key players: Bonnie Clein, Dick Carpenter and Beth Ann Carpenter.

At 7:50 A.M., Reggie Wardell and Paul Killoran, also an ED-MCS detective, drove to Indiantown Road in Ledyard to see if they could find Beth Ann.

Cynthia Carpenter, getting ready for work, answered the door.

"About three weeks ago," Cynthia said when Wardell asked if she knew where Beth Ann was, "Beth Ann went to work for a friend in London." She gave them the address. "She'll be back on December twentieth and return to England in January 1996 and stay there until March."

Wardell and Killoran began asking Cynthia about Buzz. They wanted to know what she had heard about the murder.

"Only what I've read in the papers," Cynthia said. "I read you arrested two men."

"Have you ever heard of them?"

"No. Neither has Richard, my husband, or my son, Richard."

"Have you spoken to your daughter Beth Ann recently?"

"I called her and told her about the arrests."

Cynthia went on to say that she did send Beth Ann a few newspaper clippings, but she never told her the names of those arrested, nor had she asked. Instead, Beth Ann just wanted the newspaper clippings. Wardell then got a little bit more detectivelike with his questioning. He asked whom Beth Ann was working for at the time of Buzz's murder. "Haiman Clein," Cynthia said.

Then he asked if it was possible that Beth Ann and Clein were lovers.

"I don't know that for sure," Cynthia said.

"Could these men [Despres and Fremut] have been clients of your daughter's?"

"I don't think so."

"Did Buzz ever take any money from you?"

"I don't think so," Cynthia said. "I think Beth did her banking with First Fidelity. . . . By the way, do you think that Beth and Haiman had anything to do with hiring those people who killed Buzz?"

"I'm surprised you would ask that question," Wardell said. He was shocked by her candor. "We've never implied anytime during this interview that Beth, Haiman or any one in the Carpenter family could also be involved in the death of Buzz. Is it true," Wardell continued, "that the Carpenter family wished Buzz's death because of the pain he caused the family over the grandchildren?"

"Yes. But I did call Dee Clinton and offer our condolences when I heard Buzz was killed."

The interview was obviously wearing Cynthia down some. It was running long. They were an hour into it already. As Wardell pressed, though, Cynthia kept hammering her points home. No, there wasn't a person in her family involved in Buzz's murder. No, she had no knowledge that Haiman Clein took it upon himself to carry out some wish of the Carpenter family. In fact, concerning Clein, Cynthia said, he wasn't capable of doing such a thing. He had offered the Carpenters his condolences. He had been to the house at least three times since Buzz's death and never once mentioned it. He had even brought his children over to the house to play Scrabble.

"Has Beth Ann spoken to Mr. Clein recently?"

"Before she left, she called him," Cynthia said. Then, "I told Beth that I hoped it was over between her and Haiman when she left for England."

Wardell and Killoran knew right then that Cynthia wasn't being totally truthful, because earlier she had said she didn't know for sure Haiman and Beth Ann were an item.

"Then there *was* a social relationship between Beth and Haiman, even though he is married?"

"I suspected it, but Beth never talked about it."

The phone rang at about 9:00 A.M. It was Dick. He told Cynthia he was being interviewed down the road at Colonial Tire, a local hangout he went to each morning for coffee.

After Cynthia hung up, she said she would take a polygraph to convince them that she had no knowledge of the people who planned Buzz's murder.

Before they left, Wardell gave her his business card, wrote "Kevin Kane," the New London state's attorney, across it and told her to call the state's attorney's office if she had anything more to offer.

Shortly after nine, Wardell and Killoran left. As they drove away, though, Wardell looked over at Killoran and said, "Let's wait a bit and go back and hit her with one more question."

"It was my *Columbo* move," Wardell, laughing, said later.

At 9:45 A.M., Wardell and Killoran returned. "I have one more question," Wardell said while standing at the doorstep.

"Come in," Cynthia said. "I just got off the phone with Beth and Kim. I told them that you guys thought we're involved and that Haiman has been arrested—"

"We never said Haiman Clein had been arrested."

"You said he was in custody."

"We said that other detectives were interviewing him."

"What was your other question?" Cynthia asked.

"Are you sure that Mr. Clein never mentioned anything about how or why Buzz was murdered?"

"No. The whole family thinks it was over drugs."

"Thanks."

Detective John Szamocki and a colleague had sneaked up on Dick Carpenter while he was having his morning coffee at Colonial Tire, and Dick agreed to an interview in Szamocki's vehicle in the parking lot.

They talked first about Despres and Fremut. Dick said he'd heard of the arrests—but he didn't know either man.

"How are things going?" Szamocki wondered.

"Pretty good," Dick said. "Kim is now living in Niantic with her three children. She had a 'falling-out' with Dee. I don't know what it was all about. I think Kim is going with Rob Ferguson now."

Dick then explained that Beth Ann had gone to London to work with a "friend." He said she'd be returning in December. When Szamocki asked if she'd called since she left, Dick said no. He then talked about Clein and said he didn't know if Beth Ann and Clein were intimately involved.

"Tell us about Buzz. You guys were having problems with him, true?"

"Yeah, there were problems," Dick said. He then explained that a couple of years back, Kim had been dating a sailor from Virginia who was stationed at the sub base in Groton. They were planning on getting married, but she met Buzz around the same time and called the wedding off. Dick said when he, Rebecca and Cynthia went to Hampton Beach, in New Hampshire, one weekend, Buzz, Kim and the sailor broke into his house and stole "several items," but he never reported the burglary to the cops.

Over the next hour, Dick told detectives about the custody fight that had erupted as Buzz became more of a presence in Kim's life. He went into great detail explaining just about every problem the Carpenters had had with Buzz regarding Rebecca. He made a point to say that Dee Clinton had once accused his son, Richard, and Joseph Jebran of sexually abusing Rebecca, yet DCYS concluded that it was unsubstantiated.

Dick, however, never mentioned that the Carpenters were routinely accusing Buzz of the same thing. Instead, he said he suspected Buzz of abusing *Kim*, having seen bruises on her "the size of a half-dollar." He thought Buzz was abusing drugs, too, but never saw it firsthand.

Then John Gaul's name came up. Before Dick spoke of Gaul, though, he talked about how Rebecca would call Buzz "Daddy," but he wasn't her biological father. According to Dick, Rebecca would say on occasion, "Daddy hit me." After explaining the entire John Gaul situation, Dick said Gaul dropped the idea of gaining custody of Rebecca only after Buzz threatened Tricia.

"Have you ever made a remark," Szamocki then asked, "about contracting the murder of Buzz?"

"I jokingly may have said that."

"When did you say it? Where were you?"

"I don't know . . . maybe around Christmastime, 1993, maybe January 1994. It was right here. I said it to some of my buddies at the coffee shop. I told Cynthia I'd like to 'do away' with Buzz. But no one ever took it literally. I didn't have a thing to do with this, and I know that Dee Clinton has been telling people I have."

"What do you think happened?"

"Drugs. Drug deal. Buzz used to take money from a gas station where he worked."

Szamocki got Dick to give him bank account numbers for all of their finances and signed a disclosure so they could later check to see if a large withdrawal had been made near the time of Buzz's murder.

"Tell us, Dick," Szamocki asked next, "who is it that you think most likely wanted your son-in-law dead?"

"Well, me or Cynthia would be highly probable. But it wasn't us."

"Who else, then?"

"Buck Clinton. He had an insurance policy on Buzz."

"Why did you refuse a polygraph test . . . around the time of the murder?"

"I talked it over with Beth. She told me you guys could make the outcome anything you wanted."

"That's not true, Dick."

"If you don't have anything else to go on, then I guess I'll take a polygraph."

"We'll be in touch," Szamocki said as Dick got out of the car and went back into the coffee shop.

When Reggie Wardell and Paul Killoran showed up at Haiman Clein's Pond Edge Drive home in Waterford to talk to Bonnie, she wouldn't let them in.

Wardell identified who they were and showed Bonnie his ID. "You get one shot at a witness like Bonnie," Wardell later said. "You have to be ready to ask one or two key questions. You may not get another shot after that. The witness might throw you out."

"What do you want?" Bonnie said after opening the door.

"Can we talk to you, Mrs. Clein?"

"What about?"

"It's personal—"

"What is it about?"

Wardell pulled two Polaroid photographs—Despres and Fremut—out of his pocket and showed them to Bonnie, without mentioning their names.

"Do you know these people?"

Bonnie pointed to Despres. "I know *him*." Then at Fremut. "I saw his picture in the newspaper."

Wardell asked her how she knew Despres, and Bonnie said he'd been a client of Haiman's for many, many years.

"Listen," Bonnie then said, "I shouldn't be answering any more questions. My husband's an attorney, and I'd like him present during any more questioning."

Wardell handed Bonnie his business card.

"Call us if any questions arise that you might want answers to."

Chapter 38

Within the few first weeks of being in London, working for Ali Bagherzadeh, Beth Ann began complaining about how financially strapped she was. Ali was paying her in U.S. currency and not withholding taxes, but she continued to complain about not having enough money to rent her own apartment.

Feeling a bit sorry for her, Ali allowed Beth Ann to live in the back of his office in what amounted to nothing more than a bed in an old, musty room. It was an abrupt change for someone who had come from living in luxury for so long now.

As Beth Ann began her new life, Ali immediately became impatient with her. Later, he said their relationship was "strictly platonic." Furthermore, he didn't involve himself too much in—"or care about"—her personal problems, which seemed to dominate everything she did.

But as the days passed, Beth Ann's problems became almost impossible to ignore. She ran up enormous phone bills, which she never paid, talking to Clein, and continually complained about how her life had turned out. Whenever Ali, a self-proclaimed "sap," told Beth Ann that she had to carry her weight in the office or leave, she would begin "crying and carrying on about how she had no place to live and that she had no money."

* * *

When Mark Despres found himself confined to jail for his role in Buzz's murder, having worked for Detective Chet Harris in the past as a paid informant, he decided to begin using Harris as his "go-to" person in law enforcement whenever he wanted to talk. On November 4, Despres reached out to Harris and got word to him that he wanted to open up about everything.

Harris contacted John Turner, who, along with Marty Graham, visited Despres at his new home: Walker Correctional Institution in Suffield, Connecticut.

Without any hesitation, Despres waived his rights.

The first thing Turner wanted to know was why Despres had changed his mind so suddenly.

"I've heard that Joey is talking shit, spreading rumors about me," Despres said.

"Well, let's hear what you have to say, then?"

Despres, masking his actual role, pointed the finger at Fremut and four other people, whom he refused to name. "Me and Joey killed Buzz," Despres admitted, "but Joey did the shooting."

A few days after Turner and Graham spoke to Despres, they convinced Fremut to open up even more. Whether he was going to be truthful, well, that was still to be proven. F. Mac Buckley, Fremut's attorney, had worked diligently to post bond for Fremut within the past few weeks. At $500,000, Fremut's parents had put Fremut Texaco, their house and the land they owned up as collateral, eventually getting Fremut out of jail.

At about 9:30 A.M., on November 10, Fremut and F. Mac Buckley showed up at the ED-MCS office in Norwich. Fremut agreed to waive his rights.

For four hours, Fremut talked about Despres and how they had planned to kill Buzz months before the actual murder took place. Yet as Turner listened, he knew Fremut was trying to misrepresent certain facts. When Turner pointed it out, Fremut changed his story to fit whatever scenario Turner put in front of him. At one point, Buckley warned Fremut about telling any more lies. When it came down to it, Buckley was there to cut a deal, get a reduced sentence. He told Fremut he couldn't do that if he continued to lie.

Finally, after Turner caught Fremut in a few more lies, Fremut ended up providing a detailed nine-page statement that provided Turner and Graham with a little more information. Fremut ended up implicating Despres even further, painting a more sinister, evil portrait of him.

"Mark told me he joined a Devil worship cult in Meriden," Fremut said. "As long as I have known Mark, he has always been a Christian. [But] . . . he [later] denounced God and worshiped Satan. Mark told me that these people in the cult had connections to do hits (kill people). I told my girlfriend, Cathy White, about Mark and his Devil worship."

Then he talked about how Despres planned the murder and how Dick Carpenter was responsible for setting it up through Haiman Clein.

By the time Fremut finished, and Turner and Graham had a chance to sit down and weigh his information against Cathy White's, they realized that as much as Joe Fremut wanted to downplay his role, the truth was all there: times, dates, details about guns, stalking Buzz, on and on. Joe Fremut knew things that Cathy White knew that Mark Despres knew. There was no way the three of them could have all gotten together and made their stories dovetail so perfectly.

Armed with Fremut's statement, Turner and Graham went back to Despres and told him they weren't going to tolerate his lies any longer. But if he wanted to work with them, they just might be able to do something for him down the road.

Between December 8 and December 11, Despres finally rolled over. He told them everything he could remember about the entire murder plan. Despres had even told Reggie Wardell, who had taken his statement, he was sorry for killing Buzz.

"I didn't even know Anson Clinton. I never met Anson Clinton before the night I shot him. . . . I [thought] I was getting rid of a child molester. I believed Haiman Clein when he told me that Anson Clinton was a bad guy and a child molester."

He was like a scorned child at that point, Wardell later remembered. "I wasn't so sure, though, that he was actually sorry about what he had done. But it did tell that he did it. Saying sorry was the same as a confession."

Indeed, why would someone say they were sorry for something they hadn't done?

Over a two-day period, Despres wrote a twenty-nine-page statement of fact that included just about every detail he could recall—most important, the meetings he'd had with Clein and Beth Ann. Whereas for the past few weeks Mark Despres had been protecting his son, he now admitted that Chris was there, too. To bolster his truth telling even further, Despres insisted on drawing a map of the murder scene, which matched up perfectly with the facts and photographs the ED-MCS already had.

When Wardell looked at the map Despres drew of the murder scene and put it up against all the known facts, he was overwhelmed at Despres's attention to detail.

"When I saw that," Wardell later said, "it was clear to me that Mark Despres was at that murder scene on the night Buzz Clinton was murdered."

But there was more. Besides the wealth of information they now had, the ED-MCS also had statements implicating both Beth Ann Carpenter and Haiman Clein, and it was now clear that Clein and Beth Ann had been the brains behind the entire operation from the get-go.

Once John Turner got Mark Despres to admit that his son had been present on the night of the murder, he and John Szamocki hauled Chris into the state's attorney's office for questioning.

"I'm not speaking or signing anything unless I can call my mother so she can contact my attorney," Chris said right away.

Then he demanded they order him a pizza.

"He played hardball better than the rest of them," Turner later said. "He absolutely shut up."

At some point while Chris was at the state's attorney's office, he demanded to see his father.

"He felt horrible about what he was about to do," Margaret Long later remembered. "He wanted to hear from his father that it was okay to talk."

So detectives allowed Chris to talk to Mark—but only through the doorway.

"What should I do, Dad?" Chris asked.

"Tell them the whole story. . . . Tell them the truth."

Margaret recalled later that Diana Trevethan, Chris's mother, told him not to talk unless the state was prepared to grant Chris immunity.

Within a few hours of being at the state's attorney's office, Chris had his lawyer on a speaker phone monitoring the interview. By then, Chris's attorney had already secured a deal for immunity; he was free to talk about anything without worrying about being prosecuted for his role later on.

A few days after the ED-MCS obtained signed statements from Joe Fremut and Mark and Chris Despres, a cellmate of Mark's came forward with a note he claimed Mark had written to Clein. Mark, in a last act of desperation, was trying to smuggle the letter out of prison through his cellmate, who had just been released.

"Now I don't care what it takes," Despres opened the

brief letter to Clein, "you have to get me out of here, or you will be here with me."

Then he demanded that Clein "get the money together" for his bail. If not, "my friends will do anything I say . . . your family, your girlfriend, and her brother." Despres said he was "*not* fucking around." He threatened that if Clein didn't bail him out, he would begin talking. As a postscript, Mark added: "They (his friends) will keep an eye on you till you pay—one week!"

Threatening letter or not, for Clein, the entire infrastructure of a murder-for-hire plot he had constructed from the start with Beth Ann was collapsing. Thus, there was only one thing left for Clein to do.

On December 13, John Turner finished writing Clein's ten-page arrest warrant, along with a search warrant for Clein's Old Saybrook law office. That night, Connecticut State's attorney Kevin Kane signed off on both. The arrest warrant was as detailed and meticulous as an instruction manual for an Apache helicopter. Turner left nothing out. The evidence he and his colleagues had amassed was remarkable. They had bank records, statements and a ton of circumstantial evidence that placed Clein at the forefront of what was looking like one of the most sensational murder-for-hire cases they had ever seen.

Thirty-four-year-old Sharon Brockaway was, she later admitted, Clein's "girl Friday." She was listed as a real estate assistant at Clein's law firm, but her job consisted of much more.

Brockaway looked up to Clein as a father figure. She had been a battered wife. Once, when her husband beat her, it was Clein who called the police and later "encouraged" her to have her husband arrested. Like many of her colleagues in the office, she liked Clein.

At about 11:30 A.M., on December 15, members of the state police and ED-MCS showed up at Clein's Old Saybrook office and were given permission to make entry. Clein hadn't been seen for a day or so and had been keeping a low profile since Fremut and Despres had been caught. He had been holing up in motel rooms throughout the area, hopping from one to the next to avoid contact with anyone. Brockaway, when state police asked her, said she hadn't seen him since December 14.

As the state police, detectives from the ED-MCS, and members of the Old Saybrook Police Department began rummaging through Clein's office—taking photographs, bagging items, looking through files—the phone rang. Laura Rowland, the bookkeeper, picked it up and, after speaking briefly to the caller, tracked down Sharon Brockaway.

"It's Haiman," she said, handing her the phone.

"Hello?" Brockaway said.

"Hi," Clein said.

"Hi."

"Is everything okay?"

"Not exactly."

"Are you having problems with your husband?"

"No."

"Let me speak to Marilyn."

Marilyn Rubitski had been Clein's most trusted confidante in the office. She had worked for Clein as his personal secretary for the past fifteen years. Despite her contempt for Beth Ann and the affair between her and Clein, Rubitski believed wholeheartedly in Clein. Some later said she protected him any way she could. As for Clein, he knew Rubitski would be straight with him, no matter what was going on.

"She's not available," Brockaway said of Rubitski.

"Is the office closed?"

"No."

"Is it because of snow?" Clein said, undoubtedly referring to cocaine.

"No."

"Call Axelrod."

By noon, Bob Axelrod had received a page. So he called Clein's office and spoke briefly to Brockaway.

Halfway through the phone call, a detective got on the phone and told Axelrod what was going on, adding, "We have an arrest warrant for Mr. Clein. He can surrender if he wants to."

"I'll let him know."

Dara Clein, Haiman Clein's daughter from his first marriage, had been in Chicago attending Illinois College of Optometry since 1992. Clein was proud of his daughter. She was smart beyond her years and not afraid of hard work.

The day before Clein's Old Saybrook office had been searched, Clein called Dara with what, at first, seemed like some good news.

"I'm coming to Chicago."

This wasn't necessarily an odd thing for Clein to do. In the four years Dara had been away at school, Clein had visited her on numerous occasions. The only difference this time was that it was on short notice. Whenever Clein had visited in the past, he'd always planned the trip, giving her plenty of notice about when he was coming.

On December 15, hours after the search had been concluded, Clein phoned Dara again. She wasn't home, so he left a message.

"I put some money in your bank account. Ten thousand dollars. I want you to take out ninety-five hundred. I'll be there tomorrow. I want you to give it to me then."

On Saturday morning, December 16, Clein called

again. This time, he told Dara to put the $9,500 back into her account and then take out $3,000 in cash—which she later did. During the same phone call, Clein also explained that he wouldn't be coming to Chicago after all—he now wanted her to meet him at a hotel in South Bend, Indiana, which was about ninety minutes away.

When Dara arrived and gave Clein the $3,000, she noticed right away how "upset" he looked.

"What about the rest of the money?" Dara asked. "What am I supposed to do with the seven thousand?"

"Keep a little bit for yourself, but send your stepmother fifty-five hundred."

"How?"

"Call and set it up with her. She'll give you instructions."

The next morning, they took off to another hotel in a different Indiana town about forty-five minutes away from South Bend. As they drove, Dara couldn't keep to herself what had been bothering her ever since she arrived the previous night and saw how distressed Clein had appeared.

"What's going on, Daddy?"

"I am going to be charged with murder for hire," Clein admitted.

"How . . . What happened? Tell me what's going on?"

"Someone is pointing the finger at me. His name is Mark."

"Mark?"

"The person who was murdered was hurting a child. . . ."

When they arrived at the next location, Clein told Dara it was time to split up. He had to keep on the move. She had to go back to school.

The following Monday, Dara sent a cashier's check for $5,500 to Bonnie Clein's brother's house in Massachusetts with instructions to forward it to Bonnie.

By December 17, 1995, Clein was officially a fugitive from justice, his photograph plastered all over newspapers, television stations, airports and border crossings.

As soon as the news broke, Clein's friends, family, relatives, coworkers and employees began pleading for him to give himself up. Dara worried that if her father didn't come forward soon, he would be hurt, maybe even shot. Bob Axelrod, proclaiming Clein's innocence, said that the "thought" of his client killing a "total stranger" was "ludicrous." Many were saying Haiman Clein—loving father, respected member of the Jewish community, lawyer, friend, husband, adulterer, cokehead, alcoholic, embezzler, alleged conspirator in a murder for hire— could not have been involved in such a thing.

Chapter 39

With her former lover on the run, Beth Ann had no other choice but to wait for him to call her when he reached a certain destination. Almost daily, Clein later said, he phoned Beth Ann in London. But whenever Clein began to talk about the murders, Beth Ann would hang up on him.

Christmas, 1995, was fast approaching. Penniless, Beth Ann went to Ali Bagherzadeh and asked if she could borrow some money. "I want to visit my family," she proclaimed.

Ali felt bad for her. He was a compassionate man. He had given her a place to stay. Food to eat. A job. This was it. Maybe she was making plans to leave? Thinking about it for a moment, Ali decided to lend her the money.

"I'm flying into Boston," she added.

Sometime later, Beth Ann left. Ali assumed she had gone back to the States to see her family for the holidays. With Beth Ann gone, Ali took off on a business trip.

"I wasn't sure she was coming back."

When Ali returned, he was shocked to see Beth Ann's things in the back office as though she had just returned. It had only been a few days. She was supposed to be gone for a week or two.

Confused, Ali called British Airways and Virgin Airlines to see if either airline had flights that had come in from Boston within the past two days. Neither did. Right there, he knew she hadn't gone home.

When Ali confronted Beth Ann with the information, she began crying.

"I went to Spain. I am so stressed out. I went to the Canary Islands."

"I want my money back because you lied to me."

John Turner, Marty Graham and Reggie Wardell, three ED-MCS detectives who had formed a coalition to bring down those responsible for Buzz Clinton's murder, now encountered a major snag in their investigation, which had been building momentum ever since they had obtained statements from Joe Fremut and Mark Despres. Fifty-four-year-old Haiman Clein was gone. Reports were that he had fled to his boyhood home of Florida. But no one knew for sure.

On December 21, 1995, Graham went to Robert Clein, Haiman's brother, and asked him where he thought Haiman had run to. Robert said he didn't have the slightest idea.

"Has he tried contacting you?" Graham asked.

"Nope."

But Graham had information that Robert Clein had just recently returned from Florida himself. He wanted to know why he took the trip.

"I last spoke with Haiman," he then admitted, "on December twelfth, but it had nothing to do with the case. I didn't know he had run until I read it in the newspapers. My brother never mentioned anything about the murder to me. Only that his lawyer instructed him not to talk to the police. He did, however, mention that he was a suspect."

"Do you know Mark Despres?"

"I met him a few times at Haiman's office. Haiman said he was good at fixing cars."

"What's up with Haiman and Beth Ann Carpenter?" Graham asked. "Did you know they were—"

"I will not discuss that," Robert said. Then, "Am I a suspect in this case?"

"No. We're looking for your brother."

It was a short interview. Graham could easily tell from Robert's mannerisms and careful choice of words that he was hiding something. Graham had been a cop for nearly two decades. He knew when a witness was holding something back. A good sign was when the witness would, like Robert had done, stop talking and start again all in the same breath. It meant he was thinking about what he was saying.

"He did not appear to be fully cooperative and was careful . . . about what he would discuss with me," Graham later reported.

Jose Argarim was not yet through with Beth Ann. There was something about her that kept Jose going back even after he knew she would probably let him down. While she was in London, Beth Ann and Jose had talked a few times a month to keep in touch. But that was about the extent of their relationship.

When Jose read about Clein's flight from justice and the possibility that he was somehow involved in the murder of Beth Ann's brother-in-law, he began to find out through various sources that there was a bitter family custody battle going on between the Carpenters and Clintons regarding Rebecca. So he asked Beth Ann around Christmastime what she knew about it, knowing she'd had a relationship with Clein for so long.

Beth Ann fell silent.

So Jose asked again.

She then changed the subject and refused to talk about anything having to do with Clein, Rebecca or Buzz's murder.

When he hung up, Jose had an "uneasy feeling about Beth's response," he later said. He knew something was up. "I felt that [she] knew something about Clinton's death and Haiman's involvement that she wasn't telling me."

Accountant Michael Krissell had been friends with Clein since they were kids in school. Clein had always looked to Krissell as someone to whom he could turn in a time of need. Here it was, the beginning of a new year, 1996, and Clein had been on the run for about two weeks. He had bought a car in Indiana with the money Dara had gotten for him, and after leaving Indiana, he drove directly to Miami to see Michael. Living on the run was not only a difficult, twenty-four-hour-a-day job, but it was expensive. Clein was just about tapped out of the money he'd had, his options running out.

"I'm in Miami," Clein told Krissell over the phone when he arrived in town. "I need to meet with you."

They agreed to meet across the street from Krissell's office in downtown Miami. Within moments of seeing each other, Clein told Michael everything.

"I'm on the run and wanted in Connecticut for the murder of Beth's brother-in-law. . . ."

"What?"

"Beth fled, too," Clein added.

"What are you *doing*, Haiman?"

"I have no money or credit cards, Mike. I'm living horribly."

"How have you survived?"

"Doing odd jobs."

Clein looked dirty, beaten down. He had not shaved or changed clothes in some time.

Mike Krissell was shell-shocked. He knew Clein and Beth Ann had been having an affair, and he also knew there were problems with her brother-in-law. He never believed, however, that Clein actually was going to do anything about it. The last time Krissell had seen Clein was back in 1994, shortly after the murder. Krissell had come to Connecticut to help Clein with an audit the IRS was conducting. It was then that Clein told Krissell that Beth Ann was calling him eight to ten times per day. Clein said it was "driving him nuts." Krissell even met Beth Ann several times while he was in town. Clein explained the custody battle and how he had gotten involved in the middle of it all. He told Krissell it was Beth Ann's idea to have Buzz "roughed up, beat up or taken care of." Clein said she wanted him to hire someone to do it. He was reluctant at first, he admitted, but as Beth Ann kept insisting on it, he began to think about it more seriously. As they spoke, Clein also admitted that he and Beth Ann had gotten together with the man he'd eventually hired to do it. When Mike Krissell asked what happened next, Clein told him that "the client he hired took it too far and killed [Buzz]."

When Clein met with Krissell for lunch in Miami, he reiterated what he had said almost two years earlier.

"It was Beth's idea," Clein said as he and Mike talked. "I only did it because Beth was so insistent. . . ."

"What are you going to do now?"

"I need some money."

Krissell later said he felt obligated to help Clein. Everything at that time was moving so fast for Krissell that he really didn't know what to do or say. One minute, he was sitting in his office working; the next moment, Clein was telling him he was on the run from the law along with Beth Ann because he'd hired someone to murder Buzz.

After lunch, Michael Krissell went with Clein to a local bank and withdrew $1,000.

"I'll pay you back," Clein promised before leaving.

With money in his pocket, Clein headed west for California. On his way, he was stopped in Arizona by a trooper who had spotted a headlight that was out on the car he was driving. Nervous and twitchy, Clein took a written warning and was on his way only moments after being stopped.

When Reggie Wardell reached the FBI, which had since become involved because Clein had crossed state lines, he was told that Dara Clein had admitted to meeting with her father in Indiana. The last time Dara had spoken to Clein was on December 27, 1995, she said.

With Dara's information, on January 6, 1996, the FBI tracked one Ron Coleman, from New York, who had registered at a Holiday Inn in Plymouth, Indiana, and South Bend, Indiana.

It was Clein, Detective Wardell knew as soon as he saw the name. Clein had used the same name to register at hotels in Connecticut before he took off.

Scotland Yard, in London, had been notified back in December 1995 that Beth Ann Carpenter was being investigated for the murder of Buzz Clinton. The state's attorney's office, however, didn't have enough evidence just yet to begin thinking about an arrest warrant. But Kevin Kane, Assistant State's Attorney (ASA) Peter McShane and Paul Murray, the three state prosecutors who had been working on the case with the ED-MCS all along, had an ample amount of evidence that placed Beth Ann under the same light as Clein. Still, they needed Clein to implicate her. Without his statement, they didn't have much on her at this point.

Interestingly, the state's attorney's office needed to get Beth Ann involved in the apprehension of Clein. It was no secret he was probably calling her from wherever he was hiding out. If McShane and Kane could convince her to help out, they could probably find Clein and then nail her later.

After discussing it with Hugh Keefe, Beth Ann's attorney back home, the next step was to get Scotland Yard to locate Beth Ann and talk to her.

When they found her, she agreed to help, saying Clein had, indeed, been calling her, but he was reluctant lately because he was scared of getting caught. At one time, he'd even convinced her to write down various pay phone numbers in the area where she lived in London so he could call her at different numbers. Eventually, though, Clein ran out of money and gave her phone numbers to reach him, most of which were in California.

When Scotland Yard asked, Beth Ann told them everything.

Officials at Scotland Yard, on Sunday, February 4, 1996, indicated to the FBI that Clein had made plans with Beth Ann to call her the following day. Beth Ann had given them the number Clein was going to be calling from, which was traced back to a pay telephone booth outside a 7-Eleven convenience store in Long Beach, California, just sixty miles south of Los Angeles.

Clein had been in Long Beach for about a week without anybody noticing him. The FBI had set up surveillance early in the morning on February 5 near the 7-Eleven store. They had a make on the car Clein had purchased in Indiana back in December—a blue Oldsmobile Ciera. Like the alias Clein used to check into several different hotels along his path, he used the name Ron Coleman to buy and register the car later.

With FBI agents positioned in a way that allowed them to monitor the situation, all they had to do was wait.

At about five minutes to noon, Clein pulled up in his Ciera, and FBI agents made a positive identification from a photo they obtained from the ED-MCS. A few moments later, Clein got out of his car and walked toward the phone booth. He looked scruffy and unkempt, like a homeless person, his hair matted and longer.

It was obvious, FBI agents later said, he had been living out of his car.

As Clein and Beth Ann spoke, Clein became impatient—his voice hurried and hoarse. For the first few minutes, they talked about menial things: how he was doing, how she was doing. Then, without warning, two FBI agents moved in without a word. Realizing what was going on, Clein said, "You set me up, didn't you?" to Beth Ann before he was wrestled to the ground, handcuffed and led away.

Chapter 40

Detectives Reggie Wardell and James Brady arrived in California to collect fugitive Haiman Clein on February 9. Clein was facing multiple charges—the most severe being capital felony murder, punishable by the death penalty, and conspiracy to commit murder.

Before they took off for the airport to fly back to Connecticut, Bob Axelrod warned Reggie Wardell over the phone not to talk to Clein.

"Idle conversation only," Axelrod said. "Nothing about the case."

Clein was handcuffed and his jacket draped over his wrists. When they got up to the airline counter at LAX, Clein asked Wardell where they were going to sit in the plane.

"Prisoners usually sit in the back of the plane. We'll board first, though," Wardell said.

"Well, I have frequent-flier miles," Clein said, hoping maybe he could use them to upgrade the ride back home.

Wardell didn't say anything at first. He thought it was a joke. Clein, however, gave him the impression he was serious, so Wardell went with it.

The airline knew who they were. Wardell, in a mocking fashion, asked the ticket agent if there was a chance they could get upgraded to first class.

"Our perp has frequent-flier miles!"

"Officer, I'm sorry, but we can't do that."

"Oh well," Wardell said to Clein, shrugging his shoulders.

John Turner was waiting at Bradley International Airport in Windsor Locks, Connecticut, when Clein, Wardell and Brady arrived. From there, they drove to the Westbrook State Police barracks so Clein could be officially processed.

Brian Carlson, a wealthy New York businessman with three homes—in Connecticut, North Carolina, New Hampshire—had met Clein back in early 1995. Carlson's mother needed a notary, and Carlson happened to be driving by Clein's Old Saybrook office at the time. Months later, when Carlson found himself in a battle with his mortgage company over its changing owners and not notifying him, he turned to the one lawyer he knew in Connecticut as having a stellar reputation for dealing with mortgage companies.

"He was delightful," Carlson recalled of those first few meetings with Clein. "He was a really nice guy. Farmer Brown type. Flannel shirts and jeans. Laid-back. Easy to talk to and get along with. I liked him."

When Carlson asked Clein where he stood with his mortgage company, Clein seemed excited. "We got 'em," he said.

"How much money are we talking about?" Carlson asked. If it were only a few thousand, what was the sense?

"Probably about twenty-five to thirty thousand," Clein said.

A few weeks went by, then a few months. Carlson grew impatient and called Clein to see what was happening.

"Don't pay them any money," Clein advised. Then, "But I need you to give me some money, just in case I have to make a quick deal."

"How so?"

"Well, if they want to settle right away, you're going to have to pay back all of those mortgage payments at once. I need to put twenty-five thousand in an escrow account so I can have it on hand if you're out of town. It'll just make things easier."

It made sense.

Summer 1995 turned into fall 1995, and Carlson hadn't heard a word from Clein. A letter would arrive from time to time indicating that Clein was still working the deal, but other than that, Carlson assumed Clein was making progress.

Then Clein called Carlson one day and invited himself and Bonnie to dinner over at Carlson's house. It was around Halloween, 1995.

Carlson said sure. It sounded like a good idea. They could catch up on the status of his case.

With Carlson and his wife sitting on one side of the table and Bonnie and Haiman on the other, Carlson watched as Clein's glass of vodka seemingly never ran empty throughout the night. Clein had brought a bottle of vodka and polished it off himself as the night wore on. Bonnie, rather timid in that she only spoke when she felt she was allowed to by Clein, began talking about her background.

"My father is an Episcopalian. He lives in New Hampshire," she said. "My parents are heavily involved in the church up there."

"No kidding," Carlson noted. "We own a home up near there. How 'bout that?"

"I've converted to Judaism, though," Bonnie made a point of saying. "I'm involved in a synagogue in Waterford now. All of our children are being raised under the Jewish faith." Gloating, Bonnie put her arm around Haiman, smiled, then said, "And it's all because of him."

This was an odd conversation. Only a few months before, Beth Ann and Bonnie were involved in a power struggle to win Clein's love and affection. They were fighting and yelling and having showdowns at various times and places—Clein's kids had even gotten involved. Moreover, Bonnie had slept with several of her husband's friends throughout the years, many times while he watched. Furthermore, Clein had been involved in a murder-for-hire plot. Yet here the two of them were, living it up at Carlson's house as though it were just another normal day.

In a matter of a few months, however, Brian Carlson would find out why the dinner date was so important. Clein had to keep up the facade; he had to make it appear as if he were still actively involved in his clients' legal matters, when he was actually robbing Carlson and several others blind.

Carlson had a Christmas party at his Connecticut home in mid-December 1995. Friends, neighbors, family and business associates all came. It was festive and friendly. People were caught up with the holiday spirit. At this time, Carlson had no idea that Clein was robbing him. Because the bank hadn't called looking for mortgage payments, Carlson trusted that Clein was taking care of everything.

The day before the Christmas party, Marilyn Rubitski called Carlson at his Manhattan office to tell him that Clein couldn't make it to the party. Something had come up, she said.

The next morning, Carlson snuggled up in his favorite chair by his fireplace and unfolded the morning newspaper, and there it was: HAIMAN CLEIN WANTED FOR MURDER; POLICE SEEK OLD SAYBROOK LAWYER.

"Honey," Carlson yelled into the next room, "someone finally has a good excuse for missing one of our parties."

"What?"

"Haiman Clein is wanted for murder!"

After the initial shock set in, Mrs. Carlson asked, "What

about our twenty-five thousand, Brian? What do we do now?"

The night of the party, neighbors and friends teased Carlson about his involvement with Clein. He was embarrassed, sure; but in truth, what could he do? Carlson was one more on a growing list of financial casualties Clein had accumulated throughout the years.

"It pisses me off that I gave his kid a five-hundred-dollar savings bond at his bar mitzvah. I trusted this man. He used me."

In the end, Carlson hired another attorney he had chosen out of the Yellow Pages. By chance, it happened to be Richard Paladino, a former partner of Clein's. First Paladino fixed the real estate problem Carlson had gone to Clein for in the first place; then he recouped the $25,000 Clein had stolen from his client.

In the forty days Clein had spent on the run, he traveled from Connecticut to Indiana to his boyhood home of Miami to, finally, California, where he was set up by his former lover and arrested. But now he was back in New London, facing a judge as—ironically—a criminal instead of a lawyer.

As Clein was brought into court to be arraigned, Bonnie, his loyal wife of two decades, exposed her unrelenting admiration and codependency as she smiled, waved and even blew him a kiss as he sat down next to his attorney, Bob Axelrod.

By the end of the proceedings, Judge Joseph Purtill set Clein's bond at $1.5 million. With little or no assets left— Clein had $2.81 on him when the FBI took him into custody back in Long Beach—and the bank close to foreclosure on his Waterford home, Clein certainly wasn't going to make bail.

* * *

At an intimidating six feet three inches, Assistant State's Attorney Paul Murray, at fifty, had a reputation in Connecticut for being one of the toughest prosecutors the state employed. He was stern in his arguments, forthright in his beliefs and convictions, and determined to win cases other lawyers might otherwise give up on when things didn't go their way. In his two decades as a prosecutor, Murray tried the worst of the worst: drug abusers, murderers, sexual predators.

Born in Waterbury, Connecticut, Murray went to Sacred Heart High School and the University of Connecticut; and served in the Vietnam War. Some said Murray learned his hard ways as a prosecutor working the ghettos of the state's capital, Hartford, as a police officer for five years while at the same time earning his law degree.

In the early 1980s, the chief state's attorney had formed a "five-person government corruption SWAT team" that set its sights on organized crime and corruption in state offices. The head of that committee was none other than Kevin Kane, who was now working with Murray and Peter McShane on the Buzz Clinton murder case.

When Kevin Kane went to work for State's Attorney Robert Satti, who ran the operation in New London before Kane took over in early 1995, he never thought that Murray would one day end up working side by side with him again. After both graduated from the University of Connecticut Law School in the late 1970s, they started out together in Middletown. Since then, they always seemed to run into each other somewhere along the vocation pathway.

Where Murray wore a hat of contempt for rogue cops, serial killers and child predators, at times speaking openly of his determination to rid the streets of such filth, Kane worked in the background quietly, rarely ever speaking out. When Kane went to work in New London as an assistant state's attorney in 1986, Murray went to Hartford as a special drug prosecutor. But here they were once again, together, getting ready to prosecute one of their own: Haiman Clein.

Recently Detective John Turner had uncovered a source that would eventually help the ED-MCS bust the case open even further.

On March 21, after carefully piecing together Beth Ann's role in the murder, contacting old friends and relatives, seeking to develop a motive, Turner got hold of Tricia Gaul and ended up with a four-page statement that moved the case into a completely new realm. Tricia and John Gaul were at the forefront of the custody battle between Kim and Buzz and the Carpenters. Tricia could offer an independent source of information not only to reinforce what Cathy White, Mark Despres and Joe Fremut had already stated, but also shed light on Beth Ann's role.

Around the same time John Turner took Tricia's statement, he and Reggie Wardell drove over to Dr. Matthew Elgart's office in Old Saybrook. They had gotten Elgart's name from someone close to the case who, by sheer coincidence, knew a patient of Elgart's. Mark Despres had also told them that Clein was hanging around with a "doctor in town" with whom he had snorted cocaine. Turner and Wardell knew that Elgart probably didn't know much, but he and Clein had been friends. A few simple questions wouldn't hurt. Maybe he could offer something.

After Elgart's receptionist alerted the doctor that Turner and Wardell were waiting in the reception area, Elgart appeared and asked them to walk back into the office area.

"I don't have long. . . . I have to pick someone up," Elgart said as they walked.

After walking down a short hallway, Elgart led them into an examination room that held two patients.

"Can we go somewhere a little more private?" Turner asked.

Loudly, so the entire office could hear, Turner and Wardell remembered later that Elgart then began shouting: "I hate cops! I have a real problem with authority figures because they abuse their authority and they pick on minorities."

Turner and Wardell were beside themselves. Here was a doctor shouting at the top of his lungs in his office at two detectives. It could mean only one thing: Elgart knew more than they thought; he was hiding something.

"We're just here," Turner explained quietly, "to get some background information on Haiman Clein. We've conducted interviews with people that led us to you. Relax."

"Maybe I should call an attorney."

"Who's your attorney, sir?"

"What are the questions you want to ask me?" Elgart demanded to know. He was still being loud and obnoxious, roaming now from room to room to make communicating more difficult.

"Just some background on Haiman—"

"*What* specific questions do you *want* to ask me? The police, you know, like to twist things."

"Well, sir, since you're so adamant," Turner said a bit more sternly now, "we want to know about your cocaine use with Haiman Clein. And if you have any info about the murder."

"I do not know anything about Mr. Clein. Haven't seen him in a year and a half. He was out of control."

"We know that," Turner said.

"How was Mr. Clein out of control?" Wardell asked.

"You see . . . you see how you *twist* things around," Elgart shouted. Then he walked into the area where his two patients were sitting, shouting along the way, "I hate cops! I hate cops!" Looking directly at both patients, he added, "See, they're threatening me!"

One patient laughed.

"I want an attorney present before I answer any questions," Elgart said more seriously.

"Well, maybe you *should* call one."

"I will consider this." Then he added, "I hate guns."

"I hate murder," Turner shot back immediately. "We are still going to have to speak to you." Turner handed Elgart his business card. "Call Paul Murray when you're ready to talk."

As Turner and Wardell walked out of the office, Turner stopped, turned and offered one last comment: "You're going to talk to us, Mr. Elgart. You might as well call your attorney and get it over with."

A few days after Turner and Wardell first spoke to Elgart, Elgart's lawyer phoned the state's attorney's office and indicated that Elgart was ready to talk.

Elgart's attorney was a small woman. Petite. Docile. Softspoken and frail. When she walked into the state's attorney's office, Turner explained what they wanted to talk about with her client. She agreed to let Elgart speak, just as long as she could monitor the interview.

Elgart sat at the head of the table, his attorney to his right, and Turner and Wardell to the left. For the most part, Elgart spoke of his personal history, his marriage and why he had been so attracted to having Clein as a friend.

"I was fascinated with lawyers. I was enthralled with Haiman Clein and his business and the way he worked."

In the end, though, Elgart could shed little light on the murder of Buzz Clinton.

With Tricia Gaul's statement in hand, just as Clein's probable cause hearing was about to get under way, Kevin Kane, Peter McShane and Paul Murray's main focus somewhat changed. They now strategized that they wanted to put on record evidence of Beth Ann Carpenter's participation in the crime, knowing they were likely going after her next. After several preliminary hearings, where a judge hears what evidence will be brought in, the judge allowed just about everything the state's attorney's office had requested.

This, of course, changed Clein's position entirely. Now he had to think about how he could cut a deal and maybe save his life, but he went ahead with the hearing anyway.

To set the stage, Murray called Joe Dunn, the first officer on the scene the night Buzz was murdered, Reggie Wardell and Dee Clinton, on March 28, 1996, the first day of the hearing.

Dunn, Wardell and Dee Clinton held no surprises. They were there to give the judge some background of the murder scene and Buzz's final moments.

By the end of the day, Murray called Chris Despres. As Chris spoke, a bit nervous and weary at times, he gave the judge a good indication as to why Clein should be brought to trial in the death of Buzz Clinton. Chris spoke of his father's plotting and planning Buzz's murder under the direction of Haiman Clein. He gave details. He talked about hiding the murder weapon and explained how his dad had met with Clein on several occasions.

Shocking nearly everyone in the courtroom, Chris told the judge—and the public for the first time—how his dad had offered him the opportunity to shoot Buzz, but he declined, shrugging it off as a joke.

Probable cause hearings generally last no more than a day. The state presents evidence and the court makes its decision: they either go to trial or not. In many ways, it is the same as a grand jury; the only difference being there are no jurors—only a judge.

Mark Despres had made it known that he was going to refuse to testify. In a sense, he was using his testimony as bait to save himself. But Kevin Kane, Paul Murray and Peter McShane weren't about to be bribed by a felon, so they explained to the court that they most likely weren't going to call Mark Despres.

Despres, however, was brought in to testify.

Still, under the guise of the constitutional right not to self-implicate, he refused to speak.

Between March 29 and April 2, the state brought in twelve witnesses, each putting in place his or her piece of a complicated murder-for-hire puzzle that included a bitter child custody battle between Beth Ann and her family, and Buzz and his family. By the end of the probable cause hearing, there was no doubt that Clein had played a major role in Buzz's death.

The only question that remained: who else did?

Ultimately the judge agreed. On April 3, 1996, Judge John Walsh concluded that "prosecutors presented convincing evidence" that Clein was involved in the murder.

Clein was going to trial. He would face the death penalty if convicted.

In Walsh's ruling, he believed a conspiracy existed, which was a major score for Kevin Kane, Paul Murray and Peter McShane. Because now they could bring evidence into Clein's trial that there were other people involved—mainly, Beth Ann, who was still in England.

As the judge explained his ruling, Clein and Axelrod began conversing. When Walsh finished, Axelrod indicated that his client wanted to plead out and forgo the rest of the hearing.

So Clein pleaded not guilty to capital felony murder and conspiracy to commit murder. His case would go to trial.

With Clein, Despres and Fremut in jail, all awaiting court dates, the ED-MCS began to focus on Beth Ann Carpenter and, because his name had been brought up both during the probable cause hearing and in Tricia Gaul's statement, Dick Carpenter.

Chapter 41

Beth Ann was buying time on a six-month tourist visa clock that had started ticking upon her arrival in England in October 1995. It was now well into the spring of 1996, and she still hadn't secured her stay in the country. If British immigration officials tracked her down, she would be thrown out of the country like any other illegal refugee.

When Ali Bagherzadeh had demanded his money back after Beth Ann admitted she hadn't gone back home but instead gone on holiday to the Canary Islands, he never expected her to pay up—and she never did. So with her unpaid phone charges piling up and her visa expired, Ali went to her and told her she had to leave. She had disrupted his business, his sanity, his life.

"I told immigration," Beth Ann said, "that you were my boyfriend. You need to call immigration and explain to them that you're my boyfriend."

"I will not call immigration, Beth," Ali said. "Nor will I send them a letter." Ali got louder, more forceful. "You need to call them and tell them you lied! I don't want any problems with immigration."

A day later, after realizing she probably wouldn't phone immigration, Ali phoned his lawyer and briefed him about the situation.

For the past few weeks, Ali had stopped paying Beth

Ann for the little bit of work she had been doing around the office. He was hoping it would entice her to leave.

To his surprise, though, she didn't go anywhere.

In August, Ali went to France to attend his sister's wedding. He told Beth Ann before he left that she needed to be gone when he got back.

"I should be happy about my sister's wedding," he said before leaving. "But you've got me all stressed out because you won't leave."

When he returned and saw that she was still there, "push came to shove," Ali later told police. It was time to put his foot down. "I dragged her down the stairs and out of the office with all her goods."

"How can you do this to me?" Beth Ann asked. She was crying. Begging. Pleading with him to stop. "I have no money and problems in the States—and you're doing this?"

"Leave!" Ali said again. He was angry, and he had every right to be. He had put Beth Ann up for nearly the past year. He couldn't do it anymore.

"I'll go to the police and file a complaint against you that you raped and assaulted me," Beth Ann threatened as she left.

Ali had no idea what "problems" Beth Ann was referring to back home. All he wanted was for her to be out of his life. Later, when investigators interviewed Ali and asked him what kinds of "problems" she might have been talking about, referring to Clein, Ali said the name sounded familiar, but he couldn't remember why.

"Something bizarre was going on [between them], though," he said.

One time, Beth Ann mentioned that Clein was nothing to her but an "old" and "fat" man who was "obsessed" with her. That's why I left the States!" Ali then added that Clein's secretary was obsessed with Clein, and that this same secretary was working against Beth Ann on Clein's behalf.

When John Turner subpoenaed Kim Clinton back in March to appear as a witness in Clein's probable cause hearing, he found out a few things that struck him as odd. Kim had been keeping a low profile since moving out of Dee's home. She had been dating Rob Ferguson now for a while, and it caused quite a strain between her and the Clintons. The Clintons hadn't seen their grandchildren in some time, and Kim was shacking up with one of her dead husband's best friends. To say the least, it was strange, many later said.

Kim told Turner that she had not spoken to Beth Ann since December 1995, but she was on good terms with her parents.

"Have you been reading the newspaper accounts of what's happening?" Turner then asked.

Kim said when she asked her mother to give her copies of the articles, Cynthia refused. So she was forced, she claimed, to go to the library and look them up herself.

"After reading some of the articles," Turner wanted to know next, "do you think your sister could have been involved?"

"Beth Ann does get mad."

Jose Argarim, who had been talking to Beth Ann monthly since she'd been overseas, made plans to visit her over the 1996 Christmas holiday season. By this time, Jose said later, Beth Ann had been living with "two other women," one of whom owned the house where Beth Ann was staying. Apparently, after getting thrown out of

Ali's office, she hooked up with someone she had met and talked her way into a place to stay.

It was no secret that Beth Ann was either fixated with or attracted to Middle Eastern and Far Eastern men. She had dated Joseph Jebran and Jose Argarim, and, according to Ali, an Arab himself, she didn't have any friends in England besides a few "dotty" and "shady" Arabs. The women Beth Ann ended up living with after she left Ali's office were Indians.

"She also said something about a Saudi Arabian man who was obsessed with her," Ali recalled later to police.

It's highly likely Beth Ann would have stayed with anyone who would have taken her in. And to those whom she kept as close friends, it seemed each person played some role in her agenda, whatever it was—because she lied just about to everyone she befriended in Europe.

"Beth seemed to be doing fine working in real estate," Jose recalled. "I asked [her] several times to come back to the States, and she refused, telling me that she had better opportunities in England than in the U.S."

She had been thrown out of her home, had no job and was living illegally in a country that would deport her if it had known where she was. These were hardly, one could speculate, "opportunities." On the surface of it, it appeared to be a life on the run. Otherwise, why wouldn't she return to the United States, where she had family and friends who could support her?

Money was also a concern. Where was Beth Ann getting her money? Many later said her mother had been sending her money on which to live, and allowing her to use her American Express card. Jose had also admitted to financing part of Beth Ann's life in England.

When Jose arrived during Christmas, Beth Ann asked him if he wanted to go to Saint Martin. She was going to meet her mother, she said, and grandmother. They had planned on taking a cruise.

Jose eventually went back to the States after spending a few weeks in England, but he ended up meeting her a month later, in January 1997, in Saint Martin, along with her mother and grandmother.

During the week, Beth Ann confided in Jose about a dilemma she was facing. "I can't go back to England," she admitted. "My visa ran out."

She had brought all of her personal belongings to Saint Martin. She seemed to be on the move. A gypsy. No home. No place to stay. Nowhere to go. So Argarim asked the obvious next question: "Why don't you just come back to the U.S.?"

"I might," Beth Ann said. "I really don't know where I'm going."

Two days before the Saint Martin trip ended, Beth Ann told Jose she had made up her mind. "I'm going to Ireland! They speak English there. It will be easier for me to do real estate deals."

When Jose left for home, Beth Ann, as promised, went to Ireland, as she had said, to begin looking for work as a real estate lawyer. As a perk, Ireland, if one was facing charges in the States that could lead to a death sentence, had laws restricting extradition. It was not only a great place to look for work in the real estate market—but a great place for Beth Ann to make certain her life wasn't in jeopardy. It was no secret that she was in constant contact with Hugh Keefe, her lawyer, while overseas. Both being experienced attorneys, one would have to be pretty naive not to believe they didn't discuss the fact that Ireland wouldn't extradite someone facing the death penalty.

In April 1997, Mark Despres's on-again, off-again girlfriend, Jocelyn Johnson, had her attorney send the state's attorney's office a package of documents that included self-incriminating statements written by Despres, who was seemingly digging a deeper hole for himself every time he opened his mouth.

By May, Despres, facing a possible death sentence, cut a deal with the state's attorney's office. With the opportunity to argue for less later on, Despres would get forty-five years in prison in turn for his full cooperation.

Then, with Despres on board, the state's attorney's office began to work on Clein.

Sitting in jail with a bad heart, on scores of medications, waiting for the start of his trial, Haiman Clein began to think differently about things now that Despres had agreed to cooperate. Clein was, in many ways, a weak man, growing weaker as the days in prison wore on him. Some said he was a broken man by this point, ready to throw in the towel and help himself. With Despres talking, Clein was well aware that ultimately Despres's testimony could send the proverbial last spike into his casket. He had to make a choice: either plead guilty and accept a similar sentence, or go to trial and hope like hell to reach at least one juror.

On June 12, 1997, Clein took the same deal the state's attorney's office had already given to Despres.

The ED-MCS next set its sights on Beth Ann.

John Turner had been writing Beth Ann Carpenter's arrest warrant for a few years by this point. With it signed and sealed, now all they had to do was find Beth Ann and get her back to the United States to face charges.

Ironically, the one person who would lead the ED-MCS to Beth Ann was none other than the little girl this entire ordeal had centered around for so long: Rebecca Ann Carpenter.

Chapter 42

After securing its arrest warrant for Beth Ann, the ED-MCS contacted Scotland Yard and explained how the case against her had progressed recently. In the coming months, the ED-MCS would need Scotland Yard's help in arresting, or at least finding, Beth Ann Carpenter.

Spike-haired detective David LeBlanc, an ED-MCS cop with a list of credentials to add to his comrades', had been brought into the investigation at various times for different reasons. When LeBlanc spoke to Tim Yates and David Cannon from Scotland Yard on October 21, they told LeBlanc that, according to just about everyone they had spoken to, Beth Ann had disappeared from England in late August.

"They also stated that Carpenter was psychotic, possibly suicidal, and has stolen from many of her friends," LeBlanc later wrote in this report.

Back in May 1996, Beth Ann had tried to enter England through Stansted Airport in London, but she was turned down by immigration because of "the extended amount of time she had requested to stay." British authorities felt she didn't have the "financial means" necessary to sustain a life in England for the period of time she had requested. A week later, however, she was granted entry after she returned and provided the "necessary documentation."

By October 29, 1997, the ED-MCS, after comparing this

new information with what they already knew, realized they had to find Beth Ann soon, or she just might disappear forever. So LeBlanc and Marty Graham went over to Dick Carpenter's and asked him if he'd heard from his daughter or knew where she was.

"I have not seen or spoken to [her] in two years," Dick said rather stoically, as if he were fed up with answering questions. "Talk to Cynthia. She may know. . . ."

Cynthia was at work, so LeBlanc and Graham decided to go see Kim Clinton to see if she knew anything.

"Any idea where Beth might be?" Graham asked Kim as they sat down in Kim's kitchen.

"Ireland, I think," Kim said.

"What makes you say that?"

"Rebecca came home after a visit with my parents and stated that she wanted to 'visit Aunt Beth in Ireland.'"

Graham and LeBlanc knew that kids don't normally make things up when not confronted. Rebecca had literally blurted out this information to her mother without being asked for it.

"Thanks," LeBlanc said, handing Kim his business card. "We'll be in touch. If you think of anything else, give me a call."

Later that night, Kim phoned. She had something else.

"My father just told me that my mother just left for five days. When I asked him where, he said, 'To your grandmother's house.' My grandmother's house is in South Windsor [in Connecticut]. This is highly unusual. My mother never misses work."

"Thanks, Kim."

"Wherever my mother is, David, I'm sure you'll find Beth."

When Hugh Keefe was notified later that day of the pending arrest warrant for his client, he informed the state's attorney's office he would make arrangements to have Beth Ann turn herself in.

LeBlanc and Graham weren't waiting for Hugh Keefe to make a move. Who knew how long it would take or what he was up to?

A few days before Cynthia left for Ireland, Cathy Taber, a coworker of Cynthia's, walked in on Cynthia as she was sobbing quite animatedly in an office Taber and Cynthia shared at Roncalli Health Care. It was October 28, 1997.

"What's wrong?" Taber asked, consoling her friend.

"My daughter is in trouble with some men," Cynthia said.

It was later that same night when Cynthia told coworkers she had to leave work right away to go see Beth Ann in Ireland. She didn't know how long she would be gone.

When authorities were alerted to the fact that Cynthia was somewhere in Ireland, possibly helping her daughter allude capture, it didn't take them long to get a bead on where she was.

On November 2, it was learned that Cynthia had checked into a Dublin hotel on October 30. She had paid in full for one night, the clerk said. When authorities checked her room, however, it was obvious she was using the room as some sort of front—because her bed hadn't been slept in, and her things were just lying around as if she had abandoned the place and left abruptly. Going through her things, authorities found a letter from an "attorney in Connecticut" that led them to believe that Beth Ann was wanted for murder.

It confirmed the connection.

Later, when Cynthia was asked about the trip, she claimed she went to Ireland on a "sight-seeing" trip.

It was only a matter of where and when Beth Ann was going to be captured by the Garda, Dublin's foremost law enforcement authority. Sergeants Michael Heffernan and Martin O'Neil, two of the Garda's most experienced detectives, were onto her. As soon as the opportunity presented itself, Heffernan told the ED-MCS, they would grab her. After that, it was up to the courts to decide where she went.

Contrary to what Beth Ann had told Jose Argarim, she didn't go to Ireland to look for work as a real estate attorney—at least not at first. She went to Ireland and immediately began working at the Marion Inn, a pub in Dublin. Her first job at Marion was as a waitress, but she soon requested a job that would take her out of public view: dishwasher. This abrupt request, Beth Ann's former boss Eamonn McCormack later recalled, struck him as being a bit peculiar.

"It was an unusual change," McCormack said, "because working in the kitchen was a lot harder work than that of a waitress, and a waitress makes more money. . . ."

Quite the change of careers, indeed—from a lawyer to a waitress to a dishwasher.

Beth Ann, however, couldn't practice law in Ireland without first being licensed, and she had just started taking law classes twice a week, according to McCormack, at the University of Dublin while she worked at Marion. She also told a coworker at Marion that she was just working at Marion to make ends meet. Her parents had been sending her checks from back home, but it wasn't enough money. When this same coworker asked why she had moved to Ireland from England, Beth Ann said, "Because I was involved in an accident in the UK and am now fighting a civil suit for damages." Beth Ann later would tell authorities her mother was in Ireland to help her with that civil suit.

While at school in Ireland, Beth Ann began living with a local woman who had placed an ad at the school looking for boarders. Within no time, Beth Ann was bragging to the woman about the lavish lifestyle she had left behind in America.

"She worked a lot of hours [at the restaurant]," her former roommate recalled, "and always wore jeans and a sweatshirt. She did not have a lot of clothes. . . . I was puzzled over the fact that she lived such a plush life in the States, but now was living in a small room and working in a pub washing dishes and making sandwiches."

One night, the relationship between Beth Ann and her roommate took a "drastic change." Beth Ann had been on the phone all night long, up until about 4:00 A.M.

"She was pacing back and forth," her roommate later recalled. "She was very stressed out."

Noticing the sudden change in her demeanor, the woman asked what the problem was. She never had seen Beth Ann like that.

"Nothing" was all Beth Ann said.

The next day, Beth Ann left her room with all her belongings and never returned.

A week went by. Near the beginning of November 1997, Alex Fegutou, another female coworker at Marion, arrived home from work at about 11:00 P.M. and found Beth Ann waiting outside her apartment. Beth Ann was rancid, dirty and smelled.

"Can I stay with you for a week or so?" Beth Ann begged.

"Sure . . . what's going on?"

"I'm not getting along with my roommate."

Alex Fegutou said she later found out through friends that Beth Ann had been living on the streets of Dublin, not sleeping or showering, just roaming around like a homeless person. Others said that whenever Beth Ann paid for something, she used her mother's American Express card.

During the week Beth Ann stayed at Fegutou's place,

she would leave and not come back for a day or two. Near the end of the week, she came home one night crying.

"What is it?" Alex asked.

Beth Ann just became "more hysterical" as Alex pressed her.

"Is there a problem back home, Beth?"

"It's a lot worse than that," Beth said. "My life is over."

After finding Cynthia's hotel room, the Garda was able to track down where Beth Ann had been working and staying. After watching her movements for about a week, on November 11, as Beth Ann was walking out of a local gym, the Garda moved in and took her into custody, where she was held without bail.

The arrest wasn't anything dramatic or intense—just an ending to a long and frustrating time for the ED-MCS, which had been working on finding those responsible for Buzz's murder for nearly four years now.

With Beth Ann in custody, the legal wrangling to get her extradited back to the United States could get under way.

To extradite Beth Ann Carpenter back to the United States to face charges of murder, Kevin Kane, Peter McShane and Paul Murray first had to go through the U.S. Justice Department and Office of International Affairs. The treaty the United States had with Ireland read that a person could not be extradited from Ireland if he or she was facing the death penalty. Since Beth Ann was being charged with conspiracy to commit murder, murder, and capital felony, she would indeed be facing a death sentence if convicted. But if the state's attorney's office was determined to hang the death penalty over her head, there was no chance it would see her in a U.S. court of law ever.

The first step in getting her back included Beth Ann's right to a hearing in Ireland. Kevin Kane and Peter McShane were informed that they would have to fly to Ireland and testify under oath that the person they were seeking was, in fact, the Beth Ann Carpenter Irish authorities had in custody and that she would not face the death penalty once she was extradited.

After Kane and McShane testified, the Irish courts agreed that Beth Ann should be shipped back to the United States to face charges as soon as the paperwork was in order.

Beth Ann's attorneys in Ireland, a barrister and solicitor, however, appealed the court's ruling under the guise that the prison conditions Beth Ann would face in the United States were grounds to keep her in Ireland. She would be treated improperly if extradited, they argued. Prison conditions were deplorable.

After almost a year of arguments on both sides, in late 1998 or early 1999, a high court in Ireland confirmed the court's decision, and Beth Ann was readied for a trip back home to face charges she had been trying to avoid for what amounted to almost five and a half years.

While she was being detained at Mount Joy Prison in Ireland, awaiting extradition, Beth Ann had several visitors, many of whom were her former coworkers at Marion. Charlie McCentee had met Beth Ann in 1997 while working at Marion. When he found out she had been arrested, he was curious about how she was holding up. During one visit, he came right out and asked if she was involved in the murder. It had been all over the newspapers. Before that, Charlie McCentee and his coworkers had no idea Beth Ann even had a brother-in-law who had been murdered. It was disheartening to McCentee to think she could have done it. The person he thought he knew wasn't capable of such a thing.

"I'm not involved in the murder, Charlie," Beth Ann

said. "I was having an affair with my boss at the time. He was obsessed with me. He hired a junkie for thirty thousand dollars to the kill the man."

"How did the junkie do it?" Charlie wanted to know.

"He ran him down with a car. I don't know why."

"Why did you run, then, if you didn't have anything to do with it?"

"The finger was already pointed at me. My ex-boss is cooperating and turned state's evidence against me. He was released from jail. He's setting me up. My back was against the wall. I didn't know what else to do."

"Unbelievable," Charlie said.

"My ex-boss dropped me in shit—and I'm fucked!" she added.

"What was this over?" McCentee asked. He was still confused.

"It's all over trying to get custody of a child," Beth Ann said. "The child's father was abusing her."

By mid-1999, the high court in Dublin had made its ruling on Beth Ann's appeal. It was time for her to pack her bags, and there was little that Hugh Keefe, her barrister or her solicitor could do to stop it.

When U.S. Marshal John O'Conner arrived at Bradley International Airport on June 19 with Beth Ann in tow, Marty Graham and John Turner were on hand waiting to transport her to Troop F barracks, where she would be booked, photographed, fingerprinted and sent to prison to await arraignment.

The ED-MCS had waited years for this day. Promises had been made to the Clintons that every last person involved in Buzz's murder would be brought to justice.

Today was the beginning of the end.

When Turner and Graham arrived at Troop F, the media were there waiting like salivating hyenas. As soon as Beth Ann emerged from their cruiser, camera crews and newspaper photographers snapped away as one of the most high-profile murderers the state had seen in years was transported to her new home. Not that murder wasn't common in Connecticut, but attorneys involved in murder was news . . . big news. People were shocked not only by the nature of the crime, but that it involved people who should have known better.

Lawyers.

It surprised Turner and Graham to see all the media waiting for them. It wasn't as if it had been announced that Beth Ann was being brought in. To the contrary, it had been kept under wraps. Turner himself had made sure of it.

Beth Ann's attorney, Hugh Keefe, later blasted Turner for, he said, parading his client, who had been shackled from wrist to feet, in what Keefe described as a "perp walk" for newspaper and television cameramen. Keefe was outraged that Turner apparently had tipped off reporters.

Turner, though, wasn't the type to glamorize an arrest. In fact, many of the detectives from the ED-MCS had opted to stay out of the limelight, letting troopers and local police walk up front to get their photographs taken with perps. It struck Turner as odd that Keefe had been so defensive.

On the other hand, any good detective cannot sit on what he knows to be a bogus accusation or, better yet, an outright lie. So Turner did some checking. He called the public information office (PIO) of the state police and asked if it had tipped off the media about Beth Ann's return trip back to the States.

No, the spokesperson told him. But a reporter from the *Hartford Courant,* the PIO said next, had informed them that *he* had gotten a call from Hugh Keefe's office about when, where and what time Beth Ann was going to be checking in at the "Troop F Hotel."

Chapter 43

The first order of business in the *State of Connecticut* v. *Beth Ann Carpenter* was for the court to consider the evidence against Beth Ann and determine if it was sufficient to proceed with a murder trial. She was being held on a $1 million bond at York Correctional Facility for Women in East Lyme, and there was no way she was going to be able to post it. Hugh Keefe had fought to have bail reduced, but after hearing arguments on both sides, Judge Susan B. Handy denied the request, saying how "bothered" she was by Beth Ann's having left the country at a time when suspects in Buzz's murder were being arrested.

By December 17, 1999, Judge Handy ruled that the state had enough evidence to try Beth Ann, who had just turned thirty-six, for capital felony murder and murder. Leaving the courtroom, Dee Clinton, who had waited for five and a half years to see those responsible for her son's death be brought to justice, told a newspaper reporter, "It's another good holiday. This is like . . . thank you, God."

Hugh Keefe began his campaign to undermine the state's case by saying it was building the foundation of it on a witness who was nothing more than a "liar, cheater, thief and scumbag." Indeed, Keefe knew his biggest asset was Haiman Clein's lack of credibility as a witness. Clein had robbed clients of hundreds of thousands of dollars;

he'd had sex with women while others watched; he'd allowed friends and clients to have sex with his wife; he'd admitted to conspiring with Mark Despres to have Buzz murdered; he'd been abusing drugs and alcohol for years. When Keefe got his chance to attack Clein on the witness stand, he vowed to rip his credibility apart, layer by layer, using every means possible to create doubt in the jury's mind.

And from the outset, it didn't appear like Keefe was going to have such a hard job doing just that.

Kevin Kane, however, who had taken over as lead prosecutor in the case, working diligently with Peter McShane, had his own thoughts about Clein's credibility as a witness. He admitted that Clein "had more baggage than the Ghost of Christmas Past," a trite analogy that would only grow with clichés as Kane began to present Clein to the court. But he also trumpeted the notion that if Clein was going to "manufacture a case" against Beth Ann for turning him in, he certainly would have "done a better job of it."

It was a fair argument. Clein had every possible opportunity to say anything he wanted about Beth Ann's role in Buzz's murder. Yet he gave only certain facts that when matched up against Mark Despres's, they only appeared to be more truthful. There were things Clein could have made up, and no one ever would have known—but when he didn't remember something, he told detectives and the state's attorney's office he simply didn't remember.

Kane viewed this as a positive sign of Clein's truthfulness. He felt the jury would agree.

As the case moved forward, Keefe promised to smear Clein as much as he could and prove he had acted alone in Buzz's murder because his obsession with Beth Ann had grown to such an uncontrollable level he would have done anything for her—including murder.

Be it fate or luck, during the last week of October 1999, Hugh Keefe received a letter from a convict named Paul Francis, who was serving a ninety-year sentence for killing a sixty-three-year-old Portland, Connecticut, woman and setting her house ablaze to cover up the murder.

At first blush, the letter turned out to be a defense attorney's wet dream.

After introducing himself, Francis admitted why he was incarcerated and said he had five cases pending. But then he quickly said he was writing to Keefe because of something one of his cellmates—Haiman Clein—had said to him. "I know him personally," Francis wrote. "I've talked with him at least one hundred times."

This got Keefe's attention.

"We were discussing his case," Francis continued, "when he started to cry. . . ."

According to Francis, Clein said he had "lied about Beth Carpenter and set her up because he was so in love with her and that in order to get out of the death penalty, he would do anything."

If it were true, this was exactly what Beth Ann had been saying all along: Clein had taken it upon himself to kill Buzz; she had never asked him to do anything.

"Clein told me," Francis wrote, "he took it into his own hands and set up the murder. . . ."

Francis ended the letter by stating he was coming forward only to clear an innocent woman's name.

"I have nothing to gain by this."

Months later, Francis wrote to Keefe again—but this time he perhaps sounded a little bit confused by the recent turn of events. In the interim, Keefe had sent someone to interview Francis. But Francis said he hadn't yet received a copy of that interview, which he had requested. Then he told Keefe he also wanted copies of newspaper clippings regarding Mark Despres, another cellmate of his, and "*his* willingness to testify. . . ."

Francis wanted to learn, he said, about the "deal" Despres had cut with the state's attorney's office. He was also worried about being labeled a rat inside prison.

"Can you send me statements [Despres] made? . . . If I cannot obtain any statements, I will not testify."

A week later, Francis, after receiving a letter from Keefe, wrote again. He said he had been shipped to Virginia because of overcrowding in Connecticut prisons. Then he indicated that he had received the clippings Keefe had sent him, and thanked him.

"I will be helping Beth and you. . . . I will be there for you."

On July 20, 2000, Francis wrote Keefe yet again, letting him know he was back in Connecticut, and was "still [there] for Beth." But he also mentioned, according to the state's attorney's office later, one of the main reasons why he was so interested in contacting Keefe to begin with.

"Mr. Keefe, can you help me with something? Soon I will be filing a habeas for my case. . . ." Because of that, Francis said he wanted Keefe to look for a few law students who would work pro bono for him. "I need the best place in which to receive help, for I am truly innocent."

The most pressing issue as fall 2000 approached was where the trial was going to be held. Keefe had argued that there was no way his client could get a fair trial in New London County. There had been too much publicity about the case. Keefe had submitted no fewer than three hundred newspaper articles, television news clips and radio news transcripts about the case to the court during a hearing that lasted about a week. The local newspaper, the *New London Day,* had covered the case as front-page news whenever something broke. The *Hartford Courant,* Connecticut's largest newspaper, along with the mass media coverage the case received, had also turned Beth Ann Carpenter into a sort of cult figure, following the case every step of the way. How in the world, Keefe wanted to know, was his client going to be certain an untarnished jury would be chosen? Keefe even blasted Dee Clinton at one point during the hearing, noting that she continually had told media Beth Ann was guilty.

ASA Paul Murray countered with the argument that the case had not garnered nearly half the attention Keefe was proclaiming. The coverage, Murray told the court, had been "unbiased and fair."

Murray added, "I believe the impact on New London County is virtually nonexistent."

On Tuesday, October 10, 2000, Judge Handy ruled that Beth Ann's right to a fair trial had not been jeopardized and a change of venue was out of the question. Later that day, Murray filed a motion to have Keefe disqualified from the case, arguing that Keefe had information about the case and might be called as a witness. With jury selection set to begin on November 14, nearly a month away, Murray didn't want anything to hinder the case he, his staff and the ED-MCS had been working on now for six and a half years.

Keefe, so as not to cause any further burden to his client, voluntarily withdrew himself from the case.

With Keefe out, Hubie Santos, from Hartford, a sought-after defense attorney cops feared when they got on the witness stand, stepped in and met with Beth Ann one morning. Santos was a special public defender. He wanted to talk to Beth Ann about how and why she should keep Keefe on the case. Keefe had been with her since June 1994. He knew the case; for another attorney to step in now would delay an already much-delayed trial.

Tara Knight had a movie star air about her and resembled *Legally Blonde* actress Reese Witherspoon in more ways than one. With her Marilyn Monroe–like figure, Knight, a stunning-looking blonde, was seductively attractive, charming, intelligent and crass—all in one package. Founder of Knight, Conway & Ceritelli, in New Haven, she had been appointed as Beth Ann's co-counsel during her probable cause hearing in 2000.

Unabashedly honest, Knight, who had been on Court TV and MSNBC as a legal analyst during a few high-profile cases, had a reputation for being persistent, thorough and tenacious, especially when she believed she was right.

Immediately Knight filed a motion to have Kevin Kane disqualified. Kane, Knight argued, had himself worked with Keefe in getting Beth Ann to help capture Clein, and he could be called to testify at trial also.

To make matters even more confusing, on Monday, November 6, Beth Ann's bail was reduced from $1 million to $150,000, which she quickly posted. Under the court's order, she would be monitored by an anklet and mandated under house arrest.

For the first time in years, she would be able to go home.

The entire Clinton family, as one might expect, was appalled by the court's decision. Beth Ann had already, in theory, fled the country once to avoid prosecution. What would stop her from doing it again?

From Beth Ann's view, however, one of the main reasons why she wouldn't run was that she was innocent—and a court of law, she vowed, was going to prove that.

To assure that she wouldn't flee, her entire family was stripped of their passports. The court agreed with her argument that in order to prepare for trial, the best place for her was at home, working with her attorneys. The terms of her release were as strict as any court could have ordered: She was not to leave the house except for a medical emergency. Law enforcement and court officials were given complete access to the home anytime they wanted. Any visitors to the house had to be preapproved.

Like the previous year, for the next twelve months,

both sides continued to set the stage for what one newspaper billed as "the case of [Beth Ann Carpenter's] life." One motion after the other was filed. Everything was discussed in open court, from the sexually explicit letters Clein had written to the time Beth Ann had spent overseas to letters Hugh Keefe had written to her while she was in England.

As far as Hugh Keefe and Kevin Kane's being allowed to try the case, the court finally ruled during summer 2001 that both could indeed continue. If it came down to either of them being called to testify, the court would deal with it at the appropriate time.

Chapter 44

Jury selection took a lot longer than expected. Each member of the jury had to be thoroughly questioned about his or her biases, along with how much of the media coverage he or she had been exposed to. It was a tedious process, but by the end of January 2002, a jury of eight men, four women and three alternates was chosen.

People around town were already saying it was one of the most sensational cases New London Superior Court had ever heard. The Associated Press was there, along with the local newspapers and television stations. With television cameras not allowed in the courtroom, Court TV planned to run daily updates on a Web page dedicated exclusively to the case.

An hour south of New London, in Stamford, Connecticut, however, the entire country focused on the pretrial hearings of another sensational murder trial that had been under way for nearly a year now. Michael Skakel—"the Kennedy cousin"—was being tried for the death of his former neighbor Martha Moxley, a fifteen-year-old Greenwich, Connecticut, girl who had been bludgeoned to death with a golf club on October 30, 1975. CNN, FOX News, ABC, CBS, MSNBC and Court TV were all there, broadcasting live from the scene. Dominick Dunne, a Connecticut resident and guru of true crime, was covering the trial for *Vanity Fair* magazine. Sitting alongside

Dunne on most days was his close friend Mark Fuhrman, a former detective and a writer of true crime books, who had broken the Moxley case wide open and sent it to the grand jury with the publication of his book *Murder in Greenwich*.

The allure of the Skakel trial was obvious: America was sold on anything involving the Kennedy family. To see one of them go down was to watch royalty fall from the throne. But what drew people toward Beth Ann's trial was something entirely different—something extremely rare: lawyers being accused of murder.

As officers of the court, Beth Ann Carpenter and Haiman Clein had been sworn to uphold laws and live by a court's ruling. They knew better. They were professionals. They weren't your run-of-the-mill scofflaws with criminal records. They were respected members of the community. For many people, to be involved in such a horrific crime was a sign that anyone was capable of anything.

What was even more bizarre was that a few years prior to the start of the trial, a man named Scott Pickles had been arrested and held on a bond of $3 million and was facing the death penalty for murdering his wife and two small children. Mrs. Pickles had died of multiple stab wounds to the chest and abdomen. One child had died of asphyxiation and the other of blunt trauma to the head. Pickles, like Beth Ann, was not only from Ledyard, but he had been a lawyer at one time, too. Some of the same ED-MCS detectives had even worked on both cases simultaneously.

Beth Ann had changed somewhat during the three years since she'd returned from Ireland. For one, at thirty-eight, she now had red hair that hung down below her waist. She was thin, attractive and professional-looking. And now that she had been afforded the privilege of prep-

ping her case from home, she was completely ready to do
battle with Kevin Kane and Peter McShane.

Despite her knowledge of the law or her insistence
that Clein had acted alone, Beth Ann's fate was in the
hands of Hugh Keefe and Tara Knight. To his credit,
Keefe was no slouch of a lawyer who wore cheap, wrin-
kled suits and represented lowlifes. Keefe, some said, was
one of the best criminal defense attorneys in the Northeast. He had been admitted to the bar in 1967 and
mainly had tried civil and criminal cases ever since. Since
1979, he had taught trial advocacy at Yale Law School,
one of the more prestigious law schools in the country.
In 1990, *Connecticut Magazine* named Keefe one of the
state's five best lawyers. His ties to politicians and wealth
were endless.

At about five feet eight inches, slenderly built, Keefe
wore an almost inflated-looking heap of bright rust red
hair that spoke greatly of his Irish heritage. Usually soft-
spoken and easy to get along with, he could sometimes
let his temper rear its ugly head. There was no middle
ground between Keefe and his colleagues; one either
liked Hugh Keefe and respected him or hated how he
practiced law. And, some later claimed, Keefe enjoyed
that part of the game immensely.

On February 5, Keefe filed a motion to have Chris Despres submit to a voice analysis. In what had turned out
to be a surprise move on Mark Despres's part, he had
made it known that he wasn't going to testify against
Beth Ann. In fact, he was now telling people he wanted
out of his plea bargain with the state.

Why?

Mark was saying that he wasn't the person who had
pulled the trigger on the night Buzz was murdered. Instead, he was claiming it had been Chris, his own son.

Chris Despres was not the fifteen-year-old boy he was
back in 1994 anymore. He was a twenty-two-year-old man

now. He had been married back in 1999 to Margaret Long, and had bought a house in Windsor, Connecticut, on the opposite side of the state. Further, Chris was no longer a long-haired, hippie-looking teen, full of fear and angst; he wore his hair cropped in a quarter-inch military style, and he had put on a considerable amount of weight. Rarely caught smiling, Chris had a stoic and dark aura about him. It was obvious the years hadn't been good to him. He had suffered, both emotionally and spiritually. He had spent years beating himself up over what had happened, yet he refused, a friend later said, to get any psychiatric help for it.

Mark said he had proof that his son had pulled the trigger. While confined to his cell back in the fall of 2000, Mark said he'd just happened to be listening to the Dr. Laura radio show one day and heard Chris call up and ask Dr. Laura for advice. In the process of talking to Dr. Laura, Mark was saying Chris admitted to the murder.

When Mark heard the show, he asked Jocelyn Johnson to get a copy of it. Johnson later said she went on-line and accessed Dr. Laura's Web site and downloaded a file of the show. When she told Mark she had the show on tape, Mark told her to "hold on to it."

In December 2001, Johnson, under orders from Mark, turned the tape over to the state's attorney's office. From there, John Turner took over and immediately contacted Premiere Radio in Sherman Oaks, California, the company that produced the show. It told Turner that Dr. Laura had her own Web site that might archive files, but it wasn't policy to keep files of the show on-line. Furthermore, the Web-master for the station, Radio Owen Sound, in Canada, said it "never provided audio files of the show on [its] Web site."

By the end of January 2002, Turner had a copy of the show in his hands. What he heard, however, gave him pause to speculate that the entire incident was just one more fabrication by a man who was determined to get out of jail any way he could.

"Chris . . . Chris, welcome to the program," Dr. Laura said as she finished with one caller and picked up on a "caller named Chris."

"I have kind of a weird question for your show," the caller who identified himself as Chris said. "When I was fifteen years old, I . . . I . . . I was involved with a, um . . . a murder for hire . . . and now I'm married and, well, um—"

At that point, a chagrined Dr. Laura, her voice cracking, broke in. "And what *role* did you take in this murder for hire, *Chris*?"

"I was the one that actually did it." There was brief pause. "And . . . um . . ."

"You're right!" Dr. Laura said immediately, interrupting. "This is different for the show."

The caller then laughed nervously. "I don't know if I should let my family-in-law know if I—"

"Does your wife know?" Dr. Laura asked, talking over him.

"Oh yeah. Oh yeah."

"She knew when she married you?"

"She knew when she was *dating* me."

"Huh! Gee. Okay," Dr. Laura said, and went silent for a moment. Then she became incredibly direct in her tone, almost angry. "No! I don't recommend—assuming you're a nice guy—I don't recommend that you make this public. I recommend that you get on with life . . . because the reaction [from the family] will be just like mine: I'd wish my daughter were not married to you!"

"Okay . . ."

"So, nice guy that you are, there's somebody still dead—and I have a *real* problem with that."

"I know that . . . that," the caller tried saying, but Dr. Laura wouldn't let him talk.

"I under*stand*. But I'm suggesting that this will not . . . make the relationship within the family better. So, no."

"My worry," the caller then began to say, "is that—"

Dr. Laura cut him off midsentence once again, getting louder and more defensive as she spoke. "Okay, Chris. I don't *care* that your worry is that they *might* find out something in the future. On the off chance that anybody does, you don't do it now."

The caller fell silent.

"That's my opinion," Dr. Laura said.

"Okay."

"You don't say there might be a flood," Dr. Laura added, "so I'm going to burn my house down now."

"Gotcha!"

"Okay?"

"Thank you."

After Chris hung up, Dr. Laura did one of her famous reenactments of the call. In a mocking, squeaky voice, she said, "Mommy, I'd like you to meet my boyfriend. He killed people several years ago, but he's *really* nice now." Then she spoke directly to her audience: "That would . . . make your average mother break out in hives. I'm Dr. Laura."

With the news of the tape made public, Hugh Keefe wanted Chris to submit to a voice analysis to see if he indeed had called the show. Chris had denied calling the show, and most assumed that Mark, in desperation, had put someone up to the call. Kevin Kane argued that the state's case against Beth Ann had no bearing on who actually pulled the trigger.

Still, from Hugh Keefe's standpoint, Chris was going to be a key witness for the state. Anything that could undermine his testimony might help Beth Ann.

Someone close to Chris later said there was no way it was Chris who had made that call; the mannerisms and speech patterns in the voice were definably different from Chris's. What's more, the caller had made it a point to tell Dr. Laura that the reason he was calling her show was because he wanted to come clean with his in-laws about being involved in a murder for hire. Not true. Chris's in-laws had known about Chris's involvement in Buzz's murder shortly after they met him almost four years before the call had been made. The ED-MCS had even tailed Chris's in-laws at one point. On top of that, Buzz's murder had been all over the news for years.

The most compelling evidence, however, was that Chris and his wife had split up at the time and were talking about getting divorced. In fact, a year later, in 2001, they filed for divorce. Why would the caller, if he were Chris, be worried about telling his in-laws a disturbing fact like that if he was in the process of divorcing himself from the family?

None of it made any sense.

In the end, the judge agreed, ruling that the court had no jurisdiction to make Chris submit to voice analysis.

Chapter 45

New London Superior Court is on the corner of Huntington Avenue and Broad Street in downtown New London. It has been a fixture in town for as long as people can remember. Shaped like a boomerang, the tan-brick building has four floors, with entrances in the front and back. Directly across the street is the Garde Theater. Prime Media Services, which used to be the site of Haiman Clein's law office, is directly next to the Garde. Down the block is the hustle and bustle of daily downtown life. There's a bus depot and harbor, coffee shops and delis, sport shops, bars, restaurants and office buildings.

As Beth Ann and her relatives shuffled into the courtroom, alongside Buzz's relatives and friends, to begin proceedings in the *State of Connecticut* v. *Beth Ann Carpenter*, the animosity between the families that had ignited back in 1992 seemed to build in resentment with the passing of time. The Carpenter family, many of them hugging Beth Ann in solidarity before she took a seat next to Keefe and Knight, sat directly in back of her, on the right, while the Clintons took a stronghold on the left, directly in back of Peter McShane and Kevin Kane. With only about five feet separating the families, the stares, whispers and unfriendly gestures that had become a common occurrence during preliminary hearings carried over into the start of the trial.

In fact, Court TV reporter Matt Bean later described the tension in the courtroom between the two families as a reinvention of "the Hatfields and McCoys battle" waged nearly one hundred years before in West Virginia. In that case, a dozen or so family members had been killed throughout the years of the dispute.

In this feud, it would be about only one death—the murder of Anson "Buzz" Clinton.

There are no opening arguments in Connecticut. The judge simply gives his instructions to the jury, and it's game on.

The state's first few witnesses did nothing more than establish the fact that the body of Buzz Clinton had been found on March 10, 1994. Joe Dunn, the East Lyme cop and first law enforcement person on the scene, followed a woman who had discovered Buzz Clinton's body. He told the jury how he recognized Buzz. Then, when Dunn began talking about the fight Dick Carpenter had had with Buzz sometime before Buzz's murder, Judge Robert Devlin Jr. made the jury step out of the room.

After discussing it some, Devlin said it was hearsay. The jury wouldn't be allowed to hear any of it.

Keefe and Knight had scored already.

Detective John Turner and Dr. H. Wayne Carver, the medical examiner who examined Buzz, rounded out the first day of proceedings. Both men were there to talk about the condition of Buzz's body shortly after it was discovered. Carver, when asked, said he didn't think Buzz had been run over, as Mark Despres had been saying all along. There was just no evidence, Carver insisted.

Either way, it didn't matter. Carver concluded that Buzz had been killed by several gunshot wounds to the upper body.

It was groundwork. Kane and McShane were setting the stage for what would be the toughest part of their case: explaining the bitter battle for child custody, which was, in their argument, the actual motive for murder.

On February 6, 2002, Dee Clinton, the state's first witness to that fact, began laying out how the seed of hatred for her son was planted in Beth Ann's soul merely weeks after he had met Kim and the rest of the Carpenter family.

Dee wore clothing that would become a signature of hers throughout the trial: a dark black dress she had donned at Buzz's funeral some eight years earlier. With her short-cropped graying hair, nearly unblemished skin and petite figure, for a woman in her midfifties, Dee certainly didn't come across as someone who had spent the past years wallowing in self-pity, letting the murder of her son wear her down and add years to her life. She looked more like a woman hell-bent on justice. In recent years, Dee had become an outspoken member of a support group called Survivors of Homicide. Set up in the format of Alcoholics Anonymous meetings, survivors of murdered loved ones could go to a meeting and voice their concerns, worries, fears, or just sit and talk with someone who could relate to what they were going through. The group was started in 1983 by Gary Merton, a Vernon, Connecticut, man whose teenage daughter had been murdered by a man who went on to kill again after being paroled early in the Merton death.

Just a month before the Beth Carpenter trial started, Merton stepped down as president of Survivors and Dee took over for him. In the wake of Buzz's untimely death, Dee had made a solemn pact with herself to avenge her son's death by helping others cope with the same loss.

For Dee, though, today was different: Buzz's day in court was finally here.

After establishing the fact that Buzz was her son, and that she had two other kids, Suzanne, who was now a nineteen-year-old woman, and Billy, seventeen, Dee began to talk about how Buzz had met Kim. Within moments, however, she had to ask for a glass of water, saying, "It's nerve-wracking up here."

As Kevin Kane began asking Dee about Buzz and Kim's relationship, Judge Devlin had to keep interrupting the proceedings because Hugh Keefe kept objecting. Most of what Dee had to say, Keefe was quick to point out, was hearsay. He wanted it stopped.

"Well, Your Honor," Keefe said at one point, "I ask that the court instruct her not to tell us what anyone else says."

Dee was confused. "Well, how do I do this?"

"Just try to answer the questions, ma'am," Devlin said, "without saying what other people say. . . ."

Kevin Kane continued asking questions, but Keefe kept objecting.

When Dee finally figured out how to answer Kane's questions without bringing hearsay into it, Keefe said he couldn't hear her. "I wonder if Mrs. Clinton could keep her voice up?"

As the morning wore on, Dee spoke of the first time she met Kim, then of the first time she met Rebecca.

"She had no verbal skills. She would put her head down and twirl her thumbs and wring her hair."

For the next hour, Kane had Dee outline how the relationship between Kim and Buzz and the Carpenters progressed into a nasty struggle to gain control of Rebecca, and Kim usually came out on the losing end. At one point, Kane asked Dee about a phone call Kim had made to her mother, Cynthia, regarding a night when Kim wanted to stay over at the Clintons' with Rebecca.

"Kim spoke with her mother. She started to shake. She turned white. Her whole body was trembling. And she got off the phone, and tears were in her eyes. And I said, 'What happened?' And she said, 'I have to bring [Rebecca] home.'"

Keefe objected.

It was all hearsay.

From there, Kane moved into how the verbal battles between the families erupted into an all-out court battle for custody of Rebecca, who was now eleven, and perhaps struggling to understand what had happened.

After that, Dee talked about the night Joseph Jebran brought Rebecca back to the Clintons and they noticed her swollen vagina and had to bring her to the hospital because they thought she had been molested. Keefe, time and again, objected. It seemed as though Dee was having a hard time explaining things without quoting others.

"I respectfully ask the court," Keefe said, fuming mad, "to tell her she can't keep quoting other people!"

"Please limit your testimony to what you saw . . . ," the judge urged.

"Your Honor," Dee said, "can I ask you a question? How do I get from [one place to another] without telling [you what] I was asked . . . ? I just want to do this right."

"Sure. And the only way to do it is to avoid saying what other people say. . . ."

"How do I say that, though?"

"I don't know, ma'am. The best way you can?"

"Well, I'm trying."

Dee had no bombshells to drop. She was there to describe how her son had met Kim, the relationship they had with the Carpenters and how ugly the custody battle had gotten as Kim and Buzz's relationship blossomed. The custody battle, Peter McShane and Kevin Kane knew, was the heart of their case. They had to show cause and effect. Yet there was still the lingering concern about how Beth Ann fit into the entire scope of the custody fight. Thus far, her name hadn't even come up.

So Kane had Dee describe that first day she met Beth Ann. It was a night when Beth Ann and her brother,

Richard, came over to her house to talk about Kim, Dee said.

"And could you please tell us what Beth said during that conversation?"

The court had excused the jury previously and discussed how they were going to handle the conversation Dee had had with Beth Ann and Richard. It was agreed Dee would simply tell the jury what Beth Ann and Richard had said to her and no more. Was it hearsay? Sure. But if Keefe wanted to dispute it, he would get his chance on cross-examination.

"Beth said that Kim was an unfit mother," Dee told the jury in her direct tone. "She didn't care about her daughter. . . . She sleeps with anybody, and that she's a whore. And she asked if my husband and myself could do all in our power to stop the relationship."

"Stop the relationship between whom?" Kane asked.

"Buzz and Kim."

"And did she tell you why . . . ?"

"Because Kim was a whore!"

The large pool of reporters, family members, well-wishers and trial gazers sat in awe as Dee put on record for the first time Beth Ann's anger and hatred toward Buzz and Kim's relationship.

Keefe continued objecting, stating that Dee's testimony had no bearing on his client's guilt or innocence. So what, Beth Ann didn't want her sister to date what she and her mother had described as a jobless exotic male dancer? What did any of it have to do with the case against his client?

Kane said Dee's information was not only "relevant," but several other witnesses would substantiate it.

By the time Kane was finished with Dee, she had painted an ugly portrait of rage, bitterness, jealousy and hatred toward her son by Beth Ann and her family. There was no doubt that the Carpenter family wouldn't lose any sleep over the fact that Buzz had been murdered.

It was obvious Dee held on to a bias—but one of the most important pieces of information Dee had put on record was how Buzz had made it a point to tell the Carpenters that he was planning on moving his family to Arizona to get away from what he saw as dysfunction. This, Kevin Kane would tell the jury later, was what pushed Beth Ann over the edge—the thought that she would *never* see Rebecca again.

But now it was Hugh Keefe's turn. There was still a few hours left in the day, and Keefe wanted to clear some things up.

As a defense attorney, Keefe was loud and aggressive, even forceful and threatening at times, but he was also composed and articulate. Many felt Keefe stepped over the line once in a while. And perhaps he did. Yet, when it came down to it, he had a job to do. His client was facing a life sentence for something with which she said she'd had nothing to do. Keefe was prepared to do anything he could to prove her right.

As he opened up his questioning, first saying "good morning," it was clear that just because Dee had lost a son, it didn't mean she wasn't fair game.

"Mrs. Clinton, beginning in July of '93, you say your son, Buzz, indicated an interest in moving to Arizona. Is that correct?"

"Correct."

"And did he have a job down there?"

"He had a . . . He had assurance from my husband's friend."

"Mrs. Clinton, let me ask the question again and see if you can answer it, *okay?* Did your son have a job down there?"

"I don't know."

"Did he have a lease down there for an apartment or a condo . . . ?"

"I don't know."

For about ten minutes, Keefe tried poking holes in Buzz's planned move to Arizona. He wanted Dee to admit that maybe the move wasn't set in stone, that perhaps it was just something Buzz had mentioned, like a lot of other things. But Dee held tough. She knew Buzz was serious when he said he was moving.

During the next hour, Keefe shot questions at Dee one after the other in rapid-fire repetition about most everything she had previously testified to, trying to trip her up on dates, times, places, names and anything else he could muster.

At times, Dee and Keefe went at it toe-to-toe. For example, regarding a conversation Dee had had with Beth Ann almost nine-and-a-half years ago, Keefe wanted to know if Dee thought she had a good memory.

"On certain occasions."

"But you didn't make any notes as to what Beth Ann Carpenter was telling you about *nine and a half* years ago, *did* you?"

"I don't have to write down," Dee said calmly, "where I was on September eleventh, *sir*, either, and I know *exactly* where I was on that date!"

The thrust of Keefe's questioning remained focused on Kim and the relationship she had with her parents and sister before Buzz entered the picture. Keefe was trying to let the jury know—and he did a good job of it—that Kim wasn't necessarily June Cleaver, and that her parents had every right to want a good home for their grandchild.

Near the end of the day, Keefe brought up Kim's first husband. He wanted to know if Dee had any knowledge of that relationship.

"I don't know what I knew about her relationship with her first husband. . . ."

"Do you know whether she got divorced from that first husband?"

"I'm assuming she got divorced. . . ."

"Don't assume *anything*," Keefe shouted. "Just answer my question, please."

Remaining composed, which Dee said later only added to Keefe's frustration, she said, "No, have I seen the certificate, a document?" she thought maybe an exhibit had passed through her hands explaining the divorce.

"Did she tell you she was divorced?" Keefe asked.

"Yes."

"She did?"

"But that's hearsay," Dee said with a smile.

"That's good," Keefe said. "That's what *I* kept saying."

"I know," Dee said amid laughs from the gallery, "that's how I learned it."

By the end of the day, Keefe finished his cross-examination and Kane his redirect examination. During the early part of the next morning, Keefe concluded his recross-examination and Kane a second redirect.

Dee Clinton, if nothing else, had given the jury a blow-by-blow description of the custody battle from her point of view. The jury now had an understanding of why these families hated each other so much and, possibly, why Beth Ann wanted Buzz dead.

February 8 was a Friday. Because of a holiday the following Tuesday, and the court's being closed on Mondays, it would be the last day of testimony until February 13.

Kane needed to give the jury something to think about before the break. He had set up the motive by bringing in Dee—a motive he would build upon with each witness—but he and Peter McShane needed to give the jury something more. Something tangible.

Facts.

After Dee stepped down, Linda Kidder, an attorney who had represented Kim and Buzz for a time back in 1993, took the stand to back up some of what Dee had already talked about regarding the child custody fight.

But after Kidder's brief testimony, it was time for the jury to hear exactly how Buzz was murdered—from someone who was there.

Chris Despres was dressed in a plain dark blue suit and matching tie when he entered the superior court building on the morning of February 8, 2002. As he walked through the metal detectors and headed down the hall, he said nothing. Reporters asked him questions, and spectators stared and whispered, but Chris was as stand-offish as he had ever been. It was grueling for the twenty-three-year-old. Regardless of how he felt about dear old dad, the thought of participating in the proceedings weighed heavily on him. He knew anything he said today would be used against his dad at some point later on.

According to a family friend who spent the previous night with Chris, he hadn't slept well. He had nightmares. And at one point, he even vomited.

After being sworn in, Chris explained that he now lived in Windsor, Connecticut, with his girlfriend and her son. Despite the hell Chris had gone through for the past eight years, as Kane burned through the normal introductory questions every witness was subjected to, Chris showed how composed and direct he was. He spoke loudly, clearly and tersely. Kane didn't once have to ask him to repeat himself. His answers were short and to the point. He gave only the information he knew and no more.

When it came time for Kane to bring Buzz into the

picture, Chris wasted no time telling the jury how he'd first heard Buzz's name.

"Do you recognize the name Anson Clinton?" Kane asked.

"Yes."

"And how is it that you recognize that name?"

"My dad shot him."

The gallery gasped. Dee and Buck Clinton, Suzanne and Billy, shifted in their seats, but they kept their composure. They were looking at and listening to one of the people who had last seen Buzz alive. Indeed, years had gone by, but the pain was as intense as if it happened the day before.

During the next hour, Chris explained how he and his dad had stalked Buzz. Kane had been questioning witnesses for decades. He knew how to get things out of people. Whenever he asked Chris about a certain event, he followed up with questions that made Chris recall as many details as he could remember. Details, Kane knew, went hand in hand with truth. If someone could remember without reservation the color of a car, the make and model of a car, the color of someone's hair, a person's eye color, the weather, there was a good chance he knew what he was talking about. On the other hand, if someone was trying to dance around the truth, he might likely, conveniently, just say he didn't recall.

When jurors got a chance to weigh Chris's testimony against his father's statements and the statements of Cathy White and Haiman Clein, they would clearly see how Chris's testimony dovetailed almost perfectly with that of people he didn't really know.

Kane then moved into the main reason why Chris was on the stand. He asked Chris to explain how he and his dad had met Buzz at the hotel on March 10, 1994, and how they drove in separate vehicles toward East Lyme on

I-95, but when they got to Exit 72, Mark panicked and began flashing his lights at Buzz to pull over.

"As your father was flashing the lights," Kane asked, "did you or he say anything?"

"Yes."

"Did you say anything first?"

"Yes. I asked him what he was doing."

"And what did your father tell you?"

"He said he was going to kill him."

Chapter 46

Before Chris Despres could explain to the jury what he knew about the conspiracy between Joe Fremut, his dad and Haiman Clein, the state first had to present evidence to the fact that there was a conspiracy. A witness couldn't testify to something that hadn't yet been brought out in court. So Chris had to step down from the stand in lieu of witnesses who could substantiate the state's contention that a conspiracy had, indeed, taken place. He would return, Kane and McShane promised, at a later date.

Between February 13 and 15, Teresa Jenkins, Jan Dahl (an early childhood intervention specialist with the state department of mental retardation), Carolyn Brotherton and John Gaul testified about the ongoing custody battle and bad blood between Buzz and the Carpenter family, thus adding more weight to what had become the focal point of the trial. So much so was the trial turning into a history of Rebecca's early life and the custody battle that had ensued around her, many were wondering how far Judge Devlin was going to let Kane and McShane take it. Devlin was an "extremely fair" judge, a colleague later said, "very thorough." If he felt an issue was slipping away from him in court, he'd attack it immediately. Keefe had filed a motion to suppress the state from putting forth any more statements of hostility toward Buzz made by the Carpenters, explaining without the jury present that it was "very difficult [for his client to defend herself] if witness after witness testifies about this animosity." Keefe further stated that "by osmosis" the state wanted the statements to "trickle down to Beth." Keefe was tired of it. It was time, he insisted, to get back on track with what the state actually had on his client. Forget about this custody battle business. What about the conspiracy? Where was the evidence to support it?

Kane argued that the statements were motive for murder and the jury should be allowed to hear them.

Judge Devlin said he would make a decision at a later time regarding Keefe's argument. As for right now, it was time to continue with witness testimony.

As Jenkins, Dahl and Brotherton testified over the course of the next two days, they continued to hammer home the point that the custody battle was fueled by the notion that the Carpenters didn't want their grandchild to be around Buzz for fear he was hurting her. As for Kim, several witnesses had already testified that, according to the Carpenters, she was an unfit mother. They had basically raised Rebecca from day one themselves.

But by the time John Gaul finished testifying on February 15, he put on record that the Carpenters had become so obsessed with gaining full custody of Rebecca they were prepared to do just about anything to achieve that goal. Gaul told the jury he didn't know he was Rebecca's father until *after* Kim had met Buzz, and Beth Ann and Kim then showed up at his house one day to tell him. A few weeks later, the Carpenters, Gaul recalled, began laying out their case to him, inviting him and his then-girlfriend, Tricia Baker, to their house every weekend to spend time with Rebecca. When it came time to fight legally, Gaul said, the Carpenters promised to help him financially, and they soon gave him the money to retain a lawyer. Dick Carpenter had even given him a job. Yet, when Gaul later indicated that he wasn't interested in pursuing a custody fight legally, the Carpenters ended their relationship with him and Tricia.

Joe Fremut was never considered to be one of the state's potential star witnesses. That distinction, hands down, went to Haiman Clein, who was still waiting in the wings. Joe Fremut had been evasive in the past, and he was clearly someone who, Kane and McShane speculated, could react on the stand any number of ways, none of which would help their case. For that reason, Kane and McShane floated the notion that they probably weren't going to call Fremut to testify. He had been out on bond for a while now, waiting for his own trial to begin, and there was no telling what he might say once he was sworn in.

Since the beginning of the trial, however, rumors had swirled around the courtroom like gnats that Fremut, who was supposed to turn forty-one on May 9, had been ill—extremely ill. Someone who had worked out at a nearby YMCA gym where Fremut was a frequent guest said he hadn't seen him in quite a while, and there was a good possibility he was in the hospital.

It was no secret Fremut had dated a drug-addicted prostitute, Cathy White. *Had he gotten AIDS?* some wondered. *Hepatitis? Was he using drugs himself?*

No one seemed to know.

By the second week of February, however, the status of Joe Fremut was clear. Word had come down that he had died back on February 13. It wasn't AIDS, or hepatitis, or an overdose of drugs that got him. It was cancer. Fremut had been diagnosed with bladder cancer about four months earlier, and it spread remarkably quickly and killed him.

Although Fremut's death had an impact on Kane and McShane, it wasn't that much of a setback to their case;

it was merely one more odd occurrence to add to a long list that had accumulated throughout the course of a long investigation.

For Dee Clinton, on the other hand, it was Buzz at work. From the grave, Buzz was wielding his sword, Dee later hypothesized, getting back at those who had played any part in his murder.

The one witness who could best explain how obsessive and preoccupied with Rebecca Beth Ann had become during 1992 and 1993 took the stand next. Tricia Gaul, John Gaul's wife, had met Beth Ann shortly after John had found out he was Rebecca's father. Eight years after the fact, Tricia Gaul was still holding on to the pain and hurt Beth Ann had caused her when she severed their friendship after John indicated he wasn't going to fight for custody.

Tricia was one of those perfect witnesses. She and John had had their share of trouble in their marriage, and Tricia wasn't afraid to admit that a lot of it had to do with what had happened concerning her, John, Rebecca and the Carpenters. Tricia had shown Rebecca nothing but love. If the jury was in need of latching onto a particular witness and drawing sympathy from that person, Tricia Gaul was the answer—and Kane and McShane knew it.

Kane had Tricia first detail how she had met Beth Ann and the circumstances surrounding the early part of their friendship. After Tricia explained how she and Beth Ann would talk on the phone just about every day, Kane wanted the jury to realize how quickly Beth Ann had manipulated Tricia into thinking that Buzz and Kim had lived with Rebecca in filth and that Buzz was nothing more than a child abuser.

"They lived in a shed and had no electricity," Tricia said when Kane asked her to recall an early phone conversation with Beth Ann. "Just horrible conditions. Basically, it was like a dog kennel."

"And you recall [Beth Ann] telling you that . . . ?"

"Right."

"You also said that [Beth Ann] had said there was abuse?"

"Yes."

Kane wanted to make sure Tricia—and the jury—understood what he was getting at. So he asked her again: "Is that correct?"

"She said Rebecca was being abused by Buzz."

There it was: one of the state's main reasons behind calling all of these witnesses who could explain the animosity between Buzz and the Carpenters.

Rebecca was being abused.

Beth Ann was, according to Tricia, repeatedly telling her that Buzz was abusing Rebecca—even when there was no proof to back it up. No one from the Department of Child and Youth Services had found any type of evidence whatsoever that proved Buzz had abused Rebecca. To the contrary, DCYS investigated and found Buzz and Kim to be competent parents. It was all, one could say, a figment of Beth Ann's imagination—and also, the state was beginning to show, a motive for murder.

When court resumed on February 26 after nearly a two-week break, Tricia Gaul took the stand again and spoke of how, over a period of time, Beth Ann became actively involved in helping her and John hire a lawyer so they could fight legally for custody of Rebecca. Yet, Tricia explained, Beth Ann was adamant about telling the Gauls not to let Buzz or Kim know of their involvement.

One of Kane's final questions brought back into light a central point Kane didn't want the jury to forget.

"Can you tell us whether or not the defendant expressed concern about whether the . . . whether Buzz would adopt Rebecca?"

"Yes."

"And can you tell us how concerned she was about that?"

Keefe objected to Kane's form of questioning. Keefe had been watching and listening closely throughout Tricia's testimony, catching Kane many times leading Tricia to the answers he'd wanted.

After withdrawing the question, Kane gave it another stab: "Did she express concern to you . . . Can you tell us whether or not she expressed concern to you about Buzz going away with Kim and Rebecca?"

"Yes," Tricia said.

"I object, Your Honor. That's leading! She had already answered a few minutes ago she doesn't remember anything else. And now he is just giving her these softballs, and she's agreeing."

"The objection is overruled. The answer was 'yes.' Please put your next question."

"What did she say?" Kane asked.

"They were afraid he would leave with her."

"Thank you," Kane said. "I have no further questions, Your Honor."

"Go ahead, Mr. Keefe," the judge said.

"Thank you, Your Honor."

Tricia Gaul had refused to be interviewed by Keefe's team prior to the start of the trial. It was a decision, even years later, she stuck by without reservation.

Even so, Keefe had a few things he could use to cause doubt in the jury's mind regarding Tricia's believability.

Tricia had difficulty remembering dates. Still, it wasn't as though a particular date played a significant role in her testimony. Kane and McShane had put Tricia on the stand to explain to the jury Beth Ann's preoccupation with gaining full custody of Rebecca. It wasn't anything more than that. According to what Tricia had testified to over the course of two days already, there wasn't a time she could recall when Beth Ann *didn't* carry on about Buzz, his desire to adopt Rebecca and how she wasn't going to let it happen. Dates, as it turned out, had little to do with that.

Nonetheless, dates were a foundation for Keefe to build reasonable doubt.

As he began his questioning, he would walk over and stand beside a blackboard whereupon he'd posted several dates based on Tricia's earlier testimony. Whenever he asked Tricia a question and she recalled a date that didn't jibe with what she had previously testified to, Keefe would cross it off his list.

At one point, Keefe asked in a mocking fashion, "Are you one of those witnesses who adjust your testimony depending on who is in the chair?"

"No!"

Throughout the day, Keefe badgered Tricia and, at times, even brought her to tears. He was loud and, some claimed, mean-spirited in his questioning, rarely ever letting up—even when Tricia seemed as if she were never going to stop crying.

"You are, of course," Keefe said, "biased in favor of the prosecution, aren't you?"

"I'm not biased in favor of anybody."

In the end, however, all that Keefe's hardball questioning proved was how he could trip up a witness on dates. Besides that, there wasn't much else he could get out of her. Tricia had seen firsthand, along with her husband, how obsessed and active Beth Ann and her family were in the pursuit of custody of Rebecca. And there really wasn't anyone—besides, of course, Beth Ann—who could take the stand and dispute it.

Chapter 47

When Hugh Keefe finished with Tricia Gaul, both sides argued outside the presence of the jury issues surrounding the state's next witness, Joseph Jebran.

Indeed, Beth Ann's former boyfriend, a man who had been there through it all, had filed for bankruptcy because of the debt he'd acquired while dating Beth Ann. Jebran had been accused of the alleged sexual abuse of Rebecca, and he was ready to explain just how obsessed Beth Ann had become with Rebecca.

The main thrust of the arguments centered on whether the jury would be allowed to hear about the alleged incident of sexual abuse in which Jebran had found himself entangled. There was never any proof that a sexual assault had ever taken place, and Jebran was never charged with a crime. Why even bring it up?

Judge Devlin ended up ruling that the incident had no bearing on the pending charges against Beth Ann, and statements alluding to it would not be allowed.

By Friday, March 1, 2002, Jebran was on the stand talking candidly about his relationship with Beth Ann—a relationship, he told the jury immediately, that included at one time an odd request.

"She asked me if I would take Rebecca with her and run away," Joseph said in his heavy Middle Eastern accent.

Questioning Jebran was ASA Peter McShane. Young, soft-spoken and a bit passive, McShane had a direct style to his questioning. He had been involved since day one and had done much of the research in the case. At one point, McShane, a Connecticut native and Boston University graduate, even put together a rather large timeline that detailed the case from the day Rebecca was born until Beth Ann's arrest.

McShane made a point to suggest that the kidnapping request came at around the same time that Cynthia Carpenter had dropped her custody case and was given weekend visitations with Rebecca. He wanted the jury to understand that losing the court battle was the final blow for Beth Ann, and, perhaps, the only option she felt she had left was to kidnap Rebecca and run away.

Keefe got a chance to question Jebran shortly before the lunch break, and he wasted little time trying to make a point that as a witness, Joseph Jebran should be viewed as a possible scorned lover. To show how much Jebran loved Beth Ann, Keefe submitted several letters and cards he'd written to her over the years. Was it possible that when Jebran found out she was having an affair with Clein, he set out to settle a score? Or maybe Beth Ann didn't love Jebran in the way he wanted?

Either way, Joseph Jebran shouldn't be trusted, Keefe preached.

To Kane and McShane, it was a ridiculous accusation—but one Keefe saw as an opportunity to create doubt. And doubt, when all was said and done, was the only thing Keefe and Knight had to prove.

Judge Devlin reprimanded Joseph Jebran for his bringing up the allegation of sexual abuse that Kim and Buzz had made against him. This happened after Keefe began questioning him after lunch about a statement he'd signed regarding the allegations. Jebran didn't talk in too much detail about the allegations, but he alluded to them in front of the jury.

Without the jury present, the judge had ordered him earlier not to talk about it.

After hearing Jebran disobey Devlin's earlier order, Keefe called for a mistrial. But Devlin denied it.

No harm, no foul.

Bonita Frasure, one of Clein's former law partners, followed Joseph Jebran and began to present for the state's attorney's office the next phase of its case. Clein himself was going to be called within days, Kane and McShane promised, and Frasure's testimony would begin to set up that part of the case.

Frasure gave the jury a quick account of Clein's meeting with Mark Despres and Beth Ann Carpenter in Clein's small office a few days before Christmas 1993, which would set in motion the conspiracy Beth Ann had initiated.

Over the period of the next week, the state's attorney's office presented several more witnesses who talked about how Clein had become both intimately and socially involved with Beth Ann. There wasn't much Keefe and Knight could do to attack this portion of the state's attorney's office's case besides try to play down the credibility of each witness. It was, after all, one person's word against another's. If Beth Ann wanted to contend that these people were all part of a larger conspiracy, well, she would have to get up on the stand and explain it for herself.

But as the end of February approached, there was still no indication regarding what she might do.

By March 7, the courtroom was buzzing about the one witness whom the state's case, when it came down to it, hinged upon: Haiman Clein.

Only weeks shy of his sixty-first birthday, it was easy for the gallery to see when Clein arrived in court that the years hadn't been good to him. Dressed in a white *Satur-*

day Night Fever–type dress jacket, rumpled shirt and shoddily pressed slacks, which made it obvious he hadn't worn a suit in some time, Clein was overweight and old-looking, his skin gray and pasty. Since his flight from justice back in 1996, Clein had been confined to the comforts of Connecticut's correctional system. Bonnie, his trusted wife, had divorced him in 1998, but still she stood by his side. Marilyn Rubitski, his trusted secretary, had also stood by him all these years, along with his daughter, Dara, and brother, Robert. Clein had rabbis supporting him and friends saying they couldn't believe what he had gotten himself into. One man Clein had embezzled nearly $80,000 from, someone later said, had even mentioned how he couldn't wait to buy Clein a drink once he was released from prison. Depending on whom one spoke to about Clein, he was a charmer, lawyer, friend, father, respected member of the community. Yet, others remained steadfast in their contempt, calling him an adulterer, coconspirator in a murder, embezzler, liar, thief, alcohol and drug abuser, enthusiast of kinky sex that included prostituting his wife to friends and clients. He wasn't a model citizen. He wasn't a smart man. And he surely wasn't the most credible witness one would hope to have heading into the homestretch of a murder case that was based largely on circumstantial evidence.

Nonetheless, Kane and McShane stood by their man and his accusations. They were going all the way with Clein. It hadn't mattered what he had done in his life. What mattered was that he could have chosen to make up things in light of making himself look good and Beth Ann look bad, but he chose to tell it like he remembered it, even admitting much of his own criminal and morally corrupt behavior in the process. There were times when Clein could have, both Kane and McShane continued to preach, lied about certain aspects of the case and gotten away with it. But when he didn't recall something, he simply said he didn't recall. That, the state's attorney's office insisted, played a large role in his credibility as a witness.

After spending part of the morning of March 7 detailing his professional life, Clein began to testify in candid detail over the next two days about his intimate relationship with Beth Ann and the fact that she continually brought up the bitter battle for child custody between her family and Buzz and Kim. It was, Clein said on a number of occasions, at the forefront of their lives, both professionally and socially.

Then came one of the many damaging statements, Clein would tell the jury, Beth Ann had made regarding her desire to have Buzz killed: "As long as [Buzz] is alive," Beth Ann told Clein one day, ". . . we'll never get Rebecca."

At one point, he even said that, early on, he had the impression Beth Ann had custody of Rebecca, not her parents or Kim.

As the day wore on, Clein continued to imply that Beth Ann was so anxious and worried about her niece's welfare that the only option she thought she had left was murder—and, he said, she wanted him to find someone to do it.

After Beth Ann had initially mentioned she wanted Buzz murdered, Clein said, it became a daily topic of their conversations. When he had heard enough, and had become intimate with her over a holiday in Florida, he finally came up with the idea to hire Mark Despres.

During his first few days on the stand, the jury received a pretty good picture of how the entire murder-for-hire plot had been conceived. Clein spoke in great detail about the meetings that included him, Beth Ann and Mark Despres. He spoke of the money involved. How much he trusted Despres. How he explained to Despres, because he believed it himself, that Buzz was molesting Rebecca. As

Clein spoke, jurors took notes and listened with deep curiosity. Here was a "professional" man who had employed Beth Ann, slept with her, took her out for expensive dinners and on expensive trips, explaining how she had set up this entire murder-for-hire plot.

It was extremely compelling anecdotal evidence to the fact that Beth Ann had played a role—indeed, a very *significant* role—in Buzz's murder. She didn't pull the trigger, but she pulled the strings. According to Clein, without her involvement, Buzz Clinton would still be alive.

Keefe would, of course, rip through Clein's testimony like a paper shredder once he got the chance. Keefe had already said in court on several occasions that Clein was nothing more than a liar and thief, and he had cut a deal with the state's attorney's office to save his life.

These were valid points. When it came down to it, by the end of the day on Friday, the jury had heard only half the story. In fact, the jury hadn't even yet heard that Clein had pleaded guilty already to his role in the murder and thus made an arrangement with the state's attorney's office to testify against Beth Ann in order to stave off the possibility of facing the death penalty himself—which certainly would weigh heavily on his credibility.

Even Judge Devlin wanted to make it clear.

"You haven't heard everything by a long shot," he reminded the jury before sending them home for a three-day break. "So please keep an open mind."

It was sound advice from a competent judge who had handled the trial, now nearly a month old, in a dignified and professional manner.

The chatter around town throughout the weekend was that Clein was putting the final nails in Beth Ann's coffin—and if she didn't put herself on the stand and tell her side of the story, she didn't have a chance.

Keefe and Knight had remained tight-lipped about

what they and Beth Ann had discussed in private. A defendant can decide to take the stand at any time during his or her trial. There is nothing on the books making it mandatory for a defendant to announce to the prosecution beforehand that she intends to testify.

Kane, however, had a few more things to get out of Clein before releasing him to Hugh Keefe for cross-examination. And on March 12, when court resumed, Kane went over a few menial issues he thought he needed to remind the jury of and then posed one final question to Clein.

"Mr. Clein," Kane asked, "can you tell the ladies and gentlemen of the jury why you hired Mark Despres to kill Buzz Clinton?"

"Beth asked me to," an unemotional Clein said.

"Thank you. I have no further questions."

Kane sat down next to Peter McShane and prepared for what many were predicting was going to be the lashing of a lifetime by an experienced and highly skilled defense attorney.

As Keefe stood slowly and began walking toward the bench, he put one hand in his pocket and looked down at the floor in a peaceful moment of resolve. Coming out of the gate with facts and disparaging critical analysis was something Keefe had built a reputation doing throughout the years; some maintained he'd mastered it with remarkable ease. If you were a shaky witness, you didn't want Keefe breathing down your neck and pointing his guns at you. He could slash you apart with one sentence and, as he'd done with Tricia Gaul and several other witnesses, never let up.

"So, Mr. Clein," Keefe said softly, looking up, "you *are* a murderer?"

Clein didn't answer at first and, obviously, didn't know that Keefe had in fact asked a question.

"That *was* a question," Keefe stated.

"I have been convicted of murder, yes," Clein answered. "Beth and I are murderers, correct," he added sometime later.

To show the jury how repulsive Clein's behavior had been throughout the years, Keefe listed some of them on a blackboard.

Kane objected, but it was quickly overruled.

Murderer. Forger. Thief. Tax evader. Adulterer. Drug user. An attorney who had violated his oath and responsibility to his clients by stealing their money. The list looked like a rap sheet from a career criminal. The real Haiman Clein was now being exposed.

Looking on, jurors took notes and shuffled uncomfortably in their seats. Here was, when it came down to it, a scofflaw of the worst kind who had graduated throughout the years from embezzlement to murder. Why believe *anything* he had to say?

Keefe was clever. No one denied him that. He never stuck to one specific topic too long. He liked to talk about an issue, then move on to something different. It helped to mix up a witness. If a witness was telling the truth, jumping from date to date or place to place wouldn't make much difference; the truth was the truth. If he was lying, however, it would eventually reveal itself.

By day's end, Keefe had made a few important issues clear—mainly, Clein had made an agreement with the state's attorney's office to testify against Beth Ann in order not only to save himself, but possibly to get less than the mandatory forty-five years in prison when he was later sentenced. In fact, Keefe got Clein to admit that the state's attorney's office hadn't even filed charges against him for stealing hundreds of thousands of dollars from his clients—charges, in fact, that could have sent Clein to prison for years.

Then it came time for what amounted to the most embarrassing part of Clein's five days on the stand—the infamous love letters. The jury was about to find out that Clein was not, by a long shot, William Shakespeare, bleeding his heart out on paper to the one he loved.

Keefe had Clein read from a letter dated January 24, 1994. But as Clein got to the sexually explicit parts of the letter, Tara Knight called Keefe over to their table and whispered something in his ear.

Just then, Clein was asked to stop reading, and it was decided that the letter was a bit over the top for an open courtroom. The jury would be given the opportunity, it was agreed, to read it themselves.

As the jury passed the letter around, there was no hiding the fact that Clein was coming across as a sex-crazed lunatic, admittedly high on cocaine, writing to Beth Ann about sexual fantasies many of the jurors possibly had thought only existed on the fictional pages of a porno magazine.

"Were you out of control?" Keefe asked, referring to the period in the letter.

"I must have been, as far as Beth was concerned. But I didn't think I was generally out of control, no."

"You wanted to remove any source of discomfort in her life, though, right?"

"Sure," Clein answered.

It was a fair question and an honest answer. If Keefe could convince the jury that Clein had become so obsessed with Beth Ann that he wanted her to defecate on him, as he had written in one letter, he might have done anything to make her happy. The jury needed to understand it was *possible* that Clein had taken it upon himself to have Buzz murdered when he saw how much Beth Ann was suffering over the custody battle.

Martha Jenssen, a lawyer, had been a court officer at the New London Superior Court for the past two years. With her long, dark hair, attractive figure and professional manner, Jenssen was respected by her peers and loved her job. As a court officer, she acted, as most officers do, as the judge's shadow. Her duties, among many others, included processing files, motions, orders and judgments in civil and criminal cases. In court, Jenssen sat directly next to the judge; among other responsibilities, she made sure exhibits were marked correctly and ready for court. Part of Jenssen's job also was to keep an eye on the jury to make sure it maintained a sense of integrity. If an officer overheard anything out of order from a juror, it was her job to report it.

As Jenssen was sitting, waiting for Keefe to continue with his cross-examination, she overheard a juror remark that the letter "has to be pretty bad if his assistant [Tara Knight] called him over."

When Keefe was finished with his questioning for the day, Judge Devlin made mention of the comment to the jury, reminding them that they shouldn't be discussing the case until deliberations. Still, it was an indication that the jury was itching to get this case into its hands and begin going through it. Obviously, the letter, like a lot of the evidence Keefe had presented already, was going to be crucial to Clein's credibility. And if there was one thing in Beth Ann Carpenter's corner as the trial drew to a close, it was how Haiman Clein appeared now that the jury had a complete portrait of who he truly was.

Chapter 48

For three days, Hugh Keefe questioned Haiman Clein like Clein was a prisoner of war. Just about all of Clein's previous statements had been put under a microscope and dissected word for word.

To his credit, many later said, Keefe had done a good job of attacking Clein's credibility. The true test would come later, of course. But for now, people were saying, Keefe had scored big time.

By March 13, the jury already had heard an earful of testimony surrounding DCYS's involvement in the custody battle between Buzz and Kim and the Carpenters. Keefe didn't want to bore them with more. But he still needed them to hear Beth Ann's side of an issue that the state had made into a major concern during Clein's direct examination.

Near the end of his cross-examination, Keefe somehow got Clein to admit—"I'm not sure if I saw her"—that he wasn't all that sure if Beth Ann had actually seen Mark Despres in the office on the day Clein had supposedly given Despres a photo of Buzz. Both Despres and Clein had earlier, in statements to the state police that would be available to the jury once they began deliberations, stated that Beth Ann was in the room. But now Clein wasn't so sure. He was doubting himself and his memory—which was exactly what Keefe and Knight wanted.

To tie up some loose ends, Kane recalled Chris Despres and Dee Clinton to the stand on March 19, along with Jeremiah Donovan, a local lawyer Clein had gone to in hope of retaining him for Despres, after Mark had killed Buzz. Donovan, who had been friends with Clein at one time, declined to represent Despres when he found out Clein had himself been involved in the murder. In some respects, Donovan gave the jury a bit of an outsider's point of view as to who had actually called for the murder. Kane got Donovan to admit that Clein had told him that he'd hired Despres at Beth Ann's request: "She (Beth Ann) kept after me and after me," Clein told Donovan one day. "And I finally hired Mark Despres. . . ."

Keefe had expected a much larger case from the state's attorney's office, he later said. More witnesses, more evidence, more proof that Beth Ann had been the murder-for-hire mastermind. But when the state's attorney's office wrapped its case up on March 19, over a period of sixteen days in the courtroom, it had called a total of twenty-two witnesses, two of whom were later recalled. Apparently, Kane and McShane were confident the jury was going to believe Clein. Because if it didn't, all those other witnesses really didn't matter much.

As Keefe and Knight's defense got under way on March 22, they called Thomas Cloutier, Cynthia Carpenter's attorney during the child custody fight, another lawyer (who was now a judge) who had been involved in the child custody matter. They also called Detective Marty Graham and Mary Sneed, a local tailor who had known Beth Ann for some time.

For the most part, they wanted to establish that the child custody issue the state's attorney's office had made such a big stink over during its portion of the case was nothing more than a family situation in which the

Carpenters were truly concerned about Rebecca's welfare. They wanted to show the jury that Beth Ann hadn't been as preoccupied with the situation as nearly half of the state's attorney's office's witnesses had implied. Moreover, Mary Sneed, who was "not permitted to testify about it," someone close to Beth Ann's camp later said, would have told the jury that Beth Ann had "long been thinking of going" overseas when she couldn't find a job in town after leaving Clein's law firm. More important, she even had asked Mary what she thought about London. In fact, during that same conversation, she also had told Mary that everything was "going smoothly" with regard to Rebecca. "There were no pressing problems."

Dr. Vittorio Ferrero drew the spotlight on March 22. Ferrero, Clein's former psychiatrist, had heard directly from Clein just how obsessed he had become with Beth Ann, and Keefe wanted the jury to understand it clearly.

Before the day ended, Keefe had Ferrero explain the effects of cocaine on a person's psyche. Clein had admitted to using cocaine during the time in question, and Keefe wanted to keep the focus on why a cocaine user and alcoholic shouldn't be all that useful in testifying about his actions nearly a decade ago.

After telling the jury how cocaine makes a person feel "euphoric" and "very powerful," Ferrero detailed how certain people can become "aggressive" on the drug because "they begin to believe there are plots against them. . . ." What's more, Ferrero insisted, "another complication . . . is that because of what it does to the brain, it can cause permanent damage to areas . . . that are also related to memory functions and impulse control."

"You mentioned something about feeling powerful as a side effect of cocaine use?"

"Yes."

"What do you mean by that?"

"I mean powerful in an unrealistic and inappropriate

way—that is, the person can feel there is nothing that's beyond me, there is nothing that I cannot do. I can do whatever I want and get away with it."

"Now, taking . . . Prozac and cocaine [together], and throwing in a little booze to boot, are there effects, sir, from that mix?"

"Yes."

Keefe asked Ferrero to explain.

"I would say . . . there is certainly an increased risk for damage related to memory functions."

It was possible that Clein, because he was doing many different drugs at the same time, wasn't in a position to remember accurately what had happened. Ferrero outlined rather fluently, in lay terms, that the drugs and alcohol Clein had been on had a major impact on his behavior and memory.

When Ferrero returned to the stand on March 26, Keefe quickly got him to discuss Clein's actual psychotherapy treatment: when, where, what they talked about, and how often Clein had come in for treatment.

Near the end of Keefe's direct examination, the subject of Clein's sordid sexual behavior became an issue the judge wanted discussed without the jury.

"What is it that you were going to say about Mr. Clein's sexual behavior, Doctor?" the judge asked Ferrero after the jury stepped out.

"Mr. Clein was having wild parties in his home in Old Saybrook before he lost [his home] due to financial problems. There was couple swapping at times. He had his wife have sex with friends"—reporters, well-wishers and most of the gallery nearly gasped all at once when the doctor alluded to this; in fact, the sexually explicit letters Clein had written now seemed G-rated—"sometimes several different friends. And watched it. Any part of his rationalization as to why he was doing that was [that] these people were business partners and that he needed their financial support in order to get out of financial difficulties. . . . He was showing them a good time."

Sacrificing his wife: *He was showing them a good time.*

Was there anything more to say about Clein's lack of credibility? He had sold his own wife's body and soul to friends—but not for money, for work.

Keefe's job, however, was to get this information into the hands of the jury.

Kane didn't view the situation the same way. He objected on the grounds that it had *nothing* to do with Clein's credibility. Kane suggested that Keefe just wanted to "get this in."

"His sexual practices and his sexual behavior have nothing to do with his credibility," Kane contended.

Keefe argued the "components of deceitfulness," which the court obviously had reason to question. Kane continued to say that, although most could agree it was disgusting behavior, it had nothing to do with Clein's version of the events in question.

Psychiatric information gleaned during therapy was a slippery slope. Much of it is not admissible in a court of law—hence the concern of patient-client privilege always attached to these types of arguments. But Keefe continued to beat the drum about Clein's credibility: Clein had put his own head on the chopping block by accusing Beth Ann of masterminding a murder. Anything should be fair game. Address this situation now, or have it come back on appeal.

Next there were discussions regarding Ferrero's diagnosis of Clein's antisocial disorder.

"Your Honor," Keefe said at one point after Ferrero had been asked to leave the room, "let me just say this. You have to live with what witnesses you get. I sympathize with Mr. Kane. He's got Haiman Clein. . . ."

Kane, sitting, listening without much reaction, shook

his head. Keefe was jabbing him, trying to make Clein out to be someone who shouldn't be trusted to take the garbage out, better yet make statements that could put Beth Ann in prison for life.

After a long discussion, it was agreed they would "move beyond" the topic.

No sooner did one matter get cleared up and the jury was back, did another arise after Keefe asked what turned out to be a fair and important question.

"These psychotherapy sessions that you had [with Clein]—were you able to form an opinion with respect to whether Mr. Clein was a truthful or an untruthful person?"

"Yes, I was."

"What was your opinion?"

"That he was *not* truthful."

The judge indicated to the jury that what Ferrero had just said was an "opinion," and it should be taken as such.

Opinion or not, it was coming from a reputable source.

By midafternoon, Keefe had finished his direct examination of Ferrero and Kane his cross-examination. It was up to the jury to separate truth from fact from fiction from opinion.

As March drew to a close, Keefe and Knight called several more witnesses who could throw water on the fire of the state's attorney's office's assumption that Clein had set the entire murder up under the direction of Beth Ann. No one held on to a smoking gun, but it was a way for Beth Ann's defense to offer the jury a second scenario.

Dr. Matthew Elgart, the local optometrist and one of Clein's closest friends near the time of Buzz's murder, testified how he'd snorted cocaine with Clein, offering more evidence that Haiman Clein was out of control.

One of the defense's most important witnesses to substantiate its claim that Clein had acted alone was Paul Francis, Clein's old cellmate—a guy who had written to

Keefe and told him that Clein had made up the entire murder-for-hire plot theory against Beth Ann to get back at her for turning him in. The only problem with Francis's testimony, however, was that if the jury was to believe a guy with a record as horrifying as Francis's, that same jury would have to view Clein as a monk. Lest anyone forget, Paul Francis was serving a ninety-year sentence for murdering an elderly woman.

When Francis took the stand, he testified about the letters he'd written to Keefe—but that was it, Keefe took it no further.

Kane, when he got his chance, tore right into Francis's background, having him explain how he'd been charged with burglaries, assaults, larcenies and several weapons violations, all before graduating to murder.

Francis, Kane implied, had given Keefe the goods because he wanted Keefe's law firm to represent him in an upcoming habeas corpus hearing.

In the end, though, it was up to the jury to decide.

Chapter 49

On Tuesday, April 2, 2002, Linda Yuhas, a family relations counselor, Diana Hendelman, a former friend of Beth Ann's, and Diane Contino, a real estate agent from Ledyard who knew Haiman Clein, took the stand and exposed further the fact that, according to Keefe and Knight, Beth Ann didn't have as much to do with the custody case as the state's attorney's office had been implying for the past month or so.

By midday, rumor was in the air around the courthouse like high-school gossip that Beth Ann had made a decision to take the stand in her own defense.

"No way," someone said. "She'll bury herself."

"It's her only chance," someone else commented.

Either way, it was time for her to make a decision. Soon the trial would be in the books.

If Keefe put his client on the stand, there were certain issues he was going to have to address, and from Beth Ann's point of view, she would have to try her best to clear these up. For one, how did Clein get hold of a photograph of Buzz if Beth Ann hadn't given it to him? Second, how could she imply that witness after witness were liars? There wasn't one or two people saying damaging things about her; there was a small chorus. And how, by God, would she explain away the notion of having taken off to England as soon as word hit the street that Despres and Fremut were going to be arrested in connection with Buzz's death?

All the rumors had been squelched by midmorning when the gallery looked on as Beth Ann Carpenter got up from her chair at the defense table and made her way to the witness stand. Surprisingly, she looked calm and in control. Many thought she would never do it. Yet, obviously, she had convinced Keefe and Knight that she could carry the load, and she felt confident the jury would believe what she was going to say. After all, she was a lawyer. The courtroom was not some foreign place she had only seen in movies and on television. She had experience. She knew what to say, and when to say it. Many said she was articulate, intelligent, well-liked and misunderstood.

Many others, however, swore she was manipulative, devious, cold; she had mastered the art of lying.

As every eye in the courtroom looked on, Keefe began by asking his client if she understood the charges against her. Then he wanted to know if she was involved in Buzz's murder in *any* way.

"Absolutely not," Beth Ann answered both times.

"Have you ever asked anyone in your life to murder anybody?"

"No, I have not."

"Are you a violent person?"

"No, I'm not."

"Objection," Kane said.

"Sustained."

Spending a bit of time talking about her family, Beth Ann showed impeccable memory skills regarding dates, places and details about her education—some of which took place two decades ago—and upbringing. Then Keefe had her move into her desire to practice law and her early search for a job.

"Did you ultimately apply to the law firm of Haiman Clein?"

"Yes, I did."

"And what year was that?"

Without missing a beat: "August 1992."

She said she was ultimately hired by Clein himself, then began talking about Kim and Rebecca, implying that Kim's PKU disease "leads to mental retardation" if left untreated, as well as "sexual promiscuity."

Then it was on to Kim's first husband, and several of Kim's other boyfriends, whom, she suggested, Kim had always had problems with. And because of those problems, she insisted, her parents "essentially" had to raise Kim's kids—including *Rebecca*—themselves.

After discussing briefly how the litigation process surrounding the custody of Rebecca had been initiated, she talked about Rebecca's living conditions and the visitation dispute that had erupted between Buzz and Kim and the Carpenters—plus, being a lawyer, she began helping out her parents.

"Did you want custody of Rebecca?"

"No, no."

"Have you ever wanted custody of Rebecca?"

"No, no."

"And after you moved [out of your parents' house] . . . how frequently did you see Rebecca during the years after you moved?"

"After I moved, I really—I couldn't put a number on it. I would—my mom would have fights with me because I think it was in 1993 when I missed [Rebecca's] birthday party, and I was supposed to bring the cake and I was late and I missed the birthday party. So I know I would not see her frequently because there were often arguments, and my mom would say, 'Why aren't you here? Why aren't you doing this?' I was going out. I was young. I was trying to start off doing my own thing.

"I couldn't put a number on how many times I saw her—not very frequently."

If nothing else, this was a complete playing down of her role in Rebecca's life. Rebecca was born in August 1990. By August 1993, Beth Ann had told several people about the bitter battle brewing between Buzz and her family for child custody, and she made it a daily part of her conversations with people in her inner circle—many of whom had already testified that there wasn't a moment during that period when she *hadn't* talked about getting custody of Rebecca. In fact, on August 16, 1993, she had been present at a court hearing in which Buzz acted as Kim's attorney, and later, after the hearing, she threatened his life.

According to a court employee, she had said to Buzz, "I'll kill your ass."

To say that she wasn't *that* involved in Rebecca's life at that time and was "off doing [her] own thing" was a ridiculous exaggeration at least, a lie at best.

She admitted next to speaking about the custody issue and court proceedings while working at Clein's office, but she made it sound as if she had mentioned it briefly in passing. "And if things came up, I would talk about it just like everybody talks about the things that's going on in their families or household."

"How many superior court hearings were there concerning Rebecca . . . ?"

Beth Ann didn't hesitate or even think about her answer, darting off dates with flawless accuracy. "April sixth and August sixteenth."

"Both in '93?"

"Yes. One was in Norwich and one was in New London."

"And did you attend both of them?"

"Yes, I did."

"Why were you there on April 6, 1993?"

"To support my family."

"Why were you there on August sixteenth?"

"To support my family."

"By the way, did you have any skirmish with Buzz or anybody else on either of these occasions?"

"Absolutely not. No!"

There were several witnesses who could testify differently—and they had already been interviewed by police. Some were even officers of the court. Were they liars, too? many were wondering.

When Keefe asked her if she had seen any visible signs of abuse on Rebecca, Beth Ann said, "I never saw any evidence of abuse whatsoever."

Again, just about every person close to her had disagreed. Not to mention that no fewer than three witnesses had already testified how she had talked about the abuse almost daily. Kane and McShane took notes like reporters as she spoke. Surely, the day's transcripts would make for some interesting late-night reading.

For Keefe, there was no way of getting around the fact that Clein had said Beth Ann had, point-blank, asked him to have Buzz killed one night. So Keefe decided to address the situation head-on.

"You heard Haiman Clein testify . . . that you approached him and asked him to kill Buzz. You heard him say that?"

"Yes, I did."

"He said first you asked him to do it personally. You heard him say that?"

"Yes, I did."

"Did you do that?"

"No!"

"He also said he refused to do it, certainly, so you said hire somebody or get someone else to do it, or words to that effect. You heard that?"

"Yes, I did."

"Did you do that?"

"Absolutely *not!*"

"Was there any reason that you would want Buzz dead?"

"None whatsoever."

About an hour before lunch, Keefe asked Beth Ann about Clein's drug use—she said she didn't know much about it—and how their relationship progressed from coworkers to lovers over a period of about a year. Then he had her explain away the notion that she knew Mark Despres. She admitted to being at the Christmas party in 1993 when Despres and Clein began plotting Buzz's murder. And she also said it was possible that she had even seen or met Despres at the party. She insisted, though, on having no "independent recollection" of any such meeting.

Then Keefe moved on to the infamous photograph of Buzz that Clein had said she gave him.

"Did you ever give [Clein] such a photograph?"

"Absolutely not!"

"Now, did you have photographs of Kim and Buzz?"

"I have boxes of family photographs at my house."

"And they were kept where at your house?"

She explained that all of her family photographs were kept in a closet at her condo, which gave the jury some explanation possibly as to how Clein could have gotten his hands on the photograph without her knowledge.

"Now, you say that Haiman had keys to your apartment?"

"Yes, he did."

"And did he have them for the months preceding the murder of Buzz?"

"Yes, he did."

"And you say that Haiman . . . Did he visit your apartment at will?"

"Yes!"

"Whether you were there or not?"

"Yes."

"Did he have access to everything in your apartment?"

"Yes."

With that out of the way, there was one more, little obstacle Keefe had to get around: if Beth Ann hadn't contracted for the murder, why in the world would she have stayed with Clein and continued an intimate relationship with him *after* he admitted to her that he had Buzz murdered on his own?

She wasn't denying that she knew about the murder after the fact; she was denying that she'd had anything to do with it.

"Do you remember what part of the weekend it was that Clein told you that he had arranged the murder?"

It had been a little over eight years since Buzz's murder, but Beth Ann didn't hesitate or think about her answer.

"It was a Sunday."

Keefe asked her if she remembered what time of day it was.

"It was toward the evening. It was dark, darkish hours. It wasn't bright out."

She then explained how it was the first time she had heard that Clein indeed had something to do with Buzz's murder.

"What was you reaction?"

"I didn't want to believe it. I said, 'Please, please, tell me this isn't true.' And he was laughing and he was gloating, and he thought . . . he had done this great thing. And I was just, 'You have to be crazy. You can't do this. Can't be true.'"

"Did he tell you *why* he had murdered Buzz?"

"He said, 'Don't you see? You don't have to worry about anything anymore.' He said [Buzz] was just a 'scumbag,' and that he had done the world a service."

After lunch recess, Keefe had Beth Ann discuss in a bit more detail the litigation process between the Carpenters and Kim and Buzz regarding Rebecca. When Keefe asked her about Dee Clinton's having testified that she had called Kim a whore, she denied it. When Keefe began to talk about Joseph Jebran, she wrote the relationship off as a brother-sister type of friendship. She said she had tried to make it more romantic, but the feelings just weren't there.

"Did you ever ask Joseph Jebran to take you and Rebecca and run away anyplace?"

"Never."

"Now, Beth, did you develop a friendship with Tricia Gaul?"

"I would call it more of an acquaintance, not a friendship. I mean, we went out once or twice maybe."

So not only were Haiman Clein and Dee Clinton liars, but, according to Beth Ann, Joseph Jebran and Tricia Gaul also had walked into a court of law, raised their hands, taken an oath and proceeded to lie, too. Moreover, why did she bring Tricia Gaul to Washington, DC, when she had been admitted to the bar, if she was merely an acquaintance?

For a good part of the afternoon, Beth Ann denied just about everything negative anyone had said about her. Where Clein was concerned, there wasn't anything that she would fess up to besides being obsessed with him. She said time and again that the reason she had stayed with Clein so long after the murder was because she had become codependent. She felt she couldn't live without him—that is, until she decided to turn him into the FBI while he was on the run when she was in England.

After Beth Ann played down her trip to England and Ireland as a mere working and education experience, Keefe ended his direct examination of her by asking if she had been confined to her parents' home under house arrest.

"That is correct, yeah."

One of the most remarkable aspects of Beth Ann's direct testimony was that there wasn't one time where she hadn't remembered a fact or incident. She had displayed to the jury a computerlike memory, even about events that had taken place some twenty years earlier. She answered questions with succinct, direct phrasing: dates, times, places, names. There was nothing, it seemed, Beth Ann had a problem recalling.

That, however, was all about to change.

Kevin Kane was a peaceful man. Scholarly-looking right down to his owlish glasses and Santa Claus–like white eyebrows and mustache, Kane spoke softly, rarely ever raising his voice or showing excitement. Some years ago, he'd prosecuted one of the most prolific serial killers the state of Connecticut had ever put on trial: Michael Ross, a sadistic sexual predator who had raped and murdered several young women and laughed about it afterward. Kane and Peter McShane had been instrumental in bringing Ross up on charges and, during a retrial, sending him to death row.

Beth Ann Carpenter, though, was no Michael Ross. Kane had to be careful. He couldn't come across as being overbearing and aggressive. The jury might take it the wrong way.

Because Keefe had left off with Beth Ann explaining her "trip" overseas, Kane thought it pertinent to stay on point.

"You were going to come home from Christmas break and then return to London, is that correct?"

"That's correct."

"You told other people you were going to go home for Christmas break?"

"Haiman was a fugitive!"

"Excuse me? Could you answer that, yes or no? You did not come home for Christmas break?"

"I can't answer that without an explanation."

"Did you come home in December 1995?"

"I was assisting the authorities in 1995—"

The judge broke in. "Answer the question, please."

"No, I did not come home."

Over the next few minutes, Kane showed clearly that Beth Ann never had any intention of coming home once she stepped foot on British soil. When asked if she had ever heard that Mark Despres had been arrested, she said yes.

"And did you know that he had been arrested on October twenty-eight?"

"I'm not sure that I knew the date."

"When did you first hear that?"

"I'm not sure."

For a good part of the afternoon, Kane stayed on the subject of her living in London and, later, Ireland. He wanted to know why immigration wouldn't let her back into England after she had gone to the Canary Islands.

"I don't recall."

Then he wanted to know how she got back into the country.

Smirking, she said, "A plane."

"And in what airport did you land?"

"I don't recall."

"Was it Stansted Airport?"

"I don't recall."

"You don't recall. . . . How many airports are there in the London area?"

"I believe there's four."

"Well, you landed at an airport, I take it?"

"Yes."

At about 4:45 P.M., court was suspended for the day after Keefe objected to a line of questioning that was geared toward why Beth Ann Carpenter wouldn't talk to Scotland Yard officials about Buzz's death, but was willing to aid in the capture of Haiman Clein.

The first thing Wednesday morning, April 3, 2002, Beth Ann took the stand again. So far, it hadn't gone all that badly. There were no sudden emotional breakdowns or tirades or controversial bouts of testimony. It was, when it came down to it, her word against, well, just about every witness the state's attorney's office had presented to the court.

At first, she continued testifying about her time abroad. Kane wanted the jury to believe that she had left the country to avoid arrest and, later, the death penalty, and Keefe, of course, thought he'd already proved differently.

When Kane began asking her about the context of the phone calls she was receiving from Clein while he was on the run, she again said that she couldn't "recall."

"Now, in November of '95," Kane asked about twenty minutes into his cross-examination, "end of October, early November, who did you first hear from that Mark Despres was arrested?"

"I don't recall."

"You don't recall?" Kane asked in disbelief. Then he posed the obvious next question, "Was that something that at all was any concern to you about Mark Despres's being arrested for the murder of your brother-in-law?"

"It was of *some* concern, yes."

"But not enough . . . for you to be able to now remember when you first heard he was arrested?"

"I don't recall. . . ."

Sometime later, Kane asked, "And can you tell us what you *recall* Haiman telling you about a warrant being issued for him?"

"I don't recall."

Kane then established that Clein had phoned her most of the time, not the other way around.

"And can you tell us . . . what he told you?"

"As I said, I don't recall what he said."

"You don't recall what he said?"

"No."

A bit later, "Okay, what did you say to him . . . ?"

"What did *I* say to *him*?"

"Yes!"

"I don't recall what I said to him."

Kane continued to question her about the substance of the phone calls, but she continued to say, over and over, "I don't recall." It was odd, many in the gallery said later, that she had a way of recalling issues of no significance and failing to recall issues that could be of help to the jury. For example, Kane wanted to know if she recalled telling Ali, the man she had worked for and lived with in London, that Buzz had been murdered. "I don't recall." What about telling Ali about the arrest of Mark Despres? "I don't recall."

Throughout the morning, Kane tried to get her to admit that she knew more than she was saying, but she wouldn't budge. Then he began to talk about Buzz's kids, Briana and Anson.

"You knew that at the time Buzz was killed, your sister, Kim, was pregnant, didn't you?"

"Yes."

Whenever Kane talked about the investigation portion of the case, asking her what types of questions investigators had asked her early on, she said she didn't recall.

It was obviously turning into a worthless struggle to get Beth Ann to say anything useful or important. She would talk about insignificant factoids all day long, but when it came down to anything that might shed a negative light on her . . . "I don't recall."

After being on the stand for nearly two days, about six

hours of which were under cross-examination, Beth Ann had said "I don't recall" to Kevin Kane approximately seventy times.

Under Hugh Keefe's direct questioning, however, she hadn't uttered the same phrase once.

"It was almost as if two different people were on the stand," a courtroom observer later said. "One on direct examination who had an excellent memory—and another on cross-examination who had amnesia!"

Chapter 50

A hearing took place on Thursday, April 4, 2002, regarding Dr. Robert Novelly, a psychologist whom Keefe wanted to testify about the behaviors of people who suffer from codependency syndrome. According to the defense, Beth Ann had stayed with Clein after she knew he'd had Buzz murdered because she was obsessed with him, and she needed him in her life to make her feel whole.

Kane argued that testimony about the syndrome was not recognized under state law and therefore should not be admitted.

In front of Judge Devlin, without the jury present, Novelly said that Beth Ann "may have" suffered from codependency, but he could not be positive.

Ultimately Judge Devlin said Novelly's testimony wasn't relevant and wouldn't help the jury in reaching its verdict.

Mark Despres was intoxicated with the notion of meddling in the process of justice any way he could. Rumor around the courthouse during the afternoon of April 4 was that Despres, whom Keefe wanted brought in to see if he would testify, was going to "go nuts" once he got into the courtroom. Despres had been acting erratically during the past few years—setting up, many believed, an insanity defense for himself. He had claimed he was psychiatrically impaired and suffered from several mental disorders. At times, he refused to bathe himself and was on a cocktail of medications. Thus far, however, there was little factual proof of his being mentally disturbed.

Dressed in a lime green prison jumper, his hair unwashed and tousled, in shackles, Despres was escorted into the courtroom by prison officials as onlookers and court personnel watched in trepidation. Here was the triggerman. The killer. Not the brains behind the murder, but the muscle. Despres had gained a considerable amount of weight since being incarcerated. He was big, like an out-of-shape WWE wrestler, and could have probably taken down, chained or unchained, anyone in the room he wanted.

There was an early indication that Despres wasn't going to talk, so Judge Devlin first wanted to know if he was ready and willing to cooperate.

"Would you answer questions about the case truthfully?" Devlin asked.

Despres just stared ahead in silence.

"Let the record reflect," Devlin said, "that Mr. Despres remained silent." A few seconds passed. Then, "Do you realize if you do not answer the questions, that the state could consider this a violation of your plea agreement?"

Silence.

Judge Devlin repeated to the court reporter his earlier affirmation. Then, "Do you realize that I would probably allow you to plead the Fifth?"

Silence.

Without incident, Mark Despres was then taken back to his prison cell.

Sometime later, Despres took part in a court-ordered "Competency to Stand Trial Evaluation." When he was asked where he was born, he answered, "Blue thirteen," apparently some planet he'd invented. The doctor repeated the question. "From my mother," Despres then said. No, it was a brother, "Vlad," he added. "My own last name is Cohen."

"Do you have a son of your own, Mr. Despres?"

"No, I do not."

For the past year or so, Despres had had scabs and bruises on his arms and had refused to shower regularly. Scars on his wrists indicated that he'd tried to commit suicide on at least one occasion. When asked about the scabs, Despres said, "Bugs. When they get on me, I rip them off."

"Did you make the scabs, or did the bugs cut you and make the scabs?"

"Yes."

Then doctors asked him if he understood that he was facing murder charges. He said he didn't.

"The victim of the shooting you were involved in, do you know his name?"

"Ronald Reagan."

"Do you know the role of the defense counsel?"

"To bring me sandwiches."

"What about the prosecution?"

"To kill everyone."

"The judge?"

"To make sure you're dead."

"Tell us what a plea bargain is, Mr. Despres?"

"A candy bar."

It was then explained that he should "reconsider his tactic of attempting to fake a mental illness. We're going to give you another chance to answer our questions. Now, is the judge's role to oversee the hearing or provide transportation?"

"Provide transportation."

"Is the sky blue or orange?"

"Orange."

Despres didn't want to play ball anymore. And because of his pigheaded belief that he could somehow hoodwink the system, the courts were threatening to revoke his plea bargain—which meant he would have to stand trial for his role in Buzz's murder.

In the end, doctors concluded that he "intentionally feigned or grossly exaggerated symptoms in an effort to appear seriously impaired."

The courtroom was packed and people were jockeying for position in the corridors on Tuesday, April 9, as Kane and Keefe gave their closing arguments.

Kane had a simple notion to project to the jury: Despite having "more baggage on him than a Boeing 747 on the way back carrying people from Paris," Clein should be believed because he didn't have to admit to half of what he did. He might have been a liar and a cheat, Kane said, but "compare [his testimony] to the manner in which the defendant testified."

For about thirty minutes, Kane talked about every facet of the case Beth Ann had disputed, going into great detail regarding the state's contention of motive: the custody battle over Rebecca—which was, when it came down to it, the seed of betrayal and hate.

Referring to Clein as "Mr. Wonderful" throughout much of his closing, Hugh Keefe, like an ex-spouse dealing out insults during divorce proceedings, blasted every aspect of Clein's credibility. Tara Knight, also contributing to the closing, assailed Beth Ann's taste in men by saying, "I would like to remind you that she is not on trial for staying with Clein or having bad taste in men. Every one of you," Knight said, "has stayed in a poor relationship. This is a smear campaign."

Keefe called Clein a "bum, liar and drughead."

He proposed: "If Haiman Clein is not credible, then Beth Carpenter is not guilty."

Was the jury going to believe Haiman Clein or Beth Ann Carpenter?

On April 12, a Friday, nearly a week after the jury was given the case, jury foreman Edwin Perez, as the courtroom sat on edge and a few of the female jurors began to show tears, read that Beth Ann had been found guilty of conspiring to murder her brother-in-law, Anson "Buzz" Clinton.

Beth Ann began to sob quietly. Her family, sitting in back of her, began to gasp in disbelief as one of her relatives let out a rather loud yelp.

As they had maintained throughout the trial, Beth Ann's family said nothing as they left the court in shock. The Clintons, however, all smiles, stayed and spoke openly about their delight that the mastermind behind their son's murder was going to pay for her crimes. Yet, at the same time, the conviction added little to the empty space created in their lives since Buzz had been gone.

"Buzz has been vindicated," Dee Clinton told one reporter. "He was a good, decent human being. He loved his family and his children."

After Beth Ann's sentencing date had been postponed once, she finally met her fate on August 2, 2002. Every major newspaper and television station in the state, along with the Associated Press, was in attendance to see what the court was going to hand down to the redheaded lawyer who had captured headlines for the past five years.

Judge Devlin showed little sympathy for Beth Ann Carpenter, saying that if anyone else should've known better, it was an officer of the court. Dee, Buck and Suzanne Clinton all spoke on Buzz's behalf, bringing tears to the eyes of many of Buzz's relatives in attendance. At one point, Dee even suggested to the judge that a photo of Buzz be placed in Beth Ann's cell for the entire duration of her sentence.

By far, the most emotional part of the sentencing came when young Billy, Buzz's little brother, played a videotape he'd made. It was a retrospective of Buzz's life: high school, home, work, Kim, the kids, even Buzz's pets. A song by Celine Dion played as the courtroom, judge and Beth Ann, biting her lip and blinking her eyes nervously, looked on as a homemade video depicted a man who was, at least to his immediate family, a caring, loving and unselfish human being who had been struck down just as his life was getting back on track.

Beth Ann's family continued insisting that Clein had acted alone. Cynthia Carpenter, when it came time for Beth Ann's family to speak on her behalf, said, "This is a terrible injustice. I pray daily Mr. Clein will come forward with the truth and Beth will come home where she belongs."

Shocking some, but not surprising others, Keefe introduced several police reports regarding Buzz.

"[These reports] paint a picture," Keefe argued as he handed the documents to court clerk Cameron MacKenzie, "of emotional abuse, physical abuse, threats of murder, drug abuse and drug trafficking."

In a sense, Keefe was smearing the memory of a dead man, who couldn't defend himself against the claims. Later, many outside the courtroom agreed it was blatant misuse of his authority as a lawyer. He was way out of line. Others, however, said it was standard Hugh Keefe practice.

After court, Tara Knight took questions about Keefe's putting into the record those items that cast a bad light on the victim, saying she and Keefe needed to set the record straight. Buzz wasn't the "salt of the earth,"

Knight suggested. "He was no saint." The record should reflect that.

Most everyone agreed it was a cheap shot, no matter the reason. Buzz Clinton was never on trial.

In the end, Judge Devlin sentenced Beth Ann to life in prison without the possibility of parole, plus twenty years—the only sentence he could lawfully hand down.

"This case," the judge commented—clearly dismayed, disappointed and in total disbelief of what had happened—"was about loss of human potential."

It would take almost six months to the day, but on February 4, 2003, Mark Despres, after fighting with the court over getting rid of his first attorney and obtaining another, even threatening to kill his first attorney at one point, was brought before the court to receive his sentence.

Despres was still unstable and not ready to accept responsibility for his crimes. Writing letters to the court, he would scribble little pictures of devils on the letters, perhaps attempting to seem deranged. It was clear he wanted a diagnosis of mental instability so he could get sentenced to a mental hospital instead of prison. Yet he couldn't get one doctor to agree.

For a second time, the Clinton family trekked into the courtroom and told the court how much Buzz was loved and missed. Billy Clinton again got to play his video, and Dee, Suzanne and Buck again read impact statements.

Most notably was Buck Clinton's affirmation that he wasn't willing to forget or forgive. Buck was a hard man who believed in an "eye for an eye." In his son's murder case, however, he wasn't going to get it. Deals had been made. Lives had been saved. All in the name of nailing, Kevin Kane assured the court, the one person who had masterminded the killing from the beginning: Beth Ann Carpenter.

"I say to this court," Buck Clinton said in his rugged,

emotionally wrought voice, "there is an internal burning hatred for the individuals involved in my son's murder."

Esther Lockwood, Despres's mother, read from a long and seemingly heartfelt letter she had written that explained how Mark had been abused by a father, who left when he was five, and a brother, who had also teased and beat him. She talked about how Mark was good with his hands, with kids, with kittens, and he had even dressed up as Santa Claus at times. But nowhere in the letter did Lockwood ever acknowledge that she had a grandson whom Mark had abandoned, or that Mark was sorry for what he had done.

Before the judge handed down his sentence, Mark Despres got a chance to address the Clintons.

"I hope you can find it in your heart to forgive me."

Full of rage, but sitting comfortably with his arm around his daughter, Buck Clinton yelled, "Never happen!"

Regardless of what anyone thought about Despres, Kevin Kane made a valid point when it was his turn to speak.

"He has been manipulative to the point of being treacherous. He has shown no remorse. But if it weren't for him, no one else would've been arrested or convicted."

The judge ultimately sentenced Despres to forty-five years. He could, under the state's "truth in sentencing laws," be back on the street in twenty-two years.

Buzz Clinton had been buried on March 17, 1994, St. Patrick's Day. After postponing it twice, the court, after discussing it with the Clintons, fittingly set March 17, 2003, as Haiman Clein's sentencing date.

In the end, character is everything during a trial. From the state's standpoint, Clein had shown a tremendous amount of acceptance over the years. He stood his ground, even when Keefe brought up aspects of his past that might be construed as vile, evil and disgusting, and perhaps were. But Clein had never claimed to be a priest or a rabbi; he was only saying that, without Beth Ann Carpenter, Buzz Clinton would still be alive.

Now he wanted to be paid back for his willingness to bring Beth Ann down.

The most Clein could receive was forty-five years, same as Despres. Kane, however, argued for a lesser sentence of thirty-five years. Without Haiman Clein, Kane suggested, Beth Ann Carpenter would be free.

The Clinton family, understandably, didn't agree with all of the legal jargon that had let their son's killers cut deals for reduced sentences. To them, death sentences for all of those involved in Buzz's murder would have been too lenient.

"For the truth, Mr. Clein, as a father," Buck stood before the court and read, "I thank you. But I know the real motive was to save your own hide. I will never forget, nor will I ever forgive."

Suzanne was a bit more formal and sympathetic.

"In case you didn't know, Haiman," she said, staring at Clein as he sat with his head bowed, "I loved my brother more than anyone in this world. He was always there for me." Then, a bit later, "I want you to remember my family is stronger despite all your actions. Last night, I was finally inspired. I wrote you this poem. . . ."

In the beautifully written piece titled "I Know You Thought You Could Destroy Us, but You Only Made Us Stronger," Suzanne used the title as a launching pad to tell Clein how she had felt all these years.

"As a family," she continued, "we cry together on days like today. . . . My mother is the strongest woman I know—a courageous one who fights for justice."

Dee Clinton, the most vocal of the bunch, read from a prepared statement that took about twenty minutes. After talking about how the death of her son had affected her family over the years, Dee criticized the justice system, lawyers in general, saying, "I must admit, I find it entertaining and eagerly await the positive spin we're going to hear today from [Clein's attorney]. . . ."

When it was Clein's turn to talk, he stood and, quietly, turned and looked at the Clintons.

"I'd give my life for his if I could." Then he paused, "Literally. There's no way for me to really express to them how sorry I feel."

Clein, who had been incarcerated now for six years, received thirty-five years.

It was finally over. Haiman Clein would likely spend the rest of his life in prison. Joe Fremut was dead. Beth Ann Carpenter, serving a life sentence plus twenty years, was already planning her appeal. Mark Despres, on the other hand, was sitting in his cell still trying to manipulate the system any way he could to get out of what was to him the worst environment imaginable. And it was all part of a murder-for-hire plot that had begun with the birth of a fatherless child back in 1990: Rebecca Ann Carpenter, who had turned thirteen on August 12, 2003.

Epilogue

One could argue that Circe's path, named after the Greek goddess Circe, is driven by an old cliché: "What goes around comes around." Or that what I call Circe's path is nothing more than folklore or fiction. Circe, in Homer's *Odyssey*, used poison to entice men into her web. Ultimately, once she wrapped them around her sexy little finger, she could get them to perform back-flips at a moment's notice.

To say there is a correlation between this age-old myth and Beth Ann Carpenter's life of using men in a similar fashion to get what she wanted is, some might argue, a bit of a stretch. But peel back a layer and look beyond the surface—and there is clear evidence that Circe's path exists within the confines of Beth Ann's world.

As of this writing, Beth Ann Carpenter, at the young age of thirty-nine, sits in her cell inside York Correctional Facility for Women in Niantic, Connecticut, overlooking the one spot where her life, some might say, both began and ended in the span of eight years. She now awaits word on her appeal and prepares to fight several civil suits (wrongful death) brought against her by the Clinton family and Kim Carpenter Clinton. From the north side of York, on a clear winter day, though, when all the trees are stripped naked of their leaves and th ground is brown and frozen, and the birds have gone south and the wind is bitter and howling through the cracks of the prison walls, Beth Ann, if she chooses, can look out any one of the many prison windows. And, just there, not far from a place that is now her home, where the ebb and flow of life grind on without her, about a half mile away, is the exact same location where it all began back on March 10, 1994: Exit 72, the Rocky Neck connector—the same spot where twenty-eight-year-old Anson "Buzz" Clinton, in the prime of his life, was—at the urging and planning of Beth Ann Carpenter, a jury of her peers unanimously agreed—gunned down like a helpless deer by a man he didn't even know.

So, in a sense, Circe's path, at least in theory, does exist.

Nearly everyone in law enforcement I spoke to while working on this book repeated one name to me: Inspector Jack Edwards. "He was the key to this entire investigation," a humble John Turner, along with several other detectives and attorneys, said more than once.

A retired, lifelong cop, Jack Edwards is the New London State's Attorney's Office's chief investigator and worked as the liaison between the Eastern District Major Crime Squad and the state's attorney's office during the Buzz Clinton murder investigation. Jack would, I was told, point detectives in the right direction and, so they could learn for themselves how to become better at what they did, step back. He was there to assure that detectives left no stone unturned. So when the case went to trial, hopefully, it would be open and shut.

In all due respect to Jack Edwards, a man I have never met, I didn't find his role to be all that instrumental in the story I have told here. Number one, Jack is a remarkably modest man, I'm told, and would rather not talk about his involvement in the cases he works on. Second, Jack's name appeared on not one piece of documentation I examined. I had plenty of cops tell me Jack Edwards was and is the best investigator the state of Connecticut has to offer and that he played a significant role in bringing down Beth Ann Carpenter, but again, Jack's decision not to be interviewed for this book, along with his obvious humility, stopped me from pursuing him any further.

As of this writing, Beth Ann Carpenter's attorneys have been working on filing her appeal. There is no set date for her attorneys to argue it in front of a judge, however. My professional "opinion" of how it will turn out is rather simple: *Get comfortable in prison, Ms. Carpenter, because you're going to be there for the rest of your life.*

The evidence in this case, when taken in context as a whole, is stunning. For Beth Ann Carpenter *not* to have had something to do with Buzz Clinton's murder, it would mean that not one or two people committed perjury, but just about every witness the state of Connecticut presented would have had to perjure himself or herself on the stand at some point during his or her testimony. What's important to think about is, there is no way that people who do not know each other, people who have never spoken to each other, can tell similar stories about the same events and be able to lie about them with the accuracy displayed in this case. It just doesn't happen that way. If, for example, a man in California and a man in New Jersey who don't know each other make a report about an object in the sky and describe it the exact same way, we can be certain that we've uncovered the truth about what those two people saw.

It's called objective evidence.

In my opinion, based on the interviews I have do[ne,] all I have observed and my tedious study of the pub[lic] record, Beth Ann Carpenter is, if nothing else, a liar who, perhaps, believes her own lies—nor does she have any intention of ever giving the Clinton family what they so much deserve: the truth.

Murder for hire is a complex crime. People who plan to kill other people will justify the crime any way they can to allow themselves to be able to live with what they have done. Because they often are so far removed from actually *committing* the crime, as in this case, they tend to feel as if they had nothing to do with it. Or perhaps it is just easier for them to believe they weren't part of it at all. Who knows?

Beth Ann will continue to believe that she hasn't done anything wrong—that, during pillow talk, she merely mentioned one day to Haiman Clein that the entire Carpenter family would be better off if Buzz were out of the picture. With that, she and her attorneys have repeatedly claimed, Clein took it upon himself to have Buzz killed as his "gift" to her.

What's more, Beth Ann has seemingly managed to convince her entire family of her lies. This is clearly implicit in the few press appearances members of the Carpenter family have done, namely Court TV's *Mugshots* and A&E's *City Confidential.* But the truth and, more important, the *documentation,* not to mention the absolutely misconstrued notion that so many people would perjure themselves in a court of law, are a different matter. The facts in this case speak for themselves. And it's not a matter of he said/she said; it's a matter of scores of people telling the same stories over and over and the irrefutable documentation supporting those stories.

Period.

Finally, if some readers cannot see Beth Ann's guilt or going on this journey with me throughout this k, I feel they are blinded by denial and incapable of epting the truth and *facts*—and I encourage them to contact me with *documentation* that supports proof of their *opinions*.

Beth Ann's mother, Cynthia Carpenter, received a letter from me regarding an interview I was hoping to set up with the entire Carpenter family. I called their home several times. Nobody answered my letter or returned my calls.

A nonfiction author of true crime books has to be objective, certainly. But also selective. Family members and friends of the family of those convicted are suspect sources to begin with. Many don't see the truth, or refuse to believe it. I was careful to conduct background checks on every person in this story I felt deserved to be interviewed, and I made decisions based on the many conversations I had with law enforcement, attorneys and people close to this case. If a long-lost cousin, brother, neighbor or spouse wasn't contacted by me for an interview, there was a good reason behind that decision: they were insignificant to the story and could add nothing in the form of truth. In addition, the Carpenter and Clein families had nearly a year to talk to me; neither chose to answer my letters or phone calls.

—M. William Phelps
November 2003

Acknowledgments

Every book has a few people attached to it that without whom the book would not be possible. For this, my second crime book, I am indebted to Jim Cypher.

Martha Jenssen, court officer at the New London Superior Court, was, to me, a person who always went out of her way to make sure I had whatever I needed in a timely fashion. Ms. Jenssen was extremely considerate, kind, resourceful and eager to help. Without her, this book would have undoubtedly suffered greatly. Her kindness, friendship and help was something I will never forget. I am forever grateful. Thank you, ma'am.

Court reporters Patricia Smith and Elaine Wiltsie were always considerate of my time constraints. I thank them for providing me—sometimes at a moment's notice—with all the court transcripts connected to this case.

In no particular order, I also would like to thank Detective John Turner, who is today the sergeant in charge of the Eastern District Major Crime Squad, Detectives Marty Graham and Reggie Wardell, Peter McShane, Kevin Kane, Tara Knight, Cameron MacKenzie and anyone from the New London Superior Court I've overlooked. Most were very kind. Most trusted me. I appreciate that. It makes all the difference to a writer in my position.

A special thanks to Dee Clinton, Suzanne Clinton, Buck and Billy Clinton. Some of you helped more than others, but I am grateful to you all. You are some of the strongest people I have *ever* met in my life. You have been routinely treated unfairly. Talked about by most everyone involved in this case. Castigated. Shunned. At times, made a mockery of. Yet you continue to fight for what you believe. I can only hope this book reflects a part of Buzz that you were all once witness to more than any of us.

To those of you I interviewed but changed your names in the book, thank you for taking the time to let me into your homes and tell me in candid detail about your role in this case. It takes courage and strength on your part—which you greatly showed—to trust someone like me. Thank you for your stories. I hope I haven't disappointed any of you.

A special thanks to Charlie Snyder. Your honesty and integrity should be commended. You talked about things others would not have.

Those who helped with obtaining photos, thank you. I want to also say thanks to those of you at the Hartford Public Library, New London Public Library and Ledyard Public Library for helping me locate photos, documents, newspaper articles and archives associated with the Carpenter family and Buzz Clinton. Special thanks to Marty Hubbard at the Ledyard Public Library. I need to also thank John Brand, who really put the entire photo section together for me and ended up fixing my vehicle one day when we got stranded in New London. (You're the best, John!)

Thank you Gregg Olsen and Harvey Rachlin. Also: R.K., J.G., B.W.

I cannot write a book without thanking William Acosta, a man whose gifts to this world are endless.

Kensington editor-in-chief, Michaela Hamilton, a senior editor Johnny Crime have shown me nothi but respect, guidance and support. Whether the making my words work on the page or explaining p of the business I am still trying to comprehend, I feel like I am working with the two most prolific editors in the business. Thanks both of you for always taking the time to answer my questions. A very special thanks to copyeditor S. Finnegan.

This book is dedicated to Tommy Louis ("he ain't heavy . . ."). Without his persistence, I would have never pursued this story, which was his idea from the get-go. Thanks, Tommy. I hope it lives up to what you had hoped from the beginning.

The entire Phelps family has been very supportive: thanks! Doug Leonard, a friend for years: thank you for the help during those tough times. Garry Rice, a former cop and gun expert, thanks for helping me understand the ballistics involved in this case and helping me put together the likely sequence in which Buzz Clinton might have been shot.

All my readers: Thank you for the kind letters and encouraging e-mails.

My wife: You are not only the best friend I have ever had, but my guide through life. You allow me the space and time to do my work without questioning why. You are there when things go bad, when they get worse and when everything seems to be going our way. Thank you for believing in me and not once ever asking me why I continue to do this in spite of all the negative aspects of it.

Lastly, my children. I see life in your happiness, your sadness, your stubbornness, your dreams, goals and, yes, your failures. When I look at the three of you together, the joy comes in understanding why I am alive.

If I have forgotten anyone, I sincerely apologize; it wasn't on purpose.

MORE MUST-READ TRUE CRIME
FROM PINNACLE